INTERPRETING IRISH HISTORY

Interpreting Irish History

THE DEBATE ON HISTORICAL REVISIONISM
1938-1994

EDITED BY

Ciaran Brady

IRISH ACADEMIC PRESS

This book was typeset
in 11 on 13 Ehrhardt by
Gilbert Gough Typesetting, Dublin
and first published in 1994 by
IRISH ACADEMIC PRESS
Kill Lane, Blackrock, Co. Dublin, Ireland,
and in North America by
IRISH ACADEMIC PRESS
c/o International Specialized Book Services,
5804 NE Hassalo Street, Portland, OR 97213.

A catalogue record for this title
is available from the British Library.

ISBN 0-7165-2499-6 hbk
0-7165-2546-1 pbk

Printed in Ireland by
Colour Books Ltd, Dublin

It is more of a job to interpret the interpretations than to interpret the things, and there are more books about books than about any other subject: we do nothing but write glosses about each other.

Montaigne, 'Of experience', *Essais*, Book III, xiii.

Preface

The object of this anthology is modest. It aims simply to provide a record of the debate on the character and purpose of historical writing which has occurred among Irish historians in recent decades, and of the tendencies within the practice of history in Ireland from which that debate arose. It does not attempt to provide a survey of changing views on Irish political culture in general, nor an account of the course of historiographical controversy over particular issues and events. Both of these are major topics; but they require a more intensive, monographic treatment than is offered in this collection. Here all that has been sought is to provide a register of the objectives and problems of history writing in Ireland as seen from the differing perspectives of the practitioners themselves—and of others closely involved with the discipline—over the past sixty years. It is hoped that these readings will provide both an indication of the range and depth of the issues at stake and a flavour of the strengths and limitations of the debate they have generated, and so will encourage the development of further reflection and argument.

During the course of this work I have incurred several personal debts which it is a pleasure to acknowledge. I should like to thank John Horne, David Murphy and Mary O'Dowd for much stimulating comment, to express my gratitude to my 'primary sources', Professor R.B. McDowell, Mrs Margaret Moody and Professor D.B. Quinn, and to repay two young scholars, Daithí and Jack O'Regan, for their refreshingly sceptical curiosity about the whole project. To two close colleagues, Bill Mc Cormack and Michael Quigley (one a critic, the other a geographer, but instinctive historians both), I own a particular debt for their encouragement, support and criticism at crucial stages. The essential idea for this collection originated with Brendan Bradshaw and Anthony Coughlan, both of whom have been unfailingly generous, supportive and patient. Had it not been for their noble but rash concern to delegate the task to someone apparently less engaged in the debates this book would doubtless have been better: it certainly would have appeared far earlier. That it has made its appearance at all is due largely to the persistence, flexibility and authority of Michael Adams.

C.B.

Acknowledgments

For permission to reprint the material below I am grateful to the authors and to the following journals and publishers: *Irish Historical Studies* for chapters 2, 3, 4, 10 and 12; *Hermathena* for chapter 5; Queen's University Belfast and Mrs Jennifer Lyons for chapter 6; *Historical Studies* (Melbourne) for chapter 7; *The Irish Review* for chapters 11, 17, 18; *The Irish Literary Supplement* for chapter 13; *Studies: an Irish quarterly* for chapter 14; Field Day Publications for chapter 15; *History Workshop Journal* for chapter 16.

Contents

Contributors

BRENDAN BRADSHAW is Fellow of Queen's College, Cambridge.

CIARAN BRADY is Senior Lecturer in Modern History at Trinity College, Dublin.

ANTHONY COUGHLAN is Senior Lecturer in Social Policy at Trinity College, Dublin.

SEAMUS DEANE is Professor of Irish Studies at the University of Notre Dame.

R.D. EDWARDS (1909-88) was Professor of Modern Irish History at University College, Dublin.

STEVEN ELLIS is Associate Professor of History at University College, Galway.

RONAN FANNING is Professor of Modern Irish History at University College, Dublin.

DESMOND FENNELL lectured in University College, Galway and the Dublin Institute of Technology, and is now a freelance writer and critic.

ROY FOSTER is Carroll Professor of Irish History at the University of Oxford.

ALVIN JACKSON is Lecturer in Modern History at The Queen's University, Belfast.

HUGH KEARNEY was until recently Amundson Professor of British History at the University of Pittsburgh.

F.S.L. LYONS (1923-83) was Professor of Modern History in the University of Kent at Canterbury and Provost of Trinity College, Dublin.

OLIVER MacDONAGH is Research Professor of History at the Australian Catholic University.

T.W. MOODY (1907-84) was Professor of Modern History at Trinity College, Dublin.

BRIAN MURPHY is a member of the Benedictine Community in Glenstal Abbey, Co. Limerick.

CORMAC Ó GRÁDA is Associate Professor of Economics at University College, Dublin.

KEVIN O'NEILL is Associate Professor of History at Boston College.

M.A.G. Ó TUATHAIGH is Associate Professor of History at University College, Galway.

PART I: INTRODUCTION

'Constructive and Instrumental': The Dilemma of Ireland's First 'New Historians'

CIARAN BRADY

There is a simple moral concerning the vanity of intellectual aspirations, and the nemesis they inevitably call forth, that may readily be derived from the texts collected below. It concerns a noble ambition whereby a small group of historians attempted to construct a new institutional framework which would at once radically alter the way in which historical writing was produced in Ireland and fundamentally change the way in which the Irish past and history's manner of representing it were received within contemporary Irish culture. And it concerns also a paradox whereby the grand strategies they employed to achieve their dual ends proceeded over time to subvert them.

I

In the mid-1930s Theodore William Moody and Robert Dudley Edwards, two bright and energetic young historians, near contemporaries in the Institute of Historical Research (the graduate school of the University of London), and both with substantial academic monographs about to be published, determined to bring about a revolution in the aims, methods and style of Irish historical writing.[1] In their concern to write a purer, more scholarly kind of Irish history, the two men were not alone. This, indeed, had been the aspiration of many historians of the previous generation. And in their own time they were accompanied by a talented group of scholars, notably D.B. Quinn, R.B. McDowell and Aubrey Gwynn whose own doctoral work had already set the standards they sought to uphold. But the particular revolution they sought to

---

1. Biographical studies of both men remain to be written; in the meantime much valuable information about their careers can be derived from appreciations and obituaries: see F.S.L. Lyons, 'T.W.M'.; in F.S.L. Lyons and R.A.J. Hawkins (eds.), *Ireland under the Union: varieties of tension* (Oxford, 1980), pp. 1-33, Helen F. Mulvey, 'Theodore William Moody (1907-1984): an appreciation' in *Irish Historical Studies* xxiv (1984-5), pp. 121-130, R.W. Dudley Edwards, 'T.W. Moody and the origins of Irish Historical Studies' in ibid. xxvi (1988-9), pp. 1-2, Aidan Clarke, 'Robert Dudley Edwards (1909-1988)' in ibid., pp. 121-7.

implement took a distinctly institutional—even bureaucratic—form. They began with the establishment of two paper-reading societies, 'The Ulster Society for Irish Historical Studies' founded by Moody in Belfast in February 1936 and 'The Irish Historical Society', founded by Edwards in Dublin in the following November. From the outset the societies' regular meetings were designed to have a highly academic, seminar-like tone. Antiquarian studies or general lectures rehearsing the details of well-known events or famous lives were discouraged, and papers offering a digest of new research or reporting upon work in progress by scholars trained in the various university graduate schools were preferred. From the beginning also it was intended that the two societies should act as a filtering process for papers which would eventually appear in print in a new academic periodical, *Irish Historical Studies*, which appeared as a joint publication of both societies under the joint editorship of Moody and Edwards in 1938.[2]

Irish Historical Studies was, in part, explicitly modelled on the great academic journals of Western historiography the *Historische Zeitschrift*, the *Revue Historique*, the *English Historical Review* and the *American Historical Review*. And the austere scholarly standards that were demanded of submitted papers were spelled out in detail in the formidable 'Rules for Contributors' which were circulated to would-be contributors and printed for general recognition in the fourth volume of the journal. But there was a second element in the journal's agenda additional to the propagation in Ireland of the conventional standards of academic history. This was the propagation of both the methods and the results of the academic historians' work to the widest possible audience in the shortest possible time.

'We have before us two main tasks', wrote Moody and Edwards, 'the one constructive, the other instrumental.' By the former they intended nothing other than the steady encouragement of research in hitherto unused sources or unknown topics. But under the latter heading they listed a series of features in the journal designed to further a specific pedagogic programme: articles on research methods, edited select documents, critical bibliographies and, most important of all, a special category of essays entitled 'Historical Revisions'. Articles in this section of the journal were intended to refute received wisdom or unquestioned assumptions concerning well known events, persons or processes by means of the findings of new research. They were expected to confront errors or misunderstandings directly (though not necessarily those who had perpetrated them) both in the interests of academic probity and as a

2.   For further details see Mulvey above, Moody 'Twenty years after' in *I.H.S.* xi (1958-9), pp. 1-4, Moody and Edwards 'Preface' in *I.H.S.* i (1938-9) p. 2 (reprinted below pp. 35-7) and 'Notes and News' in ibid., pp. 187, 290-9, for early lecture lists, and p. 408 for further statements of intent.

means of alerting teachers and general readers to the deficiencies inherent in the texts they had come to treat as authoritative.[3]

The idea was not new. The editors acknowledged that they had appropriated it from *History*, a periodical closely attached to the history department where they had both learned their craft, the University of London. *History* was the official journal of the Historical Association, a body established in 1906 by A.F. Pollard, the first director of the Institute in London, with the aim of developing links between the university historians and history teachers at second level. The Association, in Moody and Edwards's terms, was decidedly instrumentalist in its methods, holding regular public lectures, conferences, tours, as well as publishing in the journal, the bibliographies, research guides and historical revisions which provided models for *Irish Historical Studies*.[4] Thus from the beginning the new Irish journal was to serve two separate but, as far as the editors saw, perfectly consistent purposes: the encouragement of an open-ended research project limited only by the availability and workability of the primary sources, and the assumed responsibility of conveying the most significant results of this research in digest form for immediate use in the public or educational domain.

Over the next three decades or so Moody and Edwards pursued their dual programme of constructivism and instrumentalism through a variety of means. In 1938 the Irish Committee of Historical Sciences was established at a general conference organised jointly by both the Ulster and Irish societies as a formal correspondence committee of the Comité Internationale des Sciences Historique to keep historians in Ireland in touch with most recent scholarly developments abroad and to develop a greater international interest in the work being done in Irish universities. From the outset this new body undertook the organisation of regular general conferences of Irish historians, but in the post-war years it commenced a more ambitious series of international conferences, under a slight but significant change of title as the Irish Conference of Historians, and from the mid-1950s, the proceedings of these biennial conferences began to be published as a series under the austere and somewhat unimaginative title of *Historical Studies*.[5] Even before this, in the middle of the war indeed, the committee had established *Studies in Irish History* as a research monograph series (modelled on the highly influential Oxford Historical Monographs) which, under the general editorship of Moody and

3. 'Preface' to *I.H.S.*, below p. 35-7.
4. For the activities of the various branches of the Historical Association, see the regular reports included in the issues of *History*, new series i (1916) *et seq.*; on the purpose of 'Historical Revisions' see Pollard's 'Editorial' in ibid., pp. 1-4 and ii (1917), p. 170.
5. On the origins and early proceedings of the Irish Committee of Historical Sciences see the reports in *I.H.S.* i (1938-9), pp. 186-7, 291; the first annual report of the committee was published in *I.H.S.* ii (1940-41) and all subsequent reports have been published in the journal.

Edwards, aimed to report the fruits of new research on Irish history in a much more extensive manner and to a wider international academic readership than the necessarily smaller-scale operation of *Irish Historical Studies* permitted.[6]

At the same time the instrumentalist side of the project was being developed by the inauguration of The Thomas Davis Lectures, a series (still current) of radio lectures devoted to particular topics on themes given by experts, usually academics, but constrained by brevity to be of a general nature.[7] And in the 1960s Moody, in collaboration with Professor F.X. Martin exploited the new medium of Irish television in the cause of instrumentalism through an illustrated and immensely popular series of general lectures on 'The course of Irish history'.[8]

The constructivist and instrumentalist aims of the programme were blended in the regular appearance of 'agenda' which both men were fond of promoting either implicitly in the form of reviews of work already done or quite overtly by drafting detailed proposals for work to be undertaken in various areas. Such agenda appeared at frequent intervals in different publications, and the grandest was surely Edwards's 1978 attempt to set the research agenda until the year 2018.[9] But the most actively programmatic effort was instituted primarily by Moody in the grand prospectus he laid down for *A new history of Ireland*, a hugely ambitious project, based upon the great collective Cambridge histories, for which he finally secured public funding in the 1960s. Much of the research work on which the *New history* was to be based, Moody conceded in introducing his project, had still to be done and there were many areas where the process of discovery, argument and consensus had not yet been completed. But the *New history* itself was to act as a catalyst to these necessary stages. It was, in effect, to commence a second, highly accelerated phase of the programme launched in the 1930s by which the entire course of Irish history would be systematically reconstructed, by chronological and thematic syntheses to be produced by a generation of experienced scholars trained in the methods of the professional academic historian.[10]

6. R.B. McDowell, *Irish public opinion, 1750-1800* (London, 1944) was the first volume to appear; Studies in Irish History is now in its third series.
7. See F.X. Martin, 'The Thomas Davis lectures, 1953-1967' in *I.H.S.* xv (1966-7), pp 276-302.
8. The series was first broadcast between January and June 1966 and published in a lavishly illustrated volume by Mercier Press (Cork, 1967, 2nd edn, 1984).
9. See *inter alia* 'Agenda for Irish history' in *I.H.S.* iv (1946-7), pp. 254-69, 'Thirty years work in Irish history' in *ibid.* xv (1966-7), pp. 359-90, xvi (1968-9), pp. 1-32, xvii (1970-1), pp. 1-31, 151-87; Edwards, 'An Agenda for Irish history, 1978-2018' xxi (1978-9), pp. 3-1 9; 'Things to be done in Irish history', *Bulletin of the Irish Committee of Historical Sciences*, nos 2, 12, 21, 28 (1938-44).
10. Moody, 'A new history of Ireland', in *I.H.S.* xvi (1968-9) pp. 245-6, reprinted below, pp. 38-53.

It is perhaps odd that, despite the single-mindedness with which it was pursued for over thirty years, and the passion which both men sometimes displayed in opposing those who failed to appreciate the importance of their work, neither Moody nor Edwards elected to publish a sustained defence of the programme. There could be found, both in their public and semi-public utterances, occasional hints that something deeper than a crude unreflective empiricism had motivated their efforts. But these were never elaborated upon in print and as yet await more detailed investigation.[11] Outwardly, at any rate, Edwards remained oracular to the end. But toward the close of his career Moody attempted to provide a statement of his fundamental views on the problems of writing Irish history and his means of resolving them.[12]

It was on that occasion that he made his much celebrated and much criticised distinction between history and myth: between 'good history which is a matter of facing the facts and myth which is a way of refusing to face [them]'. On this simple basis, Moody proceeded to sketch out the two contrary but equally destructive myths which he saw as fatal to the writing of Irish history—the separatist sectarian myth, which he associated with Ulster loyalism, and the unitary, nationalist myth which was the hallmark of southern republicanism. He then provided some nuggets of information generated by recent scholarly research which he believed served to undermine both of them. And he concluded with an assertion (somewhat muted by the concession that progress thus far had been slow) that in time, under the mounting assault of the new history's batteries, these death-dealing myths of Ireland's past would eventually crumble to dust. At that point the constructive and instrumentalist programmes would converge, and the campaign launched in the 1930s would have attained its goal.[13]

Moody's valedictory testament, delivered originally to the Trinity College History Society in 1977, was not greatly troubled by theoretical sophistication. It is possible to discern in its argument some influence of the anti-idealism espoused by earlier theorists, such as Karl Mannheim and Karl Popper, in their critique of historicism. But there is no sign that Moody was responding

11. Personal recollections of Moody's former students—my own included—support the impression that he had engaged with some of the theoretical problems of writing history. His undergraduate course on 'Historiography' introduced students to the ideas of Dilthey, Croce and Collingwood. He advised me strongly to read Collingwood's *The idea of history* (Oxford, 1943) which he said exerted a deep influence upon him. Edwards frequently spoke of the importance of Michael Oakeshott as a philosopher of history (see his 'Agenda' below, p. 65). Significantly, the University of London scholar, who can hardly be described as a proponent of a 'value-free science' view of history, was invited to supply the opening paper to *Historical Studies I*, T.D. Williams, ed. (London 1955), pp. 1-19.
12. 'Irish history and Irish mythology' in *Hermathena*, 124 (1978), pp. 7-24, reprinted below, pp. 71-86.
13. Ibid., below, pp. 85-86.

—say—to Lévi-Strauss, then at the height of his influence in Ireland, for
whom such a simple distinction between history and myth would have been
absurd.[14] But despite its old-fashioned character, Moody's statement nevertheless provided the central focus of an unexpectedly rancorous debate that
took place in the decade that followed, serving at once as a rallying cry for
many academic historians who, following in the great man's path, were ready
explicitly to assert the contemporary cultural relevance of their craft, and for
their critics, both within and outside the academy, who identified it as a clear
expression of the ideological arrogance and/or innocence of an entire generation of historians.

The idea that false images of Ireland's past were undermining its present
and mortgaging its future was, of course, quite current by the time Moody
delivered his 1977 lecture. Some fluttering in the academic dovecots had
already been occasioned by the posthumous publication in 1972 of Fr Francis
Shaw's splenetic debunking of the 1916 Rising and by the historical character
of the influential polemics launched against official and popular views on the
Northern Ireland crisis by Moody's own illustrious graduate, Conor Cruise
O'Brien.[15] But until then historians had generally remained silent in public on
contemporary matters. Some like Liam de Paor, when commissioned to write
a popular introduction to the mounting troubles in Ulster, restricted themselves to a relentless historical narrative that scrupulously avoided comment
on current developments. Others like John A. Murphy, hastened to distance
themselves as professional historians from the political arguments of Cruise
O'Brien, while Shaw's article was firmly rebutted by the then doyen of modern
Irish historians, F.S.L. Lyons, in the columns of the *Irish Times*.[16]

But after Moody, inhibitions were relaxed. Lyons himself called almost
immediately for an even more thoroughgoing attack on myth by a broadfronted
campaign of new historical research into social and cultural history.[17] In the
following decade through the columns of two influential intellectual journals,
The Crane Bag and *The Irish Review*, several prominent historians including
Michael Laffan, John A. Murphy and Tom Dunne stoutly defended their

14. Moody's idea that myths should be isolated and treated as hostile to a true knowledge
which can only be derived from a rigorous application of scientifically based method may
have been influenced by Mannheim's *Ideology and Utopia* (London, 1954) and Popper's,
The open society and its enemies (London, 1945); Lévi-Strauss's explosion of the distinction
is performed repeatedly in *Structural anthropology* (London, 1969), *Myth and meaning*
(London, 1978), and *Anthropology and myth* (Oxford, 1987).
15. Francis Shaw, 'The canon of Irish history: a challenge' in *Studies*, lxi (1972), pp. 113-57;
Conor Cruise O'Brien *States of Ireland* (London, 1972).
16. Liam de Paor, *Divided Ulster* (Harmondsworth, 1969); John A Murphy, 'Nationalism
revisited' in *The Crane Bag* ii (1979), pp. 304-11; F.S.L. Lyons, 'The shadow of the past'
in the *Irish Times*, 11 September 1972.
17. Lyons, *The burden of our history*, The W.B. Rankin memorial lecture, 1978 (Belfast, 1979),
reprinted pp. 87-104 below.

discipline's obligation to question and explode misconceptions that lay at the heart of Ireland's remembered past.[18] Some of the statements made in these fora were carefully modulated and others frankly polemical: but for many the most vigorously argued position was provided by Ronan Fanning, suitably enough in his presidential address to the Irish Historical Society founded by Edwards fifty years before. In his paper Fanning trenchantly asserted his generation's responsibility of carrying forward the techniques of historical criticism inculcated by Moody and Edwards into subjects and periods which they had left untouched, lest these areas—and Fanning was particularly concerned with contemporary history—should now fall prey to myth-making by Ireland's manipulative ideologues.[19]

Like Moody, Fanning conceded that this assault on myths had hardly gotten underway. Yet the examination of myth not merely as error, but as a nefarious cultural artefact had already begun. Lyons's own *Culture and Anarchy in Ireland, 1891-1939* a survey of opposing views of Ireland's identity in the early twentieth century was one of the earliest and most controversial contributions in the field.[20] Lyons's work was supported by Roy Foster's careful tracing of the evolution of contemporary historical myths in the pages of popular nineteenth-century Irish historiography.[21] And at the same time, though working quite independently, Oliver MacDonagh, in a series of studies culminating in his *States of Mind* (1983) was elaborating a complementary account of the tortuous development of the nationalist image of Ireland through its interaction and confrontation with other self-confirming English and European myths.[22]

These examinations of the way in which conventional assumptions about Ireland's past had been shaped raised critical questions concerning the character of academic historical writing itself. But when they arose, they were, surprisingly enough, first applied in an area which had remained largely untouched by the historians' debate, the late medieval and early modern periods. Steven Ellis's 'Nationalist historiography and the English and Gaelic worlds' (1989) was an interpretative overview which sought principally to lay

18. *The Crane Bag* devoted a special issue to the topic, (vol 8, i, 1984) and published several relevant articles in other issues, esp., vols 1 (ii) and 2 (i and ii); the *Irish Review*, nos 1 and 4 (1986, 1988) devoted considerable space to the debate.

19. Fanning's paper was delivered to the Irish Historical Society in December 1986 and was subsequently published in James Dooge (ed.), *Ireland in the contemporary world: essays in honour of Garret Fitzgerald* (Dublin, 1988), pp. 131-47, reprinted below, pp. 146-60.

20. Oxford, 1979.

21. 'History and the Irish question', *Transactions of the Royal Historical Society*, 5th series, (1988), pp. 169-92; a later version is reprinted below, pp. 122-45.

22. 'Ambiguity in nationalism: the case of Ireland' in *Historical Studies* (Australia) vol. 19, (1981), pp. 337-52; below, pp. 105-121; ' "Time's revenges and revenge's time": a view of Anglo-Irish relations' in *Anglo-Irish Studies: an interdisciplinary journal* (iv), 1979, pp. 2-14; *States of mind* (London, 1983).

the foundations for his project of establishing a new framework of analysis for comparing the medieval English lordship in Ireland with the experience of English governance in Wales and in the north of England.[23] But this particular undertaking was prefaced by some brief historiographical comments wherein Ellis sought to argue that previous Irish historians had failed to appreciate the significance of the correspondences and similarities he was about to point out because they had been blinded by a dominant nationalist scheme which had required, for the purposes of twentieth-century ideology, that the medieval Irish lordships' history be treated as a distinct and separate entity without reference to similar experiences elsewhere in the area of English law and governance.

Although they provoked little more than some pleasure and some exasperation on the part of medievalists surprised to find themselves included in an exclusively nationalist historiographical tradition, Ellis's sketchy observations represented one of the first examples of an attempt to apply the myth-criticism conducted by Lyons, Foster, MacDonagh and others to contemporary historical writing as a deliberate means of undermining its interpretative credentials. And it was as such that it called forth a radical rebuttal from the early modern historian, Brendan Bradshaw, who disputed not only the terms of Ellis's central argument concerning the medieval lordship and his historiographical categories, but actually identified the article itself as a perfect example of what Bradshaw saw as a malaise that had steadily infected Irish historical writing ever since Moody and Edwards had launched their programme for a new kind of history fifty years before.[24]

For Bradshaw, Ellis's argument was the most explicit but by no means singular instance of the steady deviation of historical writing from its true subject-matter and purpose that had occurred over the previous half-century as a direct result of the austere methods, and consciously directive agenda— setting of the Moody and Edwards school. In claiming that their methods were justified as an attempt to create a 'value-free' historical science, Moody and Edwards were, Bradshaw claimed, at best intellectually and politically naive. And over time, the vanity of their efforts had became obvious in the practices of those they trained. Under the pretence of objectivity their followers had distorted or buried the heritage which the community had received from the past.[25] The fashionably sardonic tone, the narrow, calculating mode of argument and the cynical mode of assessment which the university history schools had encouraged, had served to de-sensitise modern historical writing to the sufferings and injustices of Ireland's past. This implicit desire to evade

23. *I.H.S.* xxv (1986-7), pp. 1-18, reprinted below, pp. 161-80.
24. 'Nationalism and historical scholarship in modern Ireland', in *I.H.S.* xxvi (1988-9), pp. 329-51; reprinted below, pp. 191-216.
25. Ibid., pp. 345-51, below, pp. 210-216.

the essential catastrophic character of Irish history had been compounded by an overt attack on the idea that a clear sense of national consciousness had been deeply rooted in Irish history and was not just a recent or accidental creation. The result of the historians' work therefore had been not merely to perpetuate the injustices suffered by generations past, but to denigrate the achievements and future aspirations of their successors who had successfully asserted their independence from Ireland's colonial past.

Bradshaw's intervention into what had hitherto been a somewhat halting and lop-sided debate could readily be seen to be the nemesis which the pretensions of the crusading reformers of the 1930s had finally invoked. A distinguished historian in his own right, who had undergone as rigorous a training as any professional scholar, and had already produced several studies of a boldly re-interpretative kind based upon indisputable orthodox scholarship, it was remarkable that he, rather than any critics from outside the discipline, should have been responsible for raising both the intellectual and moral stakes of the argument.[26] His article represented a qualitiative development from a growing but hitherto inchoate sense of dissatisfaction voiced in various quarters with the new public role that had been assumed by historians, and it did so primarily by lending much needed clarity, context and depth to the term most commonly employed and least often analysed in the debate concerning the historian's role in contemporary culture: revisionism.

II

Until Bradshaw the critical response to Moody's profession of faith and the similar declarations it encouraged, displayed no greater intellectual sophistication than the claims which it sought to oppose. The unfocussed and often confused nature of this initial debate was most clearly indicated by the extraordinary looseness with which the catch-all term 'revisionism' and its derivations were employed, re-appropriated and dismissed both by historians and their critics alike. The first employment of the term in the public debate remains uncertain. But the major credit for its currency probably belongs to the political and cultural commentator, Desmond Fennell, who, in a series of broadsides against the historians, enlisted it to describe that scholarship which served 'the history needs of the establishment'.[27] From the outset, however,

---

26. Bradshaw's *The dissolution of the religious orders in Ireland* (Cambridge, 1974) and his *The Irish constitutional revolution of the sixteenth century* (Cambridge, 1979) were both major studies which used well-known sources and conventional methods to open up new subjects and explode traditional interpretations. His first contribution to *Irish Historical Studies*, 'The opposition to the ecclesiastical legislation in the Irish reformation parliament' xvi (1968-9) pp. 285-31 was a highly re-interpretative article which was recognized by professional historians as a model of historical revisionism.

27. See Fennell, *The revision of Irish nationalism* (Dublin, 1989) for an account of the emergence

it seems clear, that the term was being applied in a specifically Irish context with few of the connotations it possessed in socialist political thought. Fennell's own use was, moreover, rather ambivalent. On some occasions he appropriated it for his own particular definition of a truly modernised Irish nationalism as opposed to the weaker or thoroughly deceptive manner by which it was being exploited by those whose commitment to the nation was suspect. But on other occasions his application of inverted commas and qualifiers such as 'so called', 'commonly described' etc., suggest that he was not accepting it as an instrument of definition or analysis at all, but simply taking the historians at their own estimation and inverting what they perceived to be a term of approval. That, at any rate, was how those historians who replied to Fennell chose to read his usage and several gladly embraced 'revisionism' as a simple description of the essential characteristic of the historian's work. And so whatever potential for development the argument possessed was immediately defused as the historians translated a political challenge into a mere statement of the obvious.[28]

What this sloppy confusion over terminology revealed, however, was a far deeper disjunction between the historians' perception of their practices and non-historians understanding of history's role that was fast developing under the pressure of political events in the later 1970s and early 1980s. It was at that time during intense public discussions concerning the Northern crisis and specifically during the debate generated by the New Ireland Forum with its repeated calls for a critical and consensual reappraisal all of the island's inherited traditions, that the word 'revisionism' acquired a new political valency in popular usage.[29] Yet for the historians it had long before possessed a far less problematic usage in the commonplace utterances of lecture halls, in reviews and in the prefaces to scholarly monographs to the effect that one or another assumption or conventionally held view about the past was about to be revised.

Even in this uncomplicated diction there was, of course, some genuflexion to the instrumentalist commitments of Moody and Edwards embodied in their journal's section on 'Historical Revision'. But what seemed in the 1930s to be an unproblematic combination of intellectual practice and public service had, in the highly charged political and ideological conditions of the 1970s and 1980s, come to be seen in some quarters as an unhealthy or even disingenuous position. Yet all the while the majority of practising historians failed or refused to see that such a problem existed; and insisted to the contrary that their

of the term; also idem, *Beyond Nationalism* (Dublin, 1985) and for an overview of his opinions *Heresy* (Belfast, 1993); the quotation is from 'Against Revisionism', in the *Irish Review*, 4 (1988), pp. 20-6, p. 22; reprinted below, pp. 183-90.

28. Ronan Fanning, 'The meaning of Revisionism' in the *Irish Review*, 4 (1988), pp 15-19; see also Roy Foster, 'We are all revisionists now' in ibid., 1 (1986), pp. 1-5.

29. Desmond Fennell, *The revision of Irish republicanism*, provides a useful, if somewhat subjective context for these debates.

critics' case was not merely politically motivated, but rested more seriously on a fundamental misunderstanding of what the practice of scholarly history was all about. There was no further room for argument.

From a purely professional perspective such a disengagement on the part of historians was perhaps understandable. But seen in another way it was far from satisfactory. For to many it seemed unacceptable for historians, who had often been seen to have used their professional standing to comment on a wide range of contemporary political and cultural issues, to withdraw to the defences of the academy once their claim to objectivity had been challenged in the public domain. In these circumstances it was the admission of a trained historian, Brendan Bradshaw, that the non-historical critics, whatever the limitations of their arguments, had correctly sensed something seriously amiss in the character of contemporary historical writing, and his further demonstration that these ills could be traced to the uncritically accepted assumptions of historical practice itself that radically altered the character of the debate. Not surprisingly then, it was on the larger issues raised by his critique of Ellis, rather than on the immediate dispute about the status of the medieval Irish lordship that subsequent argument developed.[30]

The event which inaugurated this second, rather more intense phase of what had now become an historians' debate was the publication, while Bradshaw's article was in the press, of the first major synthesis of modern Irish history to be produced by the present generation of Irish historians, R. F. Foster's *Modern Ireland 1600-1972*.[31] The appearance of Foster's survey established the lines of demarcation between historical revisionists and anti-revisionists in a far more public manner than had occurred before. To those who approved, Foster's work was a model of careful, dispassionate scholarship, judicious assessment and elegant compression. To those who did not, it was the epitome of revisionism, and in opposing him many critics followed Bradshaws 'metacritique' with remarkable fidelity. Some complained about Foster's style, apparently lucid and highly polished, but, they argued, deceptive in effect; and others engaged in the entertaining old word-game of isolating for comparison the adjectives and adverbs to which the author habitually resorted in order to lend weight to his assessments of events and personalities. The identification of lacunae in the narrative or imbalances in the evidence discussed were also used, following Bradshaw's argument, to suggest that the historian was underplaying or evading central but uncomfort-

30. Ellis made a spirited response in 'Historiographical debate: representations of the past in Ireland: whose past and whose present?' in *I.H.S.* xxvii (1990-1), pp. 289-308 which was largely concerned with a detailed rebuttal of Bradshaw's arguments against his comparative approach; his more general contention that historians should pay closer attention to the parallels between the development of Afrikaaner nationalism in the nineteenth century and the course of Irish nationalism has not generally been taken up.

31. London (1988).

able issues in Irish history. And finally there were those, like Bradshaw himself, who argued that Foster's old-fashioned dependence on the stock-in-trade of the historian's *modus explicandi*, i.e. complexity, contingency, accident and imperfection, offered a way of denying the possibility that the positive dynamic of a developing national consciousness could be invoked as a useful concept of historical interpretation.[32]

Some of the criticism that Foster attracted arose from normal academic disputatiousness, but in other responses a more general reaction against the representative character of his work, against his self-confident judgements and his assured manner of explanation which were assumed to be typical of conventional academic history was to be discerned. Thus it was the negative aspects of Bradshaw's critique rather than the positive proposals for an alternative kind of history which he advanced which were most readily absorbed and developed in the public arena while the underlying intellectual assumptions of those criticisms themselves were largely left unexamined.

Bradshaw's argument, for example, that the methods and attitudes of the majority of contemporary academic historians were sufficiently uniform to enable him to treat them as a single school were, despite his own qualifications, quickly translated in more general representations, into the view that there indeed existed an 'historical establishment' which served as an intellectual ancillary to the political establishment.[33] This relatively simplified 'counter-revisionist' argument arose in part from resentment at the off-handed manner in which academic mandarins sometimes in public fora had dismissed or ridiculed dearly-held beliefs about the past. But the familiar anti- intellectual suspicion that the wise men were treating the people like straw dogs was re-inforced by the association of some prominent scholars with particular political parties or politicians, by the regular appearance of others in the national media offering expert commentary on contemporary affairs, by the acceptance by historians of 'establishment' awards like the Ewart-Biggs prize (founded for the purposes of improving Anglo-Irish understanding), and by

32. Among the more considered critical responses to Foster were, Kevin O'Neill's in the *Irish Literary Supplement* (Fall 1989) pp. 1, 39 (reprinted below pp. 217-21), Kevin Kenny's in *The Recorder (a journal of the Irish American historical society)* (Summer 1990), pp. 98-105, Kevin Whelan's in *Alpha* vol 1, ii (March 1989), p. 19 and Aidan Clarke's in *The New Republic* no. 1.

33. In addition to Fennell, 'Against Revisionism' see the implications drawn with varying degrees of certitude by Declan Kiberd, 'The elephant of revolutionary forgetfulness' in Máirín Ní Dhonnchadha and Theo Dorgan (eds), *Revising the Rising*, pp. 1-20, Gearóid Ó Crualaoich, 'Responding to the Rising in ibid., pp. 50-78; Jim Smyth, ' "An entirely exceptional case": Ireland and the British problem' in the *Historical Journal* 34 (1991), pp. 999-1007; Kevin Whelan, 'The recent writing of Irish history' in *U.C.D. History Review* (1991), pp. 27-35, Padraig Ó Snodaigh, *Two godfathers of revisionism: 1916 in the revisionist canon* (Dublin, 1991).

the well-published refusal of some modern historians to associate themselves with conferences or associations which adopted a sympathetic attitude towards militant nationalism.[34]

Yet on closer analysis such an impressionistic politico-sociological theory failed to carry conviction. Crude attempts to attribute ideological or intellectual allegiance on the grounds of university affiliation, education or ethnic background now seem merely speculative, possibly offensive, and certainly not testable. But more importantly, the positing of a single dominant school of historiography—an establishment—has done great injustice to the highly variegated and innovative developments in historical research and writing which have occurred over the past half-century. The nomination of particular pioneers in this process of variegation would, in this context, be invidious. But a brief reflection on the way in which not merely historical interpretation but the actual conduct of research has been revolutionised by the contributions of scholars applying the techniques of economic, sociological and anthropological analysis should be sufficient to dispel the notion that the high political history celebrated by an earlier generation of historians still dominates the field. While more recently, the slow but steady advance of the history of women in Ireland as a distinctive body of study offers a hopeful indication that the processes of development and diversification are still very much alive in Irish academic history.[35] If an historical establishment exists today it is a far more heterodox, even fragmented, school than some non-historians would seem to believe.

The one partial exception to this rule of inclusiveness is in itself significant. For it is an instance of marginalization within the historical world which neither historians nor the majority of their critics have been anxious to consider, that is, of course, Ireland's Marxist historical tradition. From James Connolly, through Emile Strauss and Desmond Greaves to the conceptually sophisticated work of contemporary scholars like Paul Bew and Henry Patterson, Marxist scholarship has encountered considerable resistance within Irish historiography, while the generalising models of international Marxist scholars, such as Perry Anderson, Immanuel Wallerstein, Paul Hirst and Barry Hindess, have exercised even less influence on Irish historical thinking. That this neglect of Marxism can be associated with the ambivalence of many Marxists toward the problem of Irish nationalism and toward their fellow-Marxists' address to that

34. See Ó Tuathaigh, 'Irish historical revisionism' below, pp. 304-24.
35. For an important contribution to the development of women's history which sets the subject within the constructive and instrumentalist frame of the 'new history' see, Margaret MacCurtain, Mary O'Dowd and Maria Luddy, 'An agenda for women's history in Ireland, 1500-1900' in *I.H.S.* xxviii (1992-3), pp. 1-37. 'The history of women' was the theme of the Irish conference of historians in 1993, its proceedings are due to be published under the auspices of the Irish committee of historical sciences as Mary O'Dowd and Sabine Wichert (eds.), *Historical Studies XIX.*

central issue is clear from Anthony Coughlan's essay included below. But it is clear also that the failure of either of the parties in the revisionist dispute to engage in any serious way with competing Marxist models has had much to do with the relative insularity of the Irish debate.[36]

The conspiratorial notion of a closed and coherent historical establishment which has been drawn rather too easily from Bradshaw's description of a common style of analysis and expression has therefore proved unconvincing. And so too, it may seem, is the more specific charge that professional historians have sought to sustain the quite impossible pretension to be 'value free'. But again such a frequently raised criticism, it may be objected, represents merely an over-simplified version of Bradshaw's central point. It was never essential to his case that contemporary historians should claim to be value free—for clearly the vast majority of them do not, nor even that they should consciously aspire to the ideal. Rather it was his contention that the founders of modern Irish historiography certainly avowed that aspiration and, in following the methods and emulating the style which they prescribed, all subsequent historians have, willingly or not, absorbed their objectives.

III

The attitude of Moody and Edwards toward the epistemological status of history is, therefore, central to Bradshaw's argument, yet the case he has advanced in this crucial regard remains inconclusive. It is, in the first place, unclear whether Moody and Edwards ever declared their aim to be the construction of a value-free history: Bradshaw uses the term in inverted commas, but fails to supply any reference for the usage. He allows that they may merely have aimed toward that end rather than have regarded it as a realistic objective, but such a distinction he believes is analytically unimportant. Yet this disregard of a distinction between aspirations and objectives will trouble some who may argue that the difference is, in itself, the product of two entirely opposed epistemologies. A firm commitment to the aspiration of objectivity may, that is, be predicated on the assumption that, because its attainment is logically impossible, the only possibility of clarity in argument and equality in dialogue lies in a common agreement that it should always be striven for. This, for instance, was the position of Max Weber—the high-priest of value-free social science—who exerted an immense influence on twentieth-century historical practice. For Weber the systematic methodology of social science was intended to serve not as a guide to objective truth, but as a strategic weapon in his struggle against the twin enemies of nihilism and relativism.[37]

36. See Anthony Coughlan, 'Ireland's Marxist historians' below, pp. 288-305.
37. On the strategic nature of Weber's value-free methodology see Fredric Jameson, 'The

But such philosophical difficulties aside, the theoretical foundations with which Bradshaw actually accredits Moody and Edwards are ones of striking simplicity.

During their formative years as trainee historians, the two men, it appears, came under the influence of Herbert Butterfield, the remarkable British historian whose critique 'the Whig interpretation of English history'—the unquestioned belief in England's natural progress towards prosperity and liberty—stimulated their own determination to attack the Irish version of providentialism: the nationalist tradition of Ireland's steady march towards the assertion of independence.[38] There are some difficulties of timing and association in this account which need further investigation before the point is accomplished. First, it is not clear how aware the two London-based scholars were of the Cambridge don before they had commenced their work in Ireland.[39] *The Whig interpretation*, to be sure, was published in 1931, but it was of only a decade later, after the publication of Butterfield's own far from value-free, and decidedly Whiggish, book on *The Englishman and his history* (1944), that he came to have as examiner and collaborator an undoubtedly close connection with the Irish historians.[40] More seriously, the depiction of Butterfield as a defender of history as a value-free science can be easily overdrawn. For even in the early 1930s he was a passionate evangelical Christian—a lay preacher— whose polemic against the Whig historians was undertaken not to deny the role or the inevitability of moral judgement in history, but to constrain its practice by opposing those who too lightly made such judgements on the basis of hindsight and those who confidently believed that they could uncover all that history had to reveal.[41] Butterfield's influence on Irish historiography is a subject which certainly requires further investigation, but it is unlikely that

vanishing mediator; or Max Weber as Storyteller' in *The ideologies of theory; essays 1971–86* vol. 2, pp. 3–34; on the historical context of Weber's ideas, see Arthur Mitzman, *The iron-cage: an historical interpretation of Max Weber* (New York, 1970).

38. Bradshaw, 'Nationalism and historical scholarship', below, pp. 193, 197–8.

39. Bradshaw cites Edwards' son Owen's 'conviction' that the Irish historians' connection with Cambridge dates from the early 1930s, but offers no corroborative evidence to support the impression; connections between the Cambridge history faculty and the Institute of research in London do not appear to have been particularly close at this time. On Butterfield's career and outlook at this time see the editor's highly informative introductory essay in C.T. McIntire (ed.), *Herbert Butterfield: writings on Christianity and history* (Oxford, 1979).

40. Butterfield first addressed the Conference of Irish historians in 1945, his paper, 'Tendencies in historical study in England' was published in *I.H.S.* iv (1944–5), pp. 209–23 where he concluded, 'no student would be justified in saying that reflection on history or the development of historical science is calculated to lead to a cynical conclusion or a pessimistic outlook'.

41. On Butterfield's passionate commitment to evangelical Christianity throughout this time see McIntire (ed.), *Herbert Butterfield*, pp. xx–xxxix.

any examination will reveal that such a man had set out to persuade anyone
of the possibility, still less the desirability, of value-free history.

These matters are as yet speculative. But rather than following one or
other possible individual influence, it seems more plausible even now to suggest
that, in common with Butterfield and so many other historians and social
scientists throughout the West in the inter-war years, Moody and Edwards
along with the other Irish historians of their generation were confronting a
much more formidable challenge to the epistemological status of historical
practice in general than Butterfield's little polemic against the Whigs. This
was the long threatening but slowly apprehended crisis that was presented to
all historians by the European—mostly German—philosophical movement
known as historicism.

The view that historical investigation could be equated with the methods
of empirical science—a view most bluntly expressed in 1902 by the Irish
historian J.B. Bury—had been under intense attack from philosophers and
social critics long before Bury spoke. Heinrich Rickert's systematic demonstration of the incompatibility of the logic of scientific method and historical
argument combined with Wilhelm Dilthey's and Benedetto Croce's arguments
affirming the impossibility of sustaining a categorical distinction between the
contemporary mind and the fragments of the past which it sought to read as
external phenomena had seriously begun to trouble the generation of historians
who came of age around the turn of the century.[42]

Reactions among those who chose to confront these theoretical challenges
varied. At one extreme it led to an intensification of efforts to establish some
suprahistorical explanation for the tides of historical process that was demon-
strable above the flux of events themselves. Such was the response, for instance,
of Henri Berr and his colleagues in founding the *Revue de synthèse historique*.[43]
At the other extreme it led to a happy but generally unreflective acceptance
that history was, after all, simply a literary and artistic activity, an attitude
most commonly associated with G.M. Trevelyan and his manifesto acclaiming
Clio: a Muse.[44] But between these opposed positions most historians attempted
to hold a moderate line which sought at once to concede the inescapable
relativity and incompleteness of their work while making a claim to offer

42. The classic texts are Heinrich Rickert, *Kulturwissenschaft und Naturwissenschaft* (5th edn.,
    Tubingen, 1921), Wilhelm Dilthey, *Pattern and meaning in history*, ed. and trans. H.P.
    Rickman (New York, 1972), Benedetto Croce, *My philosophy* ed. and trans. E.F. Carritt
    (London, 1949); for general accounts see, George Iggers, 'Historicism' in *Dictionary of the
    history of ideas*, 2, pp. 456-68 and Leonard Krieger, *Time's reasons: philosophies of history,
    old and new* (Chicago, 1989), pp. 107-36.
43. The programmatic preface composed by Berr for the *Revue* is translated and edited in
    Fritz Stern (ed.), *Varieties of history: from Voltaire to the present* (London, 1970), pp. 250-6;
    see also Philippe Carrard, *Poetics of the new history* (Baltimore, 1992), pp. 1-28.
44. *Clio: a Muse and other essays, literary and pedestrian* (London, 1913), pp. 1-55.

statements about the past which were both internally coherent and externally defensible. In pursuit of the latter, they looked for support from a related group of social sciences, from economics, sociology, clinical psychology and the new political science. Though they clearly offered no ultimate escape from the dilemma posed to the historians, these branches of learning at least provided some logically defensible *modi operandi* which reduced the area of caprice and personal bias in historical writing and rendered historical judgements and interpretations available to more external assessment and evaluation than had been the case in the past.[45]

This was the strategy adopted most explicitly by Charles Beard, Carl Becker and their fellow 'new historians' in the United States. But it was the one followed also, though in a less overtly crusading manner, by a host of historians in Europe and England, by, for example, social and economic historians, like J.H. Clapham in Cambridge and R.H. Tawney in London and most openly by A.F. Pollard, the founding editor of that essential model for *Irish Historical Studies*, the London University-based journal, *History*.[46]

The 'highly elaborated historical science' to which Moody and Edwards made reference in the preface to their journal was not therefore perceived by their own or indeed the preceding generation of historians as an unproblematic discipline. It was rather one whose integrity had been painstakingly reconstructed over recent decades not as a crudely proclaimed 'value-free science' but as a complex and slippery body of accumulating knowledge whose statements required the closest care in formulation and development before they could sustain any claim to authority. For its promoters the new history in Ireland was not only a beginning, it was also the conclusion of a profound historical debate.

If the international atmosphere of post-historicist historical practice was not in itself sufficient to shape the outlook of Moody and Edwards and their contemporaries, cultural conditions peculiar to Ireland supplied further grounds for the establishment of a local 'new history' school. For the character of recent Irish historiography had provided a clear and highly distinctive demonstration of the historicists' case against the pretensions of history to be

---

45. For accounts of this moderate response in various traditions of historiography see Cushing Stout, *The pragmatic revolt in American history* (New Haven, 1958); Richard Hofstadter, *The progressive historians: Turner, Parrington and Beard* (New York, 1968); Peter Novick, *That noble dream: the objectivity question and the American historical profession* (Cambridge, 1988); Carrard, *Poetics of the new history;* Krieger, *Time's reasons;* and the representative selections reproduced in Stern (ed.), *Varieties of history*, esp., pp. 256-66, 304-27.

46. For the new history's influence over British historiography at this time see, Ross Terrill, *R.H. Tawney and his times*, (London, 1973) and the several reflective pieces contributed by Pollard to *History*, including, 'History and science' new series i (1916), pp. 25-39; 'Historical criticism', v (1920), pp. 21-9; 'An apology for historical research', vii (1922), pp. 161-77. For Clapham see Stern (ed.), *Varieties of history*, pp. 308-13.

an objective science. That versions of Irish history had served an important propagandist function in the movement towards Irish independence was, of course, well-known, and neither Moody and Edwards had been the first to be troubled by the problem of history's obvious ideological usefulness. At the same time, the fact that Irish history had often been written with due respect for Rankean rules and standards was something of which historians like Moody and Edwards were also well aware.[47] Yet it was also clear that this apparently sound academic history was shot through with the concerns of contemporary ideological debates in which the pretence to objectivity and impartiality was a powerful rhetorical weapon. The classic example of these encounters was the titanic struggle between W.E.H. Lecky and J.A. Froude in which both men battled about the real significance of modern Irish history—and the role of the Anglo-Irish within it—with all the paraphernalia of scholarship but with a clear ideological interest concerning the shape of contemporary British policy for Ireland that became plain for all to see.[48]

But a more recent and perhaps more disturbing instance of such present-minded academic practice was provided by clashes over the fate of the protestant reformation in Ireland which had occurred in the late 1920s and early 1930s. Again Moody and Edwards were not the first to fear the employment of academic history in the service of cultural and narrowly confessional disputes in the newly-independent Ireland: the eminent medievalist, Edmund Curtis, had warned against such developments as early as 1925.[49] But in the early 1930s, as the movement toward censorship and the closure of public debate gathered pace, the prospect that D.P. Moran's bluntly sectarian distinction between a Catholic Irish-Ireland and a Protestant Anglo-Ireland should soon infect Ireland's intellectual and scholarly life seemed increasingly likely.[50]

In the resistance against this drift toward the suppression of cultural diversity, it was, as is well known, the decades' writers and critics rather than the historians who took the lead. Most notably it was Seán O'Faolain who in

47. See their prefaces to their 1930s monographs—Moody, *The Londonderry plantation* (London, 1939) and especially Edwards, *Church and state in Tudor Ireland*, pp xxviii-xxxi; see also Moody's reflective comments in 'Twenty years after', in *I.H.S.* xi (1958-9), pp. 1-4.

48. Donal McCartney, *W.E.H. Lecky: historian and politician, 1838-1903* (Dublin, 1994), esp. chs. 4-6, 'James Anthony Froude and Ireland: an historiographical controversy' in T.D. Williams (ed.), *Historical Studies VIII*, pp. 171-90; Anne Wyatt, 'Froude, Lecky and "the humblest Irishman"' in *I.H.S.* xix (1974-5), pp 261-85; L.P. Curtis, 'Introduction' in W.E.H. Lecky, *A history of Ireland in the eighteenth century*, ed. and abridged by Curtis (Chicago, 1972), pp ix-l.

49. Curtis, 'Irish history and its popular versions', in *Irish Rosary*, xxix (1925), pp. 321-9; I owe this reference to Prof. James Lydon.

50. See Terence Brown, *Ireland: a social and cultural history, 1922-85*, (2nd edn, London, 1985), chs. 4-5; Michael Adams, *Censorship: the Irish experience* (Dublin, 1968), chs. 1-4.

a series of literary endeavours culminating in the founding of *The Bell* in 1940 forthrightly made the case that the encouragement of cultural heterodoxy was itself a nationalist issue—a necessary precondition of the gradual realization of a truly independent Ireland which was still in the process of becoming.[51] Significantly, in launching his campaign O'Faolain turned primarily not to fiction, but to social and cultural commentary and, most of all, to history. Thus in a large corpus of boldly interpretative essays, in new editions of revered Irish texts, and most importantly, in his biographical studies of major figures in Irish history, Hugh O'Neill, Daniel O'Connell and Eamon de Valera, he attempted to delineate an alternative tradition of Irish history that rested on no single or exclusive explanatory factor, such as religion, race or language, but on an accumulating series of practical responses to changed material and cultural conditions.[52]

O'Faolain proclaimed the manifesto of his new constructivist programme, in the manner of Moody and Edwards, in the preface to the first issue of his own journal *The Bell*. Introducing what appeared to be a literary magazine, O'Faolain surprisingly called for contributions not first and foremost for poetry, fiction and conventional literary criticism, but looked instead for reportage, realism and expressions of cultural diversity and dissent.

> It is our job [he wrote], to have a flair . . . for the real thing, for the thing that is alive and kicking as against the thing that is merely pretending to be alive. We have to go out nosing for bits of individual veracity, hidden in the dust heaps of convention, imitation, timidity, traditionalism, wishful thinking. In that search our only advantage is that of being professional writers. . . .[53]

What O'Faolain would demand from his contributors was not 'Art but Truth' for there were 'a hundred thousand things that are full of Art but, as for Truth, are as skinny as Famine'.

Though in his later years O'Faolain was to appear as a man disillusioned with the claims of Irish republican nationalism, he remained at this stage passionately committed to the belief that independence had unleashed opportunities for the construction of a new political culture in Ireland which might yet be fulfilled. His support of literary realism was part of this conviction, and so too his active promotion of non-fictional observation, and its most important

51. Brown, op. cit., esp., pp. 199-206; Maurice Harmon, *Seán O'Faolain: a critical introduction* (Dublin, 1984).
52. Harmon, pp. 3-57; see especially O'Faolain, *The king of the beggars* (Dublin, 1938), *De Valera* (Harmondsworth, 1939), *The great O'Neill* (London, 1942); for O'Faolain's continuing belief in the possibility of a literary re-making of Ireland, see *inter alia* his 'Standards and tastes' in *The Bell* (June, 1941), pp. 2-5.
53. 'This is your magazine', *The Bell* (December, 1940) p. 1.

aspect of all was his own historical/biographical project to re-interpret the Irish political tradition and the men who made it.[54]

In this last O'Faolain was not alone. For his own efforts at intellectual and organisational reform closely paralleled the the aims and methods of Ireland's first 'new historians'. Like him, they were also determined to devise a means of uncovering and narrating historical truths in a manner that was at once free from sentiment and bias, but available for use by all cultural traditions. Like him, they too were anxious to increase and to broaden the number of minds engaged in historical reflection and to use short interpretative articles in accessible journals to report the significance of these discoveries in the quickest possible time. And finally, like O'Faolain, they too were sufficiently confident of the contribution of their work toward the realisation of an Ireland that was yet to be, that, despite their very different cultural backgrounds, they could unite in launching their journal with the traditional prayer of Ireland's patriots: *dochum glóire Dé agus onóra na hÉireann.*[55]

IV

The point of the foregoing observations on the various contexts out of which the Moody and Edwards, initiative arose has not been simply to replace Bradshaw's speculative sketch with a more elaborate scenario, nor merely to rehabilitate the reputations of the two men as reflective scholars—a matter which, though supported by much anecdotal reminiscence, requires further study. I have sought rather to indicate the overlapping concerns of Irish cultural and intellectual life which, whatever their own impulses, made the principles and strategies of the new historians so attractive to critical intellects that were reaching maturity in Ireland in the 1930s and 1940s. The 'new history', that is to say, thrived in Irish universities not because young Irish scholars were sycophantic and uncritical lackeys of the great men, but because its underlying assumptions and aspirations continued to satisfy those engaged upon a sustained examination of the problems of Ireland's past and of its representation in the present.[56]

54. In 'Challenging the canon', his valuable section on the literary and intellectual backgrounds to the emergence of 'revisionism' in Seamus Deane (ed.), *The Field Day anthology of Irish writing*, vol. iii, pp. 561-680, Luke Gibbons rightly points to the importance of O'Faolain as a pioneer of cultural revisionism, but in drawing his examples from O'Faolain's slightly later views and in emphasising his harsh criticism of the contemporary romanticisation of Gaelic literature, history and culture, Gibbons somewhat under-rates the extent to which the proto-revisionist O'Faolain was still committed to the aspiration of a new Irish republic.

55. Edwards claimed to have been the one to have proposed the motto, but acknowledges that Moody accepted his suggestion without reservation, Edwards, 'T.W. Moody and the origins of Irish Historical Studies', *I.H.S.* xxvi (1988-9), p. 2.

56. For accounts of the influence exercised by both men over younger scholars, see Lyons,

To say that the Irish new historians were a deeply influential cultural force is not, of course, to say that they were right. But it is to suggest that when their influence and the public standing of history in general became a matter of criticism and debate in the 1970s and 1980s, something more significant than the displacement of old men from high academic office was taking place. The gathering debate over the practice of academic history has been related by commentators to the operation of several external forces, to the intractable 'troubles' in the North, to the unexpected re-examination of Irish identity that followed upon Ireland's sudden encounter with Europe, to the collapse of consensus in the light of successive governments' inability to resolve the Republic's chronic social and economic problems. Such extraneous influences doubtless exerted their sway. But the apparent failure of academic history to address these problems, or more accurately, the widespread opinion that the historians were reneging on their obligation to speak with an authoritative impartiality on these issues raised even more serious intrinsic problems within the discipline itself. For it began to appear that both in the nature of their research and in the manner in which it was presented, the later generation of historians were falling short of the founders' initial ambition to create an historical corpus which would at once allow for further investigative development and yet be of immediate educational value to the contemporary reading public.

By the later 1970s the new history's work, as Moody himself was forced to concede, had been remarkably slow in its rate of progress. The aim of recovering a hitherto unknown Irish history was far from being attained. It is true that the instrumentalist ambition of persuading history's readers to adopt a consciously critical attitude toward received versions of the past had produced some improvement in the character of school texts. But it had also generated much confusion, partisanship and mistrust among the public at large.

The disappointment of 'the new history's' pedagogic aims can in part be explained by the practical tardiness and disorganisation of the reformers themselves, as both the prospectus for *A new history of Ireland* and Ó Gráda's essay, included below, sadly reveal.[57] But deeper influences were also at work. For it is clear that the very substantial work that had actually been carried out by the historians had led not toward a new consensus, but toward increasing specialization, differentiation and exceptionalism, while the occasional movements toward convergence that had occurred turned out to be interim stages in a further process of divergence and debate that now characterised modern historical discourse. Studded with technical argument, illusions, nuances and

'T.W.M.' in Ireland under the union, pp. 1-33; Clarke, 'Robert Dudley Edwards', in *I.H.S.* xxvi (1988-9), pp. 121-7.

57. Cormac Ó Gráda, 'Making history in Ireland in the 1940s and 1950s: the saga of the *The great famine*', in *The Irish Review*, no. 2 (1992), pp. 87-107, reprinted below, pp. 269-87.

unstated empirical and conceptual assumptions the idiom of academic history had become increasingly self-referential, and by turn either hopelessly obscure or deceptively plain to the uninitiated reader.

Thus, as Brendan Bradshaw and others have contended, there had indeed arisen in recent decades a serious problem concerning the intelligibility and cultural utility of history which, whether they chose to acknowledge it or not, confronted and continues to confront contemporary Irish historians. But despite the narrow confines within which the Irish 'revisionist' debate has been conducted, academic history's present predicament is a phenomenon of a far more general character than Ireland's local difficulty. And its origins may be traced to influences rather more profound and considerably less dishonourable that many of the historians' critics have liked to suggest. They may be found, indeed, in the usually unstated assumption underlying the very strategy, sketched above, which the 'new historians' everywhere adopted to escape from the dilemmas presented to them by the sceptical, relativising challenge of philosophical historicism.

V

Having abandoned the pretensions of their nineteenth-century predecessors to act as the metahistorical interpreters of their culture, and having rejected also the possibility of emulating the logic and precision of the natural sciences, the 'new historians', in Ireland as elsewhere, rested their claim to represent a distinct and coherent body of knowledge on the integrity of good practice. The purification of method in the collection, criticism and citation of sources, primary and secondary, was the most obvious and least original element of their project. The aim to purify the language in which history was written was a second. Their mistrust of a self-conscious or literary style was the product of no pedantic delight in unashamed dullness, but rather of an acute awareness of the slippery nature of historical discourse, and a determination to prevent the deceptive rhetorics of the romantics or the scientists from creeping back in unnoticed. Thus the distinctive rhetorical tropes of the old schools, the images, metaphors, similes and symbols, which characterised their discursive strategies were to be carefully expunged from the new historical texts; and the implicitly predetermined interpretations which they supported thereby dismantled.[58]

58   The characterisation of the literary modes of nineteenth-century historiography has been borrowed here from Hayden White, *Metahistory: the historical imagination in the nineteenth century* (Baltimore, 1973); but while the new historians rarely sought to address the grand style analytically, as White has done, it was precisely against these stylistic strategies which they regarded as occlusive, mystifying and redundant that they were reacting in their insistence on the plain style, for a critical defence of this attitude by a partially reconstructed old new historian, see J.H. Hexter, 'The rhetoric of history' in Hexter, *Doing history* (Bloomington, Indiana), pp. 3-28.

Under these austere conditions of expression, few alternative modes remained. Mere chronology was an option, and in large part a necessity, for historians continued to believe that some respect for the convention of chrological sequence was required if only to make the presentation of their research intelligible. But it was, of course, insufficient. And where they sought to elevate their discourse above the plane of unglossed reportage the idiom that seemed best to provide some argumentative tissue for their disparate factual statements while threatening the least adulteration to the purity of historical language was *irony*.[59] Through irony the modern historian found a way of juxtaposing the 'new facts' generated by research with the familiar ones, or of re-organising previously unquestioned relations through the interpolation of newly acquired perspectives. But most importantly of all, the practice of irony permitted the historian to organise his discourse in a manner that commanded assent not by any external referent but by its own pellucid logic. The new facts found may not have been true in any philosophical sense, and the interpretation advanced may not have had any lasting claim to authority. But the historian had found a way of developing an argument that might secure the compliance of the most sceptical or unsympathetic reader simply through interlinked reiterations of the same formal statement, that the relationship of fact x to fact y was not necessarily good or bad, or even true or untrue, but ironic.[60]

59. Irony is, of course, a protean concept which in some hands has been used to explain the working of every form of literary expression. But the particular mode to which I refer here has been ably defined and analysed by Wayne C. Booth (*A rhetoric of irony*, Chicago, 1974) as 'stable irony', i.e. a medium of communication based upon the writer's invitation to readers to contemplate the inner, higher or contradictory meanings of the statement being made on the basis of a shared ground of experience, knowledge and judgement. The consent of readers is thus gained not by the authority of the writer as the master-manipulator of his or her material, but by their autonomous responses to the statements or related sets of statements placed before them. Booth's largely formalist critique is principally concerned with the mechanics of ironic presentation and reception, though he recognises that such engagements have been made necessary by ethical problems arising out of the epistemological uncertainty of certain modes of discourse. The ethical origin of the ironist's concern to communicate dialogically within such formidable constraints is more fully discussed in Gary J. Handwerk, *Irony and ethics in narrative: from Schlegel to Lacan* (New Haven, 1985).

60 The operation of this basic irony can be observed within historical writing on a number of levels. It is most obvious as a self-conscious style: in witty connective sentences ('This thirst for ignorance extended into some journalistic circles', J.J. Lee); in pithy interpretative summaries ('It was the only period in his life that he ever spent in prison, and the only period in his life that he ever spent in close and prolonged contact with his followers', F.S.L. Lyons); in dramatic conclusions ('But that amounts to saying that this physical force movement made its only vital conquest in the realm of the spirit', T.W. Moody); and in simple introductory gambits ('The parliament that Sidney summoned in January 1569 was used to promote a policy of conquest. It also brought out the first evidence of parliamentary opposition to the methods employed to make conquest a reality', G.A.

Irony then—occasionally exercised as an elegant and witty style, but more generally deployed as the plain and understated juxtaposition of the novel and the familiar—became a characteristic idiom of academic historical discourse. Like due respect for the rules of method and the techniques they adapted from the related social sciences, it enabled the historians to evade some of the most serious epistemological problems afflicting their study. But it was also replete with danger. Crudely applied, the ironic style easily degenerated into the merely sardonic—a facile desire to shock, amuse or deride—which, when indulged in their off-handed remarks in lecture-halls, or in print, or in their attempts to intervene in contemporary public debates, has embroiled historians in all the problems of partisanship and mistrust noted before. But more fundamentally irony as a mode of communication within historical discourse depends for its continuing effectiveness on increasing increments of knowledge. It imposes, that is, a constant requirement that the reader should know enough to get the point. And the longer the discourse persists, the more it demands that writer and reader should share a common bank of data, a shared experience of the previous stages of discussion and an agreement on the underlying terms within which further discussion will take place. It is, in short, progressively and irrevocably elitist.[61]

Here then is the paradox that from the outset lay at the heart of the 'new history's' project. A movement that began by renouncing all claims to authority based upon external referents such as artistic inspiration or scientific logic, and happily embraced the idea that (given a proper training in method), everyman might be his own historian, generated a form of discourse that in time subverted its own open-ended and egalitarian aspirations. The orchestration of a systematic programme of constructive research did not after all facilitate the instrumentalist aim of bringing the good news to the people: it actually militated against it.

Since, however, the problematic style cultivated by the Irish 'new historians' was merely a particular example of the rhetorical strategies developed by historians everywhere in the West in response to the challenge of historicism, it is not surprising that the Irish debate over 'revisionism' should appear merely as a particular example of a crisis that has confronted academic historians everywhere in the last half-century. For while few of the participants in the Irish debate have paid any notice to the parallels, the whole range of

Hayes-McCoy). But less obviously and more fundamentally it is a strategy intrinsic in the structure of re-interpretative argument, whether overtly revisionist or not, as the familiar, commonly inherited event is placed in relation to another previously unknown or perceived in a different frame in a manner that seeks to redefine and re-establish a common perception of the original instance.

61. See Booth, *Rhetoric of irony*, esp. ch. 1 and pp. 72-3; the difficulties of exclusiveness which he notices there apply with particular force where the accumulation of an agreed corpus of evidence is essential to the communication and development of argument.

issues concerning the selective use of sources, the moral obligations of the scholar, the relationship of the historians to the institutions of the state and finally the very style and tone of conventional academic writing which have been raised in Ireland since the early 1980s are precisely those which have for long been central to historical controversies elsewhere; in the debates on slavery and African-American history in the United States, on the nature of the Third Reich in Germany, on the significance of the Revolution, the Third Republic and Vichy in France, and on the status of women's history everywhere.[62]

But if the sources of Ireland's *Historikerstreit* can be shown to be both deeper and more general than the alleged moral and intellectual deficiencies of the present generation of practitioners, it seems clear also that the cures commonly advanced for Irish history's ills are hardly sufficient to heal the patient. The commonly prescribed nostrum that the narrow-minded academicians should be required to look at altogether new sources, to apply new conceptual frameworks, or pay more attention to neglected groups, places, events or ideas offers only temporary relief. For such was the very means by which the old 'new historians' once established their own claims to leadership; and thus as a rallying cry by which young tyros have traditionally mounted an assault on the bastions of some perceived historical establishment, the demand for a new kind of history seems more like a recurrence rather than a resolution of the original problem.

Yet even the more reflective calls made by Bradshaw for a new historical attitude that would be more imaginative and more empathic in its encounter with the past seem, despite their undoubted attraction, hardly more helpful. Loosely employed as a medium of criticism, such simple injunctions remain subjective, untestable and easily degenerate into a high-sounding version of unarguable bar-room abuse. But even when more carefully formulated, the prescription to empathise or imagine a little more would seem to be of relatively little heuristic value to scholars who must find their way amongst thickets of conflicting and inchoate materials that are often deceptive, sometimes unintelligible and never susceptible to absolute judgement.

Equally difficult is Bradshaw's plea for a new public history which would conscientiously rehearse the past sufferings and achievements of the Irish people in a manner that would be both instructive and re-enforcing. He has allowed in the Irish case that such people's histories might lead to the elaboration of two traditions, the nationalist and the unionist ones deplored

62. For accounts of these international debates see Novick, *That noble dream*, pp. 469-629; Charles Maier, *The unmasterable past: history, the holocaust and German national identity* (Cambridge, Mass., 1988); Guy Bourdé et Henri Martin, *Les écoles historiques* (Paris, 1983), esp. ch. 11; Henri Rousso, *Le syndrome de Vichy 1944-* (Paris, 1987); and among a large literature concerning the status of women's history, Bereneice A. Carroll (ed.) *Liberating women's history* (Urbana, Illinois, 1976) and Karen Offen *et. al.* (eds.), *Writing women's history: international perspectives* (London, 1991).

by Moody, in a manner that would be mutually beneficial. Yet the deep internal tensions inherent in both of these master traditions which might encourage such critical reflection strongly indicate that neither could for long continue to serve as categorical frameworks for public history. But why, in any case, stop at two? For it seems likely that the libertarian call to celebrate tradition merely accelerates rather than controls the centrifugal tendency, ever present in the history of historical writing, toward the production of popular accounts recounting the distinctive traditions of regions, classes, sexes and political and ideological interest groups.[63]

But least helpful of all is the radical deconstructionist view—most commonly associated with Roland Barthes and on occasion with Hayden White and sometimes threatened by history's critics in Ireland[64]—which denies all of history's claims to be a distinct and defensible form of discourse, and defines it simply as another, rather disingenuous, form of fiction, whose pretension to exercise a special privilege over others should be entirely disregarded. Thus where the public histories advocated by Bradshaw would seem to threaten Babel, the harsh judgement of the deconstructionists would appear merely to enjoin silence. In heuristic terms neither has anything constructive to offer the historians in their routine travails.

And yet, when more moderately restated, there is a manner in which both the merciless scepticism of the deconstructionists and the high moral injunctions handed down by Bradshaw seem together to suggest a way out of the modern historian's predicament. Historians could always plead immunity from the ravages of deconstruction by the claim that their discipline was enframed by a special categorical imperative that severely restricted their work and so distinguished it from the caprice of pure fiction. The obligation that compels historians to respect the laws of sequentiality—of the basic processes of chronological change—arises neither simply nor principally from the self-imposed logic of historical narrative, as some critics have argued. It is rooted more fundamentally in the universal human experience of sequential birth,

63. For an overview of Ulster unionist historiographical opinion, see Alvin Jackson, 'Unionist history' in *The Irish Review*, nos. 5 and 6 (1988,1989), reprinted below, pp. 253-68; and for a demonstration that such different traditions cannot easily allow for a peaceful co-existence in intellectual terms, see the contrasting essays by Edna Longley and Arthur Aughty and by Seamus Deane and Gearóid O Crualaoich in *Revising the rising*; international examples of such splintering are discussed in Novick, *That noble dream*, ch. 14 and Bourdé and Martin, *Les écoles historiques*, ch. 13.
64. Barthes, 'The discourse of history' trans. Stephen Bann in E.S. Shaffer (ed.), *Comparative criticism: a yearbook*, vol. 3 (Cambridge,1981), pp. 7-20; White, 'The fictions of factual representation' in *Tropics of discourse* (Baltimore, 1978), this extreme position is not, however, White's central contention; deconstruction's influence over history's critics in Ireland is most evident in Seamus Deane, 'Wherever Green is read' in *Revising the rising*, pp. 91-105, reprinted pp. 234-45 below.

suffering and death which nothing short of solipsism can deny.[65] It is, of course, beyond this basic level, in the vast realm of causation, relation, coincidence and conflict that the stuff of history is to be found, and out of which all its attendant epistemological problems arise. It is clear, for instance, that discoveries concerning one event may significantly alter the status of antecedent and succeeding ones and may in extreme cases alter their claim to be considered as instances of any historical significance at all. But in elaborating their arguments, in analytical, thematic or simply chronological terms, historians must always refer their deployments to the same basic principle of growth and decay which is the fundamental datum of every subject they study. That exercise of reference is always intensely problematic, and is the very source of the indeterminancy that characterises historical controversy.[66] For the sense of past existence, and all the motivations, desires, fears and decisions that arose from it can never be re-appropriated, only approximated and imagined.

Yet the recognition that historians can never fully apprehend but must always imagine the very processes that give value to their work should not be disabling. Rather the acceptance that the assertions, dissensions and reappraisals that constitute historical discourse are necessarily incomplete and conditional validates an attitude toward the investigation of the fragments of the past that is at once critical, self-critical and available to endless modulation and qualification. Thus the most important demand to be made of historians as they undertake the representation of their research is not that they be a little more imaginative or empathic—subjective and immeasurable desiderata which they have always attempted, with varying degrees of success, to satisfy. It is rather that they should simply be more humble: that they should acknowledge the necessary impossibility of the task upon which they have embarked. '*Tout comprendre, c'est tout pardonner*' is a maxim which has lost all conviction in our dark times. But the recognition that complete understanding can never be attained in history should be sufficient to stay the hand of judgement, and to sustain the belief that all historical judgements, whatever their provenance, are partial and imperfect.

It is only by accommodating to this necessarily inchoate position that the historians can confront not merely their political or ideological critics but the more moderate, and more theoretically serious, objections against both the text and the author which have hitherto raised the most pertinent problems for historical writing.[67] The exposure of the rhetorical subterfuges, occlusions and

65. See the thoughtful concluding discussion in Krieger, *Time's reasons*, pp. 164-71; the suggestion raised here parallels Richard Kearney's call for an overtly ethical response to the post-structuralist challenge in *The wake of imagination: ideas of creativity in Western culture* (London, 1988), pp. 386-97.

66. Ciaran Brady, 'Introduction' in Brady (ed.), *Ideology and the historians: historical studies xvii* (Dublin, 1991), pp. 6-8; Albert Cook, *History/writing* (Cambridge,1988), pp. 208-27.

67. Michel Foucault, 'What is an author?' in *Language, counter-memory, practice*, trans. D.

deflections that were characteristic of the nineteenth century prophets and scientists of history has been one of the signal achievements of post-structuralist literary criticism, and though attempts to apply these techniques to the conduct of contemporary historical writing have been surprisingly few, it seems clear that such critical approaches would prove revealing there also.[68] For the principal sin of the 'new history's' ironists lay not primarily in the elitism which their idiom inadvertently sanctioned; but in the assumption that a progressive dialogue could be generated between two equal intelligences sharing the same courses of study. The nature of historical discourse, we have now learned to recognise, has never been so simple. It cannot occur merely between contemporaries, but is shaped and sustained by a complex network of inherited ideas, assumptions and prejudices out of which no particular selection can make a special claim to objectivity. Thus whether or not the Messieurs Jourdains of the historians' audience are consciously aware of the past they have inherited or the Dry-as-Dusts of the academy affirm that they are in control of the impressions they have absorbed from their study, both are engaged in an intricate multilogue between their common inheritance of the memories, monuments and texts of the past on the one hand, and the variegated coordinates of contemporary experience within which they attempt on the other hand to anchor it.

The fact that professional historians share a common problem with those whose conscious sense of history is rudimentary or those who have extracted from the past all the select history they need may seem disturbing. But it nevertheless reveals a further requirement concerning the way in which the historians should express themselves in presenting their vicarious experience of the past. Again what is needed 'to connect' is not the voice of the prophet or the scientist, nor even the ironist; but of the experienced intelligence whose engagement with history has been tempered by the realisation that what we must demand of the past is necessarily too much, and what we can ultimately know too little.

The media by which historians may represent their pursuit of an

Bouchard and S. Simon, (Ithaca, 1977), pp. 113-38 is countered by more moderate re-statements in Hayden White, *The content of the form*, (Baltimore, 1988), esp chs 2 and 5; a useful collection of essays on the topic generally adopting a moderate post-structuralist position is Derek Attridge, Geoff Bennington and Robert Young (eds.), *Post-structuralism and the question of history* (Cambridge, 1987).

68. White, *Metahistory*, Edward Said, *Orientalism* (London, 1978) and Ann Rigney, *The rhetoric of historical representation: three narrative histories of the French revolution* (Cambridge, 1990) are all concerned with styles of history writing that have long since been regarded as suspect and anachronistic by historians themselves; significantly few analysts have yet applied their techniques to modern historical prose, and those who have seem oddly to have fastened on a sprightly, polemical and highly individual stylist, A.J.P. Taylor: White, *Tropics of discourse*, pp. 101-120, and Cook, *History/writing*, pp. 210-19; investigation of more pedestrian and conventional writers might yield less striking, but more substantial results.

irrecoverable past have yet, as Gearóid Ó Tuathaigh suggests below, to be fully explored.[69] The open adoption of fictive modes in a manner that at once acknowledges history's impotence and attempts to transcend it is a strategy that has attracted some of the bolder scholars. And the generally positive response of historians and non-historians to some of these borderland essays suggests that they have gone some distance to restoring the equilibrium of ignorance between writer, reader and their fragmentary inheritance upon which the dialogue of history depends.[70] Yet the blending of accidentally surviving reliques with imagined evidence deliberately created to fill the gaps is a strategy beset by conceptual problems, and one that requires the sustained exercise of a creative force that goes far beyond a merely well-informed talent for pastiche. The sincerity of the attempt does not guarantee its success.

On more conventional grounds it seems clear that in grappling with the epistemological problems presented by the otherness of the past, irony will remain an idiom essential to history. But it is clear also that the self-referential certitudes of irony are too enclosing and exclusive to maintain an awareness both of the essential mystery of the past and of the immeasurable influences which it yet exercises over the present. What is required, then, of the historians in the post-revisionist world is, as Ó Tuathaigh, Tom Dunne and others have argued, a more complex, more self-conscious diction that interrupts their tendency toward ironic detachment with the admission that all attempts at making sense of, or judgements about, the past are inevitably relative and conditional measures that constantly invite qualification and restatement in the dialogue between writer and reader.[71] Such humility is doubtless the appropriate moral attitude for the historians to assume as they approach the practical task of constructing their fragile representations of a lost past. But, as the instrumentalists might say, it has its uses too.

69. See Ó Tuathaigh, 'Irish historical revisionism' below, pp. 306-26.
70. Responses among historians to various literary experiments have been mixed: Simon Schama's *Dead certainties (unwarranted speculations)* (London, 1991), has been widely praised, Theodore Zeldin's total adoption of fiction in *Happiness* (London, 1989) has not. Norman Hampson's intriguing attempt to link the past, the historian and his audience in *The life and opinions of Maximilien Robespierre* (London, 1974) has had few imitators and has not excited much comment beyond the specialists.
71. See the highly suggestive comments of Tom Dunne, 'New histories: beyond revisionism; in *The Irish Review*, 12 (1992), pp. 1-12; the practical strategies proposed long ago by Nancy Streuner, 'The study of language and the study of history', in *Journal of interdisciplinary history* 4 (1974), pp. 401-15, have yet to be fully explored.

PART II: STATEMENTS OF INTENT

2

Preface to *Irish Historical Studies**

T.W. MOODY & R.D. EDWARDS

The bulk and diversity of the materials which have now to be handled by the historical investigator are such that he cannot afford to work in isolation. Historical research has become a highly elaborated science, in the practice of which the historian needs the co-operation of his fellow-workers; and if the teaching of history is not to be divorced from the results of historical research, there must be co-operation between the historian and the teacher. In Ireland, there is no periodical or institution to cater adequately for these needs. There are various bodies, central and local, such as the Royal Irish Academy, the Royal Society of Antiquaries of Ireland, the Cork Historical and Archaeological Society, the Down and Connor Historical Society, the Galway Archaeological Society, and the Louth Archaeological Society, which do valuable work in encouraging the study of particular branches and aspects of Irish history, usually in conjunction with archaeology. Their publications are full of useful information for the historical scholar, and have an established place in Irish historical literature. But in Ireland there is no counterpart to the Historical Association and the Institute of Historical Research in England, nor of the journals of these bodies, *History*, and the *Bulletin of the Institute of Historical Research*, respectively. Nor is there any periodical of the type of the *English Historical Review*, the *Revue Historique* or the *American Historical Review*. This is the more to be regretted, because in recent years the activities of the Irish Manuscripts Commission and of the Public Record Office of Northern Ireland have been making available a mass of historical material previously unknown or relatively inaccessible to the Irish scholar. It is true that some attention is given to Irish history in the English periodicals which have been mentioned, and that, in particular, the Institute of Historical Research has rendered good service in this field as in so many others. The editors of *Irish Historical Studies* take special pleasure in acknowledging their own indebtedness to that Institute, which is at once an experimental laboratory of research methods, a clearing house of historical information, and a meeting place of historians from all parts of the world. But the fact remains that the Irish historian is severely

---

* First published in *I.H.S.* 1 (1938–9), pp. 1–3.

handicapped by the absence of any journal exclusively devoted to the scientific study of Irish history. Many young historical students, graduates of the Irish universities, are engaged in scholarly work which, as things now are, has little chance of being published. The historian is human, and has small inducement to persevere with his unpaid researches, if he has no hope that the results will ever appear in print.

Irish Historical Studies, which aims at filling the gap thus indicated, is the joint product of two parallel societies, founded in Belfast and Dublin in 1936, for the advancement of Irish historical learning on scientific principles. The Ulster Society for Irish Historical Studies was first in the field, and from the beginning warmly welcomed the advent of the Irish Historical Society. The common interests and common ideals of these two bodies brought them together in an association which has resulted in the present co-operative venture. Financial support was an indispensable condition to the launching of the projected journal, and nothing gives us greater pride and satisfaction than to acknowledge the ready and generous response which the three universities of Ireland made to our appeal. The University of Dublin (Trinity College), the National University of Ireland, and the Queen's University of Belfast have each granted us equal subventions which have enabled this journal to make its first appearance in an adequate form and have ensured that it can continue long enough to prove whether sufficient public interest exists to maintain it on a self-supporting basis. The practical help which the universities have rendered is all-important; but we also value their action as an expression of their confidence in us and their approval of our undertaking. It is for *Irish Historical Studies* to justify that confidence and that approval by the quality of its contribution to Irish learning.

The needs which we are attempting to serve are various. We aim at doing, to the measure of our ability, what in England is distributed among several journals. We hope to be of service to the specialist, the teacher, and the general reader who has an intelligent interest in the subject. We have set before ourselves two main tasks, the one constructive, the other instrumental. Under the first head are to be included articles embodying the results of original research, and articles on the re-interpretation and re-valuation, in the light of new facts, of accepted views on particular topics. The latter type of article, under the title 'Historical revisions', has been standardised in *History*, the journal of the Historical Association, to whose example we gratefully acknowledge our indebtedness. We hope that this feature will prove of special value to teachers, and will help to reduce the time-lag between historical research and the teaching of history. Under the second head are to be included articles on the scope and the teaching of Irish history; articles on research methods and problems; select documents, with editorial comment; select and critical bibliographies and guides to sources, manuscript and printed; annual lists of writings on Irish history including articles in periodicals; annual lists of theses on Irish history completed and in progress in the universities of Ireland; reviews of books and periodicals dealing with, or having a bearing on, Irish history. In our review section we are anxious to include a complete record, with explanatory comments, of the work in Irish history contained in current periodicals. We aim at co-ordination and co-relation of historical work, and we hope to be a means of avoiding duplication. Only such documents as would not be likely to obtain publication in *Analecta Hibernica, Archivium Hibernicum* and the like will therefore find a place in our pages.

The response already made to our public appeal is most encouraging. We have a substantial body of enrolled subscribers, but we need many more. This journal is produced in the belief that it will attract sufficient public interest to set it on a secure and permanent foundation. Our grateful acknowledgments are due to the many publishers and learned societies who have sent us books and periodicals for review; to the *Belfast News-Letter*, the *Bulletin of the Institute of Historical Research*, the *Church of Ireland Gazette*, the *Down and Connor Historical Society's Journal*, the *Glasgow Herald, History, Ireland To-Day*, the *Irish Ecclesiastical Record*, the *Irish Independent*, the *Irish News*, the *Irish Press*, the *Irish Times*, and *The Times* (and any other newspapers and periodicals which may have been accidentally overlooked), for their courteous and helpful references to the advent of this journal; and to our publishers, Messrs Hodges Figgis. To Mr Kenneth Povey, librarian to the Queen's University of Belfast, who has given so freely of his expert advice and assistance, we owe a special tribute of praise.

We dedicate this work, as did the historians of old:

dochum glóire Dé agus onóra na hÉireann

3

A New History of Ireland*

T.W. MOODY

The completion in 1967 of thirty years of *Irish Historical Studies* has been the occasion for a stocktaking (still in progress) of the achievement of those years in Irish historiography.[1] They are coming to be seen as an era of remarkable advances in specialist research, in professional technique, in historical organisation, and in the publication of special studies, source materials, bibliographies and aids to research. Though this research has been unevenly spread, it has produced an impressive body of new knowledge on many periods and topics. The conditions for scholarly work on Irish history have thus been transformed; and there is a world of difference between the prospects for Irish historiography in 1938 and now.

The pre-1938 era in Irish historiography was characterised by scholars such as Dunlop and Wilson, Curtis and MacNeill, who, working largely in isolation, not only made important specialist contributions themselves, but also attempted boldly to construct general history on inadequate foundations. The historiography of the succeeding thirty years, centred on the history departments of the Irish universities, and enjoying for the first time the advantages of a specialist periodical, *Irish Historical Studies*, has been dominated by the need to lay new foundations, and to repair and reinforce old ones. The historians of this period have devoted themselves with energy and success to intensive research on a large range of special subjects, and have acquired a high degree of co-operation and solidarity, previously quite unknown. But their preoccupation with specialist work has meant that general history has tended to become ossified. At every level, from that of the school text-book to that of the popular survey for the general reader, the available modern publications on the general history of Ireland are still, with a few shining exceptions, highly unsatisfactory—meagre in scope, narrow in sympathy, amateur in treatment, uninformed by new research and often unreadable. The lack of good up-to-date works has given the general history of Ireland a

*   First published in *I.H.S.* xvi (1968-9), pp. 241-57.
1.   'Thirty years' work in Irish history', *I.H.S.*, xv, pp. 359-90 (Sept. 1967), xvi, pp. 1-32 (Mar. 1968).

discouraging aspect to adult readers and has created prejudice against it among young people at school and university. This has tended to restrict the supply of good teachers of Irish history at all levels and in consequence the supply of research students. Though the prestige of Irish historical scholarship has been rising and the output of specialist publications increasing, the number of scholars engaged has continued to be small and the rate of growth in the total volume of published work to be slow. The lack of good general history has thus helped to retard the progress of specialist history, the impetus to which had been in part a reaction against the writing of general history inadequately supported by research. Research itself now needs to be supported by good general history.

If history at its best is not made available to the educated public as a whole, it fails in one of its essential social functions. Till fairly recently the public interest in Irish history has been sustained by the more readable products of specialist research, by works on general topics treated in short periods, and by local history. But thanks to the efforts of a few pioneers, and especially J.C. Beckett, Irish history in the round has become acceptable to an increasing range of readers, and the demand for such work is certainly in excess of the supply. The notable and continued success of Beckett's *Short history of Ireland* (1952), and more recently the welcome given to his masterpiece, *The making of modern Ireland, 1603-1923* (1966), are good indications of the public stamina for works of historical synthesis on the highest level of scholarship. The same situation was exemplified by the reception last year of A.J. Otway-Ruthven's magisterial *History of medieval Ireland*, the only new work in its field since Curtis's book of the same name first appeared in 1923 (revised edition, 1938). The impact on the public of the cooperative work, *The course of Irish history* (edited by T. W. Moody and F. X. Martin, 1967), both as an R.T.E. television series and as a book, is a measure of the need for the broad historical survey, presented by specialists in popular form. There is, then, a growing public demand for new works of synthesis on the history of Ireland at a time when Irish historiography itself needs the stimulus of a new synthesis.

That the greatest immediate responsibility of Irish historians is the writing of general history was the key-note of a presidential address that I gave to the Irish Historical Society on 4 December 1962 under the title 'Towards a new history of Ireland'. As historians we were, I believed, called upon to give a new impetus to Irish history by promoting a history of Ireland that would span its entire course, would be broadly conceived in social, economic and cultural, as well as in political and constitutional, terms, would fully exploit the new scholarship and the new materials now available, and, finally, would be as authoritative as possible. Individual scholars working separately had already made a valuable contribution to such a history and would continue to do so. But they could not in the foreseeable future produce a synthesis such as I contemplated. That could only be achieved by a concerted effort of historical scholarship, for which the organisation that had developed among Irish historians during the past thirty years had prepared the way. I went on to outline a large-scale cooperative history of Ireland, in 12 to 14 volumes, to be written on an agreed plan by the best qualified scholars available. It should be social history in the broad sense, that is, history in which not only government but the other primary institutions of society would have their proper place and in which economic and cultural developments would be integrated with political; and it should be history in which the changing relations between society and its physical environment should receive proper attention. From existing cooperative histories of other areas we had much to learn, but we should try, with all the help and advice we could obtain from historians anywhere, to work out a model of our own. Whatever our plan of action in detail, it would require a high degree of intellectual co-operation and sharing among scholars, and this would mean a special organisation that would need financial support from somewhere, probably the state.

These proposals were well received by the Irish Historical Society and became the starting point for a good deal of discussion. Support for the suggested project was forthcoming, to a much greater extent than I had expected, from producers, and still more from consumers, of Irish history, foremost among the latter Dr C.S. Andrews, who has combined the role of man of action with life-long devotion to Clio. Criticism, of course, was not lacking. There was, it was claimed, no need for such a project. It smacked of monopoly and would discourage private enterprise. It would be disastrous to accept money from the state, and, in any case, it was unnecessary to create a special organisation for something that could be done on a purely voluntary basis. The time was not ripe for such a project: far too much specialist research had yet to be done. Besides, political history could safely be left to individual enterprise, and if there was to be a cooperative effort it should concentrate on economic and social history, in which progress has been specially slow. It would be exceedingly difficult to get Irish historians to work to any agreed plan and impossible to extract contributions from them by any fixed dates.

I recalled the counsels of despair that endeavoured to save the founders of *Irish Historical Studies* from themselves in 1937-8, and I was cheered to think that on the present occasion the pessimists were far fewer than they were then. I do not mean that the scheme was not open to criticism or that we have not profited from criticism. But much of the head-shaking and hand-wringing was due to mere apprehension or to misapprehension. The scheme had no monopolistic aim and would depend for success on the quality of the individual scholars who took part in it. There was no intention of replacing volunteers by bureaucrats, but if voluntary effort was to achieve the aim of the project in the near future then there had to be the means of ensuring co-ordination and continuity of effort in carrying it out. The editors would certainly be volunteers, but they must be supported by a full-time secretariat, and must have some permanent machinery for consultation and advice, which should be flexible and as economical of time as possible. If state support for a central organisation were to be subject to any conditions limiting the freedom of historians, it would, of course, be utterly unacceptable, but there was no reason to fear anything of the kind from an Irish government. The problem presented by the late development of Irish economic history was certainly very serious but that was surely not a reason for abandoning the whole concept of an integrated general history in favour of a general economic history. Nor was there good reason to suppose either that political and constitutional history would soon be adequately catered for, or that cultural history would not be neglected indefinitely without a cooperative effort. The objection to the proposed scheme on the grounds that it would involve endless and frustrating delay, had substance. It was not merely that some scholars were better organised and more practical than others but also that the tasks they would be facing varied greatly in intractability. There were many unsolved problems, especially in the early and medieval history of Ireland, many areas in which the treatment would necessarily be patchy and provisional, through lack of established knowledge. In the field of economic history there were vast expanses of virtually unworked territory. Ought we then to wait till all such deficiencies had been remedied before attempting an adequate general history?

Our answer was to modify the initial scheme by planning our enterprise in two stages, Stage I to extend over five years, Stage II to follow on the completion of Stage I. Time is of the very essence of Stage I, and our aim here was a general history of Ireland in two or more volumes of text, together with a volume of reference material—bibliography, chronology, succession lists, statistical tables, documents, maps, plans, and an index. To Stage II we assigned the multi-volume history of the original proposal. We would aim to publish this history as soon as possible, but each volume would appear separately as completed, whereas all the volumes of the Stage I History would be published simultaneously. We fully recognised the difficulty of inducing a score and more of contributors to observe the time-limits necessary to ensure punctual delivery of all contributions to the Stage I History, but we prepared to meet this by a combination of foresight, reason, and firmness.

The Stage I History is intended to serve two purposes: first, to provide a broad, authoritative and readable synthesis of the history of Ireland, based on the best historical scholarship now available; second, as a 'trier' for the Stage II History as to matter, method and treatment. We aim at making the Stage I work the best possible history of Ireland that can be completed in five years, and we see it as in the nature of an interim report. It may be possible, and necessary, to carry out new research on special problems (in some sense emergency programmes) for the purpose of this work, but in the main the contributors will be expected to base their narratives on research already accomplished. And this means that the ground cannot be evenly covered and that there will be many places where only provisional statements can be made. On the other hand we look to Stage II for the production of a full and definitive work, of which some volumes will probably appear soon after the publication of the Stage I History, whereas others, dependent on the carrying out of new research, may be much later in appearing. We like to think of our Stage II work as worthy of a series-title such as 'The Twentieth-century History of Ireland'. In both stages the history must be written so as to cater for the educated public, and not only for specialists. The whole enterprise rests on the conviction that history, the study of human thought and action in the stream of time, in so far as they can be reconstructed in the mind from the surviving evidence, achieves its highest fulfilment only when it is intelligible to men as such and not merely to historians.

The project I have outlined was adopted by the Irish Historical Society on 8 October 1963. In June 1964 the society arranged to transfer its sponsorship to the Irish Committee of Historical Sciences, a small but broadly-based representative body, linked with the Irish Historical Society and its counterpart in Belfast, the Ulster Society for Irish Historical Studies, and with the history departments in all the Irish universities. A special organisation for the carrying out of the project was authorised by the Irish Committee of Historical Sciences on 14 November 1964. Four historians were appointed as editors of the history—T. Desmond Williams, professor of modern history in University College, Dublin; F.X. Martin, O.S.A., professor of medieval history in University College, Dublin; J.C. Beckett, professor of Irish history in Queen's University, Belfast; and the present writer, who is also chairman of the editors. An editorial committee, consisting of the editors and nine other historians, and an advisory board, consisting of many eminent historians and other scholars who had expressed support for the project, were also set up. Financial control of the project was vested in an honorary treasurer, and we were fortunate that C.S. Andrews agreed to accept this office.

It was a cardinal point of the scheme that there must be a full-time secretariat to be the administrative arm of the editors and to provide services and facilities for the large body of scholars on whose part-time efforts the successful outcome of the scheme depended. For this and for all the necessary expenses required to translate so ambitious a scheme into practice—but not to pay any fees to contributors—we had no hesitation in approaching the government of Ireland for an annual grant (November 1963). Our application was sympathetically received by the then minister for education, Mr Patrick Hillery, and in May 1965 the editors received a firm promise of financial support. Economic stringency, however, delayed the fulfilment of this promise, and therefore stopped further progress on the project itself, till May 1967, when a small initial grant-in-aid was provided for the financial year 1967-8. With the warm-hearted support of the late Donogh O'Malley as minister for education, this was substantially increased for 1968-9. The present minister for education, Mr Brian Lenihan, has been no less perceptive of the essential character of our project than his lamented predecessor, and we confidently expect that for 1969-70 the grant-in-aid will be raised to the full amount, £8,000, that we originally sought. The grant-in-aid is subject to no conditions other than normal accounting requirements. In conformity with the spirit of the whole scheme we thought it desirable to give the government of Northern Ireland an opportunity to share in the cost of the undertaking. An application was made accordingly to the Northern Ireland minister of education, Mr H.V. Kirk, in March 1965, but in the following August Mr Kirk informed us of his regret that his ministry could not contribute to the New History.

With the initial grant from the Irish government we were enabled to provide the equipment for our intended secretariat and to meet other preliminary expenses, and during the current year we have had the good fortune to obtain accommodation for the secretariat in the house of the Royal Irish Academy, 19 Dawson Street, Dublin. In May last the editorial committee appointed as secretary of the New History Dr Liam O'Sullivan, formerly keeper in charge of the industrial, art and historical collections in the National Museum, and author of *The economic history of Cork city from the earliest times to the act of union* (1937), *The earliest Irish coinage* (1949), and a history of Irish gold and silver shortly to be published. Dr O'Sullivan took up his duties as secretary on 16 July. At this point it was thought desirable to transfer the whole project to the Royal Irish Academy. One of our most venerable institutions of learning, an all-Ireland body where members represent the whole spectrum of the sciences and humanities, the Academy has world-wide recognition and connections, and has sponsored many scholarly projects, of which its great *Dictionary of the Irish language* is a current example. In the Academy's house the New History is centrally situated, in a dignified and appropriate setting, with access to a small but invaluable working library and meeting rooms.

The decision to transfer the New History to the Royal Irish Academy was taken by the Irish Committee of Historical Sciences on 24 July 1968, when it empowered the editors and the treasurer of the New History to conclude all necessary arrangements to effect such a transfer. An agreement was reached on 16 July between the editors and the treasurer of the New History on the one hand, and the Royal Irish Academy on the other, in the form of a constitution for the New History. This was an adaptation of the scheme of organisation set up by the Irish Committee of Historical Sciences on 14 November 1964 (see Appendix A); in accordance with this constitution the

Royal Irish Academy appointed all the existing officers and committees of the New History for an initial period of five years (see Appendix B).

The New History which all these arrangements have been designed to promote is a two-stage project, of which the first stage is to result in seven or eight volumes, to be published together, and consisting of six volumes of text and one or two of reference-matter. The text volumes will be made up of two elements organised in a single series of inter-connected chapters, the 'primary narrative' and the 'complementary structure'. The primary narrative will comprise 22 periods beginning with prehistoric Ireland and ending with Ireland since 1945 (see Appendix C). It is not to be a merely political narrative but is to include topics and themes in economic, social and cultural history in accordance with the distinguishing characteristics of each period and the time-scale of the treatment. Subjects that it will not be practicable, or, because of the time-scale, possible, thus to integrate into the primary narrative, or that require some degree of specialist treatment, will be provided for in the complementary structure. This will comprise studies in such fields as regional geography, population changes, agricultural methods, trade and industry, literature and society, painting, architecture and other visual arts, music, the theatre, education, public administration, the cinema, radio and television. These studies will be distributed as interchapters among the chapters carrying the primary narrative. Besides such interchapters there will be a series of panoramic surveys or cross-sections of Irish life at strategic points in the story by historians, and also similar surveys of the Irish landscape at selected dates by historical geographers. Many varied phenomena are thus to be provided for, and all the varied components of the New History are to be brought into a coherent whole. It is important to emphasise that the primary narrative is not to be a conventional political history, interspersed with snippets of economic history, literary history, and the rest; and that the complementary structure is not to be a kind of encyclopaedia composed of tabloid histories of the economy, of literature and so on. Topics of all kinds should enter into both the primary narrative and the complementary structure wherever they assume historical importance in the time-scale and the area of activity concerned.

The demarcation of periods for the primary narrative, after discussion by the editorial committee, was finally established in November 1968 and negotiations with prospective contributors had resulted in the assignment of all but two of the periods to contributors by December 1968 (see Appendix C). The first conference of contributors was held on 27-8 December; at that point, six years after the idea was first mooted, the New History of Ireland finally passed out of the stage of discussion and preparation into that of execution and realisation. The contributors are all committed to defined sections of the scheme and to the carrying out of their undertakings in defined phases extending over five years to December 1973. The history as then completed is to be published as soon as possible afterwards.

This does not mean that the initial planning is completed. Good progress has been made in determining the composition of the complementary structure and in enlisting contributors for it (see Appendix D), but there is still much to be decided in this area. One problem that for years has baffled our efforts to find a solution has in principle been resolved. We have always insisted that economic and social history must have its place in the primary narrative, where, together with other topics outside the course of political history, it would be the responsibility of the contributors to that narrative. But in addition to this, we have also been convinced of the need for specialist treatment of economic and social history in the complementary structure. An alternative approach to this problem was put forward by Professor K.H. Connell, of Queen's University, Belfast, whose classic work on Irish population and on Irish rural society has given him a unique place as the pioneer of a new school of research in Irish economic history. Dr Connell, himself a member of our editorial committee, visualised a separate volume within the New History project, to be written by a small group of economic historians in co-operation and limited to Irish economic history since about 1760, which was all that he felt to be practicable in the near future considering the serious under-development of the subject. This did not fit in well until the concept of an integrated general history, but anxious as we were to make the best possible provision for the treatment of economic history we sought for a long time to accommodate Dr Connell's proposal within the main scheme. In the end we all agreed as the most satisfactory arrangement that his scheme should proceed without any formal connection with the New History scheme, but that there should be active informal co-operation between the two, and that some of the economic historians taking part in Dr Connell's scheme should contribute to the complementary structure of the New History. This means that there is no question of the two schemes being rivals; on the contrary they should be mutually advantageous. In the resulting histories there should be a minimum of duplication, since the economic history element in the one can be assumed as the general background for the more specialised treatment of economic history in the other.

There are several good reasons why those who are committed to the New History project can regard its prospects with a measure of optimism. If the foundations for a new historiography are far from complete, at least we have foundations well-established over a large area; we have organisation, facilities and equipment such as could not have been hoped for thirty years ago; above all we have a numerous body of original scholars committed to carrying out the scheme, who together represent an array of historical talent never before assembled for such a purpose in Ireland. We have ample precedents for successful co-operation among Irish historians, of which *Irish Historical Studies* itself is the oldest working example. The recent precedent of *The course of Irish history* is particularly encouraging, since it was the work of twenty-one scholars, it was carried out according to plan and realised the expectations of its planners, and less than sixteen months elapsed from the initial meeting of contributors to the day of publication.

If the greater part of the work done in Irish history during the past thirty years has been done by Irishmen (and in this field at least Ireland is one and indivisible), an increasing share has been taken by British, and, still more, by American, historians who now constitute an important part of the fraternity of historians of Ireland. The very existence and the steady progress of the American Committee for Irish Studies[2] are evidence of the expanding interest and activity in Irish history and literature among American scholars. The main stream of Irish historiography has been and is being enriched by valuable new research from both America and Britain, and this is an added source of strength for our New History enterprise. Recent American scholarship has also been casting new light on the Irish migration to America, on the Irish in America, and on the interrelations between Ireland and Irish-America. Much basic research still needs to be done in these fields,[3] as in the corresponding context of the Irish migration to Britain. But, thanks largely to American scholarship, the American factor in Irish history since 1800 has taken significant shape and will have its due place in the Stage I History.

Finally, among our advantages is the rapid change in the intellectual climate of Ireland, which has become incomparably more favourable to the historian's reconstruction of the Irish past than ever before The reading public is following the lead of historians in breaking away from servitude to national myths and instead has taken to studying them. As Irish economic expansion advances, and as Irishmen become more forward-looking and outward-looking, they become more, not less, interested in history and they raise new questions for

2. See L. J. McCaffrey, 'The American Committee for Irish Studies', *I.H.S.*, xv, no. 60 (Sept. 1967), pp. 446-9; Joseph M. Curran,' First Annual Report from the American Committee for Irish Studies, 1967-8', *I.H.S.*, xvi, no. 62 (Sept. 1968), pp. 204-6.

3. Many years ago I urged the need for a combined operation on the Irish migration to America by Irish and American historians working at both the transmitting and receiving end of the process ('Irish and Scotch-Irish in eighteenth-century America' in *Studies*, xxxv, no. 137 (Mar. 1946), p. 90); I still believe that this would be a rewarding enterprise. The history of Fenianism presents a challenge that might be met by a similar approach. And among many historical questions to which answers are lacking I should like to know whether the group-consciousness that was being shown in the 1890s by Americans who called themselves 'Scotch-Irish' was a reaction against that Irish-American nationalism so brilliantly interpreted by T.N. Brown (*Irish-American nationalism, 1870-1890* (1966); see *I.H.S.*, xv, 438-45); how far the two movements had common characteristics; and whether the Scotch-Irish movement supported resistance to the Irish home-rule movement which Irish-American nationalism did so much to promote.

historians to answer. The public appetite for scholarly history presented in non-specialist terms is exemplified by the remarkable vogue of the Thomas Davis Lectures, transmitted regularly on the sound broadcasting service of Radio Telefís Éireann since 1953. Many of these series have been published, especially in paperback editions, and the flow continues.[4] The changing climate of opinion also owes much to the impact of the ecumenical movement in Ireland, which has released new energies and opened up exciting new possibilities. It could hardly be said that Ireland is in the van of ecumenism, but in a surprisingly short time a great deal of theological ice has been thawed out, catholics and protestants have been engaging in the new game of dialogue, and laity and clergy have been talking to each other in public as well as in private in a way that would have seemed impossible a year or two ago. All this again has helped to create an atmosphere favourable to the pursuit of history, and especially of history as conceived and practised by the scholars who are to write the New History of Ireland.

APPENDIX A

Constitution of the New History of Ireland project as agreed between the editors and treasurer of the New History of Ireland and the committee of officers of the Royal Irish Academy on 26 July 1968

1   The New History of Ireland is a project of the Royal Irish Academy.

2   The New History of Ireland organisation comprises (a) a board of editors, (b) an editorial committee, (c) an advisory board, (d) a financial adviser, and (e) a secretariat.

3   The editors are to be responsible collectively to the Royal Irish Academy for editing the history, this responsibility including (a) the plan of the history, (b) the choice of contributors, (c) decisions regarding contributions, (d) the direction of the secretariat, (e) the nomination to all appointments in the secretariat, and (f) the presentation of an annual report to the Royal Irish Academy.

4   The editorial committee is to advise on the planning and execution of the history. It is to be kept informed of the progress of the history.

It is to make appointments to the secretariat.

4.   See F.X. Martin, 'The Thomas Davis Lectures, 1953-67', *I.H.S.*, xv, no. 59 (Mar. 1967), pp. 276-302.

It is to approve the annual budget.

The secretary of the New History of Ireland is to be secretary of the editorial committee.

It is to meet at intervals of about six months and on other occasions (especially during the planning stage of the history) as the need arises.

5   The secretariat is to include a secretary and clerical staff, who are to be appointed by the editorial committee on the nomination of the editors.
     The secretariat is to carry out the directions of the editors, and to be responsible to the editors.

6   The treasurer of the Royal Irish Academy is to receive all monies for the New History of Ireland and is to disburse them in accordance with the annual budget, on the requisition of the board of editors.
     The grant-in-aid from the Department of Education is to be paid to the Royal Irish Academy and allocated to a special account for the New History of Ireland.

7   The advisory board is to be kept informed of the progress of the history.
     It is to be consulted collectively in writing, by questionnaire and otherwise.

     Individual members are entitled to offer, or may be called on to give, advice or suggestions to the editors.

     Meetings of the board as a whole are not contemplated.

8   All appointments to the New History of Ireland organisation, except to the secretariat, are to be made by the Royal Irish Academy. They shall be made for periods of five years, or, in the case of a casual vacancy, for the remainder of the five-year period in which the vacancy exists.

9   This constitution may be amended by the Royal Irish Academy with the consent of the editors of the New History of Ireland in consultation with the editorial committee.

APPENDIX B

*Officers and committees of the New History of Ireland project
as appointed by the Royal Irish Academy on 26 July 1968*

Editors

T.W. Moody, fellow and professor of modern history, Trinity College, Dublin
T.D. Williams, professor of modern history, University College, Dublin
J.C. Beckett, professor of Irish history, Queen's University, Belfast
Rev. F.X. Martin, O.S.A., professor of medieval history, University College, Dublin

Financial adviser

C.S. Andrews, chairman, Radio Telefís Éireann

Editorial committee

The editors

John Barry, professor of medieval history, University College, Cork
Francis J. Byrne, professor of early (including medieval) Irish History, University College, Dublin
K.H. Connell, professor of economic and social history, Queen's University
R. Dudley Edwards, professor of modern Irish history, University College, Dublin
G.A. Hayes-McCoy, professor of history, University College, Galway
Oliver MacDonagh, professor of modern history, University College, Cork
A.J. Otway-Ruthven, fellow and Lecky professor of history, Trinity College, Dublin
Séamus Pender, professor of Irish history, University College, Cork
David B. Quinn, Andrew Geddes and John Rankin professor of modern history, University of Liverpool

Advisory Board

Ludwig Bieler, professor of palaeography and later Latin, University College, Dublin
James Carney, senior professor, School of Celtic Studies, Dublin Institute for Advanced Studies
Rev. Patrick J. Corish, professor of ecclesiastical history, St Patrick's College, Maynooth
Kenneth Darwin, deputy keeper of the records, Northern Ireland

Myles Dillon, senior professor, School of Celtic Studies, Dublin Institute for Advanced
    Studies
Margaret C. Griffith, deputy keeper of the records in Ireland
E.R.R. Green, lecturer in social and economic history, University of Manchester
Rev. Aubrey Gwynn, S.J., emeritus professor of medieval history, University College,
    Dublin
R.J. Hayes, director, Chester Beatty Library, Dublin
John V. Kelleher, professor of Irish literature and history, Harvard University,
    Cambridge, Mass., U.S.A.
F.S.L. Lyons, professor of modern history, University of Kent at Canterbury
Lawrence J. McCaffrey, associate professor of history, Marquette University, Milwau-
    kee, Wisconsin, U.S.A.
J.L. McCracken, professor of history, The New University of Ulster, Coleraine
R.B. McDowell, fellow and associate professor of modern history, University of Dublin
Edward MacLysaght, chairman, Irish Manuscripts Commission
P.N.S. Mansergh, fellow of St John's College and Smuts professor of the history of
    the British Commonwealth, University of Cambridge
Síle Ní Chinnéide, associate professor of history, University College, Galway
Kevin B. Nowlan, associate professor of history, University College
Brian Ó Cuív, senior professor and director, School of Celtic Studies, Dublin Institute
    for Advanced Studies
An t-Athair Tomás Ó Fiaich, professor of modern history, St Patrick's College,
    Maynooth
E.G. Quin, fellow and associate professor of Celtic languages, Trinity College, Dublin
H.G. Richardson
Michael Roberts, professor of modern history, Queen's University, Belfast
Rev. John Ryan, emeritus professor of early (including medieval) Irish history,
    University College, Dublin
G.O. Sayles, Institute of Advanced Legal Studies, University of London

APPENDIX C

A New History of Ireland, Stage I
Primary narrative—periods and contributors

1	Prehistory	M.J. O'Kelly, professor of archaeology, University College, Cork
2	5th–8th century	F.J. Byrne, professor of early (including medieval) Irish history, University College, Dublin, and Liam de Paor, college lecturer in history, University College, Dublin
3	9th cent.–1169	F.J. Byrne and Liam de Paor

4	1169–1215	Rev F.X. Martin, professor of medieval history, University College, Dublin
5	12-15–*c*.1312	J.F. Lydon, fellow, and associate professor of medieval history, Trinity College, Dublin
6	*c*.1312–1460	A.J. Otway-Ruthven, fellow, and Lecky professor of history, Trinity College, Dublin
7	1460–1534	D.B. Quinn, Andrew Geddes and John Rankin professor of modern history, University of Liverpool
8	1534–1603	G.A. Hayes-McCoy, professor of history, University College, Galway
9	1603–41	R. Dudley Edwards, professor of modern Irish history, University College, Dublin
10	1641–60	Rev. P.J. Corish, professor of ecclesiastical history, St Patrick's College, Maynooth
11	1660–1714	J.G. Simms, fellow, and lecturer in modern history, Trinity College, Dublin
12	1714–60	J.L. McCracken, professor of history, The New University of Ulster, Coleraine
13	1760–1800	R.B. McDowell, fellow, and associate professor of modern history, Trinity College, Dublin
14	1800–29	Maureen Wall, college lecturer in modern Irish history, University College, Dublin
15	1830–45	Oliver MacDonagh, professor of modern history, University College, Cork
16	1845–8	E.R.R. Green, lecturer in social and economic history, University of Manchester
17	1848–70	Cornelius O'Leary, reader in political science, Queen's University, Belfast
18	1870–91	T.W. Moody, fellow, and professor of modern history, Trinity College, Dublin
19	1891–1914	F.S.L. Lyons, professor of modern history, University of Kent at Canterbury
20	1914–21	David Thornley, fellow, and associate professor of political science, Trinity College, Dublin
21	1921–45	T.D. Williams, professor of modern history, University College, Dublin, and Kevin B. Nowlan, associate professor of modern history, University College, Dublin
22	1945–	John H. Whyte, lecturer in political science, Queen's University, Belfast

APPENDIX D

A New History of Ireland, Stage I
Complementary structure—subjects and contributors

(Note that this list is not yet complete.)

Economic and social history
L.M. Cullen, fellow and lecturer in modern history, Trinity College, Dublin
Joseph Lee, fellow of Peterhouse, Cambridge
H.D. Gribbon, Ministry of Education, Northern Ireland
Miriam Daly, lecturer in economic history, Queen's University, Belfast

Language and literature, and society
Brian Ó Cuív, senior professor and director, School of Celtic Studies, Dublin Institute
    for Advanced Studies
James Carney, senior professor, School of Celtic Studies, Dublin Institute for
    Advanced Studies
J.C. Beckett, professor of Irish History, Queen's University, Belfast
Thomas Flanagan, professor of English, University of California, Berkeley, Cal.
Conor Cruise O'Brien, Albert Schweitzer professor of humanities, New York
    University.

Visual arts and society
Edwin C. Rae, professor of art history, University of Illinois
Anne O. Crookshank, director of studies in visual arts, Trinity College, Dublin

Administration and the public services
R.B. McDowell, fellow, and associate professor of modern history, Trinity College,
    Dublin
F.B. Chubb, fellow and professor of political science, Trinity College, Dublin

Education
Tarlach Ó Raifeartaigh, chairman of the Higher Education Authority of Ireland
T.W. Moody, fellow, and professor of modern history, Trinity College, Dublin

Cinema, radio and television
H.R. Cathcart, regional officer for Northern Ireland, Independent Television Authority

The Irish abroad
T.N. Brown, professor of history, University of Massachusetts, Boston, Mass
Patrick J. O'Farrell, professor of history, University of New South Wales
Historical panoramas

John V. Kelleher, professor of Irish history and literature, Harvard University, Cambridge, Mass

Maire de Paor

Aidan Clarke, lecturer in modern history, Trinity College, Dublin

R.B. McDowell, fellow, and associate professor of modern history, Trinity College, Dublin

L.P. Curtis, associate professor of history, University of California, Berkeley, Cal.

Geography and historical geography

J.P. Haughton, fellow, and professor of geography, Trinity College, Dublin

R.E. Glasscock, lecturer in geography, Queen's University, Belfast

R.A. Butlin, college lecturer in geography, University College, Dublin

J.H. Andrews, lecturer in geography, Trinity College, Dublin

T. Jones Hughes, professor of geography, University College, Dublin

D.A. Gillmor, lecturer in geography, Trinity College, Dublin

4

An Agenda for Irish History, 1978-2018*

R.D. EDWARDS

The celebration of the fortieth anniversary of the two societies, the Irish Historical Society and the Ulster Society for Irish Historical Studies, suggests that, having looked backwards over the achievements of the first forty years, we may look forward to what might be done in the comparable future.[1]

The main achievements of these societies, the promoting of objective Irish history and the maintaining of a common cultural outlook on Irish history, were secured by the admission of Ireland as a cultural entity to the international historical organisation, the Comité International des Sciences Historiques.

The professionalism of Irish historical activities has also been the objective of these two societies through their joint journal, *Irish Historical Studies*, through the activities of the Irish Committee of Historical Sciences which they established as the Irish representative body affiliated to the international organisation, and through many other activities sponsored by their members, most notably the publication of the Royal Irish Academy's *A New History of Ireland* which owes so much to the guiding genius of the retiring president of the Irish Historical Society, T. W. Moody, of which Volume III, 1534-1691, has already appeared.

One must, however, look back further than forty years to find the beginnings of the scientific study of Irish history. By 1922 two political entities had emerged in Ireland, the first, Northern Ireland, stressing its continued association with the United Kingdom, the second committed to increasing control of its own affairs and to greater detachment from the British connection. Inevitably, Irish historians were influenced by these political developments which could have led north and south to diverge completely from one another in their research activities as well as in their organisation. Not the least of the achievements of this society and of its sister society in Belfast is that for forty years they have maintained their cultural and organisational connections. In this activity T.W. Moody's record over the last forty years is the most outstanding.

---

* First published in *I.H.S.* xxi (1978-9), pp. 3-19.
1. A paper read to the Irish Historical Society, 10 January 1978.

Soon after the establishment of Northern Ireland, David Alfred Chart was responsible for the decision to set up an archival centre in Belfast which in 1924 became the Public Record Office (PRONI) where invaluable work was carried out in accordance with the high standards employed in the Public Record Offices in these islands. A new Record Office building opened recently in Belfast specially designed to meet the requirements of archivists and historians working on the substantial body of material rescued from destruction, as well as that accruing through the development of local administration. Thus today the PRONI provides a modest exemplar for what should also be provided in Dublin, where a new record office is urgently needed and where the building which replaced the Four Courts Record Office destroyed in the civil war in 1922 still inadequately attempts to cope with the complex archival problems of the Republic of Ireland.

The Gaelic revival movement had been so much associated with twentieth-century Irish nationalism that it naturally featured prominently in the cultural plans of historians connected with the Dublin government set up by Dáil Éireann in 1919. Particularly influential was John (Eóin) MacNeill whose own achievements in establishing the scientific basis for the study of early Irish history, its laws and institutions, had profound effects upon our understanding of Irish historical development up to the collapse of Gaelic society in the seventeenth century. In 1920 Bulmer Hobson (a friend of MacNeill's), prompted J.J. O'Neill, the librarian of University College, Dublin and J.H. Delargy in an unsuccessful effort to found the Manuscripts and Records Society of Ireland. Within a short time, in 1927 and 1928, the government agreed to subsidise through the Folklore of Ireland Society (An Cumann le Béaloideas Éireann) and the Irish Manuscripts Commission (Coimisiún Laimhscríbhinní na hÉireann) publication of such material, the first with the object of collecting the oral evidence of Irish culture, the second with the object of locating, preserving, reporting on and publishing the written documentation in Irish manuscripts, particularly in the Gaelic language. This second body also came to be responsible for much of the work formerly carried out by the Historical Manuscripts Commission in Ireland.[2]

The activities of Chart and MacNeill, together with those of Delargy, the first Director of Irish Folklore, and in a lesser way, in the Dublin Record Office, of James F. Morrissey, were greatly assisted by the availability of

2. Since 1869 the Royal Commission on Historical Manuscripts, commonly called the Historical Manuscripts Commission, had reported on State Papers and other historical material not in the public record offices, but preserved in private custody, in England, Ireland, Scotland and Wales. More recently, in the United Kingdom of Great Britain and Northern Ireland, these activities led to the setting up of the National Register of Archives, which also cooperates with Dublin-centred institutions such as the National Library of Ireland and the Library of Trinity College, Dublin, as well as with the Public Record Office of Ireland.

personnel trained in recent academic developments in history and allied subjects. In Northern Ireland, this led to the revival of the *Ulster Journal of Archaeology*, with which younger academics became associated, notably Oliver Davies and E. Estyn Evans. In Queen's University, Belfast, Irish history had played little part in the Department of History. Early Irish history was customarily regarded as within the jurisdiction of the Department of Celtic, and modern Irish history was first catered for under the aegis of Professor James Eadie Todd when Robert Mitchell Henry, Professor of Latin, was acting Vice-Chancellor. It then became possible to expand the activities of a young history lecturer named T.W. Moody, who with J.C. Beckett, D.A. Chart, R.M. Henry, M.A. O'Brien of the Celtic Department, Patrick Rogers, Leo McKeown, history graduates and others set up the Ulster Society for Irish Historical Studies early in 1936. The present writer had the honour of delivering the paper at its first meeting.

In Dublin and throughout the twenty-six counties of the Irish Free State, as Southern Ireland became on 6 December 1922, it is not unfair to say that Irish historical thinking tended to continue along the lines dictated by political allegiance to nationalism. Historians joined with antiquarians in deploring the destruction of the Four Courts Record Office but prevailing popular opinion dominated public thinking in regarding the loss lightly, as but administrative debris of British rule in Ireland. While in Belfast the government was providing increasing accommodation for the new PRO, successive administrations in Dublin connived at the reduction and transfer of the Record Office staff until it became but a skeleton force incapable of attempting anything more than locating substitutes for the lost records and fearing to display any constructive ideas for future archival development. By contrast, schemes for endowing Gaelic studies preoccupied those capable of influencing government patronage until MacNeill's success in securing the establishment of the Irish Manuscripts Commission made possible the inclusion of PRO interests by the appointment of Morrissey as a member of the Commission. There was still, however, no Irish historical association, nor, as R.I. Best pointed out to T.W. Moody and to the present writer, any Irish historical review, as Kenney had noted in 1929.[3]

The first move to found an Irish historical review in March 1934 proved unsuccessful. But, two years later, after the setting up of the Ulster Society for Irish Historical Studies, the Irish Historical Society was established in Dublin, the founders including, in addition to T.W. Moody of Queen's and the present writer, a small group connected with various institutions.[4] Within

3.   J.F. Kenney, *The sources for the early history of Ireland, an introduction and guide* (New York, 1929), i, 84.
4.   Among these were: John Francis O'Doherty (Maynooth), James Carty (National Library of Ireland), James (Seamus) Pender (Royal Irish Academy), James Johnston Auchmuty (T.C.D.), Aubrey Osborn Gwynn (U.C.D.).

two years, the two societies had sponsored the first issue of *Irish Historical Studies*, having secured the support of senior academics in gaining modest subsidies from the three universities.[5] Concurrently, stimulated by Harold Temperley of Cambridge who was Chairman of the International Committee and external examiner in history in the National University, who secured the support of the head of the Dublin government, Eamon de Valera, the two societies secured international representation for Ireland as a cultural unit after the foundation of the Irish Committee of Historical Sciences. These events of 1934-8 created a corporate sense which has endured, north and south, for the last forty years.

Any agenda for the next forty years should, presumably, be presented to the Irish public in two instalments. In the year 2000, the present eighteen-year-old generation will be over forty. The teachers of today's eighteen-year-olds need to be reminded of their effectiveness or ineffectiveness when our destinies are being ruled by the forty-year-olds. It is urgently necessary to present, at least in the universities, an integrated approach to European history, including Europe's former overseas communities, if the EEC is to survive the conflicting demands of its self-centred states of today. Much evidence suggests that in Germany, France and elsewhere in continental Europe, this integrated approach is already being realised. By contrast, the extent of the commitment of the individual states in these islands to the European idea is still a matter of discussion. If Irish historians are too insular in this matter, if they do not seize the opportunity to interpret their history in its European context, they may yet have the mortification of seeing it so presented for them by the continental Europeans. We have never been sufficiently grateful to the German and French scholars for recognising our languages as an ancient contributory element in the origins of civilisation and also for their philological work in establishing the scientific bases for the study of Gaelic, Welsh and of other Celtic languages. By the year 2000 it should be apparent whether the teachers of the Irish eighteen-year-olds have equipped them adequately to take their places in Europe.

Forty years hence, the generation now being born should have become the rulers of our domestic concerns, if mankind has successfully avoided the danger of destroying all life upon earth. For this generation, the approach to world history could have vital significance if, with the other peoples in the European community, the historians have been able to record the emergence of a sense of community, and not rivalry, among the superpowers and the smaller states, and if these last have come to grips with the necessity of conceiving their status in a more modest way in international society. Continental historians can hardly

5.   Reference may here be made to W.A. Goligher and W.E. Thrift (T.C.D.); T. Corcoran, Mary T. Hayden, E. MacNeill, J.M. O'Sullivan (N.U.I.); R.M. Henry, J.E. Todd (Q.U.B.).

be blamed if they consider that the discords in our islands could impose an impossible task upon us in attempting to reconcile the absolute sovereign concepts of yesterday with the reality of today. Are we not in danger of ignoring the reality if we succumb to the temptation of underplaying the violence of these discords? Must we not endeavour to see ourselves in the wider context?

Although world history, or indeed the history of Europe, may not appear to provide many opportunities for future research in Irish history, the fact remains that future historians will fail to influence society if they cannot present the greater community locally in the first instance, educating their peoples as Europeans and ultimately as citizens of the world. Celtic imagination has often been credited with providing opportunities to see situations *in globo* less obvious to phlegmatic minds. If university professional studies can give priority to surveying general developments, the specialisations of postgraduate research, particularly for mature scholars, should offer opportunities to Irish historians to participate more fully in such activities as anthropology, archaeology and sociology, to mention but a few, which now command a wider international public which expects the support of general history.

William Hardy McNeill, the American son of an historian of Celtic penitentials, J.T. McNeill, has probably surveyed as comprehensively as anyone of the present generation the main stages of world history. He has criticised world histories written by westerners which conform either to a linear pattern deriving from Jewish and Christian ideas about God's purpose for men, or to a cyclic pattern traceable to pagan Greek speculation about cosmic time and constitutional changes in city states.[6]

McNeill's approach would suggest that the next generation will be required to devote much effort to studying the impact of China, divorced from the western European preoccupation with Jewish or Christian obsessions with divine purposes towards oriental peoples. Perhaps such study will lead to closer attention being paid to the administrative disasters of the past, when western Europe's bureaucracies became divorced from the people in the wars of religion. It might more convincingly explain the fragmentation of Europe after the Reformation. It may have to assist in preventing a third world war if the conflicting nations over most of the world continue to be led by their anonymous and faceless bureaucrats, civil and ecclesiastical. Given sufficient altruism among historians, particularly in placing nationalism in its historical context, Europe's chances of surviving to the year 2000 could be enhanced.

6.   W. H. McNeill, *A world history* (London, Oxford University Press, 1967), p. 492. See also the following works from the same author's and publisher's series ('Readings in World History'): with Schuyler Houser, *Medieval Europe* (1971); with Jean W. Sedlar, *Classical China* (1970), and *China, India and Japan, the Middle Period* (1972); with M.R. Waldman, *The Islamic World* (1973). The quotation is taken from McNeill's review of J.M. Roberts, *The Hutchinson history of the world*, in the *Times Lit. Supp.*, 27 May, 1977, p. 655.

Even if the historians play little part in it, they owe it to themselves to be ready to instruct the world community of the future. I must be forgiven if I suggest to younger colleagues that their role in society is far more decisive than that of their predecessors: it appears to me that the historian of the future must be prepared to face the challenge of the economist: the historian again becomes a prophet. He not merely fails in his duty, but he loses his public prestige if he cannot confine his predictions to the realisable.

Thus the historian can only overcome the challenge of more attractive current and future prognosticators by the stimulus of non-achievement. By achieving nothing for those concerned for the future he condemns himself to obscurity and oblivion; to being superseded by others less gifted, perhaps, but more prepared to face the challenge from the men of tomorrow seeking guidance today.

Perhaps the most urgent necessity for Irish history today is an assessment of sources from the beginning of history to the present time. The scientific developments in anthropology and archaeology have already drastically revised our approach to chronology. The Book of Invasions, *Leabhar Gabhála*, with its stately sequence of successive peoples who colonised Ireland before the Christian era, is no longer accepted as the opening chapter of Irish history. We must not, however, be satisfied with an adjustment of sources based upon the writings of Jubainville, MacNeill, Thurneysen, O'Rahilly and their disciples like Paul Walsh, Kathleen Mulchrone and D.A. Binchy on this and on the early annals.[7]

The sources must be evaluated *in toto*. The archaeological and anthropological evidence linking Ireland historically to Europe and Asia must be studied further with a view to ascertaining how far they can impose disciplinary frameworks within which our earlier source material may be appraised more critically.

The evidence from early Irish history of the first written book, the Bible,

7.   Henri d'Arbois de Jubainville, *Le cycle mythologique irlandais et la mythologic celtique* (Paris, 1884), trans. R.I. Best, *The Irish mythological cycle and Celtic mythology* (Dublin, 1903). Eoin MacNeill, 'The authorship and structure of the Annals of Tigernach' in *Ériu*, vii (1914), pp 30-113, and *Celtic Ireland* (Dublin, 1921). See also the drafts of many unpublished memoranda on *Leabhar Gabhála* and on the early annals among the MacNeill papers in the Archives Department, U.C.D. (L.A.I. Rudolf Thurneysen, 'Zum Lebor Gabála' in *Zeitschrift für Celtische Philologie*, x (1915), pp. 384-95 and *Die irische Helden und Königsage biszum siebzehnten Jahrhundert* (Hallé, Saale, 1921). T.F. O'Rahilly, *Early Irish History and Mythology* (Dublin, 1947). Paul Walsh, 'The Annals attributed to Tigernach' in *I.H.S.*, ii (1940-1), pp. 154-9; 'The dating of the Irish Annals', ibid. ii (1940-1), pp. 355-75. Kathleen Mulchrone, *Bethu Phátraic, the tripartite life of Patrick* (Dublin, 1939). D.A. Binchy, 'St. Patrick and his biographers, ancient and modern', in *Studia Hibernica* ii (1962) especially pp. 70-7. Reference may also be made to Kathleen Hughes, *Early Cristian Ireland: introduction to the sources* (London, 1972), particularly on the Book of Invasions, pp. 275, 281-3.

and its early Christian exponents, is again being explored with due regard to the successive written strata of sources in Latin as well as in the early Irish language.[8] When the strata can be evaluated in their real chronological sequence we will be in a better position to see how successive generations reinterpreted their history, and perhaps to draw more scientific conclusions.

The historian in the past has sometimes been the victim of his own expertise. Methodological developments have made historians more scientific but they may not always have realised how drastically they could be divorced from valuable sources by stressing too rigidly their exclusive reliance on contemporary documentation, or on archives, or on professional opinions, influencing them to distrust, if not reject, folk material as literary effusions. Just as studies in public opinion necessitate the evaluation of the ballad, so the whole concept of the poetic art necessitates, in successive periods, the new evaluation of literary sources if our knowledge is not to be confined to the received doctrines of the historical schools. If literature conveyed in poetry can be assessed, it should enable us to measure more precisely the manner in which literary developments communicated themselves across Europe long before we became conscious of our existence as a nation.

The supernatural powers attributed to the early Irish poets survived the coming of Christianity: at least as late as the sixteenth century there is evidence of how professional poets were prepared to invoke sanctions against law-breakers. The satire and ridicule of the poet's curse could be as demoralising as the curse of the clergy, probably as late as the nineteenth century. To ignore the necessity for appraising literary sources should no longer seem justifiable to the historian. Indeed, some attention to literature might improve the quality of historical writing. The style of the story teller, as an alternative to the austere factual statements of the documentary reporter, might well correct all but the most conservative scientists. On the other hand scientific methodology might well have its revenge if literature must now be subjected to analysis in technical terminology as complex as the type of analysis and the terminology increasingly favoured by sociologists.

In affirming the necessity to take into account the literary material, one is not underestimating the difficulties of assessment. Much of the earliest strata of primitive and old Irish still remain very obscure and some of the poetical data embodied in prose narrative suggests an even earlier stratum than the texts in which they are found. Authorship can often be in doubt where there is anonymity or attributions have been wrongly made to predominant personalities. Composite productions such as the *Leabhar Muimhneach*—the Irish Manuscripts Commission's edition by Tadhg Ó Donnchadha (Torna)

---

8.   David N. Dumville, 'Biblical apocrypha and the early Irish: a preliminary investigation', in *Proc. R.I.A.*, vol. 73, sect. C, no. 8 (1973) pp 299-338.

which was perceptively reviewed by Paul Walsh (*I.H.S.* iii [1942-3], pp. 135-43)—embodied later texts of early material such as the *Leabhar Gabhála*. Behind the tribal histories for Thomond and Desmond were the origin stories which provided some controls in assessing the stratified mythology of pre-christian invasions. In addition to earlier commentators such as Thurneysen, and MacNeill, contributions on tribal origins have more recently been made by M. Dillon, M.A. O'Brien, M.L. Sjoested and F.J. Byrne.[9]

What is next needed is a concerted move to put our earlier historical sources into a better condition for assessment. It is rather startling to realise that for some of the texts the historian usually confines his critical concepts by ignoring the original manuscripts and relying on a photocopy, a palaeographical edition, a diplomatic text or a translation. It is to be hoped that the manuscript analyses of William O'Sullivan[10] and of H.P.A. Oskamp[11] will lead historians to return to the tradition of regarding the manuscript, only, as the original source and not its copy. If the historian is to make an original contribution to his profession he should form his own impression of the original sources even though he may ultimately accept the verdict of the photocopy or diplomatic editor or translator. The concurrence of at least two independent witnesses will always be necessary in scientific history.

That is not to say that the profession will not be grateful for the work of outstanding scholars. M.A. O'Brien put students very much in his debt by his elaborate and valuable index work to the material in the first volume of his genealogical corpus.[12] Even greater would have been our gratitude had one so steeped in this rare material accompanied his text with a translation. The editors of the Book of Leinster, Osborn Bergin, Richard Irvine Best and M.A. O'Brien, have similarly provided us with their diplomatic edition.[13] Had they provided us with their translations our gratitude could hardly be expressible, even if individual scholars always remembered to make their own assessment

---

9. Myles Dillon, 'Lebor Gabála Érenn' in *R.S.A.I. Journ.*, lxxxvi (1956), pp. 62-72. M.A. O'Brien, 'Irish origin legends' in Dillon, *Early Irish Society* (Dublin, 1954), pp 36-51. Marie-Louise Sjoested, *Dieux et Héros des Celtes*, trans. Myles Dillon as *Gods and Heroes of the Celts* (London, 1949). Francis John Byrne, 'Tribes and tribalism in early Ireland' in *Ériu*, xxii (1971) 128- 66 The Book of Rights (Lebor na Cert) may represent a more sophisticated Munster claim to rulership than Leabhar Gabhála based as it was on Roman concepts of conquest. By contrast counter-obligations between kings and overkings suggest a contractual relationship in the south.
10. 'Notes on the scripts and make-up of the Book of Leinster', *Celtica*, vii (1966), pp. 1-31.
11. 'Notes on the history of Lebor na hUidre' in *R.I.A. Proc.* lxv, sect. C. (1957), pp. 117-37; and 'On the collation of Lebor na hUidre' in *Ériu*, xxv (1974), pp. 147-56.
12. M.A. O'Brien (ed.), *Corpus genealogiarum Hiberniae*, i (Dublin, 1962).
13. *The Book of Leinster* (formerly known as *Lebar na Nuachongbhála*), edited by O. Bergin, vol. i (Dublin, 1954), R.I. Best, and M.A. O'Brien, vol. ii (1956), iii (1957), iv (1965), v (1967).

of both text and translation. It is understood that Dr D.A. Binchy's edition of the early Irish laws will shortly be published. Perhaps that eminent scholar will arrange that an archivist can make available the Binchy translations even if he is too modest to publish them with the texts.

Increasingly, statisticians and sociologists are teaching us to allow for 'the margin of error' in their massive calculations. The historians can help to reduce the margin by providing them with the highest professional samples. And the trained archivist familiar with the scholar's work can so deploy his material that the consideration of his preparative studies reveals more clearly than can any published work the richness of the thought and the extensiveness of the investigations of which the material in print is but the tip of the iceberg.

The responsibility of the individual is recognised more than ever today. The historian must do his own thing. His is a threefold operation, delimiting his topic, ascertaining and assessing its source material, constructing his historical edifice. Only in a limited way should the historian involve himself in collective activities lest the result appears to be 'the agreed lie'. He must not abdicate his individual functions and in his threefold activity he must continually examine his historical conscience. Is his topic the suggestion of an independent intellect concerned about knowledge? Is it due to suggestions from others insufficiently knowledgeable about its historical context. Is his topic properly susceptible to historical treatment? Does adequate documentation exist to indicate that such treatment is possible? Does the surviving documentation permit of a double approach from internal and external sources? Is the internal documentation sufficient to enable him to treat the matter, if an institutional one, from an archival standpoint? Can the external sources be assessed in order to distinguish between one or more strata of external documentation? Can he make an historical assessment of the state of the topic as seen by successive generations of historians? Can his archival material stand up to an analysis of the circumstances in which administrative material was preserved, weeded or destroyed? Is he in a position to ascertain whether any type of records management procedure has been adopted in the processing of archival material? Before embarking on historical construction, has he taken any steps to allow for substantial gaps in documentation which is missing or which never existed? All these questions are ultimately the responsibility of the individual historian who, however, can never hope to have more than a limited achievement if he is not acclimatised to the collective enterprise. The individual requires a community at every stage in his activity if he is to understand that history is a coherence, the result of a community's interrelationships between its individuals from which a consensus often emerges. It is a truism that individual imaginations operate in different ways. The collective group can provide the individual historian with an external perspective for his own policy. Participation in an active historical seminar is a valuable exercise for the historian and enables him to test himself and his topic. He will still, of course, have to take individual responsibility as he proceeds further.

In the assessment of sources, the individual obligation of the historian to undertake a personal inspection of the originals of his documents must be affirmed. Many of the difficulties which have arisen in the past, resulting in rejection of historians' work by their critics and successors, have followed from an imaginative failure which has destroyed the credibility of their work. The historian can be grateful for the copy of his document in a transcript, a drawing, a photocopy, a microfilm, in a palaeographical or diplomatic edition, or in print. All these processes can materially ease his labours, enable him to handle his documentation more expertly, give him the confidence to perceive the historical situation in its internal and external relationships more clearly. But if he fails to make the individual contact with his material at every stage, he will ultimately be challenged for having failed in his historical duty. In all these activities, the isolated individual, confronted with mountains of material, could very well experience the feelings of despair which the researches of dedicated and enthusiastic scholars have so frequently communicated to their less energetic brethren.

Collectively, historians must perform duties for which, individually, they have little competence. The timidity of historians, particularly in Ireland, has often been alleged, and with good reason. In the twentieth century, with the consciousness that there is now a professional status for the historian, their obligations to the community in its widest sense demand that they shall express themselves in no uncertain terms about matters concerning our historical heritage, about matters relating to the preservation and availability of our sources.

As regards the sources, an immediate desideratum is an appeal to government, administrators, and repository curators in this country to establish professional archivists in charge of surviving material. The failure in this regard in the past, the failure to instruct our people as to the urgency of preserving their oral and documentary heritage, is the greatest single reason for the situation of neglect and destruction which operates under our eyes even today. In this context, historians should immediately take cognisance of Ireland's deplorable predicament in the European Community, with standards abysmally below those of the rest of the EEC states.

In terms of the collective responsibility of historians for the state of the nation, the necessities for group action may become more generally recognised if it is pointed out that the ambivalent attitudes of many civil servants towards our administrative documentation enables them to thwart all historical attempts to treat such material as part of the national heritage, which is how it is already regarded in most of the EEC countries. Most Irish civil servants, taking refuge in the British terminology of a century ago, make it difficult to secure government recognitions that the administrative material belongs to the nation, not to its transient bureaucrats. Continuing to utilise the excuse of avoiding public extravagance, our Public Record Office is still very inadequately equipped today. If it is to discharge the increasing duties demanded in the European Community, it will be obliged to depend, even more than it does today, upon the good offices of its neighbours and more immediately upon the other Public Record Offices in these islands. At London, the opening of the new Record Office at Kew makes possible a public service in information retrieval such as this country could not provide for domestic purposes, even given all the requisite facilities, before the end of the century. Here is something for the immediate agenda, if our eighteen-year-olds are to be educated to be skilled and not unskilled workers in the Europe of 2018.

Perhaps the solution is to establish a computer link to university archival centres. The progress of archival studies in this century can prove to be an invaluable experience for the historian who has frequently been accused of using his documentation, like an advocate, to win his case. Study of the approach of the archivist provides the historian with the vivid impression of the totality of material accumulated by an organisation. The result can be that the historian is emancipated from dependence on isolated ducuments and is able to trace the sequence of documentary development. This eliminates the danger of the wishful thinker attributing too much to later statements so that, without realising it, he fails to see his material in its historical context. By contrast with the select documents which the historian's construction must be based in the last resort, the archival material presents the documentary consensus.

History, then, where archival matter is available as the internal source constituent of its activity, has a higher dimensional equipment. If the historical school is fortunate enough, it can have its own archival laboratory. The problem for the future is to relate the archival laboratory to the neophyte. Students today are document-minded if only because they are stimulated by the new approach which makes available documents to enable the individual student to get some personal opportunity to appreciate material. The selection of the teacher, however, must not absolutely predominate. The pupil today may learn to appreciate history from the packaged selection of a teacher or of a repository. He is better equipped than his predecessor whose approach to history was too frequently dictated by the personal predilections of an examination-conscious tutor. At least his opportunity to develop his own personal reactions is greater. Perhaps he can now more clearly understand what his teacher is endeavouring to inculcate: history, like painting, becomes more meaningful by personal experiment. Thus he early becomes aware of the fact that history is not the agreed lie, once he can see that different reactions are permissible.

The historian, however, must be alert and independent. Although much of the training of the archivist is methodologically an advantage (particularly for young research workers) once the historian has learned the lesson of the sanctity of the archives group, he may well find himself obliged to detach himself from the attitude in a repository which respects the professional rules but does not feel obliged to relate its material to complementary material in other locations, where the sanctity of the archives group may not have been observed in the past. Furthermore, repository policy is very properly concerned only incidentally with historical processes and the archivist should not be expected to perform the functions which only the professional historian, in the ordinary course, is competent to discharge. Yet again, the archivist, unlike the historian, may be unaware of the circumstances in which administrative telescoping of past events can take place. Only a rigorous application of historical source criticism will enable the historian to safeguard himself from the uncritical acceptance of the administrator's statements regarding his material. A few examples should indicate the difficulties arising from what is here termed administrative telescoping. Perhaps they might be prefaced by a caution from Michael Oakeshott.

In *Experience and its Modes*[14] Professor Oakeshott pointed out that historians who concern themselves with origins were involving themselves in an unhistorical activity. The reminder is perhaps rather unpalatable until one recollects that, thanks to archival studies, the historian becomes aware that the documentation of 'origins' is necessarily subjective. The unpalatable reminder partly arises from the historians' awareness that origins have an interest for man, like original sin. It is hard to resist the temptation to claim historical origins, and administrators are particularly attracted to what may well confer status upon them in the eyes of the community. The result is that an administration may base its documents on fabrications or statements not founded on contemporary documentation linking their activities to those of a comparable, perhaps identical, institution in the past.

Professor F. J. Byrne, in an appendix to Dr George Eogan's description of excavations at Knowth published by the Royal Irish Academy,[15] pointed out that seventh-century kings, extending their conquests to the Knowth area, described themselves as the successors to much earlier pagan rulers. The survival of pre-Christian ruler myths into the Christian era indicates that a new administrative development sought popular approval by claiming continuity with the original occupants of this sacrosanct place.

Again, when Pope Adrian IV approved, in *Laudabiliter*, Anglo-Norman claims to Ireland, he declared, and his successor Alexander III confirmed, the authority in Ireland of Henry II in virtue of the alleged fourth-century

14. Cambridge (1933).
15. *R.I.A. Proc.*, lxvi, sect. C (1968), pp. 383-400.

Donation of Constantine of all the islands in the world to the papacy. The subsequent exposure of this Donation of Constantine as a forgery was not regarded as invalidating papal action. In its wider sense, this action would certainly have been taken as justifiable in the remarkable twentieth-century renaissance of civilisation which greatly increased administrative efficiency in western Europe, the revival of studies of imperial and canon law in that period contributing much to the ideas of absolute monarchy and a divine papacy.

Similarly, in their studies of medieval administrative and parliamentary development in Ireland, the late H.G. Richardson and Professor G.O. Sayles[16] contributed much to our knowledge of administrative developments which took place over western Europe and which were influenced by the growth of French institutions. Their contribution to the history of administration in Ireland from the twelfth to the fourteenth centuries needs to be assessed by the historian with clear ideas as to the manner in which administrative developments can be telescoped, particularly if we take into account the varying fortunes of the central government in England from Magna Carta to the deposition of Richard II. In the Irish context there is the additional danger that the historian failing to assess the sources does not take adequate account of the new thinking behind the trained administrators, usually ecclesiastics, who served either pope or king, sometimes both, exalting their masters by claiming for them a sovereignty known to Roman law but utterly repugnant to the less sophisticated community in the Gaelic tradition.

I have already referred to the imminent necessity for enlarging the university programmes in teaching history. One would hope that it would be possible before the year 2000 to take it for granted that historical schools would normally offer programmes in the history of Russia, of India, of China and of the third world. Once this has been accepted as the norm, historical research in this country will have to be prepared to cooperate with the increasing number of foreign scholars seeking guidance here, in our infinitesimal fields, for world projects in archaeology, anthropology and sociology. One shudders to think how a poor country can find its resources organised, its spending schemes controlled from skyscraper level. But Irish historians need expect no mercy if they are not prepared to accept that their quantitative and qualitative productions will have to increase fantastically if they are going to avoid being consigned to lower third-level teaching, making way for experts from more affluent nations, however inadequately equipped they may be.

Reference must also be made in this context to the necessity to plan Irish historical research at local level in cooperation with all our university staffs to carry through collective enterprises concurrently so that the time-honoured local periodicals of Cork and Galway, the *Ulster Journal of Archaeology*, the

16. See, particularly, *The Administration of Ireland 1172-1377* (Dublin, 1963).

North Munster Antiquarian Journal and many others, can cooperate in a common programme. One hopes that such cooperation could lead in time to the setting up of a series comparable to the Victoria County Histories in England. Irish historians must decide if they are capable of going beyond the county history since many counties are less than four centuries old. Lordships, kingdoms, provinces, dioceses should have considerable claims as against counties. The Irish Historical Society has every reason to be proud of the fruits of its association with the Ulster Society for Irish Historical Studies, particularly in the fine record, in which T.W. Moody's achievement is unequalled, in *Irish Historical Studies*. But this society should undertake the lead in the collective planning of regional history and there is ample scope for the total involvement for decades to come of all available scholars working systematically so that their successors may reap the fruits of a newer new history of Ireland where, perhaps, local achievements may emerge as our greatest claim to fame.

When Ireland became associated with the International Historical Congress it began to contribute annually to the International Bibliography of Historical Sciences now preparing its forty-second volume for publication. The selection of writings over the years will repay analysis if only to consider how small has been the list of Irish contributions to many aspects of historical science. Over the next forty years, simply by evaluating our own sources, by planning our potential contributions to auxiliary sciences (in particular to anthropology, to archaeology, to sociology), by completing constructive original work of the highest quality, we should be able to justify our role in European and in world history.

If our work in the future is to be commensurate with our obligations to the past, all our scholars, all the young students we can train, are needed, for we must face the fact that expansion of our work is essential. If we do not publish—and publish with distinction—we perish.

PART III: ASSUMPTIONS AND IMPLICATIONS

5

Irish History and Irish Mythology[*]

T.W. MOODY

The past is dead. Nothing, for good or ill, can change it; nothing can revive it. Yet there is a sense in which the past lives on: in works of human hands and minds, in beliefs, institutions, and values, and in us all, who are its living extension. It lives on in us, both for good and ill, shaping our lives and helping to determine our action, whether or not we know how our present is related to our past. But just as individuals cannot exist as complete persons without knowledge of their past, so human societies must have their self-knowledge if they are to preserve their corporate identity and their distinctive patterns of living. To supply this knowledge is one of the primary functions of the history of nations. But nations derive their consciousness of their past not only—and not mainly—from historians. They also derive it from popular traditions, transmitted orally, in writing, and through institutions. I am using the word myth to signify received views of this kind as contrasted with the knowledge that the historian seeks to extract by the application of scientific methods to his evidence. Myths as I define them combine elements of fact and of fiction; they are a part of the dead past that historians study, as well as being part of the living present in which we all, historians included, are involved.

All nations have their myths, which affect their corporate lives and do so most strongly in times of strain or crisis or unresolved conflict. Such myths can be sustaining or destroying, benign or malignant, influences, a stimulus to effort or an encouragement to resignation, a source of harmless amusement or an incitement to malice and hatred—or they can be a mixture of such elements. The myth-system or mythology of Ireland exemplifies all this in confusing abundance, and I want to consider some illustrative examples. Myth-making is an ancient Irish industry, of which the origin-legends and heroic tales of early and medieval Ireland are a characteristic product. But the myths I have in mind all took shape within the past four centuries, and are still more or less current.

[*] A presidential address delivered to the Dublin University History Society on Tuesday, 10 May 1977 and first published in *Hermathena*, 124 (1978), pp. 7-24.

What might be called a 'catholic-separatist' myth emerged in the early seventeenth century to explain the Irish part in the crowning struggle of Queen Elizabeth's reign to complete the English conquest of Ireland. The most formidable leader of Irish resistance to English power, Hugh O'Neill, earl of Tyrone, took care to identify his rebellion with the cause of the catholic church. And in 1600, while that rebellion was still raging, Peter Lombard (who was to become catholic archbishop of Armagh in the following year) wrote at Rome a treatise that presented it as a war of religion; which it was, but only in part. After the decisive defeat of O'Neill, an Irish exile from Cork, Philip O'Sullivan Beare, developed this theme in a book published at Lisbon in 1621, *Historiae catholicae Iberniae compendium*. How imbued this writer was with anti-protestant animus is evident from his strictures, in an unpublished work of 1625,[1] on the term 'Anglo-Ibernici' (Anglo-Irish). It was, he considered, as inappropriate to Irishmen as 'Lutheran-Irish' or 'Atheist-Irish' would be. O'Sullivan Beare was one of the founders of a long-lasting dogma that the true Irishman was both catholic and Gaelic, as he himself was. Yet the most expressive and influential element in catholic Ireland at that time was not the Gaelic or 'Old Irish' but the Anglo-Irish or 'Old English'. Descended from the medieval English colony, they were fervently loyal to the English crown, though rejecting the English reformation. Their catholicism was no less fervent and articulate than their loyalism: they and not the Old Irish were the champions of the Tridentine reforms within the catholic church. But what they demanded—in vain, as it proved—was to share political power with the new protestant colony, the 'New English', under an English and protestant king. They were bent on combining spiritual allegiance to Rome with temporal allegiance to England; and to the end of the seventeenth century, despite disastrous setbacks, they were a standing challenge to the myth that being an Irish catholic was incompatible with loyalty to the English crown. In the end, both Old English and Old Irish shared a common ruin, fighting on the side of one English king, James II, against a rival English king, William III.

The imposition of the anglican reformation by England on an unreceptive Ireland in the sixteenth century gave rise to a tremendous Irish-anglican myth. The state church, the church established by law in Ireland until 1869, was seen by anglicans as the direct descendant and true inheritor of the Christian church founded by St Patrick in the fifth century. This Patrician or 'Celtic' church, they believed, was largely independent of Rome, showed exemplary spiritual vitality, and retained an apostolic simplicity until, in the eleventh and twelfth centuries, it was brought under Roman control through ecclesiastical

1.   On 'Zoilomastix', see T. W. Moody in *A New History of Ireland*, iii, ed. T.W. Moody, F.X. Martin, and F.J. Byrne, *Early Modern Ireland* (Oxford, 1976), p. lvii.

influences from Canterbury and through the Anglo-Norman conquest. In the later middle ages this romanised and largely anglicised church was afflicted by corruption and spiritual stagnation, from which, paradoxically, it was rescued by the ecclesiastical reforms of Henry VIII, Edward VI, and Elizabeth I. If the large majority of Ireland's population refused to repudiate the papal authority and to embrace the reformed order and doctrines, this was their misfortune, and not the fault of the state or of the state church. In fact, despite the outlawry of their church and the confiscation of its property, the mass of the catholic population continued unshaken in its spiritual allegiance to Rome, and after more than three centuries, under the inspiration of a great English anglican, the state that had established the protestant episcopal church disestablished and disendowed it. Gladstone's disestablishment act of 1869 placed all churches in Ireland on a footing of complete legal equality. But Irish anglicans continued to regard their church as the true lineal descendant of the church founded by Patrick and as having the apostolic mandate for all Ireland, even though three-quarters of all its members were located in Ulster. The mythical elements in this attitude of Irish anglicans had long helped to sustain, and were in part sustained by, protestant ascendancy and a sense of protestant superiority—and they survived the extinction of protestant ascendancy in the new Irish state. But the progress of historiography and of ecumenism in Ireland has done much to moderate the anglican myth; and the bland assumptions to be found in the quasi-official *History of the Church of Ireland*, edited by W. Alison Phillips (3 volumes, Oxford, 1933-4), are not repeated by recent historical writers on the subject.

One of the most lurid and bloody events in Irish history, the rising of the native Irish in Ulster that began on 23 October 1641, produced its own instant mythology. The rising was an eruption of pent-up bitterness and resentment against the consequences of a social revolution, designed and carried out by the state. This was the Ulster plantation, which, since 1609, in a province that had been a Gaelic stronghold, established a vigorous and thrusting colony of protestant English and Scots on lands confiscated from the native and catholic population. The early months of the rebellion witnessed an upsurge of ferocious violence against settlers; thousands of them were murdered and many more died from injuries and privations. The 'massacres of 1641' were quickly publicised in Ireland and Britain as being a deliberate attempt planned by the leaders of the rising to annihilate the settlers. Contemporary reports of the numbers killed in the early stages of the rising ranged from 20,000 to 200,000—a gross inflation of the numbers of victims that was part of a propaganda campaign in the interests of further confiscation. For over two centuries protestant and catholic historians wrangled over the question both of the magnitude and the motivation of the massacres. The evidence for numbers is inadequate and immensely complex, and has not been fully explored. We are not likely ever to know with certainty how many perished, but Lecky's conclusion, reached nearly a century ago, that about 4,000 were murdered and about twice as many died, has been broadly accepted by later scholars. The same is true of Lecky's other conclusion that the massacres were not the outcome of any premeditated plan; rather they sprang from the lack of discipline and the spontaneous fury of insurgents motivated by a blinding sense of grievance, a passion for revenge, and sectarian hatred.[2]

The 1641 horror story was quickly incorporated into protestant mythology, especially that of protestant Ulster, as proof of the wickedness and savagery of Irish catholics. The atrocities were not, of course, all on one side. As soon as protestants in Ulster had recovered from the initial shock of the massacres, they retaliated in kind, a hideous example being the extermination of thirty catholic families of Islandmagee in January 1642. The most notorious incident of Cromwell's campaigns in Ireland, the slaughter of the garrison (about 2,500) and townspeople of Drogheda after he had taken the town by storm (11 September 1649), he characterised as 'a righteous judgement of God' upon 'barbarous wretches who have imbrued their hands in so much innocent blood'—that is, had been involved in the 1641 massacres.[3] The truth was that the commander and many of the defenders of Drogheda were English and that the town had never been in the hands of the insurgents. A few months later, Cromwell explained his conception of the '41 rebellion and of the massacres in a public statement that he addressed to the catholic bishops of Ireland, to whom he imputed responsibility for inciting their people to treason and outrage:

> You, unprovoked, put the English to the most unheard-of and most barbarous massacre (without respect of sex or age) that ever the sun beheld. And at a time when Ireland was in perfect place, and when, through the example of . . . English industry, through commerce and traffic, that which was in the natives' hands was better to them than if all Ireland had been in their possession and not an Englishman in it. And yet then, I say, was this unheard-of villany perpetrated by your instigation.[4]

As an example of mythology in the making this could hardly be bettered.

2.   W.E.H. Lecky, *A history of Ireland in the eighteenth century* (London, 1892), i, 46-79; Richard Bagwell, *Ireland under the Stuarts*, i (London, 1909), pp 333-5.
3.   Thomas Carlyle (ed.), *Letters and speeches of Oliver Cromwell*, ed. S.C. Lomas (London, 1904), i, 469.
4.   Ibid., ii, 8.

I turn now to a rich and many-sided mythology, that of orangeism. A quasi-official history of orangeism, by R. M. Sibbett, published in 1914-15, opens with the following:

> An orangeman who was asked how long his order had been in existence answered offhand that orangeism could be traced back to the garden of Eden. He simply meant to convey that all the essentials of a perfect nature and of an exalted religion were to be found associated in the primal day of our race.[5]

The fall of man destroyed all this perfection but in the fulness of time man's relationship with God was renewed through Christ. 'While we maintained that relationship, by faith and obedience, no one could take away our inheritance. That was protestantism and that was orangeism.' Popery, however, obscured the truth until it was challenged and its dominion in part overthrown by the reformation. Though wounded, Rome remained a powerful and vigilant enemy of the reformed religion. The orange institution, which was the means of placing the prince of Orange on the throne of England, was simply protestantism alive to its own interests and organised for its own defence.

In a less rhapsodical spirit orangeism was characterised in 1967 by the Imperial Grand Master of the Imperial Grand Orange Council of the World, Captain L.P.S. Orr, M.P. for South Down, as follows:

> No great historical movement has been more misunderstood . . . Yet it is to this movement that the world owes the establishment of the concept of civil and religious liberty. . .
>
> The famous struggle for liberty in Europe against the concept of the dictatorship of kings can be traced back to the . . . rise of the Dutch Republic against the tyranny of the Spanish sovereigns . . . Throughout this famous story runs the continuous thread of the leadership of the house of Orange from William the Silent to our own King William III. The principles of this movement (which we call orangeism because of this leadership) were constant throughout the struggle. They were to establish and protect the protestant religion (by which general term was understood not any particular sect, but the general concept of freedom of conscience in religion), and to establish civil and religious liberty.
>
> The destruction of the doctrine of the divine right of kings and the establishment in England of constitutional monarchy, while its roots in

5.   R.M. Sibbett, *Orangeism in Ireland and throughout the empire* (2 vols, Belfast, [1914-15]), i, iii-iv; and see Hereward Senior, *Orangeism in Ireland and Britain, 1795-1836* (London, 1966), pp 288-9.

English history may in fact go very deep, was none the less accomplished by orangeism; and the tradition of opposition to European dictatorship can fairly be claimed to have started with the same movement.[6]

This, I think, may be taken as an authoritative and up-to-date statement of the myth of orangeism. In its engaging mixture of fact and fantasy, of history and mythology, it admirably illustrates my theme.

William, prince of Orange, and stadtholder of Holland, who became King William III of England in 1689, certainly was a champion—tolerant, stoical, large-minded—of human liberty in a European context. He was the central figure in a European coalition, the 'grand alliance', formed to resist the aggressions of France under Louis XIV; and in accepting the crown of England offered by a parliament that had deposed the catholic King James II, William combined this role with that of defender of English constitutional liberties, including the protestant succession. But the European war in which he was the leading spirit was not a protestant-catholic struggle; for his allies included the Holy Roman Emperor and the Most Catholic King (that is, the king of Spain), and the pope himself, Innocent XI, was no less hostile than William to Louis XIV, who made the cause of James II his own. The war of the two kings in Ireland (1689-91) was a conflation of three issues: between William and James as the new and the deposed king of England, between the grand alliance and France; and between the protestants and the catholics of Ireland. For William it was, as Dr Simms has put it, a 'fringe event' in the European war.[7] The battle of the Boyne (1 July 1690), in which William showed exemplary courage and dash, though it was far from ending the war in Ireland, was seen in contemporary Europe as a victory not only for William but also for the grand alliance. In Ireland, where William had tried to avoid the image of a protestant partisan, the battle soon came to be commemorated by protestants as the symbol of a great deliverance. And well it might, because the outcome of the war between Rí Liam and Rí Séamus was to establish protestant ascendancy more securely than ever, and to confirm protestants in the ownership of nearly all the land of Ireland. The 'glorious, pious and immortal memory of the great and good King William', who 'freed us from pope and popery, knavery and slavery, brass money and wooden shoes', was an ascendancy cult during the eighteenth century, and was even invoked by the Volunteers, the embodiment of colonial nationalism in the age of the American revolution.

This eighteenth-century orange tradition, associated both with protestant ascendancy and with the constitutional liberties demanded by liberal protes-

6.   M.W. Dewar, John Brown, and S.E. Long, *Orangeism: a new historical appreciation* (Belfast, Grand Orange Lodge of Ireland; 1967), pp. 9-10.
7.   J.G. Simms, 'Remembering 1690' in *Studies*, autumn 1974, p. 231.

tants, was taken over by the secret organisation founded in 1795 as the Orange Society, later the Orange Order. The Orange Society emerged in north Armagh from the depths of communal conflict between protestants and catholics in the Ulster countryside. It was a locally-based, grassroots organisation, confronting the equally grassroots catholic Defenders, but it rapidly achieved political importance in a wider context. For it provided a counter-movement to a revolutionary challenge to protestant ascendancy from the United Irishmen. This movement, initiated by middle-class radicals, protestant and catholic, in Belfast and Dublin, headed by Theobald Wolfe Tone and William Drennan, aimed at replacing the age-long, destructive divisions between protestants and catholics by a fraternal union of Irishmen of all classes and creeds, dedicated to achieving national independence under a democratised parliament by constitutional means. These ideals never came near to being realised. After some initial success the United Irishmen found that they had to choose between abandoning their radical aims and resorting to physical force. The extreme element chose the latter alternative, the moderates withdrew, and the movement became a revolutionary conspiracy, preparing for rebellion with help from France, with which Britain was at war. At the same time the United Irishmen gained recruits in strength from among the Defenders, thereby undermining their own non-sectarian position. Instead of bringing about 'a people united in the fellowship of freedom', the United Irish movement precipitated a new upsurge of sectarian hatred and violence. This was the situation in which the Orange Society, invoking the memory of the 'great and good King William', was accepted by the Irish establishment, which initially had regarded it with dislike and alarm, as a welcome ally against the danger of political and social revolution. What had been one of a number of local peasant organisations was quickly elevated into a widely diffused institution combining protestants of all social classes, under upper- and middle-class leadership, in defence of protestant ascendancy, the constitution, and the established order. Orangeism helped to suppress the rebellion in which the United Irish movement culminated and crashed in 1798, and which led inexorably to the extinction of the Irish parliament and to the union of Ireland with Great Britain two years later.

Orangeism as institutionalised in and after 1795 became the great popular force in Irish politics and society it continued to be down to our own day. Its distinctive role was that of upholding the union as the best safeguard of protestant interests in an Ireland three-quarters of whose population were catholics with an increasing aspiration to domestic self-government in an age of growing parliamentary democracy. The Orange Order was an all-Ireland institution, but its strength lay in Ulster, where protestants constituted half the population and in economic power were immeasurably superior to the other half. Industrial revolution, pioneered and sustained by protestant initiative and protestant capital, added a new dimension to the distinctiveness of the north-east from the rest of Ireland, and turned Belfast into a prodigy of textile manufacture, ship-building, and engineering, unique in Ireland. This mushrooming industrial city absorbed great numbers of workers, catholic as well as protestant, drifting eastwards from the countryside after the great famine; and there thus arose in the citadel of Ulster protestantism a large catholic element, which by 1861 accounted for over one-third of the population. These working-class catholics, segregated in certain districts and generally occupying the least skilled and least desirable jobs, were confronted by working-class protestants, bent on maintaining economic and social superiority.

The sectarian conflict that had precipitated the Orange movement in rural Armagh in 1795 was reproduced in Belfast, which earned a grisly notoriety as the scene of intermittent sectarian violence from the 1830s. In the communal rioting that tended to become ritualised in the annual celebration of the battle of the Boyne, the Orange Order was deeply involved. In 1886, when Belfast responded to Gladstone's first home-rule bill with months of rioting (during which 32 people were killed, 371 injured, and £90,000 worth of property destroyed), the order was reanimated and its numbers enormously increased all over Ulster as it braced itself to meet the home-rule challenge. Finally, in 1912-14, the order played a leading part in the Ulster unionist preparations to resist a third home-rule measure by armed force.

The discrepancies between orangeism as viewed by a historian and as presented by orange spokesmen are both obvious and profound, and are of the essence of the Ulster predicament.

The British connection has counted for so much among protestants, and more especially Ulster protestants, that they have cultivated a myth of unique, unwavering, and absolute loyalty to the British crown. But in fact protestant loyalty has been far from unwavering or absolute. In 1639 Ulster Scots offered resistance to an oath binding them to strict obedience to King Charles I, then at loggerheads with his subjects in Scotland; and the lord deputy, Wentworth, expressed determination to make them conform or else to drive them out of Ulster back to Scotland. In the last decade of the eighteenth century liberal protestants carried their opposition to an unyielding Irish government to the point of rebellion. The disestablishment of the Church of Ireland by a reforming British government in 1869 drew a strong hostile reaction from conservative protestants and some interesting pronouncements from orange-men. Rev. John Flanagan declared at an orange soirée at Newbliss, County Monaghan, in 1869:

Protestant loyalty must make itself understood. People will say, 'Oh, your loyalty is conditional'. I say, it is conditional. . . . There is one thing upon which we can confidently throw ourselves. . . . I mean the queen's coronation oath. She should be reminded that one of her ancestors who swore to maintain the protestant religion forgot his oath, and his crown was kicked into the Boyne. We must speak out boldly, and tell our gracious queen that, if she breaks her oath she has no longer any claim to the crown.[8]

And the Grand Orange Lodge of Ireland resolved (December 1868) that:

in the event of our beloved sovereign being placed in the trying and difficult position of being called upon to refuse her assent to any measures brought before her, we hereby pledge ourselves to afford to her majesty every aid and support in our power.[9]

British resistance to the repeal, long demanded by orangemen, of the act forbidding party processions, gave rise to even stronger expressions of disenchantment; as, for example, this statement by the Omagh District Orange Lodge in 1870: 'We call on our countrymen of all creeds to join us in adopting all legal means to obtain a repeal of the union.'[10] In the home-rule crisis of 1912-14 loyalism assumed a new form when the solid mass of Ulster protestants organised themselves to frustrate a parliamentary repeal of the union by rebellion.

We . . . loyal subjects of his gracious majesty King George V . . . pledge ourselves . . . to stand by one another in defending for ourselves and our children our cherished position of equal citizenship in the United Kingdom, and in using all means which may be found necessary to defeat the present conspiracy to set up a home-rule parliament in Ireland.[11]

The situation was less Gilbertian than it seemed, for these loyal Ulster rebels were acting in collaboration with powerful conservative interests in Britain. The same was not true in 1974 when a new working-class loyalist combination successfully challenged British authority in Northern Ireland by a general strike; and it is not true today, when a second loyalist attempt to dictate terms

8. Aiken McClelland, 'The later Orange Order' in T. D. Williams (ed.), *Secret societies in Ireland* (Dublin, 1973), p. 129.
9. Ibid.
10. Ibid., p. 128.
11. Solemn league and covenant, 28 September 1912, in Curtis and McDowell, *Irish historical documents* (London, 1943), p. 304.

to a British government is being firmly resisted by that government supported by all parties in the United Kingdom parliament.[12]

Whatever the contrasts between the myth and reality of Ulster loyalism, one broad fact stands out in the perspective of Irish history: the behaviour of Ulster protestants in the 1790s in making common cause with catholics against British authority was an aberration that has never been repeated. But their loyalty to the British crown and their obedience to British authority have, in the last resort, been conditional upon their being satisfied that their vital interests were adequately protected. Foremost among these interests were their 'civil and religious liberties', which, they believed, would be fatally endangered if, instead of being part of an overwhelmingly protestant majority in the United Kingdom, Ulster protestants were to become a minority in a self-governing Ireland. If the whole of Ireland could not be kept within the United Kingdom the next best thing was to keep as much of it inside as could be effectively controlled by protestants under a subordinate parliament. This was the spirit in which devolution for the Six Counties was accepted by protestants in 1920-21 and operated by the unionist party for half a century. When in recent years protestant ascendancy in Northern Ireland was challenged by the catholic minority, the British government attempted to resolve the ensuing conflict by sponsoring a scheme of 'power-sharing' as between protestants and catholics, but it has been repeatedly frustrated by loyalist intransigence. In their determination not to yield on the issue of power-sharing some 'loyalists' have advocated total independence for Northern Ireland.

At the opposite pole to orangeism and 'loyalism', modern Irish nationalism, as formulated with conspicuous literary ability and missionary ardour by Thomas Davis and the Young Ireland group in the 1840s, has its own rich mythology. Among its myths was that of an ancient Irish nation struggling for seven centuries to recover its independence from the domination of England. Young Ireland dreamed of 'a nation once again', but it was in fact to be a new creation, a self-reliant, self-respecting community, in which all Irishmen, whatever their religion, class, or origin, would have their place, to live and work together in freedom for the common good. To promote such a union among Irishmen was the daunting task to which the Young Irelanders addressed themselves, as Tone and the United Irishmen had done half a century before. They failed to make any significant change in the divisions, above all the sectarian division, in Irish life, but they founded a myth, both magnanimous and misleading, that has never died out of Irish nationalism. It is crystallised in a characteristic poem of Davis's:

12. The loyalist strike, begun on 2 May, was finally abandoned on 13 May 1977.

What matter that at different shrines
   We pray unto one God?
What matter that at different times
   Our fathers won this sod?
In fortune and in name we're bound
   By stronger links than steel;
And neither can be safe nor sound
   But in the other's weal.

And oh! it were a gallant deed
   To show before mankind,
How every race and every creed
   Might be by love combined—
Might be combined, yet not forget
   The fountains whence they rose,
As, filled by many a rivulet,
   The stately Shannon flows.

But the hard historical fact is that it has mattered, and still matters, enormously in Ireland to which religion a man belongs. Davis, a protestant liberal, knew from painful experience that it mattered. But he shared a vision with both catholic and protestant friends in Young Ireland which the harsh realities of sectarian conflict have never extinguished. Ths Irish nation of the late eighteenth century, the nation of Grattan and Flood, of Charlemont, of Tone, the Emmets, Fitzgerald, and Henry Joy McCracken, to which Davis and his friends looked back with pride, was a protestant nation, and it had perished in the horrors of the 1798 rebellion. The Irish nation that was roused to self-consciousness by the gigantic personality of Daniel O'Connell in the 1820s was overwhelmingly a catholic nation, closely identified with the catholic church and its clergy. As the catholic church emerged out of the shadows of the penal laws to become the strongest social institution in Ireland, Irish protestants were haunted by the spectre of a catholic ascendancy replacing protestant ascendancy. They closed their divided ranks: episcopalians and presbyterians composed their differences, and joined forces in fervent support of the union and in implacable hostility to nationalism. A protestant element remained in the national movement, and in the early 1870s conservative protestants expressed their resentment against Gladstone for disestablishing the anglican church by helping to start the Home Government Association. But within a few years the broad correlation of protestants with unionists and of catholics with nationalists was reestablished, and was to be reflected in the partition of Ireland in 1920-21.

The great famine (1845-50) and the land war (1879-82) together produced a crop of strong and bitter myths. As seen by nationalists at the time and subsequently the famine was 'a fearful murder committed on the mass of the people'[13] by a heartless British government and its no less heartless adherents in Ireland, the landlords. Historical research has drawn a very different picture. The famine was too monstrous and impersonal to be the mere product of individual ill-will, or 'the fiendish outcome of a well-planned conspiracy'.[14]

> Human limitations and timidity dominate the story of the great famine, but of great and deliberately imposed evil in high positions of responsibility there is little evidence. The really great evil lay in the totality of the social order which made such a famine possible, and which could tolerate, to the extent it did, the sufferings and hardships caused by the failure of the potato crops.[15]

No doubt had Ireland had a parliament of its own, government would have been more immediately responsive to the needs of the situation. Dr P.M. Austin Bourke has shown that if all the grain crop of 1846 had been retained in Ireland, instead of only part of it, an appreciable contribution would have been made 'to bridging the starvation gap between the destruction of the potato crop in August and the arrival of the first maize cargoes [from America] in the following winter'.[16] But it remains true that the total food deficiency resulting from the potato failure in 1846 could not have been met by prohibiting the export of grain from Ireland, even if problems of acquisition, storage, milling, and distribution could have been solved at short notice.[17]

Michael Davitt and other leaders of the Land League saw the great famine primarily as the monstrous and inevitable outcome of an evil land system. In 1879 an agrarian crisis, the product of three years of exceptionally bad weather, crop disasters, falling prices, and rural unemployment, seemed to threaten a new catastrophe of the same kind. That this did not happen was due partly to improved economic conditions in Ireland since the famine, partly to the timely and realistic efforts of voluntary relief-organisations facilitated by government, and partly to the achievement of the Land League in organising a great popular agitation of tenant farmers and townspeople, relying on methods technically legal but revolutionary in spirit, to resist eviction and put pressure on the government to transform the land system on a basis of peasant proprietorship. Not only was actual starvation averted, evictions limited, and

13. R.D. Edwards and T.D. Williams (eds.), *The great famine* (Dublin, 1956), p. vii.
14. Ibid., p. xiii.
15. Ibid., pp. xiv-xv.
16. 'The Irish grain trade, 1839-48' in *I.H.S.*, xix, no. 78 (September 1976).
17. Ibid.

a new fighting spirit infused into the farmers, in dramatic contrast with their mood of resignation in the great famine, but Gladstone was convinced that only a radical change in landlord-tenant relations would restore social order. The land act that he carried through parliament in 1881 was a far-reaching victory for the farmers, enabling them to become joint owners with the landlords and preparing the way for their eventual conversion into full owner-occupiers through state-aided land purchase.

This, the greatest social revolution in modern Ireland, was associated with a mythology that has only recently begun to be examined in the cold light of history. The crisis of 1879-80 was presented by Davitt and other spokesmen of the Land League as the culmination of deep-seated evils arising out of an intolerable land system that in the famine decade had reduced Ireland's population by two millions. Landlordism was a system of legalised robbery, under which a few thousand unproductive and alien owners pocketed the lion's share of the product of 600,000 hard-working tenant farmers, the great bulk of whom paid excessive rents and, as tenants from year to year, lived under the constant shadow of the landlord's power to evict. This parasitic landlord class owed its privileged position to its historic role as the 'English garrison' in Ireland, endowed with the spoils of centuries of land-confiscation inflicted on the native Irish by the conquering English. Before this 'feudal' regime was imposed on Ireland by its conquerors the Irish knew nothing of absolute property in land, which was under 'tribal' ownership, each man having his fair share. The establishment of 'feudalism' in Ireland on the ruins sf an ancient Irish social order was thus rooted in English conquest. The feudal principle had never been recognised by the moral sentiments of the Irish people, those claim to an indefeasible interest in their holdings was therefore claim to restitution of rights of which their ancestors had been wrongfully deprived. To replace feudal landlordism by peasant proprietorship would not only remedy a monstrous social injustice, and remove the greatest obstacle to social peace and progress in Ireland, but would prepare the way for the undoing of the English conquest itself.

One fallacy in this argument is what Dr W.E. Vaughan, a pioneer in the critical investigation of estate records of the period 1830-78, calls 'the myth of the predatory landlord'. The landlords as a class were not characteristica.lly predatory nor the tenants as a class characteristically victimised. The period between the great famine and the land war was in general marked not by worsening but by improving rural conditions, and the tenants as a whole shared more fully in the increasing profits of agriculture than did the landlords. The worst faults of the landlords appear to have been not heartlessness or heavyhandedness but rather apathy and neglect, bred by encumbrances on their estates, traditions of extravagance, and the impossibility of taking a benevolent and constructive interest in a myriad of very small holdings.

The crisis of 1879-80 was not the climax of a long ferment of bitterness between landlords and tenants but the product of a combination of economic difficulties peculiar to those years, which created a situation favourable to a mass demand for 'the abolition of landlordism'. There seems no evidence of any long-standing tradition among the farmers of regarding the landlords as aliens, with no moral right to their property. On the contrary, the authority most frequently invoked for this view during the land war was not Irish but was the English liberal economist, John Stuart Mill. And as to feudalism, the total absence of it from pre-conquest Ireland is a myth partly due to the publication, under the auspices of the British government, of ancient Irish law texts in translation. Popular misconceptions derived from such sources and from historical works did much to mislead the reading public about the character of early Irish society, which Mr Donnchadh Ó Corráin has shown in a recent study to have strong resemblances to the general European pattern.

My final example of mythology is what may be called the 'predestinate nation' myth. This myth identifies the democratic Irish nation of the nineteenth century with pre-conquest Ireland, incorporates the concept of a seven (now an eight) centuries' struggle with England as the central theme of Irish history, and sees the achievement of independence in 1922 as the partial fulfilment of a destiny that requires the extinction of British authority in Northern Ireland to complete itself. Modern Irish history thus becomes, in the words of P.S. O'Hegarty, 'the story of a people coming out of captivity, out of underground, finding every artery of national life occupied by her enemy, recovering them one by one, and coming out at last in the full blaze of the sun'.[18]

This myth is incompatible with the history of social living in modern Ireland, which is far from being coextensive with a struggle for national independence; and nationalist politics have not generally been dominated by the idea of unending war with Britain until complete separation is achieved. Revolutionary nationalism as it established itself after the great famine, in the secret Irish Republican Brotherhood or fenian organisation, though professing to be democratic and though recruited principally from the working-class, never comprehended more than a small minority of Ireland's population. The movement had no social programme, and its whole political thinking was focused on a single object, absolute independence, to be achieved by physical force. It claimed that this was the real will of the Irish people, and that the I.R.B. was the infallible interpreter of that will. Yet the mainstream of Irish nationalism in the later nineteenth century ran in the moderate and constitutional channel of home rule, to be achieved by act of the United Kingdom parliament. In the first general election, that of 1885, to be held in Ireland

18. *A history of Ireland under the union* (London, 1952), p. vii.

under a relatively democratic franchise, the home rule party under Parnell won 85 of the 103 Irish seats in the United Kingdom parliament, and this pattern continued until the triumph of Sinn Féin in the general election of 1918. In 1886, when Gladstone committed the liberal party to the home rule cause, Parnell accepted his home rule scheme as a final settlement of the Irish question, and did so with overwhelming support from Irish nationalists in Ireland, Great Britain, America, and elsewhere. It was not till the home rule movement had been reduced to utter frustration by the failure of the British government to cope with Ulster unionist preparations to resist the home rule bill of 1912 by armed force that the majority of nationalists eventually transferred their support from the parliamentary party to revolutionary nationalism, which came to be symbolised by the Easter rising of 1916. And in the new twenty-six county state that emerged from the war of independence (1919-21), the tradition of parliamentary nationalism at once reasserted itself.

On the other hand the tradition of absolute predestinarian nationalism has been continued, and has been revived by the Provisional I.R.A. in its irredentist war to abolish partition. Like the fenians, they have no doubt of their moral right to wage war, in the name of the Irish people, against Britain, though they have no popular mandate to do so and though the situation has been fundamentally changed by the existence since 1922 of an independent Irish state, to which a majority of the people of Ireland belong. Whatever the cost in human suffering, demoralisation, and destruction, and in material damage, they see their campaign in Northern Ireland as justified by their own infallible interpretation of Ireland's past. When Britain has heen forced to acknowledge Ireland's right to national self-determination and has withdrawn her army from Northern Ireland, the various elements making up the Irish people will settle their differences and establish a new, democratic, independent republic of thirty-two counties. And so Ireland's national destiny will at last be fulfilled. Perhaps the most fantastic element in the Provisionals' mythology is their theory that they are waging war not on the protestant people of Northern Ireland but only on Great Britain. It is a theory for which the ground was prepared by the myth, widely cherished in the Republic till recently, that partition was wholly the creation of Great Britain and that only a British army of occupation prevented the fraternal reunion of the six separated counties with the rest of Ireland.

There has been a recent televised debate in Northern Ireland on the theme that 'Irish history will be the death of us'. If 'history' is here used as meaning the past itself, it can well be argued that the consequences of long-standing bitterness and violence will destroy us. But if 'history' is used in its proper sense of a continuing, probing, critical search for truth about the past, my argument would be that it is not Irish history but Irish mythology that has been ruinous to us and may prove even more lethal. History is a matter of facing the facts of the Irish past, however painful some of them may be; mythology is a way of refusing to face the historical facts. The study of history not only enlarges truth about our past, but opens the mind to the reception of ever new accessions of truth. On the other hand the obsession with myths, and especially the more destructive myths, perpetuates the closed mind. Irish history is far from being wholly a history of conflict, but in so far as it is so it provides little comfort for those who today identify themselves with one side or another in the great conflicts of the past. Even the perennial Irish-English dichotomy repeatedly breaks down as a principle of interpretation, from the days of the first Anglo-Norman invaders to the last hundred years, in which British people have been almost as deeply divided over the Irish question as the people of Ireland itself. Irish history has made great and unprecedented advances during the past forty years, but the effect on the public mind appears to be disappointingly slow. The business of demythologising is not the same thing as the revisionism of historians, but the two are connected. You cannot argue with a myth, but historians can, and do, argue with one another, and the result usually is that knowledge is extended and understanding deepened. The new historiography of Ireland has been making its impact on the teaching of history in the schools all too slowly, but there has been significant progress in both parts of Ireland. It is encouraging that the department of education in Dublin has significantly altered its notes for history teachers in the primary schools since the early days of the state, when it was firmly laid down that Irish history should be an instrument of national edification. The mental war of liberation from servitude to the myth is an endless, and it may be an agonising, process. It is, I believe, one in which Irish historians are called on to take an active part. We are called, if I may draw from a saying of Sir Herbert Butterfield's, to 'fight against principalities and powers, but not against flesh and blood. And ours is the work of the leaven which gradually leavens the whole lump.'[19]

19. 'Tendencies in historical study in England' in *I.H.S.*, iv, no. 15 (March 1945), n. 223. Cf. *Ephesians* vi. 12.

6

The Burden of Our History[*]

F.S.L. LYONS

When I was invited to give this lecture in memory of Brian Rankin I naturally felt very honoured. But I hope you will not misunderstand me if I say that I thought long and hard before accepting the invitation. This was not just because I realised that there would be many people here who knew him much better than I did. Although that is certainly true, I knew him well enough to have the utmost admiration for his character and his work. which in itself was a strong reason for agreeing to give the lecture. My hesitation was of a different kind. It is impossible to approach a life such as his without a strong awareness of its context, and especially of the stresses imposed upon his reconciling temperament by the conflict amid which his last ten years were spent. To speak here without referring to that conflict would not only be to ignore everything he stood for, but would also be an evasion which this particular audience would rightly resent. Yet, and here is the core of my difficulty, to speak on these matters without having been directly involved in them is to risk two equal dangers. There is first the danger of offending local sensitivities which any outsider must incur, especially if (although an Ulsterman born) he happens to live in the Republic of Ireland. And the other danger is that over the years so much has been said upon the same well-worn themes over and over again that any speech or lecture, however well-intentioned, is likely to fall leadenly upon ears dulled by constant repetition and distracted from theoretical discourses by the sounds of real battle.

Nevertheless, as you will perhaps have already concluded from the fact that I am standing here tonight, I have somehow or other resolved my problems. I have done so both because of my wish to share in commemorating Brian Rankin and because I regard it as of the highest importance to keep open as far as possible the lines of communication between north and south, by visiting as often as I can my many friends here and especially in this university which has honoured me so recently. At the same time I am determined not to sail under false colours and therefore I speak to you primarily as an historian, albeit one who has deviated into biography.

[*] The W.B. Rankin Memorial Lecture delivered on 4 December 1978 and published by Queen's University of Belfast.

The essence of the historian's calling is that while he must be imaginatively committed to his subject, he must use all the disciplines of his training to distance himself from that subject. He deals in explanations, not in solutions. He is neither judge nor prophet. His concern is with neither the future nor the present, but with the past. In this lecture, therefore, I shall not attempt to analyse the current situation, shall not forecast how it may develop, shall not produce some magical blueprint which those who have devoted all their energies to finding a way out have inexplicably overlooked. Instead, I shall be asking two questions, both more closely linked to our contemporary predicament than might at first appear.

One concerns the past itself, the other concerns the study of the past as we have engaged in it hitherto. The question about the past is simply this—have we in our entanglement with history locked ourselves into a hall of distorting mirrors so grotesque that we can no longer distinguish the realities of what has happened in this island from the myths we have chosen to weave about certain symbolic events? And my question about our study of the past is best expressed by rephrasing that question W.B. Yeats asked himself in old age about his early nationalist play, Cathleen ni Houlihan—'Did that play (or book) of mine send out certain men the English shot?' Or, to put it less emotively, have historians, in their preoccupation with particular themes, helped to shape modern attitudes and do they therefore incur a responsibility, beyond the responsibility which we all as individuals share, for the present condition of Ireland?

I said a moment ago that I was an historian who has strayed into biography and it is relevant to much of what I shall be saying tonight that the subject which now engrosses me—the life of that same W.B. Yeats who has already reared his King Charles's head in this lecture—has profoundly altered my view of Irish history. Yeats, it seems to me, is especially important not just because he exemplifies and illuminates some of the underlying cultural divisions in our society, but because in his later work he sensed that a phase of our civilisation was coming to an end and that a new phase was about to begin, probably amid violence, as that 'rough beast' he saw in the mind's eye 'slouches towards Bethlehem to be born'. At one and the same time Yeats directs our attention towards some fundamental problems which, as I shall argue, have not had due consideration from historians or others, and also reminds us that our history unfolds within the framework of the late western European civilization to which we belong.

This is by no means a lecture about Yeats's view of history, but I ask you to bear with me while I introduce my main theme by one further reference to him. The story is told of Dean Swift that he was once walking with friends outside Dublin, when he suddenly stopped short. They passed on, but realising that he was not following them one of the party went back to fetch him. 'I found him', said this friend, 'fixed as a statue, and earnestly gazing upwards at a noble elm, which in its uppermost branches was much withered and decayed. Pointing at it, he said, "I shall be like that tree, I shall die at top".' Two hundred years later, when Yeats had begun to find in the Irish eighteenth century a refuge from, and a model for, the Irish twentieth century, he took this anecdote and applied it to the medieval tower he had bought at Ballylee, that tower which served him, in his own words, as 'a powerful emblem' in some of his best poems. The tower was a ruin when he bought it, and though he restored it enough for summer use, he was never able to finish the roof and the battlements. In the first of the poems he wrote about Swift, 'Blood and the Moon', he brought the anecdote and the tower together in one tremendous question:

> Is every modern nation like the tower,
> Half-dead at the top?

It is surely a question which in one form or another we must all have asked ourselves. Many people, I imagine, would nowadays answer 'yes' almost automatically. They might even argue that half-dead at the top is, if anything, an understatement. Take any government, they would say, look at its cost, its inefficiency, its inhumanity; look at the 'leaders' of the world and their inadequacy even to identify our problems, let alone solve them; look at failures of liberal democracy, at the growth of bureaucracy, at the efflorescence of totalitarian regimes, whether of the right or of the left, all over the world; look, perhaps above all, at the destruction of natural resources and the pollution of our human environment. Can anyone doubt, these pessimists will ask, that if not already half-dead at the top we are well on the way to being wholly dead, if not by some nuclear holocaust, then by our inability to sustain an expanding population?

It would be simple, but unprofitable, to continue the catalogue indefinitely. Blaming governments is not only the too easy way out, it is also the symptom of a more deep-seated malaise, which consists rather in the abdication of private responsibility than in the breakdown of public authority. And anyway, Yeats was asking if modern *nations*, not governments, were half-dead at the top. Well, you may say, is that not nowadays a distinction without a difference? People get the governments they deserve and if what they get are half-dead at the top, doesn't that tell you all you need to know about the people?

For myself, I don't believe this. I don't believe that malfunctioning governments tell you all you need to know about the people. I don't even believe that people necessarily get the governments they deserve; rather often, it seems to me, they are stuck with governments they have had no chance of avoiding. But this said, there still remains that abdication of private responsibility of which I spoke a moment ago. Here too we could all easily compile a catalogue of woes and I imagine that for many this would include the decline of the family and the decay of parental authority; the flight from religion; the increase of undisciplined illiteracy among the young; the more unsavoury manifestations of the permissive society; the growth of vandalism; the indifference of organised groups to the needs and sufferings of those who are unable to defend themselves; the paradox of a developing mastery over nature and the growth of an ever more sophisticated science and technology, existing alongside an increasing frustration which makes the lives of so many of us boring and frivolous to a degree which our grandparents could not have begun to imagine.

I do not prolong the list, partly because it is so familiar, but more because I introduce it only for a limited purpose. My object tonight is to relate Yeats's question to modern Ireland and to see where that may take us. If I have asked you to glance briefly at the ills of society in general, rather than those of Ireland in particular, it is simply to make the obvious point that just as no man is an island, so no island is entire and sufficient unto itself. Here in Northern Ireland you have been living for ten years, as you may well have felt, at the very centre of the whirlpool, struggling always to avoid being sucked down into its uttermost depths. No one who knows anything at all about it will want to question the intensity of that terrible experience. But we have still to see it in a world perspective if we are to get it right. By this I mean two different, and to some extent opposite things.

On the one hand, it is well to remember that what you have been enduring, despite certain obviously unique features, belongs to the phase of international disorder through which we are all at present passing. This could mean that instead of struggling at the centre of the whirlpool you may in fact be circling uneasily on its outer edges, and that whether or not you are sucked into the vortex may finally depend not solely upon your own unaided efforts—crucial as these no doubt will be—but upon the ability of the world at large to bridle the contemporary anarchy and to restore not just the rule of law but the respect for ordinary humanity which has manifestly declined during our violent century.

On the other hand, there is a more constructive way of looking at this new international dimension of our lives. It has always been our besetting sin, north or south, to be so obsessed by the London-Belfast-Dublin triangle as to be often incapable of measuring our internal relationships against the broad movement of history elsewhere, or of profiting from the experience of others in not always dissimilar circumstances. Membership of the EEC has already begun to widen our horizons and more perhaps may be expected from this in the future. But apart altogether from that enlargement, an increasing awareness that terrorism is an international phenomenon and that anti-terrorist techniques are developing as a result of international experience is not without relevance for Northern Ireland. To have been, as it were, an experimental laboratory in this operation is, God knows, no comfort for the dead and the maimed, but if in due course it leads to more effective measures against this unmitigated evil, then we may feel that to belong to the wider world may have its compensations as well as its stresses.

Yet whether the international factor works for or against us will ultimately depend upon ourselves. Essentially, as I believe, it will depend upon all of us in this island gaining a clearer view of our history and a greater understanding of the burden that history has bequethed to us. This may seem a rather self-indulgent assertion. Do we not suffer from a surfeit of history, you may ask, and should we not forget the whole tedious, sordid story? But that evasion is not open to us or to anyone else. We are all what we have become and what we have become is what past circumstances have made of us. Nor, it must be said, is there the slightest sign among those who aspire to be responsible for our destiny that they intend to omit those past circumstances from their present calculations, so we had better be aware of them too.

There is, of course, another sense in which we may legitimately pray for deliverance—from the false history that has for too long masqueraded as the real thing. It has become fashionable recently to speak much of the contrast between myth and history and there have even been some gestures towards demythologising certain aspects of our past. There is now, for example, a more balanced view of what the battle of the Boyne was really about, the romantic nationalism of Patrick Pearse has come in for some fairly disenchanted criticism, and the Easter Rising of 1916 itself has begun to be seen in a colder and one hopes more objective light. These are welcome developments provided that they do not lead to the opposite extreme. What historians call revisionism is not only reasonable but necessary if it is done in the right way and for the right reasons. These are not subjectively arrived at by the light of the individual conscience, receiving from some private source a special infusion of grace. Revisionism is proper revisionism if it is a response to new evidence which, after being duly tested, brings us nearer to a truth independent of the wishes and aspirations of those for whom truth consists solely of what happens to coincide with those wishes and aspirations.

But why lecture us about the perils of revisionism, you may object, when we are living in the midst of what you yourself were among the first to call an historiographical revolution? Given that the study of our history is now on a far firmer professional base than ever before, may we not assume that the processes of revision and demythologising are in perfectly safe hands? Of course I agree, and speaking in the Queen's University it would be strange if I did not. For it was here some forty years ago that the modern movement in Irish history began and it was your own distinguished graduate and my beloved teacher, T.W. Moody, who was the mainspring of that movement as he has ever since remained.

All this I gladly concede, and yet . . . and yet . . . while agreeing that the whole subject has been marvellously transformed, I still have two serious reservations. One is that the historiographical revolution has been slow in reaching the schools. According to a survey of 1971, textbooks were still often being used in Northern Ireland which had been written thirty or forty years previously. The situation, indeed, has much improved since then and there is now available a far wider range of modern, attractively produced and reasonably objective books which should in time produce a more balanced view of the past in both parts of Ireland. But I have to add that time will be much longer than it need be if different versions of Irish history continue to be taught in different kinds of schools.

My other reservation is more far-reaching. There can be no denying that for much of the past forty years the main emphasis has been upon the rewriting of Irish political history; necessarily so, because it was around politics that the myth clustered most thickly. And of course this rewriting will continue as the opening of the archives brings the more recent past within our scope. Yet this emphasis on political history has often led to serious neglect of other kinds of history. It is still the case, for example, a generation after Kenneth Connell pioneered Irish economic history in this university, that the number of reputable economic historians in the whole island could be numbered on the fingers of two hands. But when we look beyond that—to social history, cultural history, the history of ideas—the poverty of what we have to offer is deeply disturbing. It is not long since Professor Estyn Evans, in his Wiles Lectures, castigated Irish historians *en masse* for their neglect, not only of these matters, but of the physical environment within which our past has been lived. 'It has been my contention', he said, '. . . that historical studies would be enriched if they paid more attention to habitat and heritage and that closer co-operation with geography and anthropology would be fruitful. . . . To the specialist in the history of restricted periods it may well appear that the most powerful forces in history are individual personality and free will.' 'On the larger view', he added, 'I believe that the personality of society is a powerful motive force and that it finds expression in the cultural landscape.'

Unfortunately, the case is much worse than Professor Evans imagined. Not only have historians too often disregarded the physical evidence around them, they have not even fully explored their literary evidence to give us a rounded view of our society. I do not want to overstate the case, for research is now going forward on a much wider front than formerly, but many years of specialisation are required before a more general public will get the books it so urgently needs. That is why, if for a moment we take a restricted view of cultural history as the history of the arts, we still have no comprehensive works on any major art with the possible exception of architecture. Even in literature, though it attracts a great deal of attention, there is no adequate historical survey of Irish writing. But perhaps that is not really so surprising, since we apparently can't agree on what Irish literature consists of, or in what language it should be written. Nor is this all. If we broaden our definition of culture, as we surely must, to include the whole mode of life of a community, we shall find, with some honourable exceptions, that our histories do not tell us much about many things which make up such a mode of life. And these deficiencies are equally glaring, whether we are thinking about day-to-day details of existence, or about patterns of belief, or about intellectual influences, both internal and external.

In short, though our days are filled with the actualities of communal strife, how much do we really know, in historical terms, about how a community evolves and how it interacts with, or reacts against, another community? Oh, we know about community politics all right, we know about parties and elections, about caucuses and manifestoes, and the rest of the democratic or pseudo-democratic paraphernalia. But about the essence of a community we know, I repeat, all too little outside our immediate, personal and highly fallible experience. And to cross the barriers imaginatively between one community and another is given as yet only to that small compassionate minority of whom Brian Rankin was one of the foremost in our day.

If I seem vehement in this matter, it is not that I want to belittle the valuable work already done, especially in this university and particularly in its Institute of Irish Studies, though even that has to be measured against the vast amount that has still to be achieved. Nor do I wish to take a pharisee's view of my fellow-historians. I, too, have been seduced by political history, only to find when I moved on to other fields that the foundations were often lacking and that significant generalisation was virtually impossible. But this, you may say, is for the historians to settle among themselves. Let them get on with their history of culture and not bother us until they have something to show for their labours. Fair enough, I reply, if it were only a problem for the historians. That, however, is just what it is not. For the fact that historians are inarticulate about the different cultures which collide with each other in this island is merely a symptom of a more profound ignorance which runs right through our society and is exhibited *in excelsis* on the other side of the Irish Sea.

This leads me straight to the main thrust of my argument, which is about what I shall call the disconnection in our history between politics and culture. Whether one looks at the nineteenth century arguments about Home Rule, or at the twenteith century arguments about devolution or about republicanism, the crucial questions have tended to be posed primarily in political terms. Will there be self-government for the whole of Ireland? Once partitioned, will Ireland be reunited and if so, how and when? What should be the relations of Dublin and Belfast with each other and of both with London? So the questions go on and on, and the political solutions, which are in fact no solutions, go round and round in a vacuum that seems increasingly unreal. Why is the unreal vacuum there? Why do the questions and the answers seem in the end so inane? Very largely, in my view, because over the last hundred years few people have tried to relate political solutions to cultural realities. Here in Northern Ireland, under the pressure of horrendous events, you have begun to come to terms with this problem. Indeed, a longer perspective than any we can envisage now may yet reveal that out of all the suffering of the past decade has come a far more sympathetic response to the sensitivities of the different cultures than was evident before the troubles began, or has been evident in the south at any time.

Nevertheless, we all need to know more, and our knowledge needs to be much more rational and systematic, much less intuitive and ad hoc. We require a broader frame of reference, if you like a general theory of Irish cultural development, before we can chart our course with any confidence. I say this with some diffidence, because although I cannot claim to have produced such a theory, the biography of Yeats has made me think about it to such a degree that I chose it as my theme when I gave the Ford Lectures at Oxford in 1978, a series to which I gave the sufficiently provocative title, *Culture and Anarchy in Modern Ireland*.

I mention this not merely as a free commercial, but because when I began to think about our conflicting cultures, and to survey the barrenness of the literature about them, I was driven slowly towards what I would still regard as a highly tentative and provisional analysis. It is probably very different from the analysis that a sociologist, an economist or an anthropologist would make, because I was concerned with the historic clash between cultures rather than with the delineation of cultures in, so to speak, a steady state. For this reason I avoided some of the more obvious categorisations. I did not think, for example, that the time-honoured dichotomy between north and south was good enough, or that the slightly more subtle one between east and west, favoured by some economists, was much better. The glaring contrasts between town and country, or between Dublin and the rest of the republic, or between Belfast and the rest of Northern Ireland, while certainly real, were not germane to my purpose either. So instead I tried to distinguish the clash of cultures as it occurred mainly between 1890 and 1939, two symbolic dates marking the fall of Parnell and the death of Yeats, though of course I also found it necessary sometimes to delve into a remoter past. The special relevance of this brief period was that it marked the conflict between Gaelic Ireland and Anglo-Irish Ireland which contemporaries were even then calling 'the battle of two civilizations'.

It soon became clear to me that to conceive merely of a battle between two civilizations was to miss at least half of a complex situation, just as I think that to talk, as some still do, of 'two nations' in Ireland, or even within this province of 'two communities' is to distort reality by serious over-simplification. In the end, and to cut a long story short, I emerged with a conflict between four different cultures, though I am well aware that a different principle of selection could have produced a further refined and more variegated list.

The dominant culture was, and I believe still is, the English, or as we would say nowadays, the Anglo-American culture. I call it English rather than British because, with the obvious exception of the Scottish influence in Ulster to which I shall return later, English is essentially what it was. The influence of this culture had of course always been pervasive ever since the Anglo-Norman conquest, as is evidenced in the frame of local government, in the spread of the cornmon law, and in the evolution of the Irish parliament. But this influence, which grew *pari passu* with the colonization of the country, was greatly intensified during the nineteenth century. This was due not only to the political and economic union between the two islands—though that obviously helped—but also to the industrial and transport revolutions and to the rise of modern bureaucratic government. Exposure to these various forces brought many material benefits no doubt, but in broad cultural terms the effect was to reduce the smaller island to little more than a province in the empire of Victorian taste.

The effects of this pressure were varied and immense, but one of them is particularly relevant to my purpose. The fact that it was so insistent and continuous meant that however important the reactions of the other three co-existing cultures to each other might have been, and may still be, their most significant relationship has always been with the dominant English culture. This was pre-eminently true of the old Gaelic culture which by the middle of the nineteenth century, for reasons too well-known to reiterate here, had been largely destroyed. And indeed, despite the Gaelic revival at the end of the last century and the attempt to implant the Irish language at the heart of the educational system in the Irish Free State from 1922 onwards, that Gaelic culture still hovers on the verge of extinction. Nevertheless, the idea of a Gaelic revival did become, and to a considerable extent remains, an essential element in the creation of a sense of separate identity for those who sought to escape the stifling embrace of their larger and stronger neighbour.

That separate, so-called 'Irish' identity, as it was gradually constructed during the nineteenth century, had three other characteristics which, though familiar enough, need to be mentioned briefly because they helped to develop and consolidate the differences between the exponents of this 'Irish' culture and the other cultures with which it had to compete. First, this identity came to be conceived by many as Catholic. There was a certain irony here, since the Catholic hierarchy had been one of the main agents of Anglicisation for most of the century. But once Ireland began to be regarded as a Catholic nation, there was built into this separate identity an element of puritanical exclusiveness very far from the vision of a Wolfe Tone or a Thomas Davis of an Ireland in which the different cultures would eventually be reconciled.

Secondly, this identity, though largely constructed by townbred intellectuals, assumed that its basis would always be a rural Ireland which was endowed by its inventors with traditional virtues of holiness and simplicity that might not have withstood too close an inspection of the underlying reality. Yet in another sense the emphasis upon rural Ireland, and especially upon the struggle of the small farmer to become the owner of his holding, was a right instinct, for land and the ownership of it was the fulcrum upon which much of Irish history turned. Moreover, precisely because the stress was upon ownership rather than use, the effect was to reinforce the essentially conservative nature of rural society, a society which everywhere—not least in Ulster—tenaciously preserved an attachment to the folklore, the fairy-tales and the legends that abounded in the countryside.

The third distinguishing feature of this new nineteenth century identity was the ideology mostly derived from Europe or America, to which the name nationalism was increasingly applied. Outsiders found it a puzzling term, since it apparently applied, equally and simultaneously, to treason, felony and to parliamentary agitation, yet did not inhibit large numhers of Irishmen who called themselves nationalists from serving the crown in many capacities inside and outside their own country. Perhaps it was not altogether surprising that Englishmen, faced with these confusions and seeming contradictions, tended to take it for granted that the Gaelic culture had lost its vitality and would be peacefully and rapidly absorbed by the dominant English culture.

That fate, by the end of the nineteenth century, also threatened the third of my four conflicting cultures—the one that was then coming to be called Anglo-Irish. Professor Beckett has taught us to recognise the Anglo-Irish as 'the Protestant community which dominated Ireland in the eighteenth century and those who inherited and maintained its tradition in the changed and changing circumstances of a later age'. Traditionally, they had regarded themselves as Irish without hypenation, but this had always been a dangerous assumption. By virtue of long settlement they could reasonably think of themselves as Irish no doubt, but in fact they remained *sui generis*. This was partly because they were, after all, the victors in the long process of war and conquest, but partly also because in their function as a governing class, in their intermarriage with English families, in their almost obsessive concern with having an imperial as well as an Irish role, they could easily be, and often were, represented as 'the English garrison in Ireland'.

That, too, was a most misleading description. They were, of course, colonials by origin, and like most colonials they hesitated between their country of origin and their country of settlement. To the extent that Ireland was theirs they resented their exposure to the vagaries of English politics and the unpredictability of English governments. But to the extent that Ireland was theirs only by right of precarious conquest they knew that their continued existence as a ruling elite depended upon the English power they so often disliked and despised. Yet they *were* different from the English gentry of whom they sometimes gave such a good imitation. What made them different was the Irish context within which they operated. Of this, the chief ingredients were long residence and much intermingling with the native population in a country that was unlike England in the quality of its soil and of its agriculture, in its system of land tenure, in its social organization—above all in the insecurity of life and the uncertainty of the future.

Further, they were by no means simply an ascendancy landlord class. There were clear distinctions, not only between the great families and the smaller gentry, but also between the whole landed interest and the bourgeoisie. Leaving aside for a moment the special case of Belfast, in the rest of Ireland we can distinguish a professional and entrepreneurial class to which the Anglo-Irish contributed far beyond their numbers. This was true in business, in law and medicine, in literature and the arts and, through Trinity College, in the intellectual life of the country. Indeed, it has now become almost a truism to point out how much of the literary renaissance at the turn of the century was the work of Anglo-Irish writers, mainly of the middle class, who, in launching that movement, were motivated partly though vainly by the hope of fusing the Anglo-Irish and the Gaelic cultures.

There remains the last of my quartet. Although it comes nearest home, it is the one most difficult to label. Only a reluctance to describe the whole in terms of a part prevents me from calling it Presbyterian. Yet, while it was more than that, and while I am anxious to avoid sectarian definitions, there can be no denying that it was the mingling of English and Scottish settlements in the seventeenth century that gave north-east Ulster its particularity. More concisely, one could define the evolution of the region as being the product conjointly of colonisation, of Calvinism and of industrialism. Because it was the last part of Ireland to be colonised, and because the previous population were not wiped out when they lost their land and their status, and because the newcomers included both Episcopalians and Presbyterians, the triangular friction with which we are all familiar became an integral part of Ulster history. But because the outcome was Protestant ascendancy and because the Presbyterians emerged as the largest Protestant community, the ethos of that ascendancy was predominantly Presbyterian. With the coming of industrialism this ethos became even more pronounced, since it was the Presbyterians who so largely built the docks and the shipyards and linen mills on which the fortunes of Belfast were founded. Whether on the land, or in the market-town, or in the Lagan valley, it was they who set their formidable stamp upon the quality of life. They combined for much of their history a notable liberalism in public life with a strict severity of private discipline. They were a serious people, caring for education, intent upon self-improvement and material progress, yet deeply marked by their religion. They were kindly, humorous and at the same time austere, but always responsive to their history which was at bottom a history of frontier insecurity, their mentality essentially a siege mentality, their symbolic dates 1641, 1689 and 1690.

In distinguishing these four contending cultures I have been trying to establish what I would call the essential diversity of Ireland. To those who look at the Irish past in the longest possible perspective that our knowledge of history and pre-history can construct, what may seem to them most striking about our island is what Professor Evans has called its essential unity. No doubt the unity is there in geographical and geological terms, and no doubt traces of it can be found to this day in landscape, in linguistic patterns, in rural legend and folklore, in the survival of customs and beliefs which date back to a very early stage of human settlement on this island. Yet simply to insist upon an essential unity conceived in those terms does not help us greatly in coming to grips with our present difficulties. We have to be able to contain in our minds elements both of cultural unity and of cultural diversity, and in holding the balance between these two conceptions we have to be wary of political formulations which would stress one conception at the expense of the other.

I can best explain what I mean by asking you to look briefly at how the four cultures have fared in the half-century since Ireland was partitioned. There has been, I think, a double process of simplication and of intensification. Simplication has come through the virtual elimination of the Anglo-Irish culture, and intensification through the more direct collision of the other cultures with each other after the disappearance of the Anglo-Irish culture, which had often been a mediating, even a reconciling influence. In the south, the *locus classicus* of that culture, the Anglo-Irish, increasingly on the defensive during the nineteenth century, were overwhelmed by the events of the decade 1912-1922. Cut off from Britain and sundered from their fellows in the north, they dwindled at once into a tiny minority which seemed resigned to speedy extinction. That fate, however, was slower in arriving than they had expected. Their institutions—the Church of Ireland, Trinity College, even the Masonic Order—were left untouched and they themselves were treated with the almost ostentatious tolerance which was to become the hall-mark of successive governments.

Nevertheless, these southern Protestants have played a small part in the political life of the twenty-six countries compared with the contribution they have made to business, and to the professional and intellectual life of the country. There have been some exceptions, several from my own university, but I suspect that one main reason for such consistent passivity is that the structure of poltics has made involvement difficult and distasteful. This may be changing now, but until recently the plain fact was that both the major political parties looked back to the civil war as their source of origin and this was unlikely to attract people who regarded the civil war and the preceding Anglo-Irish war with equal detestation.

Not merely the structure but also the content of public life has proved uncongenial to many southern Protestants. I said earlier that the Gaelic and Catholic character of the new state were strongly emphasised, especially during the first thirty years of its existence. This meant not only an insistence upon certain traditions that the Anglo-Irish could not share, but also the enactment of laws which, to their eyes, were both an infringement of individual liberty, and sectarian in their bias. I am referring here not merely to the much publicised issues of divorce and contraception, but also to the censorship of publications (which for many years made the south a laughing-stock in the civilized world), and more especially to the fact that the constitution of 1937 was virtually a compendium of Catholic social teaching, apparently on the assumption that it was a constitution for a Catholic people, and this although it also laid claim to a part of Ireland which was strongly Protestant.

If the Irish Free State, latterly the republic, was not wholly a Catholic state at the outset, it is in a fair way to being one now. When Dr Cruise O'Brien was lecturing here earlier this year he remarked that he left the southern Protestants out of account 'because they are as a group no longer clearly distinguishable from the rest of the population in the republic'. If this is so, and it is perhaps too sweeping, I suggest it is so largely because they have been fast vanishing from the land. This may partly have been due to emigration (though after the second world war the Protestant rate of emigration fell below the Catholic), but more likely to other causes. The chief of these were a low marriage rate, low marriage fertility (what my wife calls the regulation Protestant pair of children), an abnormally old population structure and above all a rapid increase in the number of mixed marriages of which the offspring were raised as Roman Catholics. The decline is recently said to have been halted; were this not so we might have to contemplate the virtual disappearance of the southern Protestants by the end of the present century.

If that happened, would it accentuate the Catholic and Gaelic character of the republic? Only, if at all, to a minor degree, because both those characteristics are under attack from forces that have nothing whatever to do with Anglo-Irish Protestantism. Indeed, Anglo-Irish Protestantism, which is sometimes represented as being possessed by an insatiable lust for looser marriage bonds and unlimited contraceptives, is just as conservative in its own way as the would-be Catholic-Gaelic culture that surrounds it. Both are equally hard-pressed by the dominant Anglo-American culture. We have to distinguish clearly here between official rhetoric and existing reality. It is quite true, for example, that in the republic the revival of the Irish language and of the old Irish culture generally is still an object of state policy and of private concern. Many people work extremly hard to promote this revival and in some fields—in music, drama and literature—there have been undeniable successes. And it is of course also true that the republic remains an intensely Catholic country with a high rate of church attendance and much emphasis on Catholic doctrine in personal observance and in public atiludes.

Yet all is not as it was. The Gaelic enthusaists are fighting a desperate battle against enormous odds; most people, if they were frank, would probably say that the battle was going against them. And so far as Catholicism is concerned, not only is there more open criticism of church authorities than would have been conceivable a couple of decades ago, but there is also much clearer evidence than hitherto of the emergence of a lay intelligentsia with a mind of its own. In short, Catholic conservatives and Gaelic enthusiasts are both a little like Dame Partington, striving to hold back with their sadly inadequate mops the steady rise of what Yeats long ago called 'the filthy modern tide'.

Under the combined pressures of radio, television, the cinema, pop music, sensational journalism, the paperback revolution, mass foreign travel, all the emphasis on material betterment that even modest affluence brings, it does not seem that the old Catholic-Gaelic stereotype can hold out much longer. What may take its place no one can yet say, though some of the consequences of our belated entry into the twentieth century are not very attractive. In the republic we too have our devastated inner cities, our vandalism, our broken homes, our drug and drink problems, our callousness towards the old and the helpless, we too have come of age.

Does any of this strike a familiar chord with you? Is it possible that while we have been elaborating our political differences, while Northern Ireland has been torn apart by desperadoes from both sides of the cultural divide, the filthy modern tide has all the time been washing us closer and closer together? Do we not share the same exposure to the same media, the same obsessive cult of sport as a substitute religion, the same sleasy seductions of the consumer society?

Well, yes, you may say, we do, but things are different all the same. Of course they are, not least because you have still within your frontiers the complex interaction of cultures I outlined earlier. Anglo-Americanism may be rampant, but it has not yet obliterated differences that are centuries deep. Admittedly, the Anglo-Irish culture may be in decline here also, though so long as your landed families continue to exist it cannot be written off as, in effect, it has been written off in the republic. But the pressures of the last half-century have made the Anglo-Irish culture less credible as a separate entity in Northern Ireland. Inexorably, it has been subsumed into the broader concept of an Ulster Protestant culture with strong Presbyterian overtones.

Against this amalgam it has become traditional to set the local manifestation of the Gaelic-Catholic culture, as represented by the nationalists of Northern Ireland. In many respects this community seems faithfully to mirror the native culture in the rest of the island to which it has indeed contributed much. We notice here as elsewhere the familiar marks of identification—the prominence of the church in education and in other aspects of social life, the emphasis upon the Irish language and upon Irish history and literature, the deep attachment to Irish games, all given the intensity that comes from the consciousness of existing under the shadow of what has generally been felt as a hostile or suspicious majority.

All this we know. And we know no less, indeed too well, how these divisions have been reflected in Ulster politics before and after Northern Ireland came into being. As I said earlier, I shall not be so impertinent as tu comment on those politics, but I may perhaps be allowed to emphasise once more what I have already called the disconnection which seems to exist between the underlying cultural realities and the political solutions that have been attempted in recent years. Of course, the disconnection can never be complete. Politics, after all, is about the location and exercise of power, and whoever controls power can undoubtedly exert a considerable influence upon the different cultures. Yet I cannot help feeling that this way of regarding power is becoming increasingly outmoded, chiefly because it seems so often to assume that power is exercised in some kind of vacuum, unaffected by what goes on elsewhere.

The modern world no longer allows such insulation for any country, except perhaps the very largest. Certainly it does not obtain either in the republic or in Northern Ireland. Both parts of this island are now so exposed to the dominant Anglo-American culture that I cannot see the process of absorption ever being held in check—it can never, I think, be totally arrested—unless the political arrangements of the future take a much more deliberate and sensitive account of our complex of cultures than they have so far succeeded in doing.

I have no idea what those political arrangements might be, and no fixed prejudices as to what they ought to be, but I should like, in my closing remarks, to suggest two possible fates that may be in store for us. The first fate, that of the asphyxiation of the smaller by the larger, can be briefly stated. It could very easily and quickly happen that Anglo-Americanism would extinguish what remains of our local and regional identities. This might, indeed, make for easier living, but at the cost of dire impoverishment of spirit. The things we quarrel about now may in fact have disappeared in a generation. The residue would be something so flat, stale and impersonal—for example, an architecture of indistinguishable concrete boxes, a diet of prepackaged, homogenised food, a mind–numbing mid-Atlantic television bombardment—that we might well look back nostalgically to the days when cultural differences were something to argue about because they were also something real and precious.

That is one possible outcome, and there can be no denying that the process has already gone so far that we may be powerless to prevent the filthy modern tide from submerging us altogether. If that were the only future it would hardly be worth surviving into. But there are two other forces at work in our situation which are of a different quality and promise a different future. The first is that just as the south, in the period since it achieved its independence, has developed its own recognisable identity, so too in the north we find a growing consciousness of an Ulster, if you like a 'regional' personality, which began to emerge during the second world war and has continued to develop through all that has happened since. Whether in drama or in psetry, in the novel or the short story, in painting or design, in the making of music at every level, there has been an efflorescence of talent different in three significant respects from any that has preceded it. It has much greater strength in depth; it has not emigrated but has stayed put in Northern Ireland; above all, it has transcended sectarian boundaries, working from the only assumption that is possible in the life of the mind or of the arts—that no criterion save that of excellence is to be applied. There is no time to investigate the reasons for this renaissance, fascinating as the quest would be. The crucial fact is that it has happened and that the political troubles have not extinguished it; indeed they may actually have enriched it. So that when nowadays we hear an Ulsterman— whether Protestant or Catholic—say he is an Ulsterman before he is anything else, we may feel he is obeying a true instinct in saying so.

But because an Ulsterman is an Ulsterman first, this does not necessarily mean that he is an Ulsterman only. And that is where the second of the two developments I have mentioned is relevant to my theme. It is too often forgotten that between the wars, when the political barriers between north and south were being made ever more impregnable, co-operation between the two parts of Ireland not only never ceased but spread into new fields. I am not talking now of the more obvious instances—such as that the churches crossed the great divide, or that clubs and societies did the same, or that many business enterprises took the border in their stride. I am alluding rather to the work of the historians, the geographers, the archaeologists, the folklorists, the language specialists and others who began to discover both what was common to the whole island and what was not. In doing so they demonstrated the co-existence of cultural unity and of cultural diversity, thus challenging both the exclusive-ness of Ulster nationalism and the inclusiveness of Irish nationalism. Without the recognition that cultural unity and cultural diversity constitute the burden of our history all political ingenuity seems to me vain. With that recognition, which entails a coming to terms with the realities of pluralism, it should at last be possible for us to raise our eyes from our own introverted quarrels and by learning how other pluralist societies have solved problems at least as difficult as ours, to make a more imaginative approach to our dilemma than any we have achieved so far.

This, if I may say so with deep respect, is where the work of Brian Rankin was of such immense value. You will appreciate much better than I what a heavy load he carried and how willingly he bore it. But perhaps I may be allowed to say three things about that career so selflessly spent in service. The first is that he recognised a cardinal fact about our pluralist society when he based his work upon his own community. Many have commented on how much he gave to the Presbyterian church. It was a profound understanding that led him to do this, for rootless benevolence soon degenerates into insipid dogoodism and of that no one could ever accuse him.

Secondly, it is inspiring to see how, while firmly based upon his own community, he reached out from it to work willingly and constructively with others. And here the range of his contribution was quite extraordinary, including as it did the Advisory Commission on Human Rights, the Northern Ireland Community Relations Commission, the Northern Ireland Housing Trust, the Northern Ireland Committee of the National Trust, the Senate of this university, to say nothing of his work in and for the legal profession. The list is by no means complete, but although it was so exceptional in the burden it imposed upon a single individual, it was also representative of the tradition into which he was born.

This brings me to the third point I want to make about him. What we see in Brian Rankin's many-sided sympathy is a supreme example of a quality in Ulster Presbyterianism which is nowadays too often obscured when, as Louis MacNeice once put it, 'the sun goes down with a banging of Orange drums'. The world outside is almost entirely unaware of the Presbyterian liberal tradition which has given so much to this city, to this province, to this island. It is a tradition which helped to create Belfast in the eighteenth and nineteenth centuries and to give it its cultural institutions both in education and the arts; which has been active in good works of all kinds in all seasons; which has given dedicated leadership to popular causes and which for generations maintained the practice of democratic self-government within its own community when this was not conspicuous elsewhere.

I say that this tradition is little known in the world outside. It is too little known even within these islands. While every credit should go to the Northern Ireland BBC, to Ulster Television and to the leading newspapers of the province for their success in depicting a society that marvellously continues its ordinary life in extraordinary circumstances, you will know without my stressing it, that this picture of normality functioning bravely amid abnormality is not one that is sufficiently understood elsewhere. To a limited extent it has been recognised in the republic, but in England, where the journalism of catastrophe has such hypnotic power, the idea that good can sometimes come out of Ulster has proved singularly difficult to grasp.

During my years in Canterbury, when no nightly news bulletin seemed complete without its 'fix' of Ulster violence, English public opinion had little option but to take a view of Northern Ireland as a place where bloodthirsty bigots of various obscure sects murdered each other incessantly for reasons no sane man could fathom. I longed then to say what I still say—show us the place as it really is, show it to us in all its humdrum ordinariness, its quirky humour, its stubborn contrariness, its industriousness and its integrity. Show it to us, above all, as a place inhabited not only by evil men—no one is going to deny that they exist and that they threaten all civilized life—but also by decent human beings. And we need to be shown. I myself, I freely confess, had not begun to realise the range and variety of inter-community work now going on here until I began to prepare for this lecture and to become aware of the efforts now being made towards reconciliation by so many devoted men and women. But, I repeat, this needs to be more widely known, and there comes into my mind a phrase from Arthur Miller's 'Death of a Salesman'. The poor disregarded salesman, Willie Lomas, is being defended by his wife as one of those ordinary people whose lives are lived out behind a heroic facade, turning a brave face to a world that constantly threatens to overwhelm them. Such people matter and should not be ignored. 'Attention', she says, 'attention must be paid'.

And that is why, ladies and gentlemen, when we remember the work of Brian Rankin, one of those rare people whom the world did not overwhelm, we pay it most honour, if we regard it as a light in the darkness, drawing us nearer to the reconciliation on which alone a permanent solution to our problems can be built. This is not to ignore the reality of the darkness, or to offer the easy assurance that it can be dissipated by the example, however remarkable, of one man. No rational person can deny the possibility that the darkness may yet overwhelm us, but if it is ever to be lifted, what will dispel it finally will be the dedication, not just of those who knew Brian Rankin, but also of those who are too young to have known him, to the liberal and ecumenical causes to which, and for which, he gave his life. Transcending our present tribulations and fastening our gaze upon that life, we can say with Yeats

> So great a sweetness flows into the breast
> We must laugh and we must sing,
> We are blest by everything,
> Everything we look upon is blest.

7

Ambiguity in Nationalism: The Case of Ireland*

OLIVER MACDONAGH

Ambiguity is inherent in the political process. Machiavelli's tyrant-prince is instructed to employ it. The western politician survives by its means. In four years time, it has been prophesied, this negation of God will be erected into a universal system of government.

To find ambiguity in that most political of societies, Ireland, will, then, rank as a meagre discovery. But ambiguity follows its own nature. The very concept is self-deceiving and self-concealed; and to explore so complex and deep-set an idea one operates best, perhaps, upon a well-developed subject. Of the many reasons for the range and intensity of the ambiguous in modern Ireland, I should select, as critical, its essentially colonial condition. It is true that Ireland does not conform closely to the crude stereotype. Its inhabitants, north and south, are physically indistinguishable from each other. So far from being remote from Britain, Ireland is geographically one with her on most computations, and endures more or less a common climate. One quarter of her denizens glory in the name of Britain. All of them speak the English tongue. Even those in the Republic are still largely enmeshed in the Anglo-Scottish economic system. But none of these factors, it seems to me, subtracts significantly from the colonialism inherent in Anglo-Irish relations, at any rate until well into the present century. On the contrary, each of them has contributed heavily to spreading and intensifying the phenomenon of ambiguity in Irish politics.

To some extent that ambiguity is responsive, the mirror image of British attitudes towards Ireland. By the mid-sixteenth century the Tudor *ideal* had settled down to the extirpation of the native and so-called Old English population, and the resettlement of the cleared countryside and towns by British immigrants. But despite the ventures of three centuries, from the Marian plantation of Laoighis and Offaly in 1553[1] to the Encumbered Estates

* Presidential address, section 26 ANZAAS conference, Adelaide, May 1980 first published in *Historical Studies* (Melbourne) 19 (1981), pp. 337-52.

1. T.W. Moody, F.X. Martin and F.J. Byrne (eds.), *A New History of Ireland*, vol. iii (Oxford, 1976), pp. 77-9.

Act of 1849,[2] the resources were quite inadequate for success. Neither the requisite state power nor the necessary number of adventurers was ever available. Even the most heroic of the schemes, the Ulster plantation of 1603, failed, as we know too well. even to establish a bare numerical majority of immigrants over most of the area of the province.

In these circumstances, British supremacy had to rest upon privilege of the grossest and most exclusive kind for a minority—or rather for one of the minorities, the Anglican. Even this seemed an increasingly unsafe expedient by the second half of the eighteenth century; and British control of the Irish executive, Dublin Castle, and indirect control of the Irish House of Commons at College Green (both virtually Anglican monopolies) were *pro tanto* reinforced. When in turn even these safeguards seemed insufficient, as the gale of the French Revolution was added to two other winds of change—religious indifference and the impulse to parliamentary reform—the whole tangled wool-ball was cut through by—if the bull will be allowed—the Act of Union between Great Britain and Ireland which came into force on 1 January 1801. The Act was, and remained—and so far as the six northern counties of Ireland are concerned still remains—an act of ambiguity, not to say self-contradiction. Ostensibly the union was a junction of kingdoms. In fact, after two years of confusion, the separate British executive was retained in Dublin, after the fashion of a crown colony. It was not to be expected that Irish opinion could influence the conduct of this executive. The representation of Ireland at Westminster was, in 1801, both disproportionately small, and practically confined to, and practically controlled by, a collaborationist Anglican ascendancy. No serious collision of interests seemed possible.

Even had the Irish M.P.s been hot-eyed republicans instead of loyalist landowners and lawyers they would have been hopelessly outnumbered. As Arthur Griffith put it, melodramatically, a century later, '103 Irishmen in the House of Commons are faced with 567 foreigners . . . [on a] battleground . . . chosen and filled by Ireland's enemies'.[3] But this was of course quite remote from the reality. Even in parliamentary terms the road of nineteenth century change led not to 103 but, at the highest and most extravagant computation, to 85 Irishmen conducting themselves as foreigners in the House of Commons. Their most absolute enemies there were the remaining 18 Irish members; and their best support the simple fact that the 567 were divided into parties struggling for office. This last was crucial. Parnell once said that the autocratic government of Ireland was not impossible, not even particularly difficult, but that it would never come about because of the two-party system in Great

2.   See W.L. Burn, 'Free Trade in Land: an aspect of the Irish Question', *Transactions of the Royal Historical Society*, 4th series, vol. xxi, pp. 69-71.

3.   N. Mansergh, *The Irish Question* (London, 1965), p. 226. Griffith's observation appeared in the *United Irishman* during 1910.

Britain. Once the Nationalist members were sufficiently compacted and numerous to control, at certain junctures, the balance of power, the 567 members were no longer a security against all Irish pressures. But at least as important was the British—or more exactly—the English self-image. The fundamental *legal* and *constitutional* implication of the union had been equality, or parity of treatment, for the inhabitants of the two islands. But the Act's fundamental *political* purpose was anti-separatism, which had become by the 1830s virtually synonymous with resistance to the Catholic majority in Ireland. As the relative power of the Catholics to harm increased, so also was their nature, as a subject and inherently inferior people, Occidental orientals in fact, clarified. Formally, too, unequal treatment of the two islands proved imperative. In such crucial elements of the 'age of reform' as parliamentary and local government reform, church and educational reform, the poor law and police, Irish and English legislation diverged increasingly.

Yet this, in its discriminatory aspect at any rate, could not endure. The very factor which had worked against parity in the second quarter of the nineteenth century worked in the opposite direction during the last. As Catholic-Nationalist power grew prodigiously towards the century's end, and the outworks of indirect rule through the Protestant minorities in Ireland were reduced by decades of bombardment, so killing Home Rule by kindness seemed to be the last attacking card left in the hand of even—or rather especially—the Unionist Party. Faced with the steady demonstration that four-fifths of the Irish constituencies would endorse *ad infinitum* the demand for some, ill-specified measure of autonomy, the British political classes had to find some comforting explanation. The days were gone when, in Salisbury's marmoreal phrase, 'Ireland must be kept at all hazards; by persuasion, if possible; if not, by force'.[4] The naked needs—or supposed needs—of power could no longer satisfy *amour propre*, let alone be publicly enunciated. So, political disaffection had to be attributed to social, religious or economic imparity, with the corollary of positive discrimination in terms of land tenure, state investment in economic development, Catholic education, and the like—anything rather than place Irish nationalists on a level in terms of political choice. Such were the last refuges of the Tories. But once the third Home Rule Bill was introduced in 1912, the successive tergiversations of Asquith's government, and in particular the double standards exhibited in the Curragh, Larne and Howth episodes in 1914, made it clear that the racial presuppositions of the Liberals were not in the end very different from the Conservatives.

Thus, Lloyd George's famous gibe that to negotiate with the Irish was to try to pick up mercury with a fork[5] might also have characterised the Irish nationalist conception of the brother island. One says 'brother' because,

4. *Quarterly Review* vol. cxxxiii, no. 266 (October 1872), p.572.
5. F. Pakenham, *Peace by Ordeal* (London, 1962), p. 82.

significantly, the sexual image was in constant use to express the dominator's concept of the relationship between the two islands—with the later Land Acts dimly perceived perhaps as a sort of counterpart to the Married Woman's Property Acts, and the retention of the power of political decision subconsciously validated by similar psychological mixtures of assertion and insecurity. Even the Hibernophiles might explain themselves in terms of arch femininity. Harold Begbie, the *Daily Chronicle* journalist, introduced his Home Rule tract of 1912 with Ireland

> a young and capable matron seated at her fireside, who raises her grey eyes to the visitor, and says with a whimsical and ingratiating play of laughter on her lips, 'I wish to do my own housekeeping; I think I can do it in a better way, and more cheaply, than other people can do it for me. I have no desire to fall out with my neighbours, no inclination to remember old scores against them'. The old gentlemen next door may be alarmed by this ambition, but the lady has really no more evil intent against his prosperity than to sell him the surplus of her butter and eggs.[6]

Analogy, then, often compounded ambiguity in the British attitudes to which Irish nationalism had to respond. It was a vital, though perhaps also an ultimately impossible, matter to master the multi-layered language of Westminster and Whitehall, and to decipher the code which embodied the complex and shifting roles in which current British necessity cast the Irish malcontents. Why was this vital? Because, as T.P. O'Connor once observed, Ireland under the Act of Union represented the government of one people through the public opinion of another. It was British opinion, and in the last resort British opinion working in British domestic politics, which produced political change in Ireland. From stage to stage, the fashionable Irish tactics altered, from mollification to violent outrage, and back again, and intermingled. But the strategic iron law—that all words and actions were ultimately to be evaluated in terms of their effects upon neighbouring opinion—endured. From O'Connell's efforts to construct alliances with the Whigs in 1835 to the bloody ambushes of 1920, it was English feeling which represented the target and the prize. It is this above all which explains why the exterior set of ambivalences are crucial to explaining the internal.

Let us take up the analysis of the internal at 1830 when O'Connell launched his first serious campaign for the repeal of the Act of Union. For in ambiguity as in so many other aspects of the emerging Catholic nation, O'Connell blazed the Irish trail. His parliamentary career had been prefaced by thirty years of practice at the bar, and he accepted 'the law' unquestioningly as the legitimate

6.   Harold Begbie, *The Lady Next Door* (London, n.d.), p. 24.

circumscriber of political notions and action. Behind this acceptance of the 'lawful' lay an acceptance, again as a *datum*, of all the institutions of state. O'Connell's abhorrence of what he himself called 'physical force' doctrines may also have flowed from his legalism. Conversely, the lawyer-agitator was tempted constantly to consider (and often to test in practice) the legal brinks and borderlands. Such was the mind and habit which this liberator brought to a struggle for national independence.

Why did he cast the struggle into one for repeal of the Act of Union? Strictly interpreted, repeal was politically nonsensical. The 'Grattan's parliament' of 1782 which was being sought had rested on the bases of British political control, which had in turn depended on corruption, and on the Protestant engrossment of local power and office. By 1830 both, in their pre-1800 forms, lay in that very overcrowded receptacle, the dustbin of history. It would have been quite impracticable to reconstitute the Irish parliament in the 1830s without a nationalist majority in the lower house. Exterior British control of a native cabinet was equally inconceivable. Moreover, any body dominated by O'Connell was bound to press for the full radical programme of parliamentary reform, down to universal male suffrage and equal electoral districts. He himself described the six points of the People's Charter as ancillary to the cause of repeal. It was therefore with some justice that Isaac Butt, later to invent Home Rule but at this stage the rising hope of the stern, unbending unionists, contended that

> repeal was a revolution. . . . The proposition was not to return to any state of things that previously existed in Ireland—not to adopt the constitution of any European state—but to enter on an untried and wild system of democracy.[7]

Why, then, hope for so improbable a concession as repeal? The answer is (I think) that O'Connell did not intend it as a specific proposition or demand. It was rather, in lawyer's language, an invitation to treat, an attempt to elicit a proposition from the British government. Repeal was only *apparently* a demand. In reality it represented the sloganising of pressure designed to force out a counter-offer, as is apparent in this extraordinary passage at the close of the speech in which he launched his great popular movement:

> a Parliament inferior to the English Parliament I would accept as an instalment if it were offered me by competent authority. It must first be offered me—mark that—I will never seek it . . . I never will ask for or look for any other, save an independent legislature, but if others offer

7. *Nation*, 4 March 1843, p. 327.

me a subordinate Parliament, I will close with any such authorised offer
and accept that offer.[8]

Like his successors from Parnell to Griffith, O'Connell was a separatist who
saw the measure of separation as ultimatety to be determined in Great Britain.
His demand, like theirs, was therefore expressed in essentially meaningless,
but apparently precise and precedented, abstractions.

Here then we have the prime and classic case of our phenomenon. Repeal
met all the requirements for mass agitation. Ostensibly no objective could be
clearer, or *mechanically* simpler to obtain. As a vehicle on which current wrongs
and miseries could be heaped, there was no limit to its capacity. Instead of an
impossibilist isolation, it promised an almost equally satisfying parity. Significantly, in one of his very rare elaborations of repeal, O'Connell envisaged *three*
parliaments, an Irish, a British and an imperial.[9] The crucial feature was not
the degree of independence of the Irish parliament, but its equality of standing
with the British. Conversely, the repeal movement appeared to fit a pattern
of constitutional agitation, stretching from the anti-slavery to the anti-corn law
campaign, to which the British public had become habituated. It differed
profoundly from Chartism in its rigid structure and discipline, its parliamentary capabilities, and its seemingly negative character, as a mere abolitionist
organisation aiming at a mere restoration of a *status quo*. Above all the proposed
return to 1782 permitted the notions of political independence and of fervent
adherence to the throne (and with that a sort of general absolution for all other
extravagances) to co-exist, and even be specifically connected. No contemporary appears to have remembered that the appeal from evil ministers and
cabinets to a mis-advised crown had been the first decisive move towards
revolution in the Netherlands, North America and France.

Essentially, Parnell and Home Rule was the evening performance of
O'Connell and repeal. No men could have been more different in superficial
personality or technique, the one master of verbosity, elucidation and the
theatrical, the other, of silence and repose. Their milieux too differed
profoundly, quite apart from the fact that Parnell had land to till which
O'Connell had first to map. Yet Home Rule, in Parnell's hands in the 1880s,
had all the apparent solidity but actual plasticity of repeal in the 1840s. True,
forty years of agitation had driven back the British outposts. It was quite safe
for Parnell, unlike O'Connell, to indulge in platform sedition. At the threshold
of his great decade, early in 1880, he told an American audience:

When we have undermined English misgovernment we have paved the

8.   J. Levy (ed.), *A Full and Revised Report of the Three Days' Discussion in the Corporation of
     Dublin on the Repeal of the Union* . . . (Dublin, 1843), pp. 191-2.
9.   M. MacDonagh, *The Life of Daniel O'Connell* (London, 1903), pp. 231-2.

way for Ireland to take her place among the nations of the earth. And let us not forget that that is the ultimate goal at which all we Irishmen aim. None of us, whether we be in America or in Ireland . . . will be satisfied until we have destroyed the last link which keeps Ireland bound to England.[10]

In his final days, shortly before his death in 1891, he reverted to this psuedo-violence. 'I have not misled you', he said in Dublin, 'I have never said that this constitutional movement must succeed . . . if Ireland leaves this [constitutional] path upon which I have led her . . . I will not for my part say that I will not accompany her further'.[11] Yet, as F.S.L. Lyons observes, even as he spoke these words, the familiar ambiguity remained; he still continued 'to avoid any clear commitment to the "hillside men" and to go on pinning his hopes to the next general election'.[12]

But this last type of politician's ambivalence, though striking because it involved, potentially, the lives and deaths of others and not merely their liability to taxation, is fundamentally commonplace. Far otherwise with the ambivalence of the master-concept. Carved deep into the granite of the Parnell monument, which stands appropriately enough at the culmination of O'Connell Street in Dublin, are Parnell's best remembered words, 'No man has a right to set a boundary to the march of a nation'. But no carved words record that this characteristic sibylline threat-promise had been immediately preceded by a very specific limitation of Home Rule, for the present age, to the principles and system of 1782. A few moments earlier Parnell had asked for 'the restitution of that which was stolen from us towards the close of the last century'. 'We cannot', he went on, 'ask for less than restitution of Grattan's Parliament, with its important privileges and wide and far-reaching constitution. We cannot under the British Constitution ask for more than the restitution of Grattan's Parliament'.[13] 'Restitution' was the incantation of Home Rule. It was this very word which had opened the constitution of the Irish National League, the main Home Rule organisation. Its first objective was declared to be 'the restitution to the Irish people of . . . a parliament elected by [themselves]'.[14]

---

10. R. Barry O'Brien, *The Life of Charles Stewart Parnell* (London, 1898), p. 3. Some doubt has recently been thrown on whether the words, 'the last link' were actually used—or at least whether they were ever reported, see F.S.L. Lyons, *Charles Stewart Parnell* (London, 1977), pp. 111-12.

11. *Freeman's Journal* (Dublin), 11 December 1890.

12. Lyons, op. cit., p. 614.

13. *Nation*, 24 January 1885. For an analysis of the passage, see F.S.L. Lyons, 'The Political Ideas of Parnell', *Historical Journal*, vol. xvi, no. 4, 1973, pp. 764-5. The speech was made at Cork on 21 January 1885.

14. *Freeman's Journal* (Dublin), 18 October 1882. See also Lyons, *Charles Stewart Parnell*, pp. 235-6.

Thus Home Rule, like repeal, used as its particular explanatory reference an apparently specific but essentially empty precedent. The Irish reverberations of '1782' were quite sufficient for the building of a popular front. The revolutionary potential in the idea of legislative independence was counteracted by the preservative concept of restoration; while the cruel reality of Irish sectarian hatred was masked by the association of Protestantism and patriotism implicit in the resurrection of Grattan. All this constituted little more than a stalking-horse. The fundamental purposes of Home Rule in Ireland were, under cover of a seeming political demand, to create or re-create national self-respect after two decades of humiliation and abasement, and to fuse the disparate native elements of power into a single aggressive unit.

The extraordinary success of the venture during 1879–82 so built up both the Irish party's leverage at Westminster, and Parnell's domination at home, that when Gladstone at last defined Home Rule in 1886—naturally the first man to do so was a British politician—his interpretation could safely be adopted as also the Irish view. 'I am convinced', Parnell responded to Gladstone's outline of the Bill, 'that it will be cheerfully accepted by the Irish people and by their Representatives as a solution of the long-standing dispute between the two countries'.[15] In the debate Gladstone himself looked back to 1782.[16] But not Parnell: the contrast between the vision of a dual monarchy of equal and equally autonomous nations, which that had been meant to convey, and the Dotheboys colonial assembly actually proposed in Gladstone's Bill was too painful to draw out. But, of course, the historical reality of 'Grattan's Parliament' had been a body ultimately controlled by London, and almost exclusively composed of men with a heavy stake, ultimately speaking, in the maintenance of British supremacy. The current reality of Gladstone's counter-proposition was of a native representative assembly, with a nationalist majority and no external manipulation. Naturally, with a local habitation and a name, Home Rule passed into an altogether different order of politics. It was now a lump of governmental putty, to be pummelled and kneaded, added to or torn from in committee. At the same time, we must not forget that it was the ambiguity which had produced the putty in the first place.

The pursuit of ambiguity could be extended in time. Griffith's Sinn Féin movement of 1905 looked back to the supposed dual monarchy of 1782 as well as east to the—equally supposed, perhaps—Austro-Hungarian example. But now the ambiguity of the restoration of the Irish parliament at College Green had a new, sweet use. Griffith aimed it not so much at Irish nationalists or British Liberals as at Ulster Protestants who might—he hoped—find a bridge into a new political order in the invocation of the crown and in an allegiance apparently superior to the domestic. Yet again, de Valera's desperate search

15. *Hansard*, 3rd series,. vol. cciv, 8 April 1886, col. 1134.
16. Ibid., 8 April 1886, cols. 1048, 1061.

in the autumn and early winter of 1921 for a formula which might (in the blessed phrase which had at last brought Lloyd George and the Irish to negotiation) best reconcile Irish national aspirations and Ireland's association with the empire,[17] was surely an essay in ambiguity, only this time directed primarily at his own comrades-in-arms.

Alternatively, the further pursuit of ambiguity could overleap the fence, never too stout or straight in Ireland, between pacific and violent agitation. When, for example, Thomas Davis, the virtual founding father of Young Ireland, sought in 1841 to change the basis of Irish nationalism to cultural division and conflict, all that was quite clear about the attempted substitution was the total rejection of Great Britain. Language, history, race and art, the bases of the new Teutonic concept of nationality which had inspired him, were themselves divisive elements in Ireland—not least for Davis himself, half-English by birth, Anglican in religion and practically ignorant of Gaelic. When, to take a second instance, the Irish Revolutionary Brotherhood was formed, and 'the Republic' set upon its fateful course as Ireland's destiny, the only thing that was quite clear about the new ideal was that all political connection with Great Britain must be broken. Any consideration of the shape of society or the economy, not merely in the republican Ireland of tomorrow, but even in the chained and crippled Ireland of the day, was prohibited, as inherently divisive. Thus, such abstractions as 'nation' and 'republic', were, for the anti-constitutionalists the precise equivalents of 'repeal' or 'Home Rule', for the open agitators. Ambiguity was as necessary a climbing frame for violence and extremity as for the causes of parliamentarianism and accommodation.

But it is more revealing to pursue ambiguity at a humbler level than to follow it forward in time, or laterally towards the gunmen. Beneath the grand obfuscations of the nineteenth century crusades lay a mass of minute individual ambivalence. The best means of disentangling this is perhaps to analyse its operation in the Catholic priesthood. Not that the priests were unique in their political ambiguity. On the contrary the great majority of their flocks shuttled, in precisely the same fashion, between sets of contradictory impulses. But partly because of their role as local leaders and articulators, and partly because the pressures making for contradiction were especially direct and powerful in their particular case, the priests exhibited these forms of ambiguity in a much heightened way. One of the great forces making for illusion and sophistry in Irish nationalism, the church, was tied in three particular ways to the course of caution. First, the authoritarian structure favoured age—increasingly as the nineteenth century wore on, and the average age of parish priests, none of whom retired, rose steadily. The bishops at the apex of the system were generally old men, and although there were generational modifications from

17. D. Macardle, *The Irish Republic* (Dublin, 1951), p. 513. The formula was contained in a letter of 7 September 1921 from Lloyd George to de Valera.

the extreme timidity of the early nineteenth century, and although there were always some like McHale or Croke who kept their early fire, the episcopate as a whole was most conservative. Secondly, several of the first professors at Maynooth were French emigres; and whatever of their much-vaunted importation of Jansenism, they undoubtedly stamped Gallicanism—in the sense of respect for royal institutions and lawfully constituted authority—upon the courses in dogmatic and moral theology, in which more than half the Irish parish clergy of the nineteenth century were trained.[18] Thirdly, ultramontanism, in the form of pope and propaganda, pressed the Irish clergy extremely hard towards loyalty to the crown and abstention from activism, let alone radicalism. From 1809 onwards, the British government could and did exert very great pressure upon the papacy to render the Irish church submissive; and generally Rome, with larger fish to fry in other British pans, responded readily enough. On the other hand, the Irish priests were almost without exception born, bred and schooled in the nationalism of their respective early days. Moreover, during the second and again in the last quarter of the nineteenth century, Catholicism and nationalism were virtually interchangeable terms—for the Catholic masses at least; and herein the priests' interest as an order marched with their predelictions as men. Last but far from least, by the apparent paradox which is no more than a truism after all, their local leadership of their congregations depended on their heading in the same direction. A priest deviating in public purpose from his people soon lost all influence in and even most of his income from his parish—indeed not so very long before priests challenging the Rightboys actually lost their congregations temporarily into the bargain.[19]

The clerical dilemma was particularly acute whenever Irish nationalism veered towards conspiratorial organisation or the advocacy of physical violence. Not that the constitutional movements were free from difficulty by any means. But with these evasion was generally practicable in the end. Let us take, as one example, a papal rescript of 1844, wrung from Rome by Peel and Graham.[20]

This most sternly enjoined the Irish clergy to avoid not only all political activity but also all semblance of political involvement, and, further, to dissipate all popular excitement and agitation. As it happened two of those whose speeches were selected for especial condemnation in the rescript were bishops, Higgin and Cantwell. Higgins announced publicly that he received 'the document with the profoundest respect . . . but being purely hypothetical, it

18. J. Healy, *Maynooth College: its Centenary History* (Dublin, 1895), pp. 708-14, for an account of the first chairholders.
19. J.S. Donnelly, Jr, 'The Rightboy Movement 1785-8', *Studia Hibernica*, nos. 17 & 18, 1977-8, pp. 170-1, 174.
20. J.F. Broderick, *The Holy See and the Irish Movement for the Repeal of the Union with England* (Rome, 1951), pp. 186-7, 222-3. See also C.S. Parker, *Life and Letters of Sir James Graham* (London, 1907), vol. i, pp. 401-2.

leaves matters precisely where they stood before'.[21] Cantwell (how unfortunately named!) observed that it was 'conduct and language . . . unbecoming
our sacred character, and not presence [at repeal meetings and banquets which
are] the objects of this wise and salutary precaution';[22] and like Higgins and
most of his fellow-prelates he continued to speechify and feast in precisely the
same fashion as before. The various other Roman interventions of the
nineteenth century were similarly avoided, usually by Higgins's device of
applauding the admonition but finding it irrelevant to Irish circumstances.[23]
But the secret society, the revolutionary ideal and the specifically *republican*
objective (with all its jacobinical connotations as well as its direct repudiation
of authority) were not amenable to such equivocation.

How then did the priests hold the uneasy balance when these elements
were in the ascendant in Irish nationalism? By, I would suggest, a triple
ambiguity. Its first face may be termed the 'recessional'. As particular
manifestations of nationalistic violence receded in time so might they be the
more safely sanctioned: 'the more ancient the patriots the more hearty . . .
retrospective benediction'.[24] Bloody resistance to Cromwell or the Williamites
was plainly glorious. Nor was there very long to wait before even bloody
resistance to George III was baptised. By 1848 the Wexford rising of 1798,
though execrated and repudiated by the entire Irish episcopate in its own day,
was being held up as a noble contrast to the irresponsible vapourising of the
Young Irelanders. When the Young Ireland rebellion of 1848 took place—almost literally in a cottage at Ballingarry—contempt for the 'cabbage-garden'
rising was added to the general clerical detestation of the movement. Yet thirty
years later Archbishop Croke, the bellwether of advanced clerical nationalism[25]—theoretically even a revolutionist, though a revolutionist for whom it
was always jam tomorrow or jam yesterday, but never jam today—unblushingly
praised the patriotism of the people of Ballingarry to their faces.[26] Similarly,

21. *Pilot*, 24 January 1845.
22. Ibid., 15 January 1845.
23. See, generally, O. MacDonagh, 'The Politicisation of the Irish Catholic Bishops, 1800-
    1850', *Historical Journal*, vol. xviii, no. 1, 1975, pp. 37-53.
24. J.P.P. O'Shea, 'The Priest and Politics in County Tipperary 1850-1891', PhD thesis,
    National University of Ireland, 1979, p. 197. I am indebted to Dr O'Shea's work for several
    references in the section immediately following.
25. M. Tierney, *Croke of Cashel: the Life of Archbishop Thomas William Croke* (Dublin, 1976),
    especially chs. 6 and 8.
26. *Freeman's Journal* (Dublin), 16 May 1881. In the same speech, he used a characteristically
    martial metaphor to describe the current land 'war': 'The people have their rights, and
    now that they have risen in their might, I pray them to stand by their guns'. Later in 1881
    the most celebrated instance of this form of ambiguity came in a speech delivered at
    Wexford on 9 October, 'No victory has ever been achieved on the field of battle without
    the loss of some valuable lives. You cannot make omelettes, as the French say, without
    breaking eggs . . .', ibid., 10 October 1881.

when, in the middle 1860s, the church was in full cry in denouncing Fenianism, the open 'nobility'—'nobility' was the almost inevitable encomium of dead and buried revolution—of Young Ireland was made to stand in bold relief to the hidden, dark and squalid machinations of the new conspirators. In turn, in 1886, a Nenagh priest condemning the left-wing capture of the Gaelic Athletic Association, was to declare:

> I have mentioned [the Fenians] and I ask you to give a cheer for their names. I admire those men, I know they were honest and true. Can I say the same of those who [today] . . . would lead the youth of Ireland into the way of ruin and restore again the golden age of informers?[27]

Meanwhile, the hagiography of the Irish revolutionary tradition was becoming a settled thing, enshrined in particular in T.D. Sullivan's stirring compilation, *Speeches from the dock*.[28] The classic perorations of heroic violence, from Robert Emmet's 'When my country takes her place among the nations of the earth, *then* and *not till then*, let my epitaph be written' to the 'God save Ireland' of the Manchester Martyrs in 1867—by none were these declaimed more ringingly from platforms and dining tables up and down the country than by priests and political prelates.

The second face of clerical ambivalence was the gestural, the gestures carrying no dangerous consequences within themselves. Let me employ as an illustration the visit of the Prince of Wales to Ireland in 1885, during a repressive phase. A considerable portion of the church supported a boycott of His Highness. Privately, Croke favoured receiving the prince, but he dared not fly in the face of excited popular opinion; and in public proposed, in subtle compromise, that his clergy should proffer only 'the charity of their silence'. More typical, however, of the open reaction of the patriotic priests was the call of a Fr Condon, 'shame on the Irishman who would wish to see English Royalty defiling our shores, especially when it plants its unholy presence in the person of the . . . Prince of Wales'.[29] Of course, men like Croke had to think, in high tactical terms, of the Irish party's relationship with Gladstone. But the rank and file clergy could, on the not infrequent occasions of this kind, both give vent to their inherent Anglophobia and participate in national—not to say, nationalistic—posturing in complete security.

Humanitarianism was the third stamp of priestly ambivalence. Perhaps humanitarianism is not the exact word: what one really needs is a compound embracing sympathy with suffering, the distinction between a man and his beliefs, and elemental tribal identification. In the aftermath of Fenianism, the

27. *Tipperary Advocate*, 26 November 1887, quoted in O'Shea, op. cit., p. 201.
28. T.D. Sullivan, *Speeches from the Dock—Guilty or not Guilty?* (Dublin, 1867).
29. O'Shea, op. cit., p. 299.

clergy, having anathematised it while it was a brooding force, began to bless it increasingly when extinguished. At least in the getting up of petitions for the amnesty of particular prisoners, and in chairing meetings of the Amnesty Association, large numbers of priests strove to box the Irish ideological compass. The execution of the Manchester Martyrs, who were after all avowed members of the Irish Republican Brotherhood condemned to death for the shooting of a policeman, provided the most important opening for clerical ambivalence, in the flood of funeral processions, demonstrations and requiem services which it released in 1868. 'For the first time during years', wrote A. M. Sullivan, 'the distinction between Fenian and non-Fenian Nationalists seemed to disappear'.[30] In April 1869, the *Dublin Review* neatly captured the new Janus-faced stance of the clergy: Fenianism, it said,

> has been able to present itself before the world . . . as if it had . . . the sympathy of strong sections of the Catholic clergy. This sympathy has certainly only been a kind of posthumous sympathy, limited to such objects as the saying of Masses for the souls of executed Fenians, or the collections of funds for the relief of the families of incarcerated Fenians. Still, it marks a difference . . . which it would be idle to ignore.[31]

Still more striking perhaps was the revision in the clerical attitude towards two specific Fenians as time and, later, death blurred their offences. James Stephens was the begetter of Fenianism, Charles Kickham its most fearless defender against ecclesiastical condemnation. Yet when in 1885 Stephens returned to Ireland, impoverished and rejected by the French republicans, many priests presided over the meetings of sympathy, and many contributed to the fund for Stephens's relief. As ever the well-poised Croke struck the perfect balance. In subscribing £5 to the relief fund, he eulogised Stephen's selfless patriotism, adding however that he had ever been 'a deluded lover of his country'.[32]

Similarly, by the later 1870s Kickham's anti-clericalism was slipping out of mind, and priests were lauding publicly his fortitude and self-sacrifice. Several even contributed to a testimonial raised for him in 1878, and when he died four years later and the administrator of his native cathedral town refused to receive his body in his church, other priests ostentatiously marched with the funeral, and Croke in letters to the press expressed his deep regret that malignancy had pursued a patriot after death. Croke indeed helped both

---

30. A.M. Sullivan, *New Ireland: Political Sketches and Personal Reminescences* (London, 1878), vol. II, p. 203.

31. *Dublin Review*, April 1869, pp. 494-5, quoted in E.R. Norman, *The Catholic Church and Ireland in the Age of Rebellion* (London 1965), p. 123.

32. *Freeman's Journal* (Dublin), 2 January 1887.

ecclesiastically and financially to provide a church-yard monument for Kickham soon after.[33] Death has always been—if I may put it so—a towering element in Irish life; and the funeral and the memorial were natural and much-ploughed fields for clerical ambivalence. Masses for the souls, and high crosses to the memory, of the Manchester Martyrs were exactly the sort of outlets towards which the priests, otherwise held fast in bogs of authority, theology and expedience, rushed towards, to express their veering passions.

In all this the church did not, as I have said, stand apart from the great body of its people. Its dilemmas were their dilemmas, albeit more acute in form. Its evasions were their evasions, albeit more public and more tortuous. But the very parliamentary party of the 1880s was built upon impressions of violence in the wings; and on obeisance to revolutionism, provided that it was sufficiently distant in time or sufficiently personalised in its expression. You may recall that in Parnell's pseudo-radical early speech in the United States, the phrase 'take her place among the nations of the earth' was quietly inserted No specific reference to Emmet or his armed rising was required. No Irish-American audience of 1880 would fail to catch and develop the revolutionary resonance of these words. Again, every meeting of the parliamentary party, every formal nationalist gathering of any kind, in the last two decades of the nineteenth century ended with the singing of 'God save Ireland'. Of course, this anthem displaced—and was intended to displace—'God save the Queen'. Of course, repudiation of the crown and assertion of political parity and virility were implied. But so also was the essential link between the martyrs of violence in their generation, and the agitatory warriors of the present.

In overseas Ireland, if I may so put it, the lay counterpart to clerical ambivalence was even more clearly manifest. Though for very different reasons, the constraints upon an Irish nationalist in a British colony in the 1880s were quite a close equivalent to those upon an Irish country curate. Let me take, as one vignette, St Patrick's Centenary Day in Sydney in 1888. The banquet speeches traced the line of martyrs directly and exclusively in the armed revolutionary tradition from 1798 to 1867. Then the gear was changed. Whereas, to quote one orator, 'each thrilling epoch' to the present had been 'sanctified' by a rising, the current heroes were those jailed for land agitation at Tullamore, and 'gallant Englishmen' such as Gladstone, Morley and Scawen Blunt.[34] W.P. Cawley struck the precise note of vapid bellicosity: 'Sometimes we have felt the old warlike spirit arise in us, but we have consoled ourselves with the belief that the cause of our country will be won by peaceable means'. Home Rule would come because the Irish were united under leaders they would

---

33. O'Shea, op. cit., p. 198.
34. *Freeman's Journal* (Sydney), 24 March 1888.

follow to the battlefield if necessary. We will never cease . . . until the old green flag that has been carried to victory so often over many a bloody battlefield is once more planted in the Old House [of Commons] in College Green.[35]

This stirring flight ended somewhat lamely with thanks to Messrs Toohey for a donation of £20 towards prizes for the sporting events! But when it came to James Toohey's own turn at banquet eloquence, he redressed the emotional balance by proclaiming the attachment of Irish-Australians to the 'dying words' of their 'darling patriot'—and Emmet's speech from the dock was aired yet again. But, Toohey continued, the day was almost upon them when Ireland would 'be reverenced by England as a sister, and not humbled as a slave'—highly significant if simple imagery.[36] Perhaps it can be all summed up in that the first three toasts were to the Queen, the Prince of Wales and the royal family, while Toohey's speech caused the entire company to rise to 'God Save Ireland', the dying words of other darling patriots at Manchester.

If then we feel ironic or scornful when we contemplate the systematic political ambivalence of the Irish church, we should not halt at this particular limit but extend our righteous contempt to Irish nationalism *en masse*. The priests were but the populace writ large. Not that the cold, disdainful eye should stay, even in this particular instance, at the Irish nationalists themselves. The matching ambiguities of the overlords and of the semi-*colons*—to look no further—were an integral part of the difficulty. But truly, irony and scorn would be misplaced. Pity, and tears for our fellow-shufflers, our fellow-victims of conflicting necessities, are more profitable, as well as more fitting, dispositions for historians. For to return to our starting point, we are dealing with an essentially colonial condition—or a doubly colonial one in the case of clergy with a Roman flank also to defend, or expatriates in New South Wales of whom confessions of imperial faith might be, ritualistically, demanded. The colonial condition meant dependence, and dependency enjoined at once conformity and defiance. Conformity, in some degree to be experimentally established, was necessary for survival; defiance in some degree was necessary for the self-regard which gave survival point. Increasingly the national struggle was ideational in form. Increasingly, the conflict—and also the imperial resistance—moved into the arena of subjectives, of elemental feeling and

35. Ibid.
36. Ibid. Cf. the following comment on similar activities by the exiled Irish elsewhere, from an anonymous article, 'The London Irish' in *Blackwood's Magazine*, July 1901. 'The London Irish dearly love playing at revolutionaries, but they are careful not to overdo the jest. An impressive muster can be obtained for a march with bands and banner to Hyde Park. Yet even the tearful eloquence of Mr William Sullivan or the frenzied appeals of Mr T.D. Sullivan to high heaven . . . never do more than gently tickle the listless sensibilities of the audiences.'

antipathy. Thus we should look for the explanation of nationalistic ambiguity not simply in terms of relative power, but also and perhaps even more in terms of the sensibilities of subjection.

Our two exemplars, the priests at home and the Sydney patriots, were peculiarly inhibited from sanctioning contemporary violence, conspiracy or separatist revolution. Dangerous or distasteful as these might be to other Irishmen, they were still more firmly barred to these particular bodies by ecclesiastical discipline, or by the exigencies of a colonial residence. In other words the priests and the colonials were especially weak in the scales of relative power. Yet in the case of the priests at least this especial weakness explains the especial strength of such nationalistic declarations and stances as they could adopt. Again the explanation is fundamentally simple. In part, the clergy were impelled by the old fear of public divergence from their people. In part, they followed the ordinary human path of striving to compensate for enforced restraint on one front by vehemence and exaggeration on another. But most of all the very fact that they were priests rendered them peculiarly sensitive to the perils of anglicisation, and the importance of maintaining national distinctiveness. It was no coincidence that as Irish nationalism became less formally political and more cultural and tribal in basis in the 1890s, the clergy were to the forefront in every form of practical disengagement, from the Gaelic League to the Gaelic Athletic Association, and also in identifying Gaelicism generally with Catholicity. 'And why', asked a priest ironically in a novel of the day, 'did the Almighty create the Afghan and the Ashantee? [Was it] to be turned, in the course of time into a breeched and bloated Briton? . . . England's mission is to destroy and corrupt everything she touches'.[37] It was this acute sense of Irish Catholic civilisation under threat, with British materialism and irreligion flooding in by the myriad roads of modern communications, which drove the clergy hardest towards identifying with the traditions of absolute resistance—always of course in the past or in the personal.

If this is true, and if the church was here magnifying and clarifying instead of diverging from ordinary Irish nationalism, it follows that the orthodox Irish antitheses, constitutionalism and physical force, Home Rule and a republic, open and covert organisation, and the rest, are in some respects misleading. The ambiguities of a people in a colonial state are not constants, but reflect dualisms inherent or potential in almost every individual in that community. These ambiguities are so many ciphers for decoding attitudes and even action. They are no classifying device. On the contrary, they de-classify, break up the boxes in which 'parties', 'factions', 'interests', 'sections' within a nationalism are ordinarily sorted. There is, however, the compensation that they take us to a deeper level of analysis. At this level there are no immutable commitments

37. The passage is spoken by a Fr Martin in P.A. Sheehan's novel, *Luke Delmege*, first published in 1901.

or objectives, no final differences of feeling between the contending groups. And so we are left, not with last season's pigeon-holes or glib polarities, but with the more difficult but also more truly fundamental problem of determining the reality in the ambiguous. As Yeats's final riddle in 'Among School Children' puts it:

> O body swayed to music, O brightening glance,
> How can we know the dancer from the dance?

I end with another verse, so impregnated by a sense of the tragic element in the ambiguous, which I have been attempting to convey, that beside the poet the clumsy unraveller in prose is tempted to despair. The central image in Seamus Heaney's 'Act of Union' is that of the man, Britain, fathering violently the Ulster unionists upon the woman, Ireland—no smiling matron, but a violated drab. The poem concludes with a most bitter awakening to the ambiguity, this time of conquest and colonisation itself:[38]

> And I am still imperially
> Male, leaving you with the pain,
> The rending process in the colony,
> The battering ram, the boom burst from within.
> The act sprouted an obstinate fifth column
> Whose stance is growing unilateral.
> His heart beneath your heart is a wardrum
> Mustering force. His parasitical
> And ignorant little fists already
> Beat at your borders and I know they're cocked
> At me across the water. No treaty
> I foresee will salve completely your tracked
> And stretchmarked body, the big pain
> That leaves you raw, like opened ground, again.

38. Reproduced by kind permission of Faber and Faber from *North* (London, 1975).

8

History and the Irish Question[*]

ROY FOSTER

'History is more backward in Ireland than in any other country', wrote the historian J.R. Green's Anglo-Irish widow fiercely in 1912.

> Here alone there is a public opinion which resents its being freely written, and there is an opinion, public or official, I scarcely know which to call it, which prevents its being freely taught. And between the two, history has a hard fight for life. Take the question of writing. History may conceivably be treated as a science. Or it may be interpreted as a majestic natural drama or poem. Either way has much to be said for it. Both ways have been nobly attempted in other countries. But neither of these courses has been thought of in Ireland. Here history has a peculiar doom. It is enslaved in the chains of the Moral Tale—the good man (English) who prospered, and the bad man (Irish) who came to a shocking end.[1]

Through her own works on early Irish society, Mrs Green had set herself, not to produce a scientific or a poetic history, but simply to reverse the moral of the story; and, with the establishment of the Irish Free State ten years after this outburst, events seemed gratifyingly to show that the good had come into their kingdom. The rewriting of history after this consummation, following the practice of most irredentist states, is part of the subject of this essay; but more important, perhaps, is the intention to establish such a process in a wider framework, stretching back over a longer period.

The use of history by politicians and intellectuals provides a theme which will recur: the frequent personification of 'Ireland' in nationalist writing is matched by the personal identification on the part of a long line of Irish activists of their country's history with their own identity. 'The general history of a nation may fitly preface the personal memoranda of a solitary captive,' wrote John Mitchel in his *Jail Journal*; 'for it was strictly and logically a *consequence*

* Reprinted from *Paddy and Mr Punch; connections in Irish and English History* (London, 1993); originally published in *Transactions of the Royal Historical Society*, 5th series (1988), pp. 169–92.

1. Alice Stopford Green, *The Old Irish World* (Dublin and London, 1912), p. 9.

of the dreary story here epitomized, that I came to be a prisoner.'[2] Time and again national history is presented as an actor in personal autobiography; by the same token, Irish leaders emphasized the apostolic succession of nationalism by identifying themselves with specific evangelists from the country's past.[3]

This was just one way in which past history was made to serve a legitimizing function for present commitment. In a wider sense, moral attitudes could be inferred from ideas of 'Gaelic' or even 'Celtic' practice and traditions, overlaid and corrupted by conquest. In late nineteenth-century Ireland, egalitarianism was held to have flowered in the Celtic mists, much as in England democracy was supposed to have flourished in the Teutonic forests. Professional historians can ignore both myths; Irish scholars have gone so far as to dismiss most of the canon of Irish history as conceived by the generation of 1916. However, this can itself be seen as part of the pattern whereby the study of Irish history registers, like a seismograph, the waves of politics; and the whole process can only be elucidated by considering the roots of the Irish discovery of their past, and the resulting interpretations of that past, on both sides of St George's Channel. It must also involve, at the conclusion, some consideration of very recent history, trenching upon politics. In so doing, this essay exposes itself to most of the criticisms it levels at history's treatment of the Irish question—and thus becomes part of the process.

The concept of nationalism has been defined and analysed with increasing vigour in recent years; the history of the Irish case, for obvious and pressing reasons, has been the subject of a spate of recent inquiry.[4] But when did the writing of Irish history come to have an effective political function in public discourse? The background to this is not to be found in the series of explanatory histories from the time of Giraldus Cambrensis, and including Elizabethan-Jacobean apologists like Fynes Moryson, Edmund Spenser, Edmund Campion, Sir John Davies and company.[5] The didactic nature of their work was

2. John Mitchel, *Jail Journal* (Dublin, 1918 edition), p. xlvi. All the Young Irelanders adopted this approach; see also Sir Charles Gavan Duffy's 'A Bird's-eye View of Irish History', interposed as chapter 4 of *Young Ireland: A Fragment of Irish History* (London, 1880).

3. Parnell with Grattan, for instance, and Pearse with Emmet; see D. Ryan, *Remembering Sion* (London, 1934), p. 119.

4. Sean Cronin, *Irish Nationalism: A History of Its Roots and Ideology* (Dublin, 1980); Tom Garvin, *The Evolution of Irish Nationalist Politics* (Dublin, 1981); D.G. Boyce, *Nationalism in Ireland* (London, 1982).

5. Giraldus Cambrensis (Gerald de Barry), *The Irish Historie Composed and Written by Geraldus Cambrensis* (completed in 1185) in Raphael Holinshed, *The First Volume of the Chronicles of England, Scotlande and Irelande* (1577); Edmund Spenser, *A View of the State of Ireland* (completed 1596); Edmund Campion, *A Historie of Ireland: Written in the Yeare 1571*; Richard Stanihurst, *The Historie of Ireland* (1577, Stanihurst edited Campion and Cambrensis); Sir John Davies, *A Discovery of the True Causes Why Ireland was Never Entirely Subdued . . .* (1612); Fynes Moryson, *An History of Ireland from the Year 1599 to 1603* (written c. 1617).

self-confessed, and obvious to contemporaries; their function can only be understood in terms of their time. In some quarters, much emphasis is put on the fact that these works represent English manipulation of early Irish history in order to excuse the Conquest.[6] So indeed they do; but to expect otherwise is to require a detached historical sense exercised on behalf of Irish history, at a time when it was not applied to English history, or to any other. The more sophisticated tradition which concerns us begins with antiquarian explorations in the late eighteenth century, compounded with the various senses of nationalism—colonial, Gaelic and revolutionary—stirring in Ireland at the time.

The coherent effort to establish an Irish past did, of course, rely on some of the material in the earlier histories just mentioned; but the work of the Royal Irish Academy (founded in 1786) and other learned institutions of the time was far more directly inspired by the exploration of bardic tradition, the archaeological evidence scattered profusely throughout the island, and the exploration of indigenous folk culture.[7] As elsewhere in Europe, those most enthused by the process were rarely themselves of the 'indigenous folk'; as so often in Irish history, they were largely the Anglo-Irish middle classes, and the sociological explanations for this (especially in the age of surviving, if largely ignored, penal legislation against Catholics) are obvious. But antiquarianism reacted with the discovery of folk tradition and the Ossianic cult to produce history-writing which attempted to use evidence in place of hearsay, and to present a history of the land and its various peoples, rather than a rationalization of administrative or religious policies in the guise of history.[8] Liberal nationalism both used and was reinforced by the antiquarian and romantic view of early Irish history; the capacity of the land to assimilate its invaders, a matter for censure in earlier commentaries, was implicitly now approved of.

A number of caveats should be established early on. For one thing, the scholarship of these polite enthusiasts was far from impeccable and remained prone to wishful thinking; the seductive spirit of Ossian beckoned them down false trails like a will-o'-the-wisp.[9] The real importance of the Royal Irish

6. See, for instance, N. Lebow, 'British Historians and Irish History', *Éire-Ireland*, vol. 8, no. 4 (1973), pp. 3-38.
7. See Norman Vance's pioneering article 'Celts, Carthaginians and Constitutions: Anglo-Irish Literary Relations 1780-1820', *Irish Historical Studies*, vol. 22, no. 87 (1981), especially pp. 220ff. Since this essay was first published, an important Ph.D. thesis has been written on the subject: Clare O'Halloran, 'Golden Ages and Barbarous Nations' (Cambridge, 1991).
8. Especially Charles O'Connor, *Dissertations on the Ancient History of Ireland* (1780) and Sylvester O'Halloran, *Introduction to the Study of the History and Antiquities of Ireland* (1772).
9. See Clare O'Halloran, 'Irish Re-creations of the Gaelic Past: The Challenge of Macpherson's Ossian', *Past and Present*, no. 124 (August 1989), pp. 69-95.

Academy in collecting Irish antiquities did not come until later, with George Petrie's advent to the Council in the 1830s. And a certain amount of hokum was inseparable from the fashion: the philology of Charles Vallancey, obsessed with the Punic root of the Gaelic language and culture, is one example;[10] the later controversy over the origins of the round towers another;[11] the work of Thomas Comerford, who attempted to relate Gaelic culture to that of ancient Greece, might also be instanced.[12] Nor should 'liberal nationalism' be anachronistically defined: Petrie, Caesar Otway, Frederick Burton and other enthusiasts could still be of Unionist beliefs as well as of Protestant stock;[13] and while it is always remembered that the Patriot politician Henry Flood left a celebrated bequest to encourage study of the Irish language, it is often forgotten that he did so for antiquarian, not revivalist, purposes.[14] But artistic and literary evidence shows that it was from this time that the currency of thought, running on antiquarian and historiographical lines, familiarized the Irish mind with shamrocks, wolfhounds, round towers, the cult of Brian Boru, and the image of an ecumenical St Patrick. And the historical work of Thomas Leland and John Curry combined a repudiation of the old propagandists with the discoveries of the new antiquarians to produce detailed and fairly scholarly interpretations of Irish history.[15]

By 1800 political developments in America and France as well as in Ireland itself infused a new direction into the current of historical thought; but even after the trauma of rebellion and Union, the political uses of antiquarianism and of early Irish history continued. An improving Ascendancy landlord like William Parnell-Hayes produced amateur histories with titles like *Inquiry into the Causes of the Popular Discontents in Ireland* (1805) and *Historical Apology for the Irish Catholics* (1807), in between prospecting for antiquities and restoring a seventh-century church at Glendalough.[16] The Gaelic Society of

10. Charles Vallancey, *An Essay on the Antiquity of the Irish Language, being a Collation of the Irish within the Punic Languages* (1772): see Norman Vance, 'Celts, Carthaginians and Constitutions: Anglo-Irish Literary Relations 1780-1820', pp. 266-7.
11. See Jeanne Sheehy, *The Rediscovery of Ireland's Past: The Celtic Revival 1830-1930* (London, 1980), p. 62. An antiquarian priest, Father Horgan of Blarney, finally in desperation built one himself, 'to puzzle posterity as antiquity has puzzled me'. See W.R. Le Fanu, *Seventy Years of Irish Life* (London, 1893), pp. 175-6.
12. Thomas Comerford, *History of Ireland from the Earliest Accounts of Times to the Invasion of the English under King Henry II* (1751).
13. See F. Grannell, 'Early Irish Ecclesiastical Studies' in Fr. Michael Hurley, S.J. (ed.), *Irish Anglicanism 1869-1969* (Dublin, 1970), pp. 39-50.
14. See Sir Laurence Parsons, Bt, *Observations on the Bequest of Henry Flood* (1795).
15. Thomas Leland, *The History of Ireland from the Invasion of Henry II* (1773); John Curry, *An Historical and Critical Review of the Civil Wars in Ireland* (1775).
16. See my *Charles Stewart Parnell: The Man and his Family* (Brighton, 1976), part I, chapter 2. Parnell-Hayes used illustrations from early Gaelic customs and history which show familiarity with the historiographical developments of the day.

Dublin was founded in 1807, declaring that 'an opportunity is now, at length, offered to the learned of Ireland, to retrieve their character among the Nations of Europe, and shew that their History and Antiquities are not fitted to be consigned to eternal oblivion'; other societies followed.[17] In fact, the heyday of patriotic antiquarianism was nearly past; but the heyday of patriotic historiography was at hand.

The nature of the 'patriotism', however, was not yet exclusive. From the 1830s Church of Ireland scholars devoted themselves to research into early Irish ecclesiastical history; their findings had a forum in Petrie's *Irish Penny Journal*, founded in 1840 to explore 'the history, biography, poetry, antiquities, natural history, legends and traditions of the country'. Irish Anglicans had an apologetic and propagandist motivation, besides a patriotic one; their preoccupation, then and later, was to establish their Church as the true 'Ancient, Catholick and Apostolic Church of Ireland', the uncorrupted continuation of early Irish Christianity rather than the offshoot of Tudor statecraft. This aim vitiated much of their research. Nonetheless, a tradition of restoration, fieldwork and the recording of antiquities helped towards the understanding of the past. This was greatly reinforced by editions of early Irish texts prepared by the Irish Record Commission (1810-30) and the Irish Historical Manuscripts Commission (founded in 1869), and by the facsimile edition of medieval codices issued by the Royal Irish Academy; if commentaries tended to apologetics, texts remained relatively uncorrupt. And some Irish historians at least had already been impressed by the sceptical spirit of Henri Bayle, and were determined to doubt all testimony and tradition; notably Edward Ledwich, whose *Antiquities of Ireland* consciously attempted to demolish 'bardic fictions'.[18]

These developments were accompanied by a new wave of predictable but sound histories of Ireland, too long to detail here, but vitally important in considering the early nineteenth-century background to intellectual patriotism in the age of Young Ireland. Many used original records, critically analysed; many attempted to distance themselves from contemporary political preoccupations. But the overall impression was to show early Ireland as bright with culture, not dark with barbarism. The Celt was no longer considered congenitally addicted to massacre; the methods of conquest employed by England in Ireland were generally deprecated. Such reassessments did not percolate through to the English public; but, aided by Thomas Moore and the fashion for Irish ballads, they helped to reinforce the sense of Irishness which

17. See *Transactions of the Gaelic Society of Ireland*, vol. 1 (1808). Other societies included the Iberno-Celtic Society (1818), the Irish Archaeological Society (1848), the Celtic Society (1848) and the Irish Archaeological and Celtic Society (1853).
18. Revd Edward Ledwich, *The Antiquities of Ireland* (1790). For a full critique, see D. Macartney, 'The Writing of History in Ireland 1800-1830', *Irish Historical Studies*, vol. 10, no. 40 (1956-7), pp. 347-63.

the ideologues of Young Ireland exploited so astutely in the 1830s and 1840s. On the neutral ground of 'ancient history and native art,' wrote Sir Charles Gavan Duffy long afterwards, 'Unionist and nationalist could meet without alarm'.[19] This was not, however, the case; and it is a disingenuous statement, reflecting the position of Gavan Duffy the federalist and ex-colonial governor of 1880, not of Gavan Duffy the ardent Young Irelander in 1840. Ancient history and native art could be easily manipulated (either to prove native sophistication or to indicate Gaelic propensities for unreliability and exaggeration). And even the membership cards of Young Ireland made their own statement—these were embossed with images from Irish history, thus establishing the iconography of sustained struggle which was to characterize the nationalist version of events. The figures of Brian Boru, Owen Roe O'Neill, Patrick Sarsfield and Henry Grattan were posed against harps, sunbursts and the Parliament House in College Green, wreathed by shamrocks. Young Ireland politicians like Thomas Davis graduated into politics by writing historical studies—in Davis's case a vigorous but tendentious rehabilitation of the 'Patriot Parliament' of James II.[20] And though Davis combined this with a belief in 'learning history to forget quarrels',[21] HIS SUCCESSORS TOOK A DIRECTLY CONTRARY APPROACH.

For even as the materials for studying Irish history were slowly being collected and arranged in a way that might facilitate dispassionate analysis, a biased and political priority was taking over. It is doubtful if the great antiquarians John O'Donovan, Eugene O'Curry and Petrie would have recognized themselves under the title given by the Reverend Patrick McSweeney to his study of their historical work in 1913: *A Group of Nation-builders*. But that is what constituted their importance to retrospective opinion. And history-writing after the Union, even under titles which trumpeted themselves as impartial, very often directed itself at a political moral.[22] In the campaign for Catholic Emancipation both sides used history to prove and disprove massacres and disloyalty over the centuries; during parliamentary debates 1641 and the Treaty of Limerick were as bitterly contested as the actual issue of Catholic rights in 1829, rather to the bewilderment of English Members.[23] This was emblematic of what was to come.

19. Sir Charles Gavan Duffy, *Young Ireland: A Fragment of Irish History*, p. 280.
20. *The Patriot Parliament of 1689, with Its Statutes, Votes and Procedings*, edited with an introduction by Sir Charles Gavan Duffy (Dublin, London and New York, 1893).
21. See B. Farrell, 'The Paradox of Irish Politics' in B. Farrell (ed.), *The Irish Parliamentary Tradition* (Dublin, 1973), pp. 19-20.
22. See Revd Denis Taaffe, *An Impartial History of Ireland, from the Time of the English Invasion to the Present Time, from Authentic Sources* (1809-11); cf. Francis Plowden, *An Historical Review of the State of Ireland, from the Invasion of that Country under Henry II, to its Union with Great Britain on the First of January 1801* (1803).
23. D. Macartney, 'The Writing of History in Ireland', p. 359.

Ironically, in the early nineteenth century a composite—one might almost dare to say interdisciplinary—approach to the Irish past was just becoming possible. It was represented by the epic effort put into the early work of the Ordnance Survey, which was contemporarily described as associating geography with 'the history, the statistics and the structure, physical and social, of the country'.[24] Thomas Larcom recruited scholars of the quality of O'Donovan, Petrie and O'Curry, and furnished his researchers with demanding and densely written instructions about discovering the traditions of their designated areas.[25] To explore the history of place-names alone meant embarking on something very like the history of a locality. But the finished result of this magnificent conception stopped at one parish study, finally produced in November 1837, and so loaded with accretions and detail that the original idea of accompanying every map with a similar study was abandoned.[26] The controversy over this has been long-lived and need not be disinterred here; Alice Stopford Green, who grandiloquently interpreted the Ordnance Survey team as 'a kind of peripatetic university, in the very spirit of the older Irish life', believed that their work magically 'revealed the soul of Irish Nationality and the might of its repression', and was accordingly suppressed by the government.[27] The Survey's most recent historian, in a classic study, points out the injudiciousness and impracticality of the original concept, and the shapelessness attendant upon interpreting 'modern topography' as 'ancient history'.[28] The politics of the report irrepressibly assert themselves; but its historiographical background is of at least equal significance, for here can be seen archaeology, geography and a cautious sense of historical inquiry working together.

However, as Gavan Duffy cheerfully admitted, that 'cautious and sober

24. *Dublin Evening Mail*, 27 March 1844.
25. Habits of the people. Note the general style of the cottages, as stone, mud, slated, glass windows, one storey or two, number of rooms, comfort and cleanliness. Food; fuel; dress; longevity; usual number in a family; early marriages; any remarkable instance on either of these heads? What are their amusements and recreations? Patrons and patrons' days; and traditions respecting them? What local customs prevail, as Beal Tinne, or fire on St John's Eve? Driving the cattle through fire, and through water? Peculiar games? Any legendary tales or poems recited around the fireside? Any ancient music, as clan marches or funeral cries? They differ in different districts, collect them if you can. Any peculiarity of costume? Nothing more indicates the state of civilization and intercourse. (J.H. Andrews, *A Paper Landscape: The Ordnance Survey in Nineteenth-century Ireland*, Oxford, 1975, p. 148.) The Institute of Irish Studies in Belfast has now begun the welcome project of publishing these parish surveys.
26. T.F. Colby, *Ordnance Survey of the County of Londonderry. Volume the First: Memoirs of the City and North-western Liberties of Londonderry, Parish of Templemore*. See J.H. Andrews, *A Paper Landscape: The Ordnance Survey in Nineteenth-century Ireland*, pp. 157ff.
27. Alice Stopford Green, *The Old Irish World*, pp. 56-61. Also see Michael Tierney, 'Eugene O'Curry and the Irish Tradition', *Studies*, vol. 51 (1962), pp. 449-62.
28. J.H. Andrews, *A Paper Landscape: The Ordnance Survey in Nineteenth-century Ireland*, pp. 173-7.

strain' of learning was chiefly the province of middle-class scholars, some of the gentry and dilettante Protestant clergy;[29] and the future was with Young Ireland's Library of Ireland series of pocket histories, the street ballad, the pious cliché and the historical novel (to write one of which was Davis's great unfulfilled ambition).[30] The revival of Irish historiography, which was built upon by Young Ireland, by Celtic Revivalism, and even by an impeccable Unionist like W.E.H. Lecky, was dominated by this consciousness—evident in the assumptions of learned pamphlets as in those of hedge-schools. A history lesson delivered by a teacher in a Munster hedge-school in the early nineteenth century was described by a contemporary:

> He praises the Milesians, he curses 'the betrayer Dermod'—abuses 'the Saxon stranger'—lauds Brian Boru—utters one sweeping invective against the Danes, Henry VIII, Elizabeth, Cromwell, 'the Bloody' William of the Boyne, and Anne; he denies the legality of the criminal code, deprecates and disclaims the Union; dwells with enthusiasm on the memories of Curran, Grattan, 'Lord Edward', and young Emmet; insists on Catholic Emancipation; attacks the peelers, horse and foot; protests against this, and threatens a separation from the United Kingdom. . . .[31]

This vividly depicts history being elided into politics, and into the sense of national identity built upon a powerfully articulated consciousness of past grievances as much as present discontents.

And this was the historical consciousness displayed at popular levels by the Irish to countless Victorian travellers, who, on fact-finding missions, were constantly exposed—half fascinated and half appalled—to the rhetoric of Irish nationalist history. Sometimes, indeed, they seem to have been unconsciously subjected to the Irish taste for guying their own image; the experiences of innocents like Mr and Mrs S.C. Hall, as well as those of the hard-headed Thackeray and Carlyle, record many ironies enjoyed by their unwitting expense by the cynical natives.[32] Travellers from the Continent, like de Tocqueville

29. Sir Charles Gavan Duffy, *Young Ireland: A Fragment of Irish History*, p. 75fn.
30. Ibid., p. 289. See also John Banim, *The Boyne Water* (1826), reprinted in 1976 by the Université de Lille with an introduction by Bernard Escarbelt. On the Library of Ireland, see also M. Buckley, 'John Mitchel, Ulster, and Irish nationality 1841-1848', *Studies*, vol. 65 (1976), pp. 30-44, which analyses Mitchel's contribution to the series, and D.G. Boyce, *Nationalism in Ireland*, pp. 161-2. Gavan Duffy remarked that Irish history was 'ransacked' for suitable examples and arguments (*Young Ireland*, p. 104).
31. P.J. Dowling, *The Hedge Schools of Ireland* (Dublin, 1935), pp. 111-12.
32. See Mr and Mrs S.C. Hall, *Ireland: Its Scenery, Character, Etc.* (1841-3); Thomas Carlyle, 'Reminiscences of My Irish Journey', *Century Illustrated Monthly Magazine*, vol. 24 (May-July 1882); William Makepeace Thackeray, *The Irish Sketch-book* (1843).

and de Beaumont, may not have been exempt either.[33] But de Beaumont, though he did not originate it, popularized the genocidal theory of England's historical policy towards Ireland; and the same note of vehement moralizing enters the history of his compatriot Augustin Thierry, warmly praised by Gavan Duffy.[34] Other foreign publicists entered the field, including Karl Marx.[35] And, finally, the demotic view of Irish history found its way by unlikely channels into the English consciousness.

This was not always acknowledged, at the time or since; and some of those responsible tried later to cover their tracks. Macaulay's *History* is notable for its scathing remarks on Irish barbarianism, Robert Southey's Toryism was notoriously unreconstructed, and Lord Lytton became the rabidly anti-Irish hymnologist of the Primrose League. But in youth Macaulay wrote epic poetry about the Gaelic resistance to Strongbow, Southey eulogized Robert Emmet, and Lytton produced verses commemorating Hugh O'Neill's war against Elizabeth.[36] Even as unlikely a figure as Samuel Smiles was inspired to write the history of a people whom many Victorians condemned as more opposed to self-help than any in the world. 'It is necessary that Irish history should be known and studied, for we are persuaded that *there* only is the true key to the present situation to be found—*there* only are the secret springs of Irish discontent to be traced.'[37]

33. Alexis de Tocqueville, *Voyages en Angleterre, Irlande, Suisse et Algérie*, edited by J.P. Mayer (Paris, 1958); Gustave de Beaumont, *L'Irlande sociale, politique et religieuse* (1839).

34. Sir Charles Gavan Duffy, *Young Ireland: A Fragment of Irish History*, p. 167; Augustin Thierry, *Histoire de la conquête de l'Angleterre par les Normands* (1825).

35. Marx notably in his articles in the *New York Tribune*: 'A small *caste* of robber landlords dictate to the Irish people the conditions in which they are allowed to hold the land and live on it' (11 July 1853); 'the Irish landlords are confederated for a fiendish war of extermination against the cottiers' (11 January 1859), etc. Engel's view was that 'Irish history shows one what a misfortune it is for a nation to be subjugated by another nation; all the abominations of the English have their origin in the Irish Pale.'

36. In May 1885 Lytton sent Churchill, as commissioned, 'The Lay of the Primrose', of which the last verse ran:

> When, O say, shall the Celt put his blunderbuss down,
> Cease to bully the Commons, and menace the Crown?
> When shall Erin be loyal, and Britain repose,
> Neither fawning to revels, nor flying from foes?
> That shall be, saith the Primrose, nor ever till then,
> When the country is honestly governed again,
> When the realm is redeemed from the Radical's hand
> And the Primrose comes blossoming back to the land.

  (Lytton to Churchill, 18 May 1885 (RCP 1/v/601)). It does not appear to have found its way into print.

37. Samuel Smiles, *History of Ireland and the Irish people, under the Government of England* (1844), p. iv. Cf. Sir Charles Gavan Duffy, *Young Ireland: A Fragment of Irish History*, p. 81: 'Many men refrain from reading Irish history as sensitive and selfish persons refrain

Other Victorian intellectuals felt that this was so, though the argument is not self-evidently true, and in terms of economic policy at least it may be strongly contested. But every Victorian pundit dipped into Irish history and whatever panacea they were manufacturing emerged subtly altered.[38] 'I know tolerably well what Ireland was,' confessed John Stuart Mill to an Irish economist, 'but have a very imperfect ideal of what Ireland *is*'.[39] This could stand as an epigraph for the ruminations of others as well as himself; and it was reflected in the lacunae and contradictions so evident in Mill's own writings on Ireland.[40] It has been shown how untypical was his pamphlet *England and Ireland*, when viewed in the canon of his work; but it is with this strident piece, subjecting economics to a moral and political approach to landholding, that his views on Ireland are identified. And though the pamphlet argued—and he himself reiterated afterwards—*for* the Union, its effect was to reinforce the nationalist opposition to the measure. On a different level but in a similar manner, Matthew Arnold's belief in Celtic qualities, though part of an argument for bringing Celtic culture fully into the Anglo-Saxon cultural and political system, reinforced a view of early Irish history and an interpretation of Celticism which strengthened irreconcilable ideas of separatism.[41] The most influentially misinterpreted authority, however, in this unintentional *trahison des clercs* was the historian W.E.H. Lecky.

Sitting down to write his *History of England in the Eighteenth Century* (1878-90), Lecky was increasingly preoccupied by the history of Ireland: both as an Anglo-Irishman and as a rather troubled liberal. He knew the dangers, seeing Irish history as 'so steeped in party and sectarian animosity that a writer who has done his utmost to clear his mind from prejudice, and bring together with impartiality the conflicting statements of partisans, will still, if he is a wise man, always doubt whether he has succeeded in painting with perfect fidelity the delicate gradations of provocation, palliation and guilt'.[42] His *History of Ireland*, extracted from the original production for a special edition

from witnessing human suffering. But it is a branch of knowledge as indispensable to the British statesman or politician as morbid anatomy to the surgeon.'

38. Carlyle, predictably, was the exception. Earlier he had, however, been impressed by the Royal Irish Academy museum: 'really an interesting museum, for everything has a certain *authenticity*, as well as national or other significance, too often wanting in such places' ('Reminiscences of My Irish Journey', p. 27).

39. John Stuart Mill to J.E. Cairnes, 29 July 1864, quoted in E.D. Steele, 'J.S. Mill and the Irish Question: *The Principles of Political Economy* 1848-1865', *Historical Journal*, vol. 13, no. 2 (1970) p. 231.

40. As incisively demonstrated in *ibid.*, and in 'J.S. Mill and the Irish Question: Reform and the integrity of the Empire 1865-1870', *Historical Journal*, vol. 21, no. 3 (1970), pp. 419-50.

41. See J.V. Kelleher, 'Matthew Arnold and the Celtic Revival' in H. Levin (ed.), *Perspectives of Criticism* (Cambridge, Mass., 1950), pp. 197-221.

42. His preface to the separate edition of the *History of Ireland* considers at some length the problems of writing Irish history and the steps he had taken to obviate them.

in 1892, remains a classic of liberal historiography; but despite his commitment to rationality and cool scepticism, it was dictated as much by topical preoccupations as guided by the pure light of research.[43] For one thing, he was writing *contra* James Anthony Froude, whose study of *The English in Ireland*[44] had maligned and belaboured the native Irish in a manner not to be seen again for a hundred years.[45] Lecky wrote against Froude, not for nationalist reasons, but because, as an Anglo-Irish Unionist, he feared that Froude's distortions by their very exaggeration would support the case being made by the nationalists for Home Rule. (He also worried deeply about the unintended effect of his own early *Leaders of Public Opinion in Ireland*, and opposed what would have been a very profitable reprint.) Both Froude and Lecky, in the context of the 1880s, saw their histories as relevant to the contemporary struggle for Home Rule. Froude argued, in Salisburian terms, the 'Hottentot' case of Celtic incapacity for self-government. Irish criminality 'originated out of' Irish Catholicism; Protestant virtues were commercial and social as much as religious. (This is not an anticipation of Weber and Tawney, but reflects the more exotic fact that Froude had regained his lost faith through a sojourn in a Wicklow rectory.) Culture as well as worship could be defined in religious terms, and 'Irish ideas' were a debased set of beliefs which should have been socialized out of the natives. Moreover, Anglo–Irish colonial nationalism was equally corrupt; Irish declaration that they would fight for nationhood should, then and now, be seen as bluff.

In contradicting the former statements, Lecky came near to implicitly refuting the latter: notably in his use of 'Grattan's Parliament' of 1782 to rehabilitate the Ascendancy class under siege in his own lifetime. He treated Orangeism and Protestant evangelicalism with faint distaste; this was not only a reaction against Froude, but also a reflection of the fact that he was the historian of the rise of rationalism. The exclusion of the Catholic gentry from political rights, and the ensuing development of the priest in politics, distressed him; he believed 'the secularisation of politics is the chief measure and condition of political progress',[46] by which criterion Irish politics were regressing back to infinity. But this was precisely the lesson which many of his readers did *not* learn from his book; they came away from it imbued with ideas of Irish nobility, English pusillanimity, the missed chance of 'Grattan's Parliament', and the perfidiousness of the Act of Union. Lecky himself, by

43. See A. Wyatt, 'Froude, Lecky and the Humblest Irishman', *Irish Historical Studies*, vol. 14, no. 75 (1975), pp. 267-85.
44. J.A. Froude, *The English in Ireland in the Eighteenth Century* (1872-4). There is a large secondary literature of refutation by Thomas Burke, W.H. Flood, John Mitchel, J.D. McGee and others.
45. Until, that is, E.R. Norman's *History of Modern Ireland* (Harmondsworth, 1971).
46. H. Montgomery Hyde (ed.), *A Victorian Historian: Private Letters of W.E.H. Lecky 1859-1878* (London, 1947), p. 41.

this stage of his life, did not want to see 'Grattan's Parliament' restored; an opinion with which he believed Henry Grattan would concur.[47] But the immortality of Union seemed to many the moral of his book.

It was, moreover, a moral drawn by politicians. 'I read for the History School at Oxford in the "seventies",' recalled Herbert Gladstone, 'and subsequently lectured on history. Froude, Lecky, Matthew Arnold, Goldwin Smith and John Bright brought me to conviction on Irish affairs. Four of my guides lived to be distinguished Unionists. Nevertheless, their facts and arguments led me to an opposite conclusion.'[48] Politicians of all colours had this nodding familiarity with Irish history (the most dangerous kind of acquaintance); and in private correspondence as well as public exchanges they wrangled good-naturedly about recondite issues. Thus Sir William Harcourt and Lord Randolph Churchill beguiled their time in 1889 with letters detailing the arguments for and against the honesty of Irish politicians in the eighteenth century.[49] The effect of W.E. Gladstone of his readings in Irish history was more cataclysmic. He had Gavan Duffy's word for it that Carew's campaign in sixteenth-century Munster was the closest historical parallel to the Bulgarian atrocities;[50] he had Lecky's authority for the iniquity of the Act of Union. 'He talked of the Union,' recorded Lord Derby,

> called it a frightful and absurd mistake, thought Pitt had been persuaded into it by the King, who believed it would act as a check upon the Catholics, said that every Irish man 'who was worth a farthing' had opposed it, and if he had been an Irishman he would have done so to the utmost . . . quoted as I have heard him do before, a saying of Grattan about 'the Channel forbidding Union, the Ocean forbidding separation'— which he considered as one of the wisest sayings ever uttered by man—then dwelt on the length of time during which Ireland had possessed an independent, or even a separate legislature.[51]

47. Letter to *The Times*, 9 June 1886.
48. 'The trouble with Ireland was not only social and racial. It could not be explained by unjust land laws or the sway of an alien established church. These were superadded embroilments. The root cause was English autocracy' (Herbert Gladstone, *After Thirty Years*, London, 1928, pp. 263-4.
49. See Churchill to Harcourt, 29 November 1889, Harcourt MSS 217/63, writing 'in support of a plea of "not guilty" to your charge of "bumptious ignorance",' and enclosing a pamphlet based on a speech at Perth (5 October 1889), which involved an lengthy historical exegesis on the Union. Harcourt, who had earlier stated that not 'one honest man' in Ireland approved of the measure, replied at great length, with much historical reference to back up his case (RCP 1/xiv/3340).
50. *Young Ireland: A Fragment of Irish History*, p. 93.
51. Derby's diary, quoted in J.R. Vincent, 'Gladstone and Ireland', *Proceedings of the British Academy*, vol. 63 (1977), p. 223.

Gladstone, as so many others, was dazzled by the historians' notions of 'Grattan's Parliament': the acceptable face of Irish nationalism. The Irish pamphlet literature of the 1860s and 1870s, much of it written by insecure or improving landlords, adverted constantly to this; it had been much in the minds of those who initially supported Isaac Butt.[52] Samuel Ferguson, despite Ulster and Tory associations, had once called for the restoration of 'Grattan's Parliament' (though the 'plebeianizing' nature of the Home Rule movement, and the Phoenix Park Murders, later moderated his ardour); it was a reaction shared by an important element of the gentry before the political polarization of the 1880s. The idealization of the late eighteenth century, a direct result of the way history had been written, remained.

Among those politicians whose idealized 1782, the prime example was a Wicklow gentleman whose ancestors included both a famous anti-Union patriot and the improving pamphleteer quoted earlier: Charles Stewart Parnell. He was not a reader of the literature discussed above; his strength as an Irish politician lay in his *not* knowing Irish history.[53] But his preoccupation with 'Grattan's Parliament', as invented by popular history, irritated those of his followers who had thought Home Rule through. 'There is no subject about which Mr Parnell is so ignorant as that of Irish history,' wrote Thomas O'Connor Power,

> and his contempt for books is strikingly shown in his reference to Grattan's Parliament. Mr Parnell deceives himself, through sheer indifference to history and a dislike of the trouble of inquiry into facts, when he tells us he wants Grattan's Parliament. Does Mr Parnell want a parliament in Dublin controlled by a few nominees of the British Cabinet who, under the Viceroy, constitute an Irish government in no way responsible to the Irish House of Commons? If not, then it is not Grattan's Parliament he wants, and it is not Grattan's Parliament he should ask for.[54]

But 'Grattan's Parliament', as legitimized by historians, remained the objective to be cited, for most of Parnell's audience. The idealization was based on Sir Jonah Barrington's account of an Irish nation that never was,[55] on Thomas Newenham's erroneous ideas of Irish prosperity as created by the parliament

---

52. See 'Parnell and His People: The Ascendancy and Home Rule' in *Foster, Paddy and Mr Punch*, pp. 62–77.
53. For Parnell's knowledge of Irish history, see F.S.L. Lyons, *Charles Stewart Parnell* (London, 1977), pp. 37–8 and 'The Political Ideas of Parnell', *Historical Journal*, vol. 16, no. 4 (1973), pp. 749–75.
54. *The Anglo-Irish Quarrel: A Plea for Peace* (1880).
55. *The Rise and Fall of the Irish Nation* (Paris, 1833).

of 1782,[56] on Lecky's misplaced faith in the influence of Foster's Corn Law,[57] and in the general prescription of nationalist historians that prosperity was automatically induced by native government and poverty by alien rule.

By the end of the nineteenth century, given that many such assumptions had become articles of faith for the English intelligentsia as well as the Irish people, it need not surprise us to find them governing the popular mind. What Lecky did for readers of the journals, A.M. Sullivan's *Story of Ireland* did for the general reader.[58] While Irish literacy seems to have been remarkably high in the late nineteenth century, the Irish literature which preoccupied the populace still awaits its historian; but a pioneering impressionist survey carried out in 1884 is of some interest in showing the hegemony enjoyed by Davisite poetry and history in one Cork parish. The list of histories most often borrowed from the Catholic Young Men's Society Reading-room told its own tale.[59] A popular conception of history facilitated the general view that saw the Home Rule movement as 'the heirs of all the ages that have fought the good fight after their several ways';[60] a notion which, while enabling Parnell to walk the political tightrope, was very far from the truth. And when Parnellism collapsed,

56. T. Newenham, *A Series of Suggestions and Observations Relative to Ireland Submitted to the Consideration of the Lord President and Council* (1825); for Newenham's ideas and influence, see H.D. Gribbon, 'Thomas Newenham 1762-1831' in J.M. Goldstrom and L.A. Clarkson (eds.), *Irish Population, Economy and Society: Essays in Honour of the Late K.H. Connell* (Oxford, 1982), pp. 231-47. His ideas were repeated in Alice Murray's influential *Commercial and Financial Relations between England and Ireland from the Period of the Restoration* (London, 1903).

57. 'One of the capital acts in Irish history; in a few years it changed the face of the land and made Ireland to a great extent an arable instead of a pastoral country.' The case against this and other misconceptions is trenchantly summarized by Joseph Lee, 'Grattan's Parliament', in B. Farrell (ed.), *The Irish Parliamentary Tradition*, pp. 149-50. 'Foster's Corn Law did not reverse an existing trend: at the very most it slightly accentuated it.'

58. First published 1867: acutely analysed in D.G. Boyce, *Nationalism in Ireland*, pp. 247ff.

59. J. Pope-Hennessy, 'What Do the Irish Read?', *Nineteenth Century*, vol. 15 (January-June 1885), pp. 920ff:

> Abbé MacGeohegan's *History of Ireland from the Earliest Times to the Treaty of Limerick*, with John Mitchel's continuation; D'Arcy McGee's *History of Ireland to the Emancipation of the Catholics*; Duffy's *Four Years of Irish History*, with the preceding fragment, *Young Ireland*; A.M. Sullivan's *Story of Ireland*; Justin H. McCarthy's *Outline of Irish History*; Lecky's *History of the Eighteenth Century*; Walpole's *History of Ireland to the Union*; O'Callaghan's *History of the Irish Brigade in France*; Justin McCarthy's *History of Our Own Times—*, these are the most read; but the works of Macaulay, Hallam, Froude, with Father Tom Burke's *Refutation of Froude*, are read also. In biography Madden's *Lives of the United Irishmen*, *The Life and Times of Henry Grattan*, Moore's *Life of Lord Edward Fitzgerald*, Wolfe Tone's Memoirs, Mitchel's *Jail Journal*, Maguire's *Father Mathew* seem to be favourites (p. 926).

60. *United Ireland*, 13 August 1881.

the popular conception of history instantly located the catastrophe in the context of a long succession of Saxon (rather than Anglo-Irish) betrayals.

Sinn Féin was to prove the successor movement to the Irish Parliamentary Party, but in everyday ways which were strategically underplayed at the time;[61] its emphasis was rather upon a specific reading of history. The founder Arthur Griffith's ideas of autarky in economics and Gaelic purity in politics fused an idealization of 'Grattan's Parliament' with a belief in Celticism which brought together the teachings of nineteenth-century historians, ancient and modern: the very name of his first weekly, *United Irishman*, was a reference to Mitchel and Tone, and the politics of Sinn Féin synthesized constitutionalism with implicit violence.[62] Griffith's 'Hungarian policy' of boycotting institutions in order to win separate but equal status under the crown was itself based upon misapplied historical parallels: as George Bermingham acidly pointed out, if Griffith was really following the Hungarian model, he should have seen that the equivalent of the Magyars were the Anglo-Irish.[63] But Griffith, and still more his contemporaries among nationalist ideologues, defined 'Irish' in a way that implied, or even stated, its congruence with 'Gaelic' and 'Catholic'. And this sectional reading, the result of sectional history, set the tone of twentieth-century nationalism.

It was an identification which contradicted the official spirit of Young Ireland, but which had achieved dominance in the late nineteenth century, for political and educational as well as intellectual reasons.[64] Its articulation by the

61. See David Fitzpatrick, *Politics and Irish Life 1913-1921: Provincial Experience of War and Revolution* (Dublin, 1977).
62. See D. Macartney, 'The Political Use of History in the Work of Arthur Griffith', *Journal of Contemporary History*, vol. 8 (1973), p. 67. It is worth, however, quoting Griffith's utilitarian view of the ends of education:

> The seconday system of education in Ireland . . . was designed to prevent the higher intelligence of the country performing its duty to the Irish state. In other countries secondary education gives to each its leaders in industry and commerce, its great middle class which as society is constructed forms the equalising and harmonising element in the population. In Ireland secondary education causes aversion and contempt for industry and 'trade' in the heads of young Irishmen, and fixed their eyes, like the fool's, on the ends of the earth. The secondary system in Ireland draws away from industrial pursuits those who are best fitted to them and sends them to be civil servants in England, or to swell the ranks of struggling clerkdom in Ireland.

(*The Sinn Féin Policy*, Dublin [n.d., but delivered as a speech to the first annual conference of the National Council, 28 November 1905].)
63. George A. Birmingham, *An Irishman Looks at His World* (London, 1919), pp. 12-13.
64. In 1868 Gerald Fitzgibbon's pamphlet *Ireland in 1868* (noted by Marx as the distillation of the Ascendancy case) emphasized the complete lack of tension between Protestant and Catholic at university, on the Bench and in professional life; but the same author's *Roman Catholic Priests and National Schools* (1871) held that the denominational nature of national schools had bred the idea of the true Irishman as Catholic and Celtic, and driven a wedge

Gaelic Revival has been ably analysed, though there were elements of pluralism and inclusivism present which have sometimes been underestimated.[65]

Shaw remarked that 'there is no Irish race any more than there is an English race or a Yankee race [but] there *is* an Irish climate which will stamp an immigrant more deeply and durably in two years, apparently, than the English climate will in two hundred';[66] but this reading of Irish history went as unheard as the expostulations of John Eglington, George Russell, W.B. Yeats and others who saw themselves as no less Irish for being of identifiably settler descent. What happened instead was that the period of nationalist irredentism saw the culmination of historical writing which mined the past for political continuities and extrapolations.

Patrick Pearse was the prime mover in this process, and in recent years much has been done to clarify the bases upon which he built his view of history: a visionary world of early Celtic tradition where racial identification was automatic, a national sense was the paramount priority, and the sacrificial image of the ancient hero Cúchulainn was inextricably tangled with that of Christ.[67] Not only Pearse's youthful *Three Lectures on Gaelic Topics* (1897-8), but all he wrote and taught up to his execution in 1916 owed far more to John Mitchel and the Library of Ireland than to the researches of Eoin MacNeill, whose path-breaking lectures to early Irish society were delivered in 1904 and published two years later.[68] Pearse's use of Irish history was that of a calculatedly disingenuous propagandist; it was this that enabled him, for instance, so thoroughly to misinterpret Thomas Davis.[69] But if it is argued—as it might be—that the importance of Pearse's distortions is diminished by the fact that he was very far from being an accepted historian, it is instructive to turn back to Alice Stopford Green.

Daughter of an archdeacon in County Meath, and wife of the greatest popular historian of an age, Mrs Green moved from revising her husband's

65. See 'Varieties of Irishness' in *Paddy and Mr Punch*, pp. 21-39.
66. G.B. Shaw, *Prefaces* (London, 1938 edition), pp. 443-4. Cf. E. Estyn Evans, *The Personality of Ireland: Habitat, Heritage and History* (revised edition, Belfast, 1981), pp. 43-4, where an elegant demonstration is given of the 'mongrel' nature of the Irish 'race'.
67. See Fr. Francis Shaw, 'The Canon of Irish History: A Challenge', *Studies* vol. 61 (1972), pp. 133-52; Ruth Dudley Edwards, *Patrick Pearse: The Triumph of Failure* (London, 1977); J.V. Kelleher, 'Early Irish History and Pseudo-history', *Studia Hibernica*, no. 3 (1963), pp. 113-27.
68. On MacNeill, see Michael Tierney, *Eoin MacNeill: Scholar and Man of Action 1876-1945*. (Oxford, 1981), especially pp. 90-6.
69. He identifies Davis with a commitment to physical force in *Political Writings and Speeches* (Dublin, 1924), pp. 323-4; but Davis, especially in a celebrated essay 'Moral Force', specifically denied that this was an answer. See B. Farrell, 'The Paradox of Irish Politics', p. 19.

works to writing medieveal history on her own account, and ended as a formidable and partisan advocate of Irish nationalism. This identification was reflected in works like *The Making of Ireland and Its Undoing* (1908), *Irish Nationality* (1911) and *A History of the Irish State to 1014* (1925). A Freudian, or a seeker after symbols, might note that from the age of seventeen she spent seven years in semi-blindness, and during the ordeal relied upon an already well-stocked mind and a remarkable memory; for her view of Irish history represented a similarly restricted vision, and an ability to feed omnivorously on preconceptions. The concept of 'the Irish national memory', indeed, recurs obsessively in her works;[70] she may be seen as a representative of those Ascendancy Irish whose insecurity drove them to extremes of identification, much as the urban nationalist intellectuals of the era embarked upon a *narodnik* search for 'the West'. Mrs Green's pre-invasion Ireland was a classless, egalitarian 'Commonwealth', where 'the earliest and the most passionate conception of "nationality" flourished';[71] 'democratic' continuities were asserted, the purity of 'Gaelic' culture emphasized, and the moral as well as aesthetic superiority of 'Gaelic civilization' trumpeted.[72] Despite her declarations in introductions and footnotes of indebtedness to Eoin MacNeill, the scholarly subtlety and tentativeness of his approach to the early Irish past had no part in Mrs Green's productions; and probably for that reason they entered the mainstream of Free State culture.

Here they remained, despite the accumulated findings of historians who showed that land patterns in early Christian Ireland argued for a landholding system very far from her vision of Gaelic society,[73] that the so-called High-Kingship of Ireland did not exist before the middle of the ninth century,[74] and that—as MacNeill indicated in 1904—the received framework of early Irish history was an invention of chroniclers from the ninth century and later, working assiduously for the glorification of their patrons. If, however, Mrs Green was fooled by what a later historian has crisply called 'the concoctions of the Annals',[75] she had a real and immediate reason for being thus fooled: the desire to establish a legitimate continuity for Irish separatism.

70. See, for instance, *A History of the Irish State to 1014*, pp, ix, 85, etc.
71. *A History of the Irish State to 1014*, ch. 6.
72. See especially *Irish Nationality*, pp. 13, 14, 20-21, 28, 76, 95, 165.
73. Notably the work of Kathleen Hughes; for a summary, see E. Estyn Evans, *The Personality of Ireland: Habitat, Heritage and History*, pp. 58-9.
74. See especially, D.A. Binchy, 'The Origins of the So-called High Kingship' (Statutory Lecture, Dublin Institute of Advanced Studies, 1959).
75. J.V. Kelleher, 'Irish History and Pseudo-history', pp. 120-2, for the case against the 'Book of Rights' and other sources as twelfth-century creation. 'So extensive was the revision of historical evidence that we have, I would say, about as much chance of recovering the truth about early Christian Ireland as a historian five hundred years from now would have if he were trying to reconstruct the history of Russia in the twentieth century from the broken sets of different editions of the Soviet encyclopaedia.'

George Russell, on the other hand, knew and accepted that his view of early Ireland was legendary and symbolic, and thus 'more potent than history'.[76] But the spirit of the Free State was more in accord with Mrs Green's literalism. Thus the *Catholic Bulletin*, bemoaning modern times in 1925, reflected Mrs Green's vision when it remarked, 'It is very different in Ireland now to those old days when the poorest Catholic family would, on assembling in the evenings, discuss scholastic philosophy and such subjects'. And in the same year the same journal recommended Daniel Corkery's *Hidden Ireland* to 'G.W. Russell and his clique . . . they will there see how the Gael, the one Irish nation with the Irish literature, regards and dealt with and will deal with that mongrel upstart called Anglo-Irish tradition and culture.'[77]

What followed was the institutionalization of a certain view of history in the Free State, as instructed by the Department of Education from 1922, and memorialized in textbooks that did duty for the next forty years. Teachers were informed that 'the continuity of the separatist idea from Tone or Pearse should be stressed'; pupils should be 'imbued with the ideals and aspirations of such men as Thomas Davis and Patrick Pearse'.[78] Thus history was debased into a two-dimensional, linear development, and the function of its teaching interpreted as 'undoing the conquest'; even the architecture of the Irish eighteenth century was stigmatized as ideologically degenerate. One must be wary of falling into the same trap as those who, by condemning the sixteenth- and seventeenth-century historians, imply that scientific objectivity was possible at that time; textbooks in British schools in the 1920s and 1930s were hardly models of fairminded detachment. Moreover, in the new state of Northern Ireland, the recommendations of the Lynn Committee (established in 1921) reflect an equally strong sense of history as a tool, or weapon, to be manipulated through the schools.[79] But the popularization of invented tradition in the Free State and the Republic served a directly political function important enough to bear analysis; and it came about as the result of a longer process than is sometimes assumed.

Moreover, the process itself created some contradictions and paradoxes. One is that the exclusive glorification of one strain in Ireland's complex history

76. Æ (George William Russell), 'Nationality and Cosmopolitanism in Art' (1899), reprinted in *Some Irish Essays* (Dublin, 1906), p.18.
77. *Catholic Bulletin*, February and June 1925, quoted in Margaret O'Callaghan, 'Language and Religion: The Quest for Identity in the Irish Free State' (MA thesis, University College Dublin, 1981).
78. Ruth Dudley Edwards, *Patrick Pearse: The Triumph of Failure*, p. 341.
79. 'We think that the powers of the ministry to regulate and to supervize the books used in schools should be very strictly exercized in the matter of historical textbooks. No books bearing on the subject of history should, without previous official sanction, be permitted to be used in any schools under the Ministry.' Quoted in John Magee, 'The Teaching of Irish History in Irish Schools', *Northern Teacher*, vol. 10, no. 1 (1970).

caused as a reaction the equally tendentious glorification of another. Thus the record of the 'Anglo-Irish' was equally idealized in different quarters, sentimentalizing the Bourbon spirit of a class notable in the main for its philistinism and bigotry, which, when the testing time came, failed in everything—social duty, political imagination and nerve.[80] More important for our purpose is the major paradox: the fact that the institutionalized debasement of popular history was accompanied from the 1940s by a historiographical revolution in academic circles which, within twenty-five years, reversed nearly every assumption still being made by the textbooks. The foundation under Eoin MacNeill of the Irish Manuscripts Commission in 1929 had something to do with this; so did the formation of the Ulster Society for Irish Hstorical Studies, and the Irish Historical Society, a few years later. Bureaucratic philistinism, and an idiosyncratic attitude to the availability of government records, provided obstacles in North and South—as they still do. But a school of Irish history evolved at the research level which transcended traditional divides within Southern society and culture, as well as across the new border.[81]

By the 1960s the work of a whole generation of scholars had exploded the basis for popular assumptions about early Irish society, the conquest, the plantation, the eighteenth-century parliament, the record of landlordism, and most of all the continuities between the various manifestations of nationalism: in some cases, reverting to ideas held in the past by minority opinion but contemptuously dismissed.[82] By the mid-1960s, coinciding with signs of realism and adaptation in Irish politics, a number of indications presaged the establishment of a new interpretation of Irish history as a complex and ambivalent process rather than a morality tale. The Institute of Irish Studies was founded in Belfast in 1965, with the object of co-ordinating research in

80. This is reflected by the adoption among historians of George Russell's *Irish Statesmen* as the agreed source for quotations showing the sanity and cosmopolitanism of the Anglo-Irish in the Free State; but as O'Callaghan ('Language and Religion: The Quest for Identity in the Irish Free State', n. 85) reminds us, it spoke for far fewer of them at the time than did the less liberal *Church of Ireland Gazette* or *Irish Times*.

81. For a retrospect and a commentary, see Robin Dudley Edwards, 'An Agenda for Irish History', *Irish Historical Studies*, vol. 21 (1978-9), pp. 3-19; above, pp. 54-67.

82. The case for interpreting the Land War of 1879-82 as a revolution of rising expectations was asserted by Barbara Solow, *The Land Question and the Irish Economy 1870-1903* (Cambridge, Mass., 1971); Paul Bew, *Land and the National Question in Ireland 1858-1882* (Dublin, 1978); W.E. Vaughan, 'An Assessment of the Economic Performance of Irish Landlords 1851-1881', in F.S.L. Lyons and R.A.J. Hawkins (eds.), *Ireland under the Union: Varieties of Tension* (Oxford, 1980), pp. 173-200; James S. Donnelly, *The Land and the People of Nineteenth-century Cork* (London, 1974), and others. But it is also to be found in contemporary texts like Anna Parnell's astringent *The Tale of a Great Sham*, edited by Dana Hearne (Dublin, 1986), and in Terence McGrath's *Pictures from Ireland* (1880), which described the Land War in terms of an adroit takeover by the middling tenantry, manipulating a credit squeeze.

different disciplines. An important report on the teaching of history in Irish schools appeared in 1966.[83] The next year, a new Irish history school textbook was launched which at last replaced the didactic tracts that had done duty for decades.[84]

Most symbolically, the commemoration of the 1916 rising produced some unexpected historiographical results. One was a work by an impeccably nationalist scholar which portrayed Dublin Castle in 1916 as characterized by well-meaning muddle and a vague acceptance of the desirability of Home Rule.[85] More strikingly, a Jesuit historian, commissioned to write an article on Patrick Pearse to celebrate the anniversary, produced an intemperate and violent attack on Pearse's preference for striking a rhetorical blow against an England that had put Home Rule on the statute book, instead of taking on the Ulster Volunteers who had prevented its implementation; and went on to denounce Pearse's falsification of past history in the interests of present politics.[86]

Not the least significant thing about this outburst, however, was the fact that the article was deemed unsuitable for publication in 1966, and saw the light of day six years later, only after its author's death. By then, the results of simplistic historical hero-cults had become obvious in the carnage of Northern Ireland. When the seventy-fifth anniversary of 1916 arrived in 1991, it was treated by the Irish government as a sensitive issue, to be approached in a deliberately restrained way—very different from the unequivocal celebrations of 1966. This caused a small-scale but vociferous old-Republican reaction—according to the *Sunday Tribune* the initial demonstration in 1990 featured not historians but out-of-office politicians, freelance journalists, ex-1960s activists (including quaintly, a Pop Art painter), and the members of the Short Strand Martyrs Memorial Flute Band.

And this points up the paradox mentioned earlier. It would be tedious as well time-consuming to detail the areas of Irish history where old stereotypes

83. See Report, 'The Teaching of History in Irish Schools', 1966, in *Administration*, journal of the Institute of Public Administration, Dublin (Winter 1967), pp. 268-85. This committee included historians who were influential in the new school of history-writing and emphasized throughout the need for impartiality and an international perspective. Also see John Magee, 'The Teaching of Irish History in Irish Schools'.

84. T.W. Moody and F.X. Martin (eds.), *The Course of Irish History* (Dublin, 1967). Previously the field had been held by M. Hayden and G.A. Moonan, *A Short History of the Irish people from the Earliest Times to 1920* (Dublin, 1921) and J. Carty, *A Junior History of Ireland* (Dublin, 1932).

85. L. Ó Broin, *Dublin Castle and the 1916 Rising* (Dublin, 1966).

86. See Fr. Francis Shaw, 'The Canon of Irish History: A Challenge', and for comments, F.S.L. Lyons, 'The Dilemma of the Irish Contemporary Historian', *Hermathena*, vol. 115 (1973), p. 53; Ruth Dudley Edwards, *Patrick Pearse: The Triumph of Failure*, pp. 341-2; Terence Brown, *Ireland: A Social and Cultural History 1922-1979* (London, 1979), pp. 287-9.

have been questioned. This has been done with the aid of sociology, geography, economics, and most of all a new approach to statistics. Mentalities, Protestant as well as Catholics, have been examined. In the early period the Irish Sea has been reinterpreted as the centre, not the frontier, of a cultural area. In the plantation era, patterns of settlement and the very framework of dispossession have been revised. Divergent local socio-economic and political cultures have been analysed; our sheer ignorance about, for instance, the effects of the Famine have been stringently exposed. In recent years Irish historians have presented their readers with a version of ancient Ireland where some estates were worked by slaves,[87] and of early Christian Ireland where much of the damage to churches was done not by invaders but by marauding rival abbots;[88] we have even been shown a Dermot MacMurrough who is not the villain of the piece.[89] To take another period, the Fenians have been presented as 'easily recognisable and fairly typical mid-Victorians', using the movement as a vehicle for leisure activities and not particularly committed to Republicanism;[90] the emigrating Irish have been defined as 'among the greatest supporters of the second British Empire and the Commonwealth'.[91] Sinn Féin has appeared as a similarly utilitarian and ideologically uncommitted machine for the brokerage of local power politics;[92] the Land War has been seen as 'sacrificing economic progress on the altar of Irish nationalism';[93] and 'traditional Ireland', so far from a frugal rural community exempt from the taint of materialism and modernization, has been explosively derided by an Irish economic historian as 'full of rats who just did not know how to race'.[94]

It might be assumed that the point had been reached for which Shaw hoped in the 1920s, when he wrote of the national history:

> There are formidable vested interests in our huge national stock of junk
> and bilge, glowing with the phosphorescence of romance. Heroes and
> heroines have risked their lives to force England to drop Ireland like a
> hot potato. England, after a final paroxysm of doing her worst, has

87. E. Estyn Evans, *The Personality of Ireland: Habitat, Heritage and History*, p. 59.
88. A.T. Lucas, 'Plundering of Churches in Ireland' in E. Rynne (ed.), *North Munster Studies* (Limerick, 1967), pp. 172-229.
89. F.X. Martin's 1975 O'Donnell Lecture presented this unexpected picture.
90. See R.V. Comerford, 'Patriotism as Pastime: The Appeal of Fenianism in the Mid-1860s', *Irish Historical Studies*, vol. 21, no. 87 (1981), pp. 239-50.
91. D.H. Akenson, *Occasional Papers on the Irish in South Africa* (Grahamstown, S.A., 1991), p. 30. (The generalization refers to the whole Empire, not just to South Africa.)
92. David Fitzpatrick, *Politics and Irish Life 1913- 1921*.
93. Barbara Solow, *The Land Question and the Irish Economy 1870-1903*, p. 204, and R.D. Crotty, *Irish Agricultural Production: Its Volume and Structure* (Cork, 1966).
94. Joseph Lee, 'Continuity and Change in Ireland 1945-1970' in *Ireland 1945-1970* (Dublin, 1979), p. 177.

dropped Ireland accordingly. But in doing so she has destroyed the whole stock-in-trade of the heroes and heroines . . . We are now citizens of the world; and the man who divides the race into elect Irishmen and reprobate foreign devils (especially Englishmen) had better live on the Blaskets where he can admire himself without disturbance. Perhaps, after all, our late troubles were not so purposeless as they seemed. They were probably ordained to prove to us that we are no better than other people; and when Ireland is once forced to accept this stupendous new idea, goodbye to the old patriotism.[95]

What happened, at least until very recently, seemed a contrary process: academic revisionism has coincided with popular revivalism. The version of Irish history presented in P.S. O'Hegarty's influential *Ireland under the Union* persisted: 'the story of a people coming out of captivity, out of the underground, finding every artery of national life occupied by the enemy, recovering them one by one, and coming out at last into the full blaze of the sun . . .'[96] This version long remained in vogue among politicians and popular historians (and *a fortiori* television historians). The simplified notions have their own resilience: they are buried deep in the core of popular consciousness, as recent analysis of folk attitudes in rural Ireland has shown.[97] The point should also be made that the triumph of revisionism in Irish academic historiography is a particularly exact instance of the owl of Minerva flying only in the shades of nightfall: events in the island since 1969 have both emphasized the power of ideas of history, and the time it takes for scholarly revolutions to affect everyday attitudes. Nor have Irish readers always been particularly anxious to explore the historical analysis offered by scholars from other countries.[98] But the discrepancy between beliefs in the university and

95. G.B.S. [Shaw], 'On Throwing Out Dirty Water', *Irish Statesman*, 15 September 1923; quoted in F.S.L. Lyons, *Culture and Anarchy in Ireland 1890-1939* (Oxford, 1979), p. 165.

96. Dedicatory preface to *A History of Ireland under the Union* (Dublin, 1952). It might be added that this is a work of wide reading and dense texture, in which original documentation and personal reminiscence is used to powerful effect; but it is none the less pervaded by obsession.

97. See H. Glassie, *Passing the Time: Folklore and History of an Ulster Community* (Dublin, 1982), p. 83, which records the 'education' transmitted in rural Fermanagh: ' "it took the boys in Fenian days to carry it on until the Men Behind the Wire came. . . . The old fight had to be fought, and it had to be fought from the days of eighteen and sixty-seven, and indeed it went back further. Seventeen and ninety-eight, that was the first Rising. That's what you want to know: the background to everything." ' Also see ibid. pp. 639ff., for observations about the keeping of 'alternative history' in local communities. In a similar manner, the memory of dispossession lasted on at atavistic levels, noted by Arthur Young, and often since (see, for instance, Tom Garvin, *The Evolution of Irish Nationalist Politics*, p. 16).

98. The work of M.W. Heslinga, *The Irish Border as a Cultural Divide* (Assen, Netherlands,

outside it raises some questions. The transition from piety to iconoclasm may
have been too abrupt for the change to percolate through immediately. Still
the depressing lesson is probably that history as conceived by scholars is
different to what it is understood to be at large, where 'myth' is probably the
correct, if over-used, anthropological term. And historians may overrate their
own importance in considering that their work is in any way relevant to these
popular conceptions—especially in Ireland. The habit of mind which preferred
a visionary Republic to any number of birds in the hand is reflected in a
disposition to search for an Irish past in theories of historical descent as bizarre
as that of 'the Cruthin people' today,[99] the Eskimo settlement of Ireland
postulated by Pokorny in the 1920s,[100] the Hiberno–Carthaginians of Vallancey,
or the Gaelic Greeks of Comerford.

Such as the attitude goes with the disposition to legitimize, to praise and
to blame, conspicuously evinced by the old traditions of Irish history-writing.
The same pieties are still reiterated buy self-appointed 'anti-revisionisms', but
it is noteworthy that they restrict themselves to delivering the same generalizing
lecture in different places, or concentrating on small theological disputations
based on highly selective readings: whereas the general histories published in
the last decade have begun to reflect the interrogations of academic research.
Not only do these now reach a wide market, in a country which reads about
itself obsessively; there is also every sign that a new generation finds the old
disputes and obsessions less and less relevant to immediate problems. In this,
like much recent scholarship, they incline towards the line of Goldwin Smith,
articulated by his study of *Irish History and Irish Character* in 1861: 'There is
no part of all this which may not be numbered with the general calamities of
Europe during the last two centuries, and with the rest of these calamities
buried in oblivion.' Elsewhere in his rather weary and acerbic, but essentially
sympathetic, study, the same author remarked that the 'popular writer on Irish
history' should 'pay more attention than writers on that subject have generally
paid to general causes, [should] cultivate the charities of history, and in the
case of the rulers as well as the people, [should] take fair account of misfortunes

1962), has received less attention than might be expected; and Erhard Rumpf's pioneering
Nationalism and Socialism in Twentieth-century Ireland, published in German in 1959, had
to wait until 1977 for an English translation (under the imprint of Liverpool University
Press). When carrying out research, Dr Rumpf was told 'by an authority on Irish politics'
that he could not hope to analyse the dynamic of Irish nationalism: 'There was no
sociological, sectarian or class problems or angle in the Sinn Féin movement, or any part
of it, from beginning to end' (p. xv).

99. I. Adamson's book *Cruthin: The Ancient Kindred* (Newtownards, 1974) is interpreted by
Unionist ideologues as arguing for an indigenous 'British' people settled in Ulster before
the plantations.

100. Elegantly mocked by E. Curtin in the *Irish Statesman*, 7 November 1925: 'We must beat
our harps into harpoons and our wolfdogs into walruses.'

as well as crimes'.[101] Professional Irish historiography has turned this corner; but the question which may interest future historians is why the 'popular Irish history' took so long to follow.

101. Goldwin Smith, *Irish History and Irish Character*—'an expansion of a lecture delivered before the Oxford Architectural and Historical Society at their Annual Meeting in June 1861' (1861), preface and p. 193.

9

'The Great Enchantment': Uses and Abuses of Modern Irish History[*]

RONAN FANNING

In the present situation, with the dire past still overhanging the dire present, the need to go back to fundamentals and consider once more the meaning of independence, asserts itself with almost intolerable urgency. The theories of revolution, the theories of nationality, the theories of history, which have brought Ireland to its present pass, cry out for re-examination and the time is ripe to try to break the great enchantment which for too long has made myth so much more congenial than reality.

So wrote F.S.L. Lyons in one of three lectures broadcast in December 1971 to commemorate the fiftieth anniversary of the Anglo-Irish Treaty of 1921.[1] The power of myth likewise loomed large in T.W. Moody's 1977 address 'Irish history and Irish mythology' which took as its point of departure that 'all nations have their myths, which affect their corporate lives and do so most strongly in times of strain or crisis or unresolved conflict'.[2] Again, Roy Foster, in his 1982 address on 'History and the Irish question', has suggested that 'the depressing lesson is probably that "history" as conceived by scholars is a different concept to "history" as understood at large, where "myth" is probably the correct, if over-used anthropological term'.[3] These three passages, drawn from the writings of three of the most eminent representatives of three successive generations of modern Irish historians, testify to a striking characteristic of modern Irish historiography: a continuous compulsion to confront myth and mythology.

---

[*]   First published in James Dooge (ed.), *Ireland and the Contemporary World: Essays in honour of Garret Fitzgerald* (Dublin, 1988), pp. 131-47; an earlier draft of this paper was delivered as the presidential address for 1984-86 to the Irish Historical Society on 21 January 1986.

1.   F.S.L. Lyons, 'The meaning of independence' in Brian Farrell (ed.), *The Irish parliamentary tradition* (Dublin, 1973), p. 223.

2.   Above, pp. 71-86, esp. p. 71.

3.   Above, pp. 122-45, esp. p. 144.

I mean by 'myth' any historical narrative which is either imaginary or fictitious or both, either in whole or in part. Some myths are founded on popular and often ancient traditions, 'transmitted orally, in writing, and through institutions'.[4] The myths with which I am particularly concerned may be of much more recent origin. Some of these myths were created or are sustained for contemporary political purposes. Those who seek sedulously to preserve the integrity of such myths—as well as those who strive to erect counter-myths in their place—want to legitimise their political purposes by cocooning them in the comforting cloak of a mythical past. Hence, although the aims of the constitutional politician committed to the idea that nothing can be gained by violence are diametrically opposed to the aims of the paramilitary spokesman convinced that his organisation's objectives can only be gained by physical force, both are anxious to plunder and to prostitute the past for their purposes in the present. The more intense the contemporary conflict between such competing legitimacies, the greater the temptation.

One immediate cause of this obsession with the mythological which is so characteristic of modern Irish historiography is the recrudescence of political violence in Ireland since 1968. But, before looking more closely at how the contemporary crisis in Northern Ireland has reinvigorated the debate about Irish history and Irish mythology, we should recall that the tension between the scholarly practice of history and the immediate political concerns of the society has not always been so great.

Indeed that tension was markedly less acute when the founding fathers of modern Irish historiography, Theo Moody and Robin Dudley Edwards, established the Irish Historical Society in Dublin and its sister-society the Ulster Society for Irish Historical Studies in Belfast exactly fifty years ago. *Irish Historical Studies*, the joint journal of the two societies, was first published in 1938 under their joint editorship and, in that same year, Moody and Edwards were prime movers in the establishment of the Irish Committee of Historical Sciences which has since provided for the representation of Irish historical interests of the Comité International des Sciences Historiques.

But this bald rehearsal of the main events in the Irish historiographical revolution is less germane than its timing. The years 1936 to 1938 witnessed a constitutional revolution in independent Ireland when the settlement embodied in the Anglo-Irish Treaty of 1921 was torn up and replaced by the External Relations Act of 1936, the 1937 Constitution and the Anglo-Irish agreements of 1938 which, in the eyes of most Irish republicans, legitimised the authority of the state for the first time since independence. The corollary was the erosion of the ideological base of those who claimed the right to take up arms against the state. 'When the Irish people had established freely a state in accordance with their wishes', Eamon de Valera told the Dáil as he

4. Moody, loc. cit.

introduced the Treason Blll in 1939, 'those who tried, by violent means, to overthrow that state should be held here, as in other countries, to be guilty of the most terrible crime of a public character which is known in civilised society.'[5]

The advent of World War II, moreover, further reinforced the state's authority north as well as south of the border, however much Irish neutrality when contrasted with Northern Ireland's contribution to the British war-effort may have widened the partitionist divide. The successful implementation of internment without trial south and north—not merely during the war but again during the IRA's border campaign of 1956-61—was but one of the more obvious manifestations of this phenomenon. Historians practising their procession in Ireland in the quarter of a century inaugurated by 1938 thus did so in curiously unchanging political circumstances. It has become fashionable to characterise the forties and the thirties as the most deplorably stagnant of decades and it can scarcely be doubted that the isolation from professional colleagues abroad imposed upon Irish historians was unhealthy. Nor did the scarcity of resources and, in particular, the paucity of jobs for historians in university departments of history make for the most stimulating of intellectual environments.

In retrospect, however, it seems to me more appropriate to identify stability rather than stagnation as the most remarkable feature of the intellectual and political landscape against which Irish historians pushed forward the boundaries of their historiographical revolution. The point is well illustrated by the sentence with which another of Moody's contemporaries and principal collaborators, J.C. Beckett, chose to conclude his widely acclaimed one-volume history *The Making of Modern Ireland* when it was first published in 1966. He then wrote: 'though the settlement [of 1920-22] left a legacy of bitterness issuing occasionally in local and sporadic disturbances, it inaugurated for Ireland a longer period of general tranquillity than she had known since the first half of the eighteenth century'.[6] Today such a statement might well provoke incredulity if not, indeed, derision—at least among non-historians. For *today* our present vision is not reassured by tranquillity so much as dimmed by the blood since shed. Today the Northern Ireland crisis in its present phase has already endured for some eighteen years—longer than the period spanning the 1798 rebellion, the creation of the United Kingdom of Great Britain and Ireland under the terms of the Act of Union of 1800 and the rising of Robert Emmet; longer than the episodic revolts of Young Ireland and the Fenians in mid-nineteenth century; longer than the Irish revolution even if that revolution is most generously interpreted as having a continuous existence from 1916 to

5.   Ronan Fanning, *Independent Ireland* (Dublin, 1983), p. 133.
6.   J.C. Beckett, *The Making of Modern Ireland 1603-1923* (London, 1966), p. 461.

1923; longer, arguably, than all of these episodes taken together. A historian writing today under Professor Beckett's title might instead conclude that the events of 1968-9 inaugurated in Ireland longer period of violence than she had known since the seventeenth century.[7]

Yet it is, I think, important to recognise that few historians would have withheld assent from what Professor Beckett wrote, when he wrote it; we cannot otherwise recognise the starkness of the contrast between the perception of the mid-sixties and the perception of the mid-eighties. That contrast is especially striking if one compares the perception of the young. Few of today's younger generation—and no one younger than twenty-one—have any conscious memory of a time when Ireland was at peace. For them (and the phenomenon will inevitably become still more striking with each passing year) Professor Beckett's tranquillity is as much a part of the past as the Government of Ireland Act of 1920 or the treaty of 1921.

But, before returning to our exploration of how the Northern Ireland crisis has influenced what I have described as the Irish historiographical revolution, let us look at the original limits of that revolution as conceived by its participants.

Perhaps the single most important limitation was the imposition of a terminal date after which the writing of modern Irish history was deemed undesirable, at least in the pages of *Irish Historical Studies*. The constitution of *Irish Historical Studies* enacted in 1938 that no articles should be published in the journal which had reference to Irish politics after 1900 and the editors were bound to exclude or amend any passage which was at variance with this rule.

The justification for such a rule seemed self-evident. The official records for the government of the United Kingdom of Great Britain and Ireland in the twentieth century remained closed. So, too, were the major political collections, most of which were still in private hands and had yet to be entrusted to the charge of archivists or deposited in libraries, let alone thrown open to historians. The history of the first decades of the twentieth century could not be properly written, so the argument ran, because the archival record upon which it must be based was unavailable.

There remained, moreover, the vast task of 'revealing Irish history'[8] of the earlier centuries and this was the battleground on which professional historians first assaulted myth and mythology—the first monographs published

7. This was not, however, Professor Beckett's conclusion. The final sentence in the second, revised edition of the book, published in 1981, reads: 'But the settlement, whatever its final outcome, did at least inaugurate for Ireland a longer period of general tranquillity than she had known since the first half of the eighteenth century' (p. 461).

8. See Helen Mulvey, 'Theodore William Moody (1907-84): an appreciation', *I.H.S.*, xxiv, no. 94 (1984-5), p. 123.

by Edwards and Moody related to the sixteenth and seventeenth centuries respectively.[9]

But the mythologies of twentieth-century history carry a heavier political charge which must be distinguished from the mythologies of a time beyond the memory of the living. By postponing the writing of twentieth-century history professional historians deferred coming to terms with the dilemma arising from the new and much more potent trappings that mythology assumed under the impact of the Irish revolution of 1916-23.

In the first decades of the twentieth century not only nationalist mythology but what Moody has described as the 'mythology of Orangeism'[10] were utterly and irrevocably transformed. Nationalist mythology became, firstly, an integral part of the ideology of a successful revolution and, latterly, the ideology of the only nation-state newly established in Western Europe in the twentieth century. Viewed from the nationalist perspective, the opposing mythology was similarly transmuted into the ideology of a no less successful counter-revolution. From the unionist perspective that transmutation provided the ideological foundations for the establishment of Northern Ireland, just as the similar transmutation in nationalist mythology provided the ideological underpinnings for the independent Irish state, notwithstanding the shattering impact of civil war on the coherence of that ideology.

The erection of what were in effect two competing state ideologies on this small island renders the achievement of Moody, Edwards and their collaborators, in so swiftly establishing a single unified structure embracing north and south for the study of Irish history, all the more remarkable. And it takes away nothing from that achievement to point out that it would have been still more difficult—even, perhaps, impossible—to attain had they felt constrained immediately to address themselves to the mythological-cum-ideological conflict of the first decades of the twentieth century.

That task was rightly postponed until the archives for these years were progressively unveiled. The British Public Records Act of 1958 implemented a 1954 recommendation to the British government that cabinet papers and departmental records should become available fifty years after their creation. This provision was liberalised in 1966 when records were opened to the end of 1922 and, again, when the Public Records Act of 1967 replaced the fifty-year rule with a thirty-year rule.[11] Given Ireland's status as part of the United Kingdom of Great Britain and Ireland until 1922, these releases of what, of course, are now British records paved the way for writing a more definitive history of the Irish revolution, notwithstanding the continued prescription of

9. R.D. Edwards, *Church and state in Tudor Ireland* (Dublin, 1935) and T.W. Moody, *The Londonderry plantation 1609-41* (Belfast, 1939).
10. Moody, 'Irish history and Irish mythology', above, p. 75.
11. *Hansard*, 5th series, vol. 749, cols. 25-28; 26 June 1967.

periods of forty years and longer for certain Irish records dealing, in the phrase of the then British Attorney General, with 'what are commonly called "the troubles".'[12] The fact that release of these records about the 'troubles' of the past was so soon followed by the 'troubles' of the present has, I believe, more profoundly influenced the writing of twentieth-century Irish history than most historians care readily to recognise.

As a general rule Northern Ireland governments followed these British examples in releasing their records in the Public Record Office in Belfast. Irish governments, however, were less easily swayed by Lord Acton's maxim which that same British Attorney General quoted at Westminster in 1967: 'to keep one's archives barred against historians is tantamount to leaving one's history to one's enemies'.[13] Thus, although the volume of relevant records housed in archives in Ireland was much smaller, their release was much slower—so much so that F.X. Martin's publication in 1961 of two memoranda by Eoin MacNeill which he had unearthed in the National Library[14] was widely regarded as a major turning-point in the historiography of the 1916 Rising. Sensitivities surrounding the civil war contributed to the reluctance of successive Irish governments to open official records and the first release of the cabinet records of independent Ireland was delayed until 1976. Although, as a matter of practice, the Taoiseach's Department has subsequently released its own records under a thirty-year rule there has been no statutory obligation upon it to do so. Indeed even today we still await the enactment of the National Archives Bill belatedly introduced in the Senate in 1985, and recently initiated in the Dáil. In practice, however, the thirty-year rule provided for in that Bill has already won increasing acceptance among those who have custody of departmental and other official records. The relevant article of *Irish Historical Studies*'s constitution now provides that 'no article shall be published on a topic having reference to Irish politics later in date than thirty years prior to the publication of the article'.

But, until 6 March 1978, when that amendment was introduced, 1925 was the terminal date adopted by *Irish Historical Studies* and one has to ask why it was that the Irish *historical* establishment moved more slowly in the matter than even the Irish, let alone the British, political establishment. Scholarly inertia is doubtless one answer. Acute awareness of political sensitivities in an organisation which embraced north and south, and similar sensitivity to the scars left by the Irish civil war—well symbolised by the destruction of so many irreplaceable records in the Public Record Office in Dublin's Four Courts at the outset of that war in 1922—are others.

12. Ibid., col. 34.
13. Ibid., col. 27.
14. See Helen Mulvey, 'Twentieth-century Ireland, 1914-70' in T.W. Moody (ed.), *Irish historiography 1936-70* (Dublin, 1971), p. 109.

That said, it remains remarkable how few professional historians in Ireland have become involved in writing twentieth-century political history.

One reason is that there was no time for historians to produce anything approximating to a definitive history of the Irish revolution before old mythologies were revived and new mythologies created by the eruption of violence after 1968. A comparison of the two collections of essays on Irish historiography published by the Irish Committee of Historical Sciences in 1971 and 1981 respectively is instructive on this point.[15]

Also noteworthy is how high a proportion of the best work on the revolutionary period has been produced by non-Irish-born historians attached to universities outside Ireland—the major works of Joseph Curran, David Fitzpatrick, David Miller and Charles Townshend are examples which spring readily to mind.[16] Many of the books written by Irish authors working in Ireland, moreover, have been produced by historians who have received no formal historical training at undergraduate and postgraduate level and who are not attached to university departments of history. The valuable volumes produced by Dr Leon Ó Broin are a case in point.[17]

How does one explain this apparent disinterest in, not to say neglect of, the revolutionary period on the part of professional historians holding academic appointments in Ireland? Part of the explanation undoubtedly lies in the fact that Edwards, Moody and others of their generation had already fixed upon their own areas of research interest before the materials for writing revolutionary history became generally available. It is in the nature of postgraduate supervision, moreover, that the interests of the supervisor often become the interests of the supervised.

Another factor was the extraordinarily short interval which elapsed between the release of records for the revolutionary period and the introduction first of the fifty-year rule and then of the thirty-year rule which threw open to would-be researchers into twentieth-century Irish history a vast new field of endeavour extending far beyond the revolutionary period.

But the most significant factor in deflecting the energy of historians not merely away from the history of the revolution but away from all political history was the growing vogue for social and economic history. Conscious of the much greater strides made by social and economic historians working outside Ireland and relieved of the insularity and isolationism imposed by

15. See Mulvey, loc. cit. and David W. Harkness, 'Ireland since 1921' in Joseph Lee (ed.), *Irish historiography 1970-79* (Cork, 1981).

16. Joseph Curran, *The birth of the Irish Free State 1921-23* (Alabama, 1980); David Fitzpatrick, *Politics and Irish life 1913-21* (Dublin, 1977); David Miller, *Church, state and nation in Ireland 1898-1921* (Dublin, 1973); Charles Townshend, *The British military campaign in Ireland 1919-21* (Oxford, 1975). David Fitzpatrick has since joined the Modern History Department of Trinity College, Dublin.

17. See especially, *The Chief Secretary: Augustine Birrell in Ireland* (Dublin, 1969).

World War II and its immediate aftermath, Irish historians began belatedly to respond to the prevailing trends in international historical scholarship. They were reacting, too, to the intolerable confines of the narrowly traditional political history taught in Irish schools and still promulgated by the Department of Education in Dublin in the 1950s. Nor should one forget the reaction against the political in favour of the socio-economic which permeated the better-educated strata of Irish society after the publication of *Economic Development* in 1958, which was also reflected in the perception that Seán Lemass's priorities as head of government were very different from Eamon de Valera's traditionalist values.

This, then, was the background to the establishment in 1970 of the Economic and Social History Society of Ireland which sprang from the Economic History Society's conference of 1967. The first number of the new Society's journal, *Irish Economic and Social History*, was published in 1974.

The initiative thus taken by leading Irish economic historians such as Louis Cullen and Ken Connell was the most important new departure in Irish historiography since the events of 1936-8. Cullen and Connell, in short, did for their generation of historians what Moody and Edwards had done for theirs. The most notable feature of Irish historiography in the past decade has been the proliferation of publications on socio-economic history. Leslie Clarkson, writing in 1980, suggested that 'over 1,000' items had been published since 1968 on Irish economic and social history.[18] One consequence is that many of the most able and energetic historians attached to the history departments of Irish universities now specialise in socio-economic history and so, inevitably, do their best graduate students.

The growing predominance of socio-economic history uncannily coincided with the eruption of violence in Northern Ireland, which in turn triggered the renewed debate on the relationship between history and mythology of which the three addresses from which I quoted at the outset are an integral part. Historians and historiographers alike should, I believe, be suspicious of coincidences and we must ask whether there is any causal connection between the contemporary crisis in Northern Ireland and the enthusiasm for socio-economic, at the expense of political. history. My own belief is that there is indeed such a connection. One by-product of the political stability in both parts of Ireland for thirty years after 1938 was the hardening of the implicit assumption among all but the most pessimistic of historians that political violence on any significant scale in Ireland was a thing of the past. This assumption was reinforced by the heady optimism which characterised the Lemass-O'Neill era of the early sixties. It followed that few historians doubted that what they denounced as mythology was a creed outworn which, sooner

18. See Joseph Lee, 'Irish economic history since 1500' in Lee, op. cit., p. 173.

or later, would be overwhelmed by the weight of publications amassed by the professional advocates of academic history.

The peace and stability of the forties and fifties reinforced by the optimism of the sixties made for a mentality conducive to what the British historian Herbert Butterfield designated the Whig interpretation of history: the tendency 'to praise revolutions provided they have been successful, to emphasize certain principles of progress in the past and to produce a story which is the ratification if not the glorification of the present'.[19] The problem, argued Butterfield, must be treated 'as an aspect of the psychology of historians'.[20]

The psychology of Irish historians as it evolved in the thirty years after 1938 ill-fitted them for research into the history of the Irish revolution. They shared the political sensitivities of their generation and, even had the records been available, they were not temperamentally disposed to seize upon such subjects, say, as the role of physical force as a factor in the achievement of Irish independence as their chosen subject of research.

Assumptions that peace and stability would endure were shattered between 1968 and 1972 when the fifty-year-old system of government and politics in Northern Ireland was first destabilised and then destroyed. In the process, moreover, allegedly antiquated and decaying mythologies again acquired an ideological importance of the highest political significance The effect upon historians, as upon all Irish intellectuals, was obviously immense and, even in the case of so pre-eminent a historian as F.S.L. Lyons, could be traumatic.

Indeed Lyons's revulsion from 'the great enchantment' derives, it seems to me, from his own disenchantment and disillusion at the latest savage twist in Irish history. Disenchantment permeates the pages of his last book, *Culture and anarchy in Ireland 1890-1939* (Oxford, 1979). My own unease when I reviewed that book was graphically, if perhaps unconsciously, illustrated by the picture on the dustjacket of the hardcover edition—unprecedented, to the best of my knowledge, in so academically earnest a series as the Ford lectures; namely a photograph of armed British troops manning a barricade in Talbot Street during the Easter Rising. The juxtaposition of photograph and title invites the inference that culture resided only behind the barricade, 'anarchy' outside, held back by the Kiplingesque 'tommies'. Nothing in the text sets out to overturn such inherent Anglo-Saxon attitudes.

Irish or, as Leland Lyons would have it, Gaelic sensibilities on the other hand are treated much less tenderly and he is clearly unsympathetic towards the amalgam of Gaelic-Catholic culture which became predominant after independence. Indeed when he writes that 'much of the cultural history of Ireland in the twentieth century was to be the history of [the] disenchantment'

---

19. Herbert Butterfield, *The Whig interpretation of history* (London, 1973 edt.), p. 9. This analogy was suggested to me by Dr Vincent Comerford.
20. Ibid.

of the Anglo-Irish, one senses that he numbers himself among the ranks of the disenchanted.

Nowhere is this more plain than in his profoundly pessimistic conclusion: that the 'true anarchy'

> during the period from the fall of Parnell to the death of Yeats . . . was not primarily an anarchy of violence in the streets, of contempt for law and order such as to make the island, or any part of it, permanently ungovernable. It was rather an anarchy in the mind and in the heart, an anarchy which forbade not just unity of territories, but also 'unity of being', an anarchy that sprang from the collision within a small and intimate island of seemingly irreconcilable cultures, unable to live together or to live apart, caught inextricably in the web of their tragic history. (p. 177)

Pessimism is an occupational disease of all historians and Leland Lyons's generation of modern Irish historians, traumatised by the upheavals in Northern Ireland, may be peculiarly prone to infection. But the note sounded in this concluding passage and elsewhere is less of pessimism than of near-despair. Despair about the condition of the society whose recent history he is concerned to chronicle at best limits the historian's perspective; at worst, to succumb to despair is the greatest sin the historian can commit, for it ends in the paralysis of the historical imagination.[21]

My comments came belatedly to Leland Lyons's attention a mere three months before his tragically premature death in 1983 and prompted him to a characteristically courteous respond which serves as a monument to how Ireland's most eminent twentieth-century historian reacted to the predicament with which I am here concerned. *Culture and anarchy*, he acknowledged,

> ends in pessimism and yes, I was pessimistic when I wrote it and am still more so now. . . Does pessimism paralyse the historical imagination? Sometimes I think yes. . . but on balance I *don't* feel paralysed and only feel that I might be paralysed if I believed in progress. Since I don't, I find ample scope in trying to come as close as possible to 'how it actually was'—of course, not very close. I would really find it hard to be both a concientious historian and an optimist—there I diverge from Yeats who was ultimately, I think, an optimist.[22]

---

21. These paragraphs are taken from my review recorded on 12 January 1983 and broadcast on RTE's radio programme, *Bookweek*.
22. F.S.L. Lyons to the author, 20 June 1983.

Few would contest that pessimism makes for a hardier and healthier cast of mind than optimism for the historian striving to resist Irish forms of the Whig interpretation of history. But the pessimism of the historian who believes the worst will happen must be distinguished from the pessimism of the historian who witnesses the worst happening and believes there may be still worse to come. Social and economic historians, it seems to me, are more immune to paralysis of this latter and blacker brand of pessimism because their subject does not impose the same necessity to grapple with the use of myth in political ideology that confronts political historians.

Witness, for instance, the positive, vigorous tone of David Fitzpatrick's conclusion to his recent essay on 'Unrest in rural Ireland': 'Let us grit our teeth, master the typologies of the sociologist, yet retain spirit enough to raise a small hurrah if the Irish case manages to wriggle out of its comparative straitjacket.'[23] No enervating pessimism here, but rather the self-confident energy of a subject claiming its rightful place in the international discipline of which it is a part.

Historians of twentieth-century political history, in stark contrast, must grit their teeth and boldly assert that very uniqueness of the Irish experience which Dr Fitzpatrick so wisely warns his colleagues against.

The point may be simply made. Nowhere else in the European, North American or antipodean democracies does the writing of twentieth-century history demand so constant a confrontation with mythologies designed to legitimise violence as a political weapon in a bid to overthrow the state. If those engaged in the practice of political history feel compelled to seek the company of historians from other lands in their quest for the consolations of comparative history they might be better advised to turn to the Middle East. They might turn, in particular, to Bernard Lewis's brilliant passage which draws our attention to those who

> would rewrite history not as it was, or as they have been taught it was, but as they would prefer it to have been. For historians of this school the purpose of changing the past is not to seek some abstract truth, but to achieve a new vision of the past better suited to their needs in the present and their aspirations for the future. Their aim is to amend, to restate, to replace, or even to recreate the past in a more satisfactory form.

And it is Lewis who also reminds us that 'those who are in power control to a very large extent the presentation of the past and seek to make sure that it is presented in such a way as to buttress and legitimise their own authority,

23. *Irish Economic and Social History*, xii (1985), p. 104.

and to affirm the rights and merits of the group which they lead'.[24]

One could scarcely find a more succinct statement of what motivated the Irish political establishment after 1969 to adopt that interpretation of modern Irish history commonly described as 'revisionist'.

If I have said nothing until now about 'revisionism' it is because it seems to me to be a term as often abused as it is over-used, a term which is of greater political than historiographical significance. Thus while 'revisionist' may be a perfectly apt term of abuse for defenders of the republican ideological commitment to physical force to use about those nationalists who seek to undermine that tradition, it makes much less sense in the mouth of a professional historian who knows that much of the history of the revolution of 1916-22 has yet to be written, let alone rewritten.

Nevertheless even the most lordly and remote of modern Irish historians cannot afford to ignore the charge of revisionism if only because it carries, and is intended to carry, pejorative connotations which are designed to erode his professional authority in the popular mind. Put another way, the dynamic which sustains the current debate about revisionism is the conviction of many politicians and of still more intellectuals that modern Irish history is too *politically* important to be left to the charge of mere academic historians. Historians who would dispute this contention might ponder the phenomenon of poets and painters, philosophers and literary critics—even an occasional barrister!—queuing to pronounce upon subjects which properly (although not, of course, exclusively) fall within the historian's domain. Examples abound in the pages of the now defunct *Crane Bag* and in that journal's collateral descendants, the Field Day pamphlets.

But the very odium some attach to the epithet 'revisionist' betrays their ideological motivation. For what they fear is not the revision of the facts but of their faith, regardless of whether their totems are orange or green. Theirs are not the open minds of those genuinely engaged in the activity of historical discovery, but the closed minds of those desperately determined to preserve their ideology intact.

Historians must never forget that the ideologists, and not the mythologists, are their most dangerous enemies. In extreme cases the ultimate triumph of ideology may mean that none but invented history will remain. One need look no further than the Soviet Union and the writing and rewriting of history there since the victory of communism after 1917 for a vivid example.

These are weighty matters and the extra burden imposed by the most modern Irish political history upon those who write and teach it is, I believe, a further factor which impels many historians to the study of different subjects and of more distant times. Although that burden must never be exaggerated

24. Bernard Lewis, *History — remembered, recovered, invented* (Princeton, 1975), pp. 55, 53.

lest it be less lightly borne, the tasks of disentangling the recent political past from the anguished and violent present make psychological demands which many of the most brilliant and reflective scholars find abhorrent.

But, in our present predicament, it seems to me that we have no alternative except to reassert the primacy of political history and to serve as chroniclers of contemporary history. To say this is not to derogate from the high achievement of our colleagues working in social and economic history or in other centuries. It is rather to seek their support in endorsing Joe Lee's ringing declaration that the supreme challenge facing the Irish economic historian at the end of this century is simultaneously to extend and transcend the boundaries of his subject.[25]

'An important aspect of the historical process', argued Herbert Butterfield, 'is the work of the new generation for ever playing providence over even the disasters of the old, and being driven to something like a creative act for the very reason that life on the old terms has become impossible'.[26] Although 'disastrous' is much too harsh an epithet to ascribe to the initial reluctance of Moody, Edwards and their colleagues to write the most recent political history of Ireland, the new generation of modern Irish historians cannot fairly plead their necessities precisely because the conduct of history on the old terms had indeed become impossible.

We must take new bearings, not least because of the enormous public appetite for information about our most recent political past. That appetite is most marked in the young, both in and out of universities, and we will fail to satisfy it at our peril. Many of those who will enter our lecture theatres next year were as yet unborn in 1968 and the present generation of students were then mere infants. None can recall a time when Ireland was at peace. Such a time is, for them, part of history.

Historians cannot escape the duty of treating as history what is already so widely perceived as history no matter how difficult or distasteful that duty might be to discharge. And the difficulties are indeed immense. No relevant cabinet minutes or other confidential government records emanating from Dublin, London or Belfast are available, or will become available before 1999—and that is assuming the general application of a thirty-year rule which may well prove a presumptuously extravagant assumption. For the most part all that is available is the public record. We are told what governments and other interested parties (parliamentary or para-military) want to tell us. We know what we read in the newspapers when, as even undergraduate students of political history are aware, the first rule is never to believe what you read in the newspapers. Any historian of Anglo-Irish relations who has examined

---

25. Lee, loc. cit., p. 196.
26. Butterfield, op. cit., p. 59.

the archival record—whether for 1921 or for 1938 or for 1949—is conscious of the chasm separating what happens behind closed doors from newspaper accounts of what allegedly happens behind closed doors.

Newspapers, like radio and television, are partial in two senses. Partial, obviously, in that their accounts are invariably incomplete. Partial, too, in that politicians and public servants who leak stories to the media do so not to serve the interests of any objective historical truth but to disseminate whatever variant to that truth best suits immediate and essentially propagandist purposes. This is not, of course, to dispute that such inspired leaks may be a useful source for historians who accept that politicians are concerned with managing and manipulating the historical account rather than with unbaring it. The historian who knows which journalist or which broadcaster receives most favoured treatment from which politician or civil servant enjoys a distinct advantage over the historian who has no such knowledge. Such knowledge will not necessarily reveal what is happening but it may well reveal what Downing Street or Stormont Castle or Iveagh House want to happen or what they want the public to think is happening.

But, flawed and inadequate though it may be, that history must be written because, for the moment at least, it is the best contemporary history we have. The point was well made by Leland Lyons here in University College Dublin when he addressed the History Society in November 1971 on 'the dilemma of the Irish contemporary historian':

> we have a plain duty to address ourselves to contemporary history even in its most controversial aspects, but to do so in full knowledge of the deficiencies of the genre, and with our gaze fixed upon strictly limited objectives. . . . Our principal business for years ahead will simply be to elicit the facts of which we are at present woefully ignorant, and to set out those facts in the clearest and least sensational prose we can achieve. For those who come after us will the work of analysis and synthesis be principally reserved. If by patient excavation and resolute refusal to study the recent on any but the terms dictated by our discipline, we contribute a little towards the restoration of sanity in this island, then we shall have done all that honour demands—more, perhaps, than we dare hope.[27]

The alternatives seem even more starkly unacceptable today than they appeared fourteen years ago, which is why we must prepare for a task which will often be pedestrian and frequently unpalatable. But to shirk that task would materially contribute to conditions fertile for the creation of new mythologies. Few academic historians will seek professional profit, still less

27. *Hermathena*, vol. cxv (Summer 1973), pp. 55-6.

intellectual pleasure, in recounting the grisly catalogue of horrors extending over the last eighteen years. But, with us or without us, that tale will still be told. If we seek refuge at the top of our ivory towers and shrink from telling it, it will fall to those with less tender intellects but with staunch political purposes to take our place.

10

Nationalist Historiography and the English and Gaelic Worlds in the Late Middle Ages*

STEVEN ELLIS

Much more so than in modern times, sharp cultural and social differences distinguished the various peoples inhabiting the British Isles in the later middle ages. Not surprisingly these differences and the interaction between medieval forms of culture and society have attracted considerable attention by historians. By comparison with other fields of research, we know much about the impact of the Westminster government on the various regions of the English polity, about the interaction between highland and lowland Scotland and about the similarities and differences between English and Gaelic Ireland. Yet the historical coverage of these questions has been uneven, and what at first glance might appear obvious and promising lines of inquiry have been largely neglected—for example the relationship between Gaelic Ireland and Gaelic Scotland, or between Wales, the north of England and the lordship of Ireland as borderlands of the English polity. No doubt the nature and extent of the surviving evidence is an important factor in explaining this unevenness, but in fact studies of interaction between different cultures seem to reflect not so much their intrinsic importance for our understanding of different late medieval societies as their perceived significance for the future development of movements culminating in the present. In sum the historiography of these societies is whig in emphasis: historians have been preoccupied not so much with what appeared important to contemporaries as with the emergence of modern political entities—England or Britain or Ireland—out of the medieval states and societies which preceded them.

It is of course a major function of historians to explain the relationship between the past and the present so as to clarify and extend our understanding of both, but there is a danger that by concentrating overmuch on this process historians may end up not explaining the present but rather oversimplifying the past. The pattern of recent research would suggest that this danger is acute for late medieval Ireland,[1] although many of the criticisms which can be levelled

---

* First published in *I.H.S.* xxv (1986-7), pp. 1-18.
1. See in particular the works cited below, nn. 5-8.

at Irish historiography apply in some measure to the treatment of other areas.[2]
The aim of the present paper is twofold: to offer a critique of the present
nationalist historiography of late medieval Ireland and to make some suggestions towards the creation of an alternative framework for the writing of its
history.

The influence of modern Irish politics on the historiography of late
medieval Ireland has been unfortunate. It was understandable that in the
aftermath of the establishment of the Irish Free State in 1922 the previous
balance between what might be described as nationalist and unionist historiographical traditions should be upset. Where the unionist tradition had stressed
Ireland's position within the British Isles, the little England across the Irish
Sea, the backwardness and instability of Gaelic Ireland, and the benefits which
the *pax Normanica* had brought to the island,[3] historians like Edmund Curtis
concentrated on such topics as friction between the Westminster and Dublin
governments, the Gaelic revival, the Great Earl uncrowned king of Ireland,
the blended race, and the fifteenth-century home-rule movement.[4] In this way
they were able to provide the fledgling Irish Free State with respectable
medieval precedents. Yet history thrives on controversy, and it might have
been expected that the political partition of the island, reflecting the persistence
of both nationalist and unionist traditions, would have stimulated a more
balanced study of its history. For the modern period this may be true, but
sixty years on, though their unionist counterparts are long dead, many of the
nationalist concepts and perspectives of late medieval Ireland are unfortunately
still with us.

Some of the cruder claims have of course been modified: the home-rule
movement has become a separatist movement, the blended race is now a
'middle nation', and the Great Earl—if we ignore this mistranslation as a
Gaelic equivalent of 'Ethelred the Unready'—has been demoted to all-but-
king.[5] Yet nationalist concepts and themes—the 'gaelicization of the Anglo-

2.   Some modifications in the present Anglo-centric presentation of the late medieval English
     polity are suggested in S.G. Ellis, 'Crown, community and government in the English
     territories, 1450-1575' in *History*, lxxi (1986), pp. 187-204.
3.   See, e.g., G.T. Stokes, *Ireland and the Anglo-Norman church* (London, 1889); G.H. Orpen,
     Ireland under the Normans, 1169-1333 (4 vols, Oxford, 1911-20); Philip Wilson, *The
     beginnings of modern Ireland* (Dublin, 1912); Robert Dunlop, *Ireland from the earliest times
     to the present day* (Oxford, 1922); F.E. Ball, *The judges in Ireland, 1221-1921* (2 vols, London,
     1926).
4.   *A history of medieval Ireland* (London, 1923; 2nd ed., 1938) See also A.S Green, *The making
     of Ireland and its undoing, 1200-1600* (London, 1908); Eoin MacNeill, *Phases of Irish history*
     (Dublin, 1919).
5.   J.P. Lydon, *The lordship of Ireland in the middle ages* (Dublin, 1972), ch. 9; *Ireland in the
     later middle ages* (Dublin, 1972), ch. 5; 'The middle nation' in J.F. Lydon (ed.), *The English
     in medieval Ireland* (Dublin, 1984), pp 1-26.

Irish', the 'synthesis of the Gaelic and colonial traditions', 'Hiberniores ipsis Hibernis', and the declaration of the 1460 parliament[6]—remain surprisingly resilient. There are even hints of more thorough-going historiographical developments along these lines. A purported analysis of 'Hiberno-Norman civilization' on the eve of the Tudor conquest hardly proceeded beyond coining the name,[7] but leading Gaelic historians have recently gone so far as to propose the abandonment of 'the distinction between "Gaelic" and non-"Gaelic" Irish society' as 'a bit of inherited old rope which has nothing to contribute to Irish medieval studies, methodologically or otherwise'.[8]

It is not of course suggested here that modern historians have been content merely to develop approaches indicated by Curtis. In particular, there have been important advances in our knowledge of the lordship's adnministrative structures and government, of developments within the Gaelic polity, and some important studies of war and society in English and Gaelic Ireland.[9] There is even perhaps an increasing awareness that recent work on Ireland under the three Edwards cannot easily be squared with traditional perspectives on the expansion and decline of English lordship in medieval Ireland. Nevertheless, the dominant interpretative framework remains a national one: it inclines to treat the island as a political rather than a geographic entity, its history shaped by interaction between inhabitants, and the impact of outside factors ignored or dismissed as deleterious.

This imbalance is at times artificially perpetuated by the development of terminology which is, to say the least, needlessly confusing to outsiders. Apparently their migration across the Irish Sea transformed regional councils into presidencies, scutage into royal service, and purveyance into cess; yet the English versions of these terms were also current in Ireland. The settlers are variously described as 'Anglo-Norman', 'Anglo-French', 'Anglo-Irish', 'Hiberno-Irish', 'Hiberno-English' and 'Old English', hut seldom the 'English'

---

6. K.W. Nicholls, 'Anglo-French Ireland and after' in *Peritia*, i (1982), p. 394, reviewing Art Cosgrove, *Late medieval Ireland, 1370-1541* (Dublin, 1981); Art Cosgrove, 'Hiberniores ipsis Hibernis' in Art Cosgrove and Donal McCartney (eds.), *Studies in Irish history presented to R. Dudley Edwards* (Dublin, 1979), pp. 1-14; idem, 'Parliament and the Anglo-Irish community: the declaration of 1460' in Art Cosgrove and J.I. McGuire (eds.), *Parliament and community: Historical Studies XIV* (Belfast, 1983), pp. 25-41.

7. R. Dudley Edwards, *Ireland in the age of the Tudors; the destruction of Hiberno-Norman civilization* (London, 1977).

8. Gearóid Mac Niocaill, 'Gaelic Ireland to 1603' in Joseph Lee (ed.), *Irish historiography, 1970-79* (Cork, 1981), p. 4; Nicholls, loc. cit.; Donnchadh Ó Corráin, 'Bibliographica' in *Peritia*, i (1982), p. 411.

9. See especially A.J. Otway-Ruthven, *A history of medieval Ireland* (2nd ed, London, 1980); H.G. Richardson and G.O. Sayles, *The Irish parliament in the middle ages* (Philadelphia, 1952); Lydon, *Lordship of Ireland*; K.W. Nicholls, *Gaelic and gaelicised Ireland in the middle ages* (Dublin, 1972); Robin Frame, *English lordship in Ireland, 1318-1361* (Oxford, 1982).

which they called themselves;[10] even though for royal officials such contemporary subcategories as 'the English of Ireland' and 'the English of England'
were usually unnecessary. By contrast, however, the term 'Irish' is loosely and
ambiguously used to mean, at different times, both Gaelic' in a cultural sense
and 'Irish' in a geographical sense, even though contemporary Gaelic society
maintained a firm distinction between *Gaelach* and *Éireannach*.[11] In these
circumstances, it is understandable that Dr Penry Williams, whose specialist
knowledge of Tudor Wales was employed to such good effect in his masterly
study, *The Tudor regime*, should dismiss Ireland with the remark that it 'would
have needed a book to itself, so different were Irish society and Irish
government from English'.[12]

The themes chosen and the terminology employed thus go a long way
towards predetermining the thrust of traditional arguments. Briefly, this is
that English rule in Ireland was inherently unstable because the colonial
community, isolated from its cultural homeland, became increasingly 'gaelicised', developing an Irish outlook and interests which conflicted with the
crown's. This intractable problem could only be held in check by repeated
royal interventions, but when after 1534 a serious attempt was made to
incorporate Ireland more fully into the Tudor state, a complete breakdown
between crown and community soon occurred. By 1570 English rule in Ireland
was rapidly approaching its classic form—a despotism dependant on a standing
army and English officials, with very little indigenous support, amid mounting
opposition by Gaelic and Old English nobles who were increasingly united by
common interests and the catholic religion.[13] Moreover, given this emphasis
on themes which are utterly different from the commonplaces of English
historiography, it is not surprising that English historians, glad to be discharged
from responsibility for charting developments in yet another borderland, have
readily accepted that Ireland was indeed an exception to the pattern of
development in regions like Wales and the north. And for different reasons,
the other group of historians who might have offered a corrective to this
whig-nationalist interpretation have shown equally little interest in the
medieval lordship. Ironically, the relationship between the modern and

10. As an ignorant foreigner, I have hitherto followed established conventions. Nevertheless,
    the term 'Anglo-Irish' has other meanings, and its use, even as a short-hand for 'the English
    of Ireland', misleadingly suggests the early emergence in England of a much more precise
    sense of English identity than the wide, primarily cultural sense of 'Englishness' which
    prevailed in the late middle ages. The terms 'Anglo-Norman', 'Anglo-French' and
    'Hiberno-Norman' are in any case hardly appropriate to the later period. See also Michael
    Richter, 'The interpretation of medieval Irish history' in *I.H.S.*, xxiv, no. 95 (1984-5), pp
    289-98.
11. E.g. *A.C.*, pp. 442, 642, 708.
12. (Oxford, 1979), p. vii.
13. A recent restatement of this view is Edwards, *Ireland in the age of the Tudors*.

medieval partitions of the island is such that the present republic includes all the more densely colonised areas of the medieval lordship, while Northern Ireland was formerly one of the least anglicised areas. Thus, rather than developing pre-1922 unionist perspectives of the medieval lordship within the English state, historians of the unionist tradition have generally preferred to explore the politically more congenial problem of why, since 1603, parts of Ulster have developed differently from the rest of the island.[14]

In sum, the concern with the pre-history of Irish nationalism has been allowed to prejudge the issue of the island's separate development in the late middle ages. Irish history looks different because its historians incline to treat developments there in isolation, particularly from those in Britain. Take, for example, one of the most familiar developments of the period, the so-called 'Gaelic revival'. The movement is nowhere defined but supposedly 'explained' by coining the term 'gaelicisation' to refer to a mysterious process whereby the settlers became 'more Irish than the Irish themselves'. Culturally, there may be some merit in the term, but, after the introduction of the galloglass in the later thirteenth century, there were apparently no significant politico-military developments within Gaelic Ireland which would justify its use. It is true that Gaelic nobles began to wear armour, build castles and adopt the military techniques of the invader, but such developments might equally well be called 'anglicisation'—a term which has been surprisingly neglected. Indeed a leading authority on the revival has recently conceded that it remains 'in many ways [a] baffling phenomenon'.[15] Nevertheless, most of its salient characteristics, as it affected English Ireland, were also evident in another English borderland, the Welsh marcher lordships. These included a 'crisis' and 'decay' of lordship, depopulation and falling land values, the reversion of arable land to pasture, increased population mobility, the flight of labourers and bond-tenants, and the penetration of Welshmen and Welsh customs into English districts.'[16] Yet no historian would describe this as 'wallicanisation': manifestly, despite the truism, we are in fact dealing with an English decline, in that the root causes of the recovery of land by Gaelic chiefs and the cultural assimilation of outlying parts of the English lordship were changes within the English territories and mostly changes occurring outside Ireland altogether. At the least, we need to consider how far the fall in prices, rents and land values in the lordship, the crisis in the towns and the decline of manorial

14. Perhaps one reason why nationalist interpretations of medieval Ireland have not in the circumstances achieved an outright monopoly is that among modern historians specialising in Ireland, 1169-1603, the handful whose background and training were not nationalist have included such prolific writers as A.J. Otway-Ruthven, H.G. Richardson and G.O. Sayles, David Quinn and Robin Frame.
15. Nicholls, 'Anglo-French Ireland', p. 392; idem, *Gaelic & gaelicised Ire.*
16. See, most recently, R.R. Davies, *Lordship and society in the march of Wales, 1282-1400* (Oxford, 1978), ch. 15.

farming, all of which have been well documented for late medieval England, were part of a more general European phenomenon rather than something which can be exclusively attributed to a Gaelic revival.

Only by pursuing such comparisons much more consistently can the real differences in the Irish situation be identified. Much of what at present passes for comparison hardly proceeds beyond the comparatively settled society and administratively more favourable environment of England south of the Trent. Yet England was not culturally uniform, and many of the supposedly distinctive features of English society in Ireland find parallels elsewhere. On the Anglo-Scottish border, for example, historians have noted the emergence in the fourteenth and fifteenth centuries of kinship units termed 'surnames' which were very similar to highland clans. Whether English or Scottish, these surnames accepted joint responsibility for injuries, collectively sought vengeance for wrongdoing, and also developed their own theories of landholding and inheritance in opposition to feudal forms. These developments, however, are attributable to the increasing weakness of royal authority and social insecurity in the period, such as also occurred in the Irish lordship at this time, not borrowings from Gaelic Scotland.[17] Similarly, the unlawful taking of distresses about which there were so many complaints in Ireland was also a problem in the Welsh marcher lordships. There, magnates such as the duke of Buckingham insisted for financial reasons on Welsh law and custom in dealing with their Welsh tenants, but the well-known observation that the earl of Kildare used both English and Gaelic law 'which[ever] he thought most beneficiall, as the case did require', is cited as evidence of 'gaelicisation'.[18] Moreover, the monetary compositions which in the Irish lordship frequently replaced the draconian penalties prescribed by English criminal law were probably in part an Irish manifestation of a general weakness in the common law system which was evident in other areas of weak government. It is notable that in its attitude to the land law the Englishry of Ireland was generally more conservative.[19] But, in any case, partible inheritance was quite common in England, especially among upland communities.[20]

17. T.I. Rae, *The administration of the Scottish frontier, 1513-1603* (Edinburgh, 1966), pp. 5-11; J.A. Tuck, 'Northumbrian society in the fourteenth century' in *Northern History*, vi (1971), pp. 22-39; Philip Dixon, 'Towerhouses, pelehouses and border society' in *Archaeological Journal*, cxxxvi (1979), pp. 240-52. See also the seminal article by Robin Frame, 'Power and society in the lordship of Ireland, 1272-1377' in *Past & Present*, no. 76 (Aug. 1977), pp. 3-33, which first suggested some of the arguments developed in this article.

18. Hore & Graves, *Southern & eastern counties*, p. 162; Nicholls, *Gaelic & gaelicised Ire.*, p. 48. Cf. T.B. Pugh, *The marcher lordships of South Wales, 1415-1536: select documents* (Cardiff, 1963); Davies, *Lordship & society*, pp. 144-5, 162, 407-8, 449-50.

19. Cf. R.A. Griffiths, 'Wales and the marches' in S.B. Chrimes, C.D. Ross and R.A. Griffiths (eds.), *Fifteenth-century England, 1399-1509: studies in politics and society* (Manchester, 1972), pp. 154, 155; S.G. Ellis, *Reform and revival: English government in Ireland, 1470-1534* (London, 1986), pp. 121-3, 139.

The point is not that there was no interaction between English and Gaelic culture in Ireland, but that departures in the lordship from southern-English norms are not necessarily the product of Gaelic influences. Until we have for the lordship detailed studies of those problems which bulk large in histories of other European countries—such questions as the rule of law and the rise of absolutism, taxation and representation, warfare and the growth of state bureaucracy, and crown-community relations—we are not in a position to do justice to such themes as the Gaelic revival and 'Anglo-Irish separatism'.

In the circumstances, there is perhaps something to be said for setting aside considerations of how Ireland's Gaelic inhabitants and English settlers became Irishmen and looking more carefully at how they considered themselves. In 1552 the geographer Sebastian Munster noted in his *Cosmography* that 'formerly regions were bounded by mountains and rivers . . . , but today languages and lordships mark the limits of one region from the next, and the limits of a region are the limits of its language'.[21] How relevant are these remarks to Ireland? Notwithstanding considerable research on the impact of Gaelic society on English rule in Ireland, little effort has been made to relate this question to the similar problem faced by the Scottish monarchy. For example, the well-known remarks in 1380 of John of Fordun, the Aberdeen chronicler, might almost have been made about Ireland:

> The manners and customs of the Scots vary with the diversity of their speech. For two languages are spoken amongst them, the Scottish and the Teutonic, the latter of which is the language of those who occupy the seaboard and plains, while the race of Scottish speech inhabits the highlands and outlying islands. The people of the coast are of domestic and civilized habits, trusty, patient and urbane, decent in their attire, affable and peaceful, devout in divine worship yet always prone to resist a wrong at the hand of their enemies. The highlanders and people of the islands, on the other hand, are a savage and untamed nation, rude and independent, given to rapine, easy-living, of a docile and warm disposition, comely in person but unsightly in dress, hostile to the English people and language and, owing to diversity of speech, even to their own nation, and exceedingly cruel.[22]

20. D.M. Palliser, *The age of Elizabeth: England under the later Tudors, 1547-1603* (London, 1983), pp. 162-3, 175-6; Scott Harrison, *The Pilgrimage of Grace in the Lake counties, 1536-7* (London, 1981), p. 7; S.J. Watts, 'Tenant-right in early seventeenth-century Northumberland' in *Northern History*, vi (1971), esp. pp. 69-71.

21. Cited in Geoffrey Parker, *The Dutch revolt* (London, 1979), p. 35.

22. Cited in T.C. Smout, *A history of the Scottish people, 1560-1830* (2nd, paperback ed., London, 1972), p. 39.

Chronicles in Ireland and Scotland usually referred to this savage people as Irish or Scots depending on their place of residence. But even English observers could occasionally do better than this, as when, with reference to the lordship of the Isles in 1545, it was reported that a new king had arisen in Scotland out of 'the Scottyshe Irysshe'.[23] As is well known, the two regions shared a cornmon Gaelic language with standard literary forms and local dialects which for long remained mutually intelligible. Gaelic chiefs of later medieval Ireland continued to recruit mercenaries from Scotland, and there was from the later fourteenth century substantial colonisation by Gaelic Scots in north-east Ulster.[24] Indeed the lordship of a senior branch of the Clan Donald, MacDonald of Dunivaig and the Glens of Antrim, spanned the North Channel, and its head was sometimes *Rí Innse Gall* in this period.[25] Yet Gaelic specialists have so far shown little interest in investigating exactly how comparable were the clan system, landholding, law and other Gaelic customs common to both regions. Had Gaelic Scotland and Ireland achieved a political unity under an *ÁrdRí na nGael* in the sixteenth century, instead of being absorbed into separate kingdoms, would historians have had any difficulty in explaining this development on the basis of a common culture in the later middle ages?

There is of course an occasional admission that the Scottish Highlands were 'an integral part of the Gaelic Irish [*sic*!] world';[26] but the implications of this seem to have been missed. The traditional concepts of Ireland (apostrophised as *Inis Banba* or *Inis Fáil*) with a high kingship and a 'national history' about its occupation and defence were by the fifteenth century no more than propaganda, displayed in poetry. Rather, loyalties in the Gaelic world were primarily local and dynastic, and in so far as the Gaelic Irish possessed a collective sense of identity, this was based on race and culture, characteristics which were shared with Gaelic Scotland.[27] In publishing his

23. *L. & P. Hen. VIII*, xix (ii), no. 795.
24. Edmund Curtis, *Richard II in Ireland, 1394-5* (Oxford, 1927), pp. 58-9, 88; D.B. Quinn and K.W. Nicholls, 'Ireland in 1534' in *New hist. Ire.*, iii, 17; W.C. Dickenson, *Scotland from the earliest times to 1603* (2nd ed., London, 1965), p. 5. See also the remarks in Cosgrove, *Late medieval Ire.*, pp. 83-5.
25. John Bannerman, 'The lordship of the Isles' in J.M. Brown (ed.), *Scottish society in the fifteenth century* (London, 1977), pp. 212-13, 222; Alexander Grant, *Independence and nationhood: Scotland, 1306-1469* (London, 1984), pp. 212-13; Jean Munro, 'The lordship of the Isles' in Loraine MacLean of Dochgarroch (ed.), *The middle ages in the Highlands* (Inverness, 1981), pp. 33, 35.
26. Nicholls, *Gaelic & gaelicised Ire.*, p. 3. Cf. Brian Ó Cuív, 'The Irish language in the early modern period' in *New hist. Ire.*, iii, 527.
27. See esp., Brendan Bradshaw, *The Irish constitutional revolution of the sixteenth century* (Cambridge, 1979), pp. 15- 27, 179-80. Donnchadh Ó Corráin, 'Nationality and kingship in pre-Norman Ireland' in T.W. Moody (ed.), *Nationality and the pursuit of national independence: Historical Studies XI* (Belfast, 1978), pp. 1-35, argues for an Irish sense of

Gaelic translation of the Book of Common Order in 1567, Bishop John Carswell claimed that he wished to counteract the many 'vain hurtful lying worldly tales composed about . . . Fionn MacCumhaill with his warriors', and he clearly intended his book to be read in Ireland as well as Scotland.[28] The Gaelic annals of Ireland persisted in dividing the island's inhabitants into *Gaeil* and *Gaill* even though, as has recently been observed,[29] the geographic term *Erennchaib* was available and occasionally used. This was no doubt because the occasion and opportunities for common action against outsiders were far outweighed by the continuing relevance and importance of this ethnic division. Moreover, many of the obits of Gaelic *literati* continued to describe them as 'cend scoile Erenn ocus Alban', 'ollam Erenn ocus Alban re sinm' or 'oide fer nErenn ocus nAlban re dán'; and even lesser lights freely migrated across the North Channel.[30]

Arguably, it was only in the late sixteenth century, when Gaelic Ireland came under serious political pressure from the Elizabethans, that conditions developed which were more conducive to the emergence of a distinctive Gaelic Irish identity, separate from Scots Gaelic, in opposition to the English. The annals sometimes qualified *Gaeil* with *Erenn* or *Alpan*, but this may be no more significant than contemporary English talk about northerners and southerners. They frequently also distinguished between 'English hobs' and 'Irish dogs' as *Saxain* and *Gaill*, but not consistently so.[31] To Gaelic speakers a worthwhile distinction could be made between *Gaill* (who generally understood their language and customs) and *Saxain* (who did not); but occasional usages such as 'muinter Righ Saxan' with reference to both *Gaill* and *Saxain* resident in Ireland suggest that they were also aware of an essential unity between the two groups.[32] Perhaps *Saxain* were seen as a sub-category of *Gaill*, but we really need to know more about the precise meaning of *Gaill* in the medieval annals. Certainly, there are occasional hints that the *Gaeil* of late medieval Ireland (or rather the learned classes who passed to and fro between Scotland and Ireland) thought more in terms of a common Gaelic world surrounded by *Gaill* than an Irish polity threatened by Englishmen.

identity and 'otherness' in pre-Norman Ireland, but refers only incidentally to Gaelic Scotland (p. 23, n. 89: grant by Ruaidrí Ua Conchobair to teach the students of Ireland and Scotland, 1169).

28. Cited in Bannerman, 'Lordship of the Isles', pp. 235-6, 238.
29. Cosgrove, *Late medieval Ire.*, p. 79.
30. *A.L.C.*, ii, 176, 290, 364. Cf. ibid., ii, 416: an attack by the Clann-Duiphshith of Scotland, with their Scottish and Irish kin, on O'Conor Don.
31. See Bradshaw, *Irish constitutional revolution*, p. 27; Cosgrove, *Late medieval Ire.*, p. 74, but cf. *A.L.C.*, ii, 460 ('Éire uile ar na gabáil le Gallaibh in bliadhain sin [1584], innus ccur cuirset oineach ocus uaisle fer nErenn ar gcul'). The English nicknames are of course those proscribed by the statutes of Kilkenny.
32. *A.C.*, p. 684.

The Annals of Ulster in particular form an important historical source about
the western isles; and there is also the revealing entry of 1540 in the Annals
of Connaught, with its clumsy reference to a Scottish race and Scottish politics
more generally; 'Ri Alpan do chor gharma sr maithib an chinidh Alpanaigh et
a techt chuigi aran cuan a roibhe se, et dul annsa loing a roibhe an Ri doibh
et an Ri da ngabail itir Gall 7 Ghaoídel, 7 na Goill do lecin amac a cinn tamaill
'na diaigh sin'.[33]

Politically too there are good reasons for considering developments from
a Gaelic, rather than Irish, perspective. One of Edmund Curtis's shrewder but
less influential suggestions was that the earldom of Ulster constituted an
'Anglo–Norman wedge driven' into 'the old Gaelic world of Erin and Alba'.[34]
In fourteenth-century Scotland, however, historians have noted a Gaelic
resurgence, with the expansion in the power of the Clan Donald lords of the
Isles to exercise a supremacy over the other chiefs of the west (and, we may
add, north-east Ulster).[35] This resurgence followed the decline of the earldom
of Ulster, the collapse of Norse power in the isles, and the resumption of
strong connexions with Gaelic Ireland. In the late middle ages the western
isles, annexed from Norway in 1266, were of course seen as part of Scotland,
as indeed was Rathlin Island,[36] and the lord of the Isles usually acknowledged
the king of Scots as his overlord. But as an absentee Lowlander intervening
in a clan-based society, the king of Scots was no more able to make a reality
of his claims than was the English lord of Ireland following similar acknowledgements by chiefs in Ireland.[37] Moreover, as the Elizabethans quickly
discovered, part of the resilience of Gaelic Ireland under threat in the sixteenth
century stemmed from its strong links with the western isles which could only
be broken by a coordinated campaign of the Tudor and Scottish governments,
a practical proposition only after the union of the crowns in 1603. Thus if the
Gaelic revival in later medieval Ireland did not follow from any important
politico-military developments in Ireland, it may be that it occurred because
there was in reality one Gaelic world and because in both Scotland and Ireland
for the first time since the ninth century Gaelic chiefs were able to make more
efficient use of existing resources. Conversely, the revival of strong government
in England under the Yorkists and early Tudors (1461-1547) and in Scotland
under James III and James IV (1460-1513) put pressure on the Gaelic polity;

33. *A.U.*, passim; A.C., p. 716. Cf. ibid., pp. 398, 406, 410; *A.L.C.*, ii, 136, 324; Ó Cuív, 'Irish
    language', 519, 523, 527, 541.
34. Curtis, *Med. Ire.*, p. 211. Cf. Frame, *English lordship in Ireland*, pp. 131, 151-2.
35. Grant, *Independence & nationhood*, ch. 8; Smout, *History of the Scottish people*, p. 40;
    Dickenson, *Scotland*, pp. 41-2.
36. Cyril Falls, *Elizabeth's Irish wars* (London, 1950), p. 155.
37. Bannerman, 'Lordship of the Isles', pp. 211-19; Grant, *Independence & nationhood*, pp.
    212-20; Munro, 'Lordship of the Isles', pp. 26-35.

it led in Ireland to a resurgence of English power during the Kildare ascendancy and in Scotland to the final forfeiture and suppression of the lordship of the Isles.[38] Arguably, the major significance of these events has been overlooked because they cut across traditional perspectives centring on change within Ireland.

Ultimately, however, politics in the Gaelic world were localised and dynastic; events in Munster rarely had much impact in Ulster, so that the effects of the distortion or omission of wider perspectives have not been too disastrous. The English lordship of Ireland, however, was part of a much wider group of territories, in which the English crown and court culture acted as a strong centralising force. Thus it is seriously misleading to discuss its internal history or interaction with Gaelic Ireland either without reference to develop- ments elsewhere in the English territories or with the crown, court and political community treated as an external factor. This is not to deny the value of local or regional studies, which indeed are especially valuable in the context of the lordship's comparatively fragmented society: but the English context remains basic to an understanding of many aspects of politics and society in the lordship.

Perhaps this argument might best be supported and clarified by a brief comparative survey of another developing nation-state and a more extended consideration of the lordship's development in the century before 1534, the period for which nationalist interpretations are most firmly entrenched. The 'decentralized particularist structure'[39] of contemporary France is an historical commonplace, even though France was not untypical in this respect. Almost the only factor common to its different provinces was the monarchy: there was no common law, but each province had its own customs and privileges, and the king specifically confirmed those of newly-acquired territories. Justice was equally decentralised: outside the royal demesne, local seigneurs linked by feudal ties to the crown retained substantial judicial as well as political autonomy; and as new provinces were added, separate provincial *parlements* were established, distinct from the *parlement* of Paris, as sovereign royal courts. Likewise, the *pays d'états* each had their own provincial estates which controlled taxation and were therefore far more important than the cumbersome, underdeveloped estates-general. French was the language of the court, but it was not widely understood outside northern France. Indeed, according to Eugen Weber, as late as the nineteenth century one quarter of all Frenchmen understood no French at all; others had learned it as a foreign language but normally spoke Oc or Flemish or Breton or a local *patois*: they did not consider themselves French, for France was a distant country around Paris, and the south in particular considered itself bound to France as Ireland was to

---

38. Dickenson, *Scotland*, pp. 5, 37-41, 274-98; Ellis, *Reform & revival*, passim.
39. J.H. Shennan, *Government and society in France, 1461- 1611* (London, 1969), p. 5 and passim for the following remarks.

England.[40] Compared with this, the late medieval lordship was closely integrated into the English polity!

Nevertheless, at first sight, received ideas of neglect, decline, degeneracy and 'Anglo-Irish separatism' seem to have much to commend them. Successive kings apparently had little time for Ireland; events clearly showed that royal control over the Dublin administration was inadequate; the spread of Gaelic customs in border areas especially seemed to continue; and a separate parliament, coupled with the increasing local domination of the lordship's separate administrative institutions, provided a strong impetus towards the growth of a distinct Anglo-Irish sense of identity. Clearly, if conditions in England south of the Trent were the norm, the geography, cultural balances and localised power structures of the lordship presented royal government there with quite extraordinary problems.

Yet, even after the loss of English Gascony and Normandy, England south of the Trent constituted less than half of the English polity; and the other borderlands provided many parallels to the purported peculiarities of English Ireland. Indeed, what was exceptional about the lordship was not exceptional conditions there but simply the particular *combination* of exceptions to southern English norms. Under the Lancastrians, the lordship's claims to a recognised place within the English polity must have seemed fairly secure. Alone of the territories outside England, it was subject to English common law and so to English legislation. English was the dominant spoken language, the king's subjects there regarded themselves as Englishmen, and its administrative institutions were more closely modelled on those in England than elsewhere. The lordship was of course part of a separate island and had a land frontier with Gaelic Ireland, but it was not unique in this: the kings of France and of Scots were accounted much more formidable adversaries threatening the continental territories and the north of England respectively. Even when English kings considered England's real position as an island power, instead of their own continental claims and aspirations, much of English foreign policy was directed to controlling the narrow seas against invasion by maintaining blocks of territory on both sides of the English Channel.[41] Control of the major Irish ports and the southern and eastern coastline there was a useful link in this chain of defences, but there was less reason strategically or commercially to extend this control to the comparatively remote and infertile Gaelic west or north.

Thus, since there was no major external threat to crown interests in Ireland, scarce resources could safely be diverted to address more pressing problems elsewhere. Nor is there much real evidence to support notions of an internal

40. Eugen Weber, *Peasants into Frenchmen: the modernization of rural France, 1870–1914* (London, 1977), chs 6–7.
41. M.G.A. Vale, *English Gascony, 1399–1453* (Oxford, 1970), esp. p. 1.

threat from a shrinking Pale and 'Anglo-Irish separatism'. The theory of a shrinking Pale mistakes the fifteenth-century definition of this entity for its decline and depends on a misreading of a statute of 1488.[42] 'Anglo-Irish separatism' is more complicated. As has recently been argued, the decline of a cross-channel nobility may well have altered the shape of politics in the fourteenth-century lordship, but this does not mean that the political community there was increasingly isolated from its cultural homeland, speaking some archaic dialect which was unintelligible on the mainland.[43] Just as the sea united Ulster with the western isles, it also linked the lordship's port-towns with those of western England.[44] In any case, mid fifteenth-century politics there were dominated by those great Irish magnates, Richard duke of York, John Talbot first earl of Shrewsbury, and James Butler fourth earl of Ormond, whose son was created earl of Wiltshire in 1449; and if this was somewhat exceptional, cross-channel landowning remained a significant factor in politics until the 1536 act of resumption.[45] In a short excursus on Ireland in his *Anglica historia*, Polydore Vergil wrongly but revealingly attributed the civility of the lordship's population to their frequent contact with England. They were gentle and cultured, lived an English manner of life, were obedient to the king and mostly understood the language; but he was much less charitable about the barbarous Cornishmen whom he described as the fourth people inhabiting Britain.[46] Anglo-Irish ties were also strengthened from the later fifteenth century with the increasing resort of gentlemen's sons to the universities, Inns of Court and to court itself. Indeed, this was one facet of the strengthening of royal control and governmental reform which was a feature of the reigns of Edward IV and Henry VII in the lordship as elsewhere.[47]

Similarly, manifestations of political dissent are readily explicable within

42. S.G. Ellis, 'Parliaments and great councils, 1483-99: addenda et corrigenda' in *Anal. Hib.*, no. 30 (1980), pp. 104-5; idem, *Reform & revival*, pp. 50-52.

43. Frame, *English lordship in Ireland*, esp. ch. 2. Cf. Alan Bliss, 'Language and literature' in Lydon (ed.), *English in medieval Ireland*, pp. 27-45, and my review of it in *Studia Hib.*, xxiv (1984), forthcoming.

44. Although the fact has generally escaped attention, the towns of the Yorkist and early Tudor lordship were both prosperous and plentiful by comparison with those of other English borderlands. See S.G. Ellis, *Tudor Ireland: crown, community and the conflict of cultures, 1470-1603* (London, 1985), ch. 2; Palliser, *Age of Elizabeth*, ch. 7.

45. Otway-Ruthven, *History of medieval Ireland*, ch. 11; S.G. Ellis, 'Parliament and community in Yorkist and Tudor Ireland' in Cosgrove & McGuire (eds.), *Parliament & community*, pp. 52-3; idem, *Tudor Ireland*, pp. 131, 135.

46. *Anglica historia*, ed. D. Hay (London, 1950), pp. 78-80, 90-94, 108; Anthony Goodman, *A history of England from Edward II to James I* (London, 1977), p. 7, n. 4.

47. Green, *Making of Ireland*, ch. 8; Helga Hammerstein, 'Aspects of the continental education of Irish students in the reign of Queen Elizabeth I' in T.D. Williams (ed.), *Historical Studies VIII* (Dublin, 1971), pp. 137-53; N.P. Canny, *The formation of the Old English élite in Ireland* (Dublin, 1975), pp. 26-31. For administrative reform, see Ellis, *Reform & revival*.

this framework. The Irish parliament did of course provide the government's critics with a separate forum. (It is a moot point whether in this period peers like Lord Ormond represented Irish grievances in the English parliament, as did peers for other regions unrepresented in the cormnons there.)[48] Yet the prcoccupation of historians with political crises such as the 1460 declaration and the 'rival' parliaments of 1478 obscures the essential harmony of crown-community relations, rather like Sir John Neale's interpretation of parliament in Elizabethan England.[49] The fifteenth-century Irish parliament was above all an administrative board, with only minor, and local, legislative functions before 1494. It was important and successful precisely because it was an instrument of royal government, and as such it helped to extend royal control rather than to promote separatist tendencies. Subsequently, Poynings' law determined which executive, Dublin or London, should control parliament and also the nature of its work, but talk about the law reducing 'the role of the Irish parliament to one of servility' is beside the point.[50]

The emergence of an Old English élite is a well-attested development in the politics of later Tudor Ireland, and clearly it built on the political vocabulary of an earlier age. But if ideological differences between Old and New English were only becoming important under the later Tudors, of what consisted this 'Anglo-Irish identity' a century earlier? The use of the term 'Anglo-Irish' to describe the Englishry of Ireland is in many ways a hindrance rather than an aid to understanding because it introduces an artificial distinction in terms of crown-community relations between one regional élite and the rest. In practice the king's dependence for the lordship's good government on a magnate like the earl of Kildare, the methods by which he attempted to influence the earl, and the responses which this elicited, were no different from his relations with the Percy earl of Northumberland in the government of the north.[51] Moreover, political dissent in the late medieval lordship took three main forms, all of which were to be found elsewhere within the English polity.

Most commonly, there were the noble feuds, notably the Talbot-Ormond dispute and the Geraldine-Butler rivalry. As with Courteney *versus* Bonville in the south-west or Neville *versus* Percy in the north, the king intervened to

48. Representation in the English commons was of course confined to England until Henry VIII's reign and was weighted in favour of the south, with Cheshire and Durham unrepresented Thomas, 7th earl of Ormond, was summoned to the upper house as a baron.
49. Cf. Art Cosgrove, 'A century of decline' in Brian Farrell (ed.), *The Irish parliamentary tradition* (Dublin, 1973), ch. 4; G.R. Elton, 'Parliament' in Christopher Haigh (ed.), *The reign of Elizabeth I* (London, 1984), esp. pp. 79-84.
50. Margaret MacCurtain, *Tudor and Stuart Ireland* (Dublin, 1972), p. 7. Cf. Ellis, 'Parliament & cornmunity'.
51. See especially M.E. James, *A Tudor magnate and the Tudor state: Henry, fifth earl of Northumberland* (York, 1966). The evidence on which the following interpretation of the lordship's history is generally based is set out in Ellis, *Tudor Ireland*, chs. 3-5.

prevent such disorders from becoming a serious threat to public order, and particularly heinous enormities or prolonged strife would earn a summons to court to allow personal arbitration by the king.[52] Conditions in Ireland exacerbated the seriousness of such feuds because in a marcher region of comparatively discrete lordships, the magnates and their connexions were particularly necessary for defence: a disgruntled earl of Kildare could incite Gaelic chiefs and semi-autonomous border lineages within his orbit of influence to attack his political rivals in the lordship. Yet Kildare's conduct hardly differed from that of Lord Dacre of the North, whose compact landholding and connexion in northern Cumberland made his cooperation essential for the defence and good government of the West March towards Scotland.[53] In 1525 Thomas, third Lord Dacre, was dismissed as warden-general for allegedly associating with the notorious Charlton surname and encouraging them against the Northumberland gentry.[54] In April a campaign had been instigated by Cardinal Wolsey against the thieves of Tynedale, a lawless district of the Middle Marches which had been statutorily incorporated into the shire of Northumberland in 1495: Wolsey's servants reported that the thieves were now 'contented to obey the kinges highness' and to make amends, provided 'their pledges nowe in prison be deliuered at large'. Yet 'two great capeteynes emonges them' remained obdurate, of whom one, Hector Charlton, claimed to be Dacre's servant 'and that he neuer wold submyte hym selffe to tyme he see the seid Lord Dacre'.

> We haue nott maid eny roodes vpon theym or distroyed their countre as yett, for that all this tyme we haue by our messyngers motioned theym to obey the kinges highnes as trew subiectes . . . Their chief relief and comforth at euery inuasions to be maid vpon theym is to fflee in to Scotland and then to be well and surety resaued; and at all their excourses vpon the kinges trewe subiectes thei bring with theym grete nombre of Scottis.[55]

52. See especially, M.C. Griffith, 'The Talbot-Ormond struggle for control of the Anglo-Irish government, 1414-47' in *I.H.S.*, ii, no. 8 (Sept 1941), pp. 376-97; Martin Cherry, 'The struggle for power in mid-fifteenth-century Devonshire' in R.A. Griffiths (ed.), *Patronage, the crown and the provinces in later medieval England* (Gloucester, 1981), pp. 123-44; R.A. Griffiths, 'Local rivalries and national politics: the Percies, the Nevilles and the duke of Exeter, 1452-1455' in *Speculum*, xliii (1968), pp. 589-632; M.A. Hicks, 'Dynastic change and northern society: the career of the fourth earl of Northumberland, 1470-89' in *Northern History*, xiv (1978), pp. 78-107.

53. For the Dacre connexion, see M.E. James, *Change and continuity in the Tudor north: the rise of Thomas, first Lord Wharton* (York, 1965), app. i. For his estates, see also S.E. Cott, 'The wardenship of Thomas Lord Dacre, 1485-1525' (unpublished M.A. thesis, University of Manchester, 1971), pp. 7-11.

54. Cott, op. cit., p. 81; James, *Change & continuity*, pp. 8-9.

55. B.L., Cotton MS, Caligula B.I., ff 46ᵛ-7 (*L. & P. Hen. VIII*, iv (i), no. 1289).

Did the Harrolds and Lawlesses of the Dublin marches behave any differently?

Shortly after the attempt to rule the lordship through Piers Butler, eighth earl of Ormond, instead of Kildare (1522-4), a similar experiment saw Henry Clifford, first earl of Cunlberland, replace Dacre as deputy-warden of the West March. The experiment failed for very similar reasons: Clifford had no lands in Cumberland and, without Dacre co-operation, could no more rule the marches from Skipton castle than could Ormond the Pale from Kilkenny castle.[56] He was replaced by William, fourth lord Dacre, in 1527, but the feud continued and soon involved Sir William Musgrave, who was appointed constable of the isolated crown outpost of Bewcastle over Dacre's head in 1531.[57] Deteriorating relations with Scotland forced Henry VIII to temporise, particularly during the Anglo-Scottish war of 1532-4: a *casus belli* was the old dispute about whether the town and priory of Cannonby, which claimed to be Scottish but which lay between the English march to the south and the 'debateable land' of the West March, was properly part of Scotland or of the 'debateable land' between the two realms.[58] Henry needed Dacre to support his claim, but, immediately the war ended, Dacre was arrested in May 1534 on a charge of treason. Allegedly, he had *inter alia* negotiated a private arrangement with Scots enemies of Liddesdale, notably the independent Armstrong clan which frequently encroached on the 'debateable land', whereby they were promised indemnity and freedom from reprisals for any raids made upon Musgrave's lands.[59] In fact the charges against Dacre were of a very similar nature to those levelled against the Fitzgeralds before the Kildare rebellion. Musgrave asserted that 'the cuntrey has been so overlayd with the lord Dacres they thowght there was non other kyng'; and although Dacre escaped the Fitzgeralds' fate, he was dismissed from office, disgraced and heavily fined.[60] In borderlands like the far north and the Pale marches, a magnate had to cultivate relations both with the king's enemies and the nominally English upland lineages in order to rule effectively; but the corollary was that the border magnates would sometimes use these contacts in less desirable ways.

Closely linked to the magnate feuds as a source of disorder within the king's dominions were the strong regional loyalties which manifested themselves in many areas. In part these stemmed from the great noble connexions, but distance from London and the court in the south-east was important, and cultural differences were clearly also a factor in Cornwall, Ireland and Wales.

56. *L. & P. Hen. VIII*, iv (i), nos 10, 220, 405, 1223, 1429, 1779, 2176.
57. James, *Change & continuity*, pp. 9-10.
58. W. MacKay MacKenzie, 'The Debateable Land, in *Scot. Hist. Rev.*, xxx (1951), pp. 109-25.
59. James, *Continuity & change*, pp. 16-19. See also G.M. Jackson, 'The wardenship of William Lord Dacre, 1527-1534' (unpublished B.A. dissertation, University of Manchester, 1972).
60. Ibid.; P.R.O., S.P. 1/84, p. 199, cited in James, *Change & continuity*, p. 17.

For example, within England itself, Englishmen were categorised as north-erners or southerners, while the Englishries of Ireland and Wales were seen as Irish or Welsh. Yet the sense of separate regional identities which these terms presupposed was by no means inconsistent with a developed sense of an English national identity and political nation. This sense of English nationality was of course centred on England, and southern England in particular, but it was not primarily geographical. Rather, it comprehended the king's freeborn English subjects throughout the realm of England and its dominions, who were officially described as Englishmen. Bondmen, Gaelic Irish resident in the Englishry, and the native Welsh enjoyed a lesser status, which also differed from that of aliens born outside the crown territories.[61] Lamenting England's divisions reflected in the Lincolnshire revolt of 1536, Richard Morison argued that 'it were wel in Englande if we were all called Englyshemen of this countrey or that . . . and not these northern men, these southerne, these western'; while one of the orders issued to Henry VIII's army in 1513 was that no man reproach another 'because of the countree that he is of, that is to say, be he French, English, Northern, Walshe, or Irysh'.[62] Thus, while the king's subjects in Ireland might be described colloquially as Irish,[63] they remained officially English lieges who regarded themselves as Englishmen, spoke English and used English law and customs.

In this wider sense, an English identity was an important political phenomenon to which the crown appealed in its dealings with foreigners, whereas regional animosities were a significant, but latent, factor in internal administration of which the crown had to take account. Thus, although in theory the king's commission was all-sufficient, it was an unwritten law of English government that the rule of counties lay with their native élites. The intrusion of outsiders was regarded as exceptional and created friction; when Richard III went further and attempted systematically to place his northern adherents in control of unreliable and hostile southern shires, this was seen as tyranny.[64] In a crisis, regional sentiments might be starkly asserted, as frequently during the Wars of the Roses, and also during the Pilgrimage of Grace with its demand for a free parliament at York or Nottingham, with the north properly represented, and that for all sub poenas except treason appearance should be required only at York.[65] In the same way, the systematic intrusion into the Dublin administration of clerks and captains from England

61. These points are developed in Ellis, 'Crown, community and government'.
62. A.J. Kempe (ed.), *The Loseley manuscnpts* (London, 1835), pp. 114-15; [Richard Morison], *A remedy for sedition*, ed. E.M. Cox (London, 1933), p. 41. I am grateful to Keith Thomas for these references.
63. For example, Harris, *Hibernica*, i, 30.
64. A.J. Pollard, 'The tyranny of Richard III' in *Jn. Med. Hist.*, iii (1977), pp. 147-66.
65. Anthony Goodman, *The Wars of the Roses* (London, 1981), pp. 224-6; Anthony Fletcher, *Tudor rebellions* (3rd ed., London, 1983), ch. 4 and docs 2-11.

predictably created friction between 'English' and 'Irish' in the lordship. In different ways, Richard of York in 1460 and Thomas Lord Offaly in 1534 were able to manipulate this sense of regional identity to their own ends. And when, as in the case of Lord Grey in 1478, an ill-equipped outsider was peremptorily inserted as lord deputy into an administration already troubled by rivalry between Geraldines and supporters of the English-born bishop of Meath, trouble of a different sort could ensue.[66] Before the emergence in the mid-Tudor period of new concepts of nationality based on the *patria*, and with it the denial to the Old English of Ireland of their English identity, the use of terms like 'the Anglo-Irish community' and an 'Anglo-Irish identity' have, at best, a dubious validity as a short-hand to denote the regional identity of the English of Ireland within the context of the English political nation. What was at stake was not 'English interference' in, or 'English domination' of, an 'Anglo-Irish community',[67] but the king's occasional failure to govern the Englishry of Ireland in accordance with accepted English norms.

The third form of political dissent in the late medieval lordship were the various political rebellions which punctuated the 1460-1534 period. Interestingly, the lordship seemingly produced no major movement of social and economic protest, perhaps because outside the more densely settled but geographically separate regions of the Pale, south Wexford and the Ormond district, the Englishry comprised an English aristocracy over a Gaelic peasantry which was politically no more active than in the Gaelic lordships. Yet, as in England, the traditional factions and feuds of the region's nobility spilled over into national politics through their alignment with opposing sides in the Wars of the Roses. In this contest the lordship was an important prize because of its strategic location, constitutional status and reserves of manpower This was most clearly shown in 1487: a Yorkist pretender was crowned king of England in Dublin, with Henry Tudor powerless to intervene, and attempted to repeat Richard of York's strategy of 1460 by invading England with an army of German and Gaelic mercenaries, supplemented by Pale levies. These levies must have constituted the only substantial contingent of conventional English bills and bows in the entire army: but despite the well-attested English xenophobia, the army seemed sufficiently authentic in aims and appearance to secure substantial support in England and came close to overthrowing Henry VII.[68] Indeed Yorkist intrigues supported by the Fitzgerald earls in 1460, 1487,

66. Ellis, *Tudor Ireland*, pp. S4-64. Cf. Memoranda roll, 18 Edward IV m. 26 (P.R.O.I., Ferguson roll., iii, f. 221v): the bishop of Meath's servant resisted Lord Treasurer FitzEustace when he distrained for rent, threatened 'quam cito hoc fecerit, tam cito decapitus erit' and asserted that the bishop was governor of Ireland.
67. Bradshaw, *Irish constitutional revolution*, ch. 9; Ellis, 'Crown, community and government'. Cf. Lydon, *Ireland in the later middle ages*, pp. 144-5; Bradshaw, op. cit., pp. 29-30.
68. M.T. Hayden, 'Lambert Simnel in Ireland' in *Studies*, iv (1915), pp. 622-38, Goodman, *Wars of the Roses*, pp. 99-107.

1491 and possibly also in 1470, and the Lancastrian risings of 1462 in Meath and Kilkenny cannot be explained simply in terms of local politics. Feelings ran much deeper than this—as with William Butler, clerk, who was imprisoned in 1470 for calling Lord Treasurer Portlester a traitor and who in 1487 was attainted of treason by 'Edward VI's' parliament for adhering to Henry Tudor.[69] Such conspiracies were both possible and dangerous, not just because royal control in the lordship was comparatively weak, but because local politics were linked to national politics and disturbances there could and did spread to the mainland.

Nevertheless, because the lordship's political community was English, it responded to the same methods by which the Yorkists and early Tudors aimed to consolidate their control over other outlying parts of the English territories. Moreover, the fact that successive kings should attempt to govern by these methods is itself significant: as in England, administrative reform, bonds, acts of resumption and against retaining were all methods by which Henry VII attempted to re-establish peace and good government in Ireland.[70] Above all, however, good government depended on good relations with the nobles, a fact which is readily apparent from Henry VII's dealings with Gerald Fitzthomas, eighth earl of Kildare—if we set aside anachronistic ideas which credit Henry Tudor with wishing to establish 'direct rule' and the artificial distinction between 'Anglo-Irish' influence and English control. The failure in the period 1485–95 of the first Tudor to establish a working relationship with Kildare led to feuds, conspiracies and political instability in the lordship which Gaelic chiefs were not slow to exploit: by contrast, Kildare's reappointment as governor following the Salisbury settlement of 1496 inaugurated a period of stability which was without parallel in the late medieval lordship and which saw the major demonstrations of the earl's power and influence which characterised the Kildare ascendanoy.[71] Yet Kildare's restoration occurred not because the king was forced to fall back on an unreliable noble following the failure of a classic Tudor experiment in bureaucracy under Poynings (1494–5), but because the preferred option of rule through the local magnate was now presented in a reliable and trusty form. Likewise, the events of 1478–9, when interpreted in this context, can be seen as a similar crisis in Kildare's relations with Edward IV, and they were solved in a similar manner and with similar

---

69. Memoranda roll, 10 Edward IV m. 8 (P.R.O.I., Ferguson coll., iii, f. 221); Parliament roll, 8 Henry VII c. 22 (P.R.O.I., RC 13/9).
70. S.G. Ellis, 'Henry VII and Ireland' in J.F. Lydon (ed.), *England and Ireland in the later middle ages* (Dublin, 1981), pp. 237–54. See also *Cal. anc. rec. Dublin*, i, 171 (bond of nisi by the city of Dublin in 1,000 marks, 1488); and (against retaining) *Cal. pat. rolls, 1485–94*, p. 316; Statute roll, 10 Henry VII, c. 12 (*Stat. Ire.*, i, 45–6).
71. Ellis, *Tudor Ire.*, chs 2–4, 6, passim. For the Salisbury settlement, see Agnes Conway, *Henry VIII's relations with Scotland and Ireland* (Cambridge, 1932), pp. 226–9.

consequences for the lordship's political stability in the years 1479-83.[72]

In reality, the decline of royal subventions and of 'English interference' which characterised the lordship during the Kildare ascendancy reflects its relative stability, peace and prosperity, and the general satisfaction of successive kings with this state of affairs. It was not a dereliction of royal duty in the face of peculiar problems which the king and council scarcely understood.[73] Conversely, the fall of the Fitzgeralds in 1534 which, according to the received interpretation, provided Henry VIII with the long- awaited opportunity to introduce 'direct rule', was in fact a disaster for royal government, as the king quickly discovered.[74] The political eclipse of the lordship's leading family was a major factor in the 'mid-Tudor crisis' as it affected Ireland, and the crown was thereby encouraged to experiment with unorthodox methods of government which seriously exacerbated, if they did not actually create, an Irish problem. Thus the abandonment in Ireland of the traditional methods by which the Tudors were successfully assimilating outliers like Wales and the north, in favour of a strategy of military conquest, was chiefly a cause rather than a consequence of the island's separate development. But the real significance of such developments is obscured by attempts to present them as products of long-term processes which saw the gradual emergence of an Irish nation.

In sum, the adoption for late medieval Ireland of an anachronistic, Hibernocentric perspective, with associated nationalist themes, is a conceptual trap similar to that discerned by J.H. Hexter in A.F. Pollard's work.[75] Since the perspective and concepts chosen owe more to modern aspirations than contemporary preoccupations, nationalist interpretations necessarily reveal steady 'progress' towards an independent Ireland. But the validity of such concepts can only be tested by discussing developments in English and Gaelic Ireland in their respective contexts of the English and Gaelic worlds.[76]

72. Ellis, *Reform & revival*, pp. 15, 18, 24-8, 37, 46, 69; idem, *Tudor Ire.*, pp. 61-4.
73. Cf. Charles Ross, *Edward IV* (London, 1974), pp. 203-4.
74. Cf. MacCurtain, *Tudor & Stuart Ire.*, pp. 6-21.
75. 'Factors in modern history', in J.H. Hexter, *Reappraisals in history: new views on history and society in early modern Europe* (2nd ed., Chicago, 1979), pp. 26-44
76. Earlier versions of this paper were delivered, in whole or in part, at meetings of the Royal Society of Antiquaries of Ireland, the student history societies at Trinity College, Dublin, and St Patrick's College, Maynooth, and the Irish Historical Society. I am very grateful for the comments and criticisms offered there.

PART IV: CRITICAL PERSPECTIVES

Against Revisionism[*]

DESMOND FENNELL

In his stimulating contribution to the Garrett FitzGerald *festschrift*,[1] Ronan Fanning quotes Bernard Lewis as saying that 'those who are in power control to very large extent the presentation of the past and seek to make sure that it is presented in such a way as to buttress and legitimise their own authority. . . .' I would add 'and the policies they are pursuing'. Fanning comments: 'One could scarcely find a more succinct statement of what motivated the Irish political establishment after 1969 to adopt that interpretation of modern Irish history commonly described as "revisionist".' In other words, so called "revisionist" history has served the history needs of that political establishment. I agree, and would simply specify that it has met that establishment's need for a history that would 'buttress and legitimise' its major departure from the nationalist ideology on which the state was founded, and the attitudes and policies following from this; particularly its suspension of the demand that Britain withdraw from Ireland, its assumption that Britain's attitude towards Ireland is benevolent, and its collaboration with Britain against the nationalist armed rebellion in the North.

However, since I am opposed to revisionism, and intend to oppose it here, I must also advert to, and take to heart, something that Fanning says later in that same essay. He says that 'The very odium some attach to the epithet "revisionist" betrays their ideological motivation. For what they fear is not the revision of the facts but of their faith, regardless of whether their totems are orange or green. Theirs are not the open minds of those genuinely engaged in the activity of historical discovery, but the closed minds of those desperately determined to preserve their ideology intact'. Now, in passing, I am struck there by the transformation which revisionism seems to have undergone from a version of Irish history that has served the needs of a political establishment to one that is professed by fear-less men, *not* worried about their faith, who are pursuing truth sincerely and with open-mindedness. Perhaps, of course,

*   Reprinted from *The Revision of Irish Nationalism* (Dublin, 1989), pp. 62-70; an earlier version appeared in *The Irish Review* 4 (1988), pp. 20-26.
1. ' "The great enchantment": Uses and Abuses of Modern Irish History' in James Dooge, ed., *Ireland in the Contemporary World. Essays in Honour of Garret FitzGerald* (Dublin 1986); above, pp. 146-60.

it is not a transformation, but simply that revisionism, for Fanning, is both those things simultaneously! More to the point, however, I find, on examining my conscience, that his pen-sketch of *some* of the opponents of revisionism does not fit me.

I know that new historical facts are continually being discovered and I welcome this. I am not afraid that any discovery of new facts will shake my belief in the essential tenets of Irish nationalism, for those tenets are not a myth depending on an act of faith, but practical moral convictions that are held, *mutatis mutandis*, by people everywhere—convictions concerning a nation's right to freedom, the wrongness of its being subject to another nation, and the rightness of resisting and rebelling against such oppression. Nor, finally, am I, nor have I been, desperately determined to preserve intact the Irish nationalist ideology that was transmitted to me in my youth and enunciated publicly all around me up to 1969 and after that.

From 1969 onwards, first with three articles in the *Irish Times* in August of that year, later in my *Sunday Press* column and elsewhere, and finally in my book *The State of the Nation* and my written and oral submissions to the New Ireland Forum, I pioneered and won acceptance for the revision of certain inessential tenets of traditional Irish nationalism, most notably, the contention that the territory of Ireland determines membership of the Irish nation—when in fact this is determined by a shared historical experience and a shared consciousness; the related proposition that all the inhabitants of the Six Counties belong to the Irish nation—rather than constituting, as they do, an Irish community and a British community; and the designation of a reunited Ireland as the primary aim of Irish political nationalism. For that I substituted 'the recognition of the Irish nation, or the Irish identity, throughout Ireland, but specifically, now, in the north-eastern counties,—a united Ireland being the ideal way of securing that, but not the only way. In this sense, I, too, have been a crusading revisionist, but with this difference from the historical revisionists: I have revised, for the most part, the living nationalist doctrine, not the history of modern Ireland and of Irish nationalism; and I have revised with a sense of piety towards our nationalist past, with allegiance to the essential tenets of Irish nationalism, and with critical respect for contemporary Irish nationalism, however embodied or expressed. In short, with a disposition regarding those matters typical of many Irish men and women, but not shared by the revisionist historians.

What is the popular image of historical revisionism in Ireland today? A retelling of Irish history which seeks to show that British rule of Ireland was not, as we have believed, a *bad* thing, but a mixture of necessity, good intentions and bungling; and that Irish resistance to it was not, as we have believed, a *good* thing, but a mixture of wrong-headed idealism and unnecessary, often cruel, violence. The underlying message is that in our relations with Britain on the Irish question the Irish have been very much at fault. This is the popular image of historical revisionism, but it will be evident, when I quote you a passage from the mild revisionist—mild at the time at least—F.S.L. Lyons, that it is not far from the reality. The passage introduced the article by Fanning which I have referred to, and supplied it with its title, 'The great enchantment'. In a radio lecture in 1971 Professor Lyons said:

> In the present situation, with the dire past still overhanging the dire present, the need to go back to fundamentals and consider once more the meaning of independence, asserts itself with almost intolerable urgency. The theories of revolution, the theories of nationality, the theories of history, which have brought Ireland to its present pass, cry out for re-examination, and the time is ripe to break with the great enchantment which for too long has made myth so much more congenial than reality.[2]

Leave aside that political call 'to break with the great enchantment', meaning presumably the Irish Revolution's dream of a prosperous independent Ireland and a recreated Irish mind and culture. That dream of becoming a normal European nation had, in Professor Lyons' view, addled our minds and rationality. Note, rather, his theory of historical causation, his moralising interpretation of cause and effect in recent Irish history. Ireland had been brought to its present pass (that is, the violent chaos in Northern Ireland and its spillovers), not by Britain's conniving with the Ulster unionist rebellion of 1912 and ignoring the will of most of the people of Ireland, and particularly of the nationalist Irish in the Six Counties; nor by the scandalous fifty years of British rule in Northern Ireland; nor again by the continuing refusal of Britain, even in 1971, to recognise the Irish nation and its rights there. No, Ireland had been brought to its present pass in the North by theories of revolution, of nationality, and of history, which we Irish had entertained and must now re-examine; the present dire situation had been caused, in other words, by *ourselves*, by the ideas and convictions inspiring our freedom struggle, by our nationalism. The cause of the present evil was not the wrong mind and action of British imperialist nationalism, but the wrong ideas and action of our liberationist nationalism.

This example of historical revisionism illustrates its key features well. It is not, primarily, the presentation of new facts, nor again, as some revisionists would have us believe, the refutation of factually false historical 'myths'. Primarily, it is a new *moral interpretation* of the known major facts, and the

2.   Published as F.S.L. Lyons, 'The Meaning of Independence' in Brian Farrell (ed.), *The Irish Parliamentary Tradition* (Dublin, 1973), p. 223.

general course of events, especially in the last century and a half—with the help occasionally of new minor facts, or a new treatment of already blown minor facts. More precisely, it is a new allocation, with regard to the known major facts and the general course of events, of *rightness* and *wrongness*, as between the ideas and actions of the Irish and the intentions and actions of the British (or Ulster British).

The net tendency of this re-allocation is a threefold discrediting. It tends, in the first instance, to discredit the basic, motivating tenet of historical Irish nationalism, namely, that British rule of Ireland (or of part of it) was—regardless of exonerating factors—morally wrong, and that the Irish resistance to it was—regardless of blemishes—morally right; secondly, and thereby, to discredit the Irish nationalist tradition, and particularly what was by European and world standards its *genuinely* nationalist wing, the republican tradition ('genuinely' nationalist because it sought a nation-state rather than regional self-government); and finally, then, to discredit the main achievement of that republican nationalist tradition, the Irish Revolution. Revisionism, both in its ultimate thrust, and as a matter of objective fact, is the historiography of the Irish counter-revolution.

I am suggesting, in other words, that it is untrue to regard it simply as a re-writing of history in reaction to the events in Northern Ireland after 1969, and with the aim of depriving the republican rebellion there of moral legitimacy. In the Republic, from the early 60s onwards, with British, American and German capital providing the wealth which Sinn Féin economics had failed to provide, and the rise to power in Dublin of a new élite of businessmen, bureaucrats, media people and politicians who adopted swinging London as their cultural and moral lodestar, a journalistic campaign got underway against everything which de Valera and his era stood for, from the Constitution back to and including 1916. This reflected and expressed the new élite's scepticism about the value of the revolution and of the Irish nation-state itself, and its growing hostility to both of them. When, accordingly, in 1970-71, the Irish Government, faced with open warfare in the North, decided to treat, not Britain, but the IRA as the malign factor, this Dublin counter-revolutionary movement saw its opportunity and seized it. By simultaneously fomenting revulsion against the republican rebellion, and representing it as the outcome of the nationalist ideology which had inspired the revolution and was incarnate in the Republic, it persuaded many and paralysed many others. It was at this stage, and objectively therefore as servants of the counter-revolution, that the academic historians, within the universities and outside them, began to formalise what had existed previously largely in journalism and chat-shows.

When I said earlier that I was opposed to revisionism, I was exaggerating somewhat. I am not opposed to the *writing* of such history, as I am not opposed to the writing of any kind of history, if its factual narrative is substantially true, and its interpretation, moral or otherwise, clearly argued. But I reject the pretension of revisionist history to be a value for the nation. I oppose its recommending itself, or its being accepted, as the proper or true history of modern Ireland. First, because I believe that its moral interpretation is not correct; second, because such history does not serve the well-being of the nation. The first of those reasons is, by its nature, open to debate—I have stated my position, which, as it happens, accords with that of the world in general with regard to Irish-British relations up to and beyond the revolution. My second reason, however, is not debatable.

Every nation in its here and now, the people who make up the nation now, have needs with respect to their national history. They need for their collective well-being an image of their national past which sustains and energises them personally, and which bonds them together by making their inherited nation seem a value worth adhering to and working for. (Of course, for their national well-being, they need to have this complemented by a similarly fortifying image of the present; but my point is that they need in the first place that kind of image from their history.) The modern Irish nation—the new Irish nation formed from the late eighteenth century onwards—was provided with such a history by scholars whose aim was, often explicitly, to supply it with such a history in place of the nationally useless and undermining histories or pseudo-histories of Ireland written by Englishmen. And this new Irish nation would not have formed, and made the very notable mark which it did make on the world, without that history-writing.

The kind of history-writing which sustains, energises and bonds a nation, and thus serves its well-being, can be briefly described. It shows the nation, in its past, involved in a continuous or near-continuous pattern of meaning in which the nation, represented by its state (if it had one), and/or by great men, women and movements, brave soldiers, righteous civilian insurgents perhaps, was always, in some sense, right-minded and right-acting, and occasionally morally splendid. (I say 'in some sense', for the designated mode of right-mindedness and right action varies from nation to nation and, often enough, between an earlier and later period of a national history.) Within that general framework of meaning and moral interpretation, generations of historians can follow each other, or historians of the same generation differ; revision can succeed revision, new facts be integrated, perspectives change, images of outstanding historical figures or movements get transformed. Many particular moral interpretations can alter. Factual truth can be pursued scrupulously, and the more factually true the history, the better for the nation. But always, in the end, if the history is to serve the nation's well-being, the framework of meaning and of moral interpretation which I have sketched above will be maintained and renewed.

Obviously, I am talking about a science of history which is also an art: an art like that of those composers or musicians who, in successive generations, with meticulous dedication, and each differently than his contemporaries, rearrange an old tune or song. But this art comes easily, and without betrayal of self, but rather with affirmation and satisfaction of self, to those historians whose passion for factual truth and conscientious moral judgment is equalled by their piety for the nation's pattern of historical meaning, and their regard for what their fellow-countrymen, and they themselves, need from their national history for their minds and hearts—being, as they are, ineluctably, English, Irish, French or Egyptian human beings.

Mark well, I am not saying that historians *must* have this disposition, and *must* practise this art of reconciling their concern for factual truth and correct moral judgment with the pattern of meaning and moral interpretation which their predecessors and the people, working together, have established. I am saying simply that historians so disposed, who practise this art, contribute to the well-being of the nation, and that those not so disposed, and who therefore do not practise this art, do no. Fortunate the nation whose historians are mainly of the former kind, unfortunate the nation in which historians of the latter kind predominate.

The Irish nation, as it moved into the 1960s and 70s, possessed an established framework of historical meaning and moral interpretation. Its continuous pattern of meaning from the eighteenth century onwards—the only thread of *national political* expression running through this period—was its liberationist nationalism. This, along with its poverty and its Catholicism, had given Ireland its character in the world. In the eyes of the great majority of people, South and North, it was this historic nationalism which had brought the nation to where it was and which pointed towards its future political completion. Two main strands ran through it up to the Treaty of 1921: nation-state or republican nationalism, which organised for armed insurrection; and a nationalism of less than that—Repeal, Home Rule—which we can call devolution nationalism, and which pursued parliamentary methods. Both strands were motivated by the same objective conditions of the nation and the same moral convictions about the wrongness of English rule and the right of Ireland to freedom—though they defined 'freedom' differently. The two strands bickered; they also intermingled and overlapped, in sentiment and song and literary sustenance. They joined in Parnell's New Departure, commemorated the '98 Rising together, and, after 1916, fought electorally for the nation's soul. Out of the victory of republicanism came a revolutionary combination of parliamentary and physical force methods which led to the establishment of the Irish nation-state; and in that state, under the aegis of mainstream republican nationalism, parliamentary democracy triumphed and endured, and die-hard republicanism was outlawed.

That was the pattern of meaning leading from the past to the present which most Irish people saw, vaguely or clearly, in their history. In that continuous pattern they saw the nation, represented by great men, women and movements, righteous insurgents, and brave soldiers, inspired by right ideas and acting rightly. They saw this with pride. They cherished songs, poems and other writings emanating from this inheritance, and they revered countless places, buildings and relics which it had imbued with value. The revisionist historians, instead of maintaining this framework of meaning, moral interpretation, and anchored value, and renewing it through industrious and creative revision, set about demolishing it. Their articles, books, radio talks and speeches represented the Irish nationalist tradition, and in particular its revolution, as radically flawed by wrong ideas and wrong action, to such a degree as to make it something we should be ashamed of. 'Forget', they told the Irish and the world of Africa and Asia, America and Europe, 'that you saw in the Irish Revolution one of the great liberating landmarks of this century, and treasured the names of MacSwiney and de Valera. It was all a mistake, a huge blunder, something we should not have done, or at least not that way.'

In short, the revisionists provided a history which, far from sustaining, energising and bonding the nation, tended to cripple, disintegrate and paralyse it. It was as if a counter-revolution, come to power in Moscow, should re-write Russian history so as to denigrate the October Revolution, all that led to it, and all that flowed from it. Just as such a history would not serve the well-being of the Russian nation, so this Irish revisionist history has not served the well-being of the Irish nation, but has served and promoted its ill-being, and the ill-being of its nation-state, which we are all experiencing and which many of our educated young people are running from in disgust.

The best defence of their history-writing which the revisionists can offer is that its moral judgments of historical Irish nationalism are correct, and that, in the exceptional circumstances of recent years, history-writing could best serve the nation and the state by undermining the moral legitimacy which the Northern rebels against British rule might draw, or seem to draw, from history. But this is an absurd argument; for, leaving aside whether the revisionists' historical moral judgments are correct, it says, in effect, that a history (theirs, namely) which undermines the moral legitimacy of the national revolution, and of the state which emerged from it, is at present the best way history can serve the national interest!

Quite apart from its intrinsic absurdity, however, such a defence raises many questions. Questions about the revisionists' common sense and knowledge. Do they really imagine that the IRA in the North sit cowering in their burrows and trenches fearful of some new blast of revisionist history from UCD? Are they not aware that the principal motivation of these Irish men and women is drawn from the national and social circumstances in which they live—and that their rebellion could have been ended long ago simply by changing those? Questions about moral legitimacy. Is it morally legitimate for Irishmen who are living in freedom to try to undermine the rebellion of Irishmen and women who are not? Was it, in the 70s, morally legitimate to try to undermine a rebellion which, in the 80s, has led to an Anglo-Irish Agreement that some revisionists, like most people, regard as a good thing? Is it morally legitimate for historians to use history-writing for dabbling, amateurishly, in contemporary politics, and that at the cost of offering their nation a meaningless and disabling past, such as English historians, hostile to Ireland, once offered it?

There, I believe, lies the nub of the matter.

12

Nationalism and Historical Scholarship in Modern Ireland*

BRENDAN BRADSHAW

The object of the present essay is to suggest that the mainstream tradition of Irish historical scholarship, as it has developed since the 1930s, has been vitiated by a faulty methodological procedure. The study falls into two parts. The first considers a similar exercise conducted in this journal by Dr Steven Ellis in 1986.[1] The intention here is to suggest that Ellis's analysis of the problem is misconceived. The second part seeks to explore the problem 'as it really is' and ultimately to prescribe a remedy. Continuity between the two parts is provided by the fact that the issue comes down to a consideration of the place of nationalism as a formative influence on modern Irish historical scholarship. In short, Ellis sees nationalism as a productive force in this connexion and identifies 'whig-nationalist' preconceptions as the basic source of confusion. The first part of this study, therefore, is concerned to refute that analysis and to show that the evidence adduced by Ellis does not sustain it. The second part argues that the modern tradition actually developed in self-conscious reaction against an earlier nationalist tradition of historical interpretation and aspired to produce 'value-free' history in accordance with the criteria of scientific research elaborated in Herbert Butterfield's *The whig interpretation of history*. It will be argued that that is precisely the problem.

I

Ellis rests his case on a study of the recent literature on the history of late medieval Ireland. He identifies three main features of the analysis found there as evidence of whig-nationalist misconceptions. One is the fundamental error, as he believes, of adopting Ireland as the substantive entity for investigation. To do so, he argues, is to assume an anachronistic perspective. Ireland had no meaningful historical existence in the late medieval period. It was merely a

---

* First published in *I.H.S.* xxvi (1988-9), pp. 329-51.
1. Steven G. Ellis, 'Nationalist historiography and the English and Gaelic worlds in the late middle ages' in *I.H.S.*, xxv, no. 97 (May 1986), pp. 1-18; see above, pp. 161-80.

geographical expression, part of a borderland which demarcated two politico-cultural zones; one English, under the jurisdiction of the English monarch; the other formed by the Celtic peoples on the Atlantic fringe. These two zones, Ellis urges, provide the historically meaningful territorial entities of the period. They, therefore, constitute the proper objects of historical investigation rather than the national territorial units which emerged in the early modern period.[2] Ellis's two other examples of whig-nationalist bias relate to the conceptual categories in which historians of late medieval Ireland conduct their analyses. One is the notion of Gaelicisation. The term was coined to denote a process which historians envisage as central to the English crown's Irish problem at this period, namely the erosion of the English colony through the advance of the Gaelic septs, on the one hand, and, on the other hand, through the capitulation of the colonists to native ways. Here, Ellis suggests, nationalistically-inclined historians have fallen into the classic trap against which Butterfield warned of finding in the evidence what they are predisposed to see, the congenial prospect of a Gaelic resurgence.[3] In reality, according to Ellis, the evidence merely signifies a process of adaptation whereby the colonists adjusted to the exigencies of border conditions while retaining their sense of Englishness and loyalty to the crown. He notes the occurrence of the same phenomenon in other border territories which, significantly, he suggests, has not attracted nationalistically-loaded terms such as Cambrianisation or Scoticisation. Ellis's third example related to the area of ideology. Here he finds evidence of whig-nationalist bias in the use of the term 'Anglo-Irish separatism' in analysing the political ethos of the colonial community at this time. The term is intended to describe an aspect of the colonial mentality which found expression in periods of crisis in Anglo-colonial relations, and which has been taken to reflect a sense of alienation from the metropolis, and an awareness of a unique colonial identity based on the special nature of the community's historical experience, its cultural distinctiveness and, above all, its separate constitutional system as a lordship under the English crown. In fact, Ellis suggests, the evidence tells overwhelmingly against the existence of a separate colonial identity at this time. The colonists themselves defined their identity as English: the emergence of the distinctive Anglo-Irish appellation lay far in the future. The defining mark of their ideological stance was loyalism—loyalty to the crown and to the English political community. And the rhetorical gestures that occasionally occur in the course of political crises have been misinterpreted. Anglo-Irish separatism, Ellis contends, like the Gaelic resurgence, had no historical reality in this period. Both are projections

2. Ellis, 'Nationalist historiography', pp. 6-10; above, pp. 167-71. A similar case is argued, though with English whig-nationalism in mind, in Hugh Kearney, *The British Isles* (Cambridge, 1989), pp. 1-9.
3. Ellis, loc. cit., pp. 2-7; above pp. 162-7.

of a nationalist frame of reference on to a period well before the thing itself had achieved any historical existence.[4]

In responding to Ellis's thesis, therefore, the first task is to examine the conceptual categories which Irish medievalists bring to bear on their analyses and to show the value of these as tools for elucidating the situation 'as it really was'. In that way, it will be possible to reject, as a *non-sequitur*, criticism of these as anachronistic products of whig-nationalist bias.

To begin with, something must be said in defence of the study of late medieval Ireland as a substantive entity. The defence need not rest on the fact, which, in any case, Ellis seems to have overlooked, that Ireland was not a mere geographical expression at this period. It also enjoyed constitutional existence as a lordship under the English crown. Be that as it may, it seems more useful to approach the question at a more general level in terms of the intellectual viability of investigating historical entities in a state of potential rather than actual existence. In this connexion, the remark has recently been made, by way of riposte to Butterfield's strictures against a present-centred historical perspective, that 'the most obvious of all historical questions is: "How did we arrive at the condition we are now in?" '[5] A glance at the practice of historians of other European countries serves both to bear out that observation and to reduce the logic of Ellis's case to absurdity. Are we to conclude automatically that the medieval historians of Spain, Italy and Germany—to name but a few—have succumbed to whig-nationalist anachronism in choosing to study the history of territories that had yet to attain political coherence in their period? The answer is, of course, that the proof of the pudding is in the eating—which takes the discussion to a consideration of the conceptual categories devised by Irish medievalists for the purpose of elucidating the evidence.

Examining the instances cited by Ellis in the context for which they were intended, it is clear that they provide well-adapted tools of analysis, not anachronistic perceptions projected from a modern nationalistic standpoint. Thus, the reality of the situation which the term Gaelicisation was coined to describe entailed more than mere functional adaptation. The state of 'degeneracy' to which it refers, and about which contemporary officialdom expressed so much concern, was alarming precisely because it entailed a transformation of colonists, in effect, into 'mere Irish', through the adoption of the specifically Gaelic features of the border culture—language, manner of dress, social

4.   Ibid., pp. 10-18; above, pp. 172-80. In this regard Ellis's argument complements that of Robin Frame for an earlier period in *English lordship in Ireland, 1318-1361* (Oxford, 1982).
5.   A. Rupert Hall, 'On whiggism' in *Journal of the History of Science*, xxi (1983), pp. 45-59 at pp. 53-4. For a more extended exploration of the methodological problem involved, see Adrian Wilson and T.G Ashplant, 'Whig history and present-centred history' in *Hist. Jn.*, xxi (1988) pp. 1-16.

conventions. The process here described is, in fact, the familiar phenomenon of anthropological studies, acculturation, i.e. the cultural assimilation of a minority social group when directly exposed to a flourishing majority culture.[6] The term Gaelicisation well describes the specific content of the process of acculturation as it occurred in late medieval Ireland. Its use, therefore, is entirely compatible with an unbiased, scientific approach to the evidence.

Similarly, 'separatism' well describes an important current that developed within the political consciousness of the colonial élite in the late medieval period. Ellis is assuredly mistaken here in insisting that the colonial community constituted no more than a regional variant within a pan-English social group comprehending the crown's entire medieval patrimony. That a clear distinction was made between the colonists and any such regional sub-group is indicated by the contemporary designation which applied to the former the qualifying epithet 'by blood', thus setting them apart from the normal English 'by birth'. Crucial to the distinction, it should be emphasised, was the awareness, not simply of territorial separation, but of constitutional separation as well. The colony constituted a lordship appended to the English crown but not to the English realm—and the colonists showed themselves highly sensitive to the distinction.[7] And all of this was reinforced in practice by effective political separation since, in virtue of its unique constitutional status, the colony possessed an institutional system parallel to the one in England and thus enjoyed a form of devolved government unknown elsewhere in the crown's dominions. Set against that background, the existence of a current of separatism within the political mentality of the colonial élite is reasonably discerned in the abundant evidence of colonial chauvinism directed against the metropolis, and the occasional protestations of institutional autonomy at times of crisis in Anglo-colonial relations. In this case also, the conceptual category serves usefully to illuminate the significance of the evidence in its contemporary context. Once more the analytical approach of modern Irish medievalists is seen to be entirely compatible with an unbiased, scientific approach to the evidence. That being so, it is clear that Ellis's conclusion of nationalist bias does not follow from the evidence he adduces.

At this point, it becomes necessary to pursue the argument from categories to personalities. That is in order to test a notion of environmental conditioning which seems to weigh heavily with Ellis. His views on this subject are

6. This phenomenon of 'degeneracy' was first fully delineated in the statute of Kilkenny (1366), the terms of which were to be reiterated in parliamentary legislation thenceforward down to the Reformation parliament (1536-7). For a discussion of Anglo-Irish degeneracy in terms of the anthropological concept of acculturation, see J.A. Watt's analysis in Art Cosgrove (ed.), *A new history of Ireland*, ii (Oxford, 1987), pp. 308-13, 386-8.
7. For a succinct discussion of the constitutional point, taking account of recent debates, see Art Cosgrove, 'The Yorkist cause, 1447-60' in ibid., pp. 557-68 at pp. 564-6.

pinpointed in a passage in which he ponders the question of how the historical writings that differ from the whig-nationalist norm are to be explained—he acknowledges the existence of a small minority of Irish historians who have resisted the blandishments of whig-nationalism. He finds the answer in 'background and training'. Moulded outside the social and intellectual matrix of the majority Irish community, a small minority of modern Irish historians were preserved from nationalist indoctrination and were thereby enabled to swim against the tide of the dominant historiographical tradition.[8] The argument is plausible. What follows is intended to show that it is confused by testing the thesis from two convergent directions, the effect of which will be to lead the discussion to a more positive line of enquiry concerning the historical circumstances which have conditioned the development of Irish historical scholarship in the modern period.

Turning first to Ellis's elect few, the roll call of these which he provides indicates what he has in mind by a background preserved from nationalist indoctrination. The small group of undoctrinaire historians are either, like himself, English by birth and education; or else they belong to the Irish minority community, are of British stock and were educated at one of the two traditionally protestant universities. The trouble with Ellis's thesis is that it contains too many anomalies. The last three occupants of the chair of medieval history at Trinity College, Dublin, can be taken as examples. The late Jocelyn Otway-Ruthven is assigned by Ellis to the list of those who were preserved from nationalist bias by background and training. Yet her distinguished predecessor, Edmund Curtis, and her no less distinguished successor, James Lydon, figure prominently among the exponents of the whig-nationalist tradition, even though conditioned by the same social and intellectual environment.[9] The confusion is highlighted from the opposite direction, so to speak, by considering an historian whose background and training serve to consign him to the majority nationalist tradition. This is Dr Art Cosgrove of University College, Dublin. Cosgrove features prominently among Ellis's exponents of whig-nationalist historiography. And it is certainly the case that his recent survey, *Late medieval Ireland, 1370-1541* (Dublin, 1981), gives prominence to the themes of a Gaelic resurgence, of Gaelicisation and of Anglo-Irish separatism.[10] All of that notwithstanding, Cosgrove does not cut a persuasive figure as a whig-nationalist historian. That is because his work fails to reflect the cast of thought associated with the epithets conjoined in Ellis's label. By definition whig-nationalism must be taken to designate an

8. Ellis, 'Nationalist historiography', p. 4, n. 14; above, p. 165.
9. Compare ibid., p. 4, n. 14 and pp. 2-3. Although Lydon was an undergraduate at University College, Galway, his postgraduate study was at the University of London.
10. For Ellis's identification of Cosgrove as a serious offender, see 'Nationalist historiography', p. 2, n. 6; above, p. 163.

historical approach characterised, on the one hand, by a teleological orientation, by a preoccupation with long-term significance, with the evolutionary thrust of the historical process, and on the other hand, by value judgements grounded upon a nationalist ideology. Cosgrove's interpretative approach fails to conform to the expected pattern in either respect. His discussion is firmly bounded by the chronological frame within which his study is set: there is never a glance towards the farther horizons. The exposition is carefully balanced. The tone is detached and non-judgemental. Most especially, his work is free of the kind of anachronistic misconceptions that Ellis associates with whig-nationalist historiography. His treatment of the themes of Gaelicisation and separatism are presented against the background of a highly complex and fluid political environment and balanced against the countervailing current of colonial cultural prejudices. Similarly, in treating the Gaelic resurgence he gives full weight to its political and ideological incoherence.[11] In short, Cosgrove's work clearly fails to conform to the category to which Ellis assigns it. The question raised by all of this, therefore, is whether Ellis himself was misled by anachronistic preconceptions in his approach to the work of the modern school of Irish historians. The cases examined here cast serious doubt on his culturally determined classifications and seem to point towards a more complete reality.

The way is now clear to test the third aspect of Ellis's thesis, his account of the historical circumstances which, he suggests, conditioned the emergence of a tradition of whig-nationalist historiography in the modern period. This will be found to clinch the indictment. Ellis sees the modern school of Irish historiography as a product of political circumstance. It emerged, he believes, in the aftermath of the foundation of the state in 1922 as a sort of intellectual adjunct. Its function, in short, was to create and propagate a version of Irish history responsive to the ideology of the triumphant nationalist monoculture. And it continued as it began; the monoculture provided the incubus for historiography which, in turn, served to perpetuate the monoculture's mythology. Here, Ellis suggests, lies the key to the historiography of the medieval period as it developed within the ambience of the nationalist monoculture; it was directed towards providing 'the Irish state with respectable historical precedents'.[12] The thesis has a persuasive simplicity—gained, as so often, by a lamentable disregard for the actual evidence. In setting the record straight

11. Cosgrove, *Late medieval Ireland. 1370-1541*, esp. ch. 5. The same measured approach characterises his historiographical study of the theme of 'Hiberniores ipsis Hibernis' in Art Cosgrove and Donal McCartney (eds.), *Studies in Irish history presented to R. Dudley Edwards* (Dublin, 1979), pp. 1-14.

12. Ellis, 'Nationalist historiography', p. 2; above, p. 162. The circularity of Ellis's argument at this crucial point should be noted: the modern school of Irish historiography is nationalist because the establishment of the nation-state in 1922 created the need for a nationalist school of Irish historiography. No consideration is given to the historical circumstances in which the modern school originated.

it is useful to lead in by referring once more to the work of Art Cosgrove. As representative of the mainstream historiographical tradition, it holds a twofold interest. On the one hand, to draw out the implications of the point made earlier, it fails to confirm Ellis's view of the aspiration which has moulded that tradition, namely, to provide the modern nation-state with an historical lineage. On the other hand, it draws attention to a moulding influence on the tradition which Ellis seems to have overlooked in his preoccupation with whig-nationalism. That is the aspiration towards a study of the past 'for its own sake' based on a scientific examination of the documentary sources. The key to Cosgrove's approach to the history of late medieval Ireland is to be found in the ideology of professionalism which has gained increasing hold on Irish historical scholarship for the past half-century and more.

The circumstances in which this development took place are crucial to an understanding of the ethos of the modern historiographical tradition. The story still awaits its historian. However, the broad outlines have become sufficiently clear in recent years mainly through the accounts provided by the late Professor Robin Dudley Edwards who was intimately involved in the episode.[13] Two major developments were set in train by the opening decades of the century. One was the establishment of chairs and lectureships in history at the universities and other third-level institutions.[14] However, the decisive development, as it now seems, was the training of the leaders of a new generation of Irish historians in England in the early 1930s, at first, mainly at the London Institute of Historical Research and later at Cambridge. The accounts mention Edwards, T.W. Moody, D.B. Quinn and, in the following decade, T. Desmond Williams.[15] Two features of this episode must be emphasised as decisively influencing the course of future developments. One is the cultural mix represented by the group: closely associated with Trinity, University College, Dublin, and Queen's, Belfast, it reflected in social terms the middle-class milieux of the three confessional communities of the island, protestant, catholic and dissenting. This goes far to explain the pervasive influence of the approach to the history of Ireland which they came to promote. On the completion of their training all four were soon ensconced in academic posts at their old

13. The main source is R.W. Dudley Edwards and Mary O'Dowd, *Sources for early modern Irish history* (Cambridge, 1985), pp. 201-13, esp. pp. 208-11. An earlier sketch was provided by Edwards in the early pages of his 'An agenda for Irish history, 1978-2018' in *I.H.S.*. xxi, no. 81 (Mar. 1978), pp. 3-19; see also the personal communication of David Quinn to Steven Ellis in Ellis, 'The economic problems of the church: why the Reformation failed in Ireland' in *Journal of Ecclesiastical History*, xli (1990). Cf. Edwards, 'T.W. Moody and the origins of *Irish Historical Studies*' in *I.H.S.*, xxvi, no. 101 (May 1988), pp. 1-2.

14. Edwards & O'Dowd, *Sources*.

15. Ibid.; James McGuire, 'T. Desmond Williams (1921-87)' in *I.H.S.*, xxvi, no. 101 (May 1988), pp. 3-7; Aidan Clarke, 'Robert Dudley Edwards (1909-88)' in ibid., xxvi, no. 102 (Nov. 1988). pp. 122-3.

colleges and with remarkable rapidity came to dominate teaching and research at the main centres of historical studies in Ireland. This feature also holds a special significance for the nature of the ideology which they came to promote as practising historians. Their shared experience of professional training—fostered a sense of a common professional identity and a common commitment to professional values transcending the diversity of cultural backgrounds. Henceforth, there would be neither protestant, catholic nor dissenter *qua* historian but a common academic profession. That attitude found its most influential expression in the launching of *Irish Historical Studies* in 1937-8 as the common forum of professional historical scholarship in Ireland.

The second feature of significance relating to the formative experience of these future founders of the modern school of Irish historical scholarship concerns its specifically technical content as a preparation for the enterprise of historical scholarship as such. In this regard it is clear from later personal reminiscences that the effect was to engender two principles as the basis on which Ireland's past was henceforth to be studied as a properly professional discipline. One is the principle of a scientific research technique: the application of the various research procedures developed in the previous half-century for the recovery, control and criticism of the historical sources. The second principle refers to the area of hermeneutics—the bedevilling problem of historical interpretation. In that connection it is highly relevant to note the mood of revisionism which established itself among a new generation of historians in England from the early 1930s onwards, for, in a form adapted to Irish circumstances, it seems to have provided the source of the hermeneutical principle to which the new breed of professionals in Ireland committed themselves. Ironically, to deliver the *coup de grâce* to Ellis's thesis, the reaction now gaining ground in England was heavily influenced by a young Cambridge historian named Butterfield, by means of a brilliant historiographical polemic published in 1931 under the title of *The whig interpretation of history*.[16] The application of Butterfied's highly influential thesis to the state of historical studies in Ireland was not far to seek. It lay in the public history moulded by the nationalist movement and promoted at a popular level ever since the days of O'Connell and Young Ireland. In self-conscious reaction, therefore, against the popular mythology generated by the agitation for national independence since the early nineteenth century, the principle of 'value-free' interpretation

16. On the impact of Butterfidd's polemic, see John Tosh, *The pursuit of history* (London, 1984), p. 122. Owen Dudley Edwards has expressed to me his conviction, based on his father's later reminiscences, that the well-known 'Cambridge connection' with Irish historical research dates from these early years. The link, prominently involving Butterfield and T. Desmond Williams, is clearly evident from the following decade (McGuire, 'Williams'). Aidan Clarke's perceptive memoir stresses the formative influence on Edwards of his research supervisor, Canon Claude Jenkins (Clarke, 'Edwards', p. 122). Clarke's account complements the one offered here.

was espoused by the new breed of Irish academic historians as the basis on which a properly professional historiography was to be developed in modern Ireland.[17] More than half a century before Ellis's clarion-call went forth to rid the interpretation of Irish history of whig-nationalist misconceptions, that task had already been taken in hand.

II

It seems fair to claim that the 1930s saw the launching of Irish historical studies on a professional basis—with all due credit to earlier anticipations and to the developments which established the necessary institutional framework. The hallmark of the new professionalism was the monograph, the specialist study based on systematic archival research and replete with a critical apparatus. Even if that form was not unknown before the 1930s, the sheer competence of the new practitioners, in contrast to the clumsiness and perfunctoriness of the old, marked the advent of a fully professional methodology.[18] Fifty years on, the gains can be counted in terms of the mining of the archival resources which has proceeded steadily ever since, in the stream of books, articles and research theses which has added massively to the stock of historical knowledge, and, *pace* Ellis, in the expurgations from the historical record of those legends, anachronisms, idealisations and sheer confusions, to which the writing of history, before the development of a scientific methodology, was acutely vulnerable. The advances, therefore, have been considerable. And it is altogether proper that in recent years the achievements of the early pioneers have been acknowledged in the form of academic honours, *Festschriften*, and the marked esteem of younger colleagues. Nevertheless, there is also a cost to be counted. And fifty years on seems not an inopportune time to do so. That is the task to which the rest of this study is devoted.

In doing so, I intend, like Ellis, but from a different standpoint, to question the basis on which the tradition established itself. In short, my intention is to challenge the interpretative principle of value-free history and to suggest that it has served to inhibit rather than to enhance the understanding of the Irish historical experience. It will soon become clear that the analysis provided here has incurred an intellectual debt in a surprising quarter—to Herbert Butterfield, whose *Whig interpretation* seems to have provided the rationale for the

17. As above, n. 13. On the pre-existing nationalist interpretation, see R.F. Foster; 'History and the Irish question' in *R. Hist. Soc. Trans.*, 5th ser., xxxiii (1983), pp. 169-92 at pp. 174-7; above, pp. 122-45 at p. 123-6.
18. In that regard the first fruits of the training of the early pioneers set exemplary standards: R. Dudley Edwards, *Church and state in Tudor Ireland: a history of the penal laws against Irish catholics, 1534-1603* (Dublin, 1935); T.W. Moody, *The Londonderry plantation: the city of London and the Irish Society, 1609-41* (Belfast, 1939); D.B. Quinn, 'Tudor rule in Ireland, 1485-1547' (unpublished Ph.D. thesis, University of London, 1933).

value-free approach to Irish history in the first place. Butterfield's subsequent historiographical reflections, which serve to modify and to clarify the original thesis, have received less attention generally and, in particular, have made no perceptible impact on the ideology of professionalism as it developed in Ireland. What follows provides, in part, a belated attempt at assimilation. The procedure, then, will be to subject the mainstream tradition of modern Irish historical scholarship to critical scrutiny in order to identify the limitations inherent in the principle of value-free history as these have revealed themselves in practice. Here invidious generalisations will have to be risked, concerning which it is hardly necessary to say that they are not intended to apply with equal force and in every instance to individual practitioners of the *genre*. They are intended rather to categorise flaws associated with the scholarship of the mainstream tradition—by and large and more or less—as it has developed over the first half-century of its existence.

By way of a preliminary skirmish, a comparatively trivial point may first be made concerning form rather than substance. That is the sheer dullness of the clinical style to which value-free historical discourse lends itself. No doubt, lack of literary verve is not a shortcoming only of practitioners of the value-free mode. Suffice it to say, on the other hand, that Butterfield was sufficiently exercised by the prospect, as an inherent hazard of the method, to address himself to the problem specifically in *The whig interpretation*, and that one of the founding fathers of the modern school in Ireland was moved to acknowledge it, as a practical consequence, in the work of his major collaborator and, by implication, in his own.[19]

Discussion of the criticisms of substance against the principle of value-free history must begin at the refined level of epistemology with the objection, now widely acknowledged, that it fails to take account of the intellectual processes by which the historical past is reconstructed and represented. These involve the exercise of personal judgement and, therefore, of subjective assessment, at every stage: in the selection of evidence on the basis of its perceived relevance; in its arrangement in accordance with a perceived pattern of coherence; in its contextualisation in the light of its perceived historical significance.[20] No doubt, the inescapability of subjective assessment does not necessarily invalidate the inspiration towards value-free interpretation. However, it serves to emphasise the difficulty of translating the principle into practice and draws attention to an epistemological trap to which the value-free approach is peculiarly vulnerable, the operation of unrecognised or, at least, unacknowledged bias.

19. Butterfield, *Whig interpretation*, ch. 5. See Edwards's comment on Moody's *Londonderry plantation:* 'it might be suggested today that dullness was the price paid at times for . . . objectivity' (Edwards & O'Dowd, *Sources*, p. 209). The same comment might be made about Edwards's *Church and state*.

20. Tosh, *The pursuit of history*, ch. 7; John Passmore, 'The objectivity of history' in Patrick Gardiner (ed.), *The philosophy of history* (Oxford, 1974), pp. 145-60.

The danger is that the espousal of the value-free principle may simply result in practice in value-based interpretation in another guise. That precisely is the burden of the case made out here against the historiography of the value-free school in Ireland. The evidence as it presents itself in the scholarship of the school will be discussed under two main categories. One concerns sins of omission, so to speak. The intention here is to demonstrate the inherent limitations of the value-free principle as a means of examining the Irish historical experience insofar as it has led to the neglect of a central aspect of that experience. The category of sins of commission, on the other hand, is concerned with the ways in which the value-free principle has proved actively destructive as a basis on which to investigate and to interpret Ireland's historical past. In both respects, the critique is fundamentally indebted to an insight of Butterfield which proved seminal for the development of his later thought on the historian's task. That concerns the differing nature of the interpretative challenge posed to the historian by the historical process in its catastrophic and in its benign aspects.

Most fully in *Christianity and history*, Butterfield drew attention to the special interpretative challenge posed by the history of communities, such as the Jews, whose past has been peculiarly marked by catastrophe. That such a challenge is posed to the historian of Ireland will hardly be disputed, seared as the record is by successive waves of conquest and colonisation, by bloody wars and uprisings, by traumatic social dislocation, by lethal racial antagonisms, and, indeed, by its own nineteenth-century version of a holocaust.[21] It is here, in responding to the interpretative challenge posed by the catastrophic dimensions of Irish history, that the sins of omission of the value-free school are to be observed. These may be pin-pointed by reference to the approach of the school to three episodes in particular which have definitively shaped the course of modern Irish history: the conquest of the early modern period; the accompanying process of dispossession and colonisation; and the calamitous nineteenth-century famine. The shortcomings of the value-free approach manifest themselves in these instances in the form of a number of interpretative strategies which have the effect of filtering out the trauma.

One such is tacit evasion. This can be observed in a particularly blatant form in the response of the value-free school to the violence of the conquest. The suppression of the Kildare rebellion in 1534-5 with which, however unintentionally, the history of the early modern conquest begins, ushers in a phase of unprecedented ruthlessness in the crown's reaction to dissent in Ireland. The tone was set by the ironically-styled 'pardon of Maynooth' in

21. Herbert Butterfield, *Christianity and history* (London, 1949), ch. 4. The reference to the mid-nineteenth-century famine is intended to refer to the scale of a disaster which was, it is clear, humanly avoidable; it is not intended to carry connotations of genocide. See Cormac Ó Gráda, *Ireland before and after the Famine* (Manchester, 1988), esp. ch. 3.

1535, by the indiscriminate massacre of civilians and garrison alike at the Fitzgerald castle of Carrickogunell later the same year, and by the execution of Silken Thomas and his five uncles at Tyburn in 1537, despite their surrender on terms.[22] This combination of atrocity *ad terrorem* and blatant disregard for the conventions of the code of honour was to recur with dismaying regularity down to the end of the sixteenth century. An instance which attracted particular notoriety in the Europe of the Counter-Reformation was the massacre of Smerwick in September 1580.[23] However, the international attention attracted by Smerwick is largely explained by the inclusion of a contingent of Spanish reinforcements among the victims. It scarcely ranks as the most shocking of the atrocities perpetrated by the Elizabethan *conquistadores*. It is surpassed for sheer villainy by the ambush and extermination of the O'More rebels inveigled to a parlay at Mullaghmast in 1577; and deeper depths of inhumanity were plumbed in the massacre of the defenceless women and children of the McDonnells by Essex and his freebooters on Rathlin Island in 1575.[24] Against that background the notorious Cromwellian massacres at Drogheda and Wexford in 1649 take their place, not as uniquely barbaric episodes, but as part of a pattern of violence which was central to the historical experience of the inhabitants of the island in the early modern period.

On the other hand, it is historiographically important to note that in this regard the Irish experience was not, in itself, a unique phenomenon. It was shared by those countries of northern and eastern Europe which were engulfed by the so-called 'wars of religion' in the aftermath of the Reformation—culminating all too appropriately in the horrors of the Thirty Years War—and, *a fortiori*, by those countries further westward engulfed by that other manifestation of early modern Europe's aggressive spirit, the westward enterprise of conquest and colonisation.[25] However, the effect of the wider

22. On this episode, see Brendan Bradshaw, *The Irish constitutional revolution of the sixteenth century* (Cambridge, 1979), pp. 172-7. For a revisionist interpretation of the government's Draconian reprisals, see Ellis, 'Henry VIII, rebellion and the rule of law' in *Hist. Jn.*, xxiv (1981), pp. 513-31.

23. A recent account which highlights this theme with particular reference to Smerwick is Richard Berleth, *The twilight lords: the epic struggle of the last feudal lords of Ireland* (London, 1979), pp. 162-76. Significantly for the case argued here Berleth is an American author and a populariser rather than a professional historian. His account owes nothing to the Irish school of value-free history.

24. A definitive account of the massacre at Mullaghmast is now provided in Vincent Carey, 'Gaelic reaction to plantation: the case of the O'More and O'Connor lordships of Laois and Offaly, 1570-1603' (unpublished M.A. thesis, St Patrick's College, Maynooth, 1986). The massacre at Rathlin Island is treated in Nicholas Canny, *The Elizabethan conquest of Ireland: a pattern established* (Hassocks, 1976), pp. 141-53.

25. The 'darkness' of this phase of European history is emphasised in Henry Kamen, *The iron century* (London, 1976), esp. pt IV. See also J.R. Hale, 'Sixteenth-century explanations of war and violence' in *Past and Present*, no. 51 (1971), pp. 3-26. On the ruthlessness and

historical perspective, as can be seen, is not somehow to diminish the significance of the Irish catastrophe but rather to increase in historiographical interest as—uniquely after all—the compounded product of religious conflict and colonial conquest. And, by the same token, the effect is also to highlight the failure of the modern school of Irish historical scholarship to respond to the interpretative challenge posed by this central aspect of the Irish historical experience in the early modern period. The failure is well exemplified in three recent publications: two survey histories by established scholars in the field and a collection of essays reporting the contributions of a new generation of early modernists. All three are designed to convey to an undergraduate readership an understanding of early modern Irish history based on the knowledge and insights provided by modern critical scholarship.[26] Revealingly, therefore, none of the three engages with the phenomenon of catastrophic violence as a central aspect of the history of the conquest: it receives occasional perfunctory reference in one and scarcely any mention at all in the others.[27] These representative texts serve to pinpoint, therefore, one form of tacit evasion practised by the modern school of Irish historical scholarship in responding to the interpretative challenge posed by the catastrophic dimension of Irish history: the simple expedient of ignoring the evidence.

The same expedient, though in a somewhat more subtle form, characterises the historiography of colonisation. In this regard, the way was led by T.W Moody whose *Londonderry plantation* in 1935 provided a model for the study of plantation down to Perceval-Maxwell's study of the plantations in Ulster in 1973.[28] In these the analysis concentrates on the social and economic history of the new settlements, thereby—wittingly or otherwise—marginalising the history of the dispossessed and the explosive socio-political implications of colonisation. More recent studies of plantation, however, have offered a new interpretative approach which enables these issues to be encompassed, at least obliquely, while at the same time filtering out the trauma. The strategy adopted in these—also favoured in recent discussions of the crown's brutal expression

violence of the conquest and colonisation of North America, see Francis Jennings, *The invasion of America* (Chapel Hill, N.C., 1975), esp. chs 9, 17, 18.

26. S.G. Ellis, *Tudor Ireland: crown, community and the conflict of cultures, 1470-1603* (London, 1985); Nicholas Canny, *From Reformation to Restoration* (Dublin, 1988); Ciaran Brady and Raymond Gillespie (eds.), *Natives and newcomers: essays on the making of Irish colonial society 1534-1641* (Dublin, 1986).

27. Ellis refers to the phenomenon more frequently than the others, but fails either to examine it or to indicate its central significance. Elsewhere Ellis has attempted to explain away the Draconian reprisals following the Kildare rebellion by the interpretative strategy of 'normalisation' (Ellis, 'Henry VIII & the rule of law'). Canny's sin is all the greater for the fact that his early monograph on the Elizabethan conquest was a pioneering examination of the phenomenon (Canny, *Elizabethan conquest*, ch. 6).

28. Moody, *Londonderry plantation*; Michael Perceval-Maxwell, *The Scottish migration to Ulster in the reign of James I* (London, 1973).

of eighteenth-century violence—is one of normalisation: the abnormality is analysed in terms of a more normal historical process. Thus, as treated in the recent monographs of Gillespie and MacCarthy-Morrogh, the colonisation of east Ulster and Munster respectively becomes a mere matter of internal British migration, part of a vaguely suggested larger pattern of continuing settlement.[29]

Finally, the trauma of the nineteenth-century famine reveals, perhaps more tellingly than any other episode of Irish history, the inability of practitioners of value-free history to cope with the catastrophic dimensions of the Irish past. Here, confronted by an episode which does not easily lend itself to treatment by 'evasion' or by 'normalisation' as in the case of conquest and colonisation— because disaster forms the substance of the event—the response of the value-free school has been, in the main, as in the case of the violence of the conquest, one of sheer neglect. Thus in the half-century after the emergence of the new school in the mid-1930s only one academic study of the Famine appeared, a collective volume, edited by Edwards and Williams in 1956.[30] And when eventually a second brief study appeared, thirty years after the first, yet another strategy was deployed to distance the author and her readers from the stark reality. This was by assuming an austerely clinical tone, as befitting academic discourse, and by resort to sociological euphemism and cliometric excursi, thus cerebralising and, thereby, desensitising the trauma.[31]

In short, confronted by the catastrophic dimension of Irish history, the discomfiture of the modern school of value-free historians is apparent. So is the source of their discomfiture: a conception of professionalism which denies the historian recourse to value-judgements and, therefore, access to the kind of moral and emotional register necessary to respond to human tragedy.[32] Thus

29. Raymond Gillespie, *Colonial Ulster: the settlement of east Ulster, 1600-1641* (Cork, 1985); Michael MacCarthy-Morrogh, *The Munster plantation: English migration to southern Ireland, 1538-1641* (Oxford, 1986). A third recent monograph, Philip Robinson, *The plantation of Ulster* (Dublin, 1984), does discuss the 'native dimension' but as a marginal issue. A more satisfactory treatment—the exception which proves the rule—is provided in Aidan Clarke, 'Pacification, plantation and the catholic question, 1603-23' in T.W. Moody et al (eds.), *A new history of Ireland*, iii (Oxford, 1976), pp. 187-231. For a penetrating critique of the 'normalising' approach, see Hiram Morgan's review of Gillespie and MacCarthy-Morrogh in *Journal of Ecclesiastical History*, xxxix (1988), pp. 128-31. For reference to 'normalising' interpretations of eighteenth-century Irish violence, together with a critique of this approach, see Thomas Bartlett, 'An end to moral economy: the Irish militia disturbances of 1793' in *Past and Present*, no. 99 (1983), pp. 41-64 at p. 42.

30. R.D. Edwards and T. Desmond Williams (eds.), *The Great Famine* (Dublin 1956).

31. The study in question is Mary E. Daly, *The Famine in Ireland* (Dundalk, 1986). These criticisms have been powerfully argued by Cormac Ó Gráda in a review of Daly's book in *I.H.S.*, xxv, no. 99 (May 1987), p. 333, and more fully in his *Ireland before and after the Famine* (Dublin, 1988), esp. ch. 3, and 'For Irishmen to forget?: recent research on the great Irish famine' (University College, Dublin, Centre for Economic Research Working Paper 88/3).

32. The same point is made in relation to the concern of professional social and political

inhibited, their treatment of the catastrophic dimension of Irish history fails on two counts. First, the effect of their reticence has been to marginalise a central dimension of the Irish historical experience and, indeed, in some cases virtually to write it out of the record. To that extent, the effect of adherence to value-free interpretation has been to limit and, thereby, to distort the perception of the past. The second failure relates to the social implications of the first. For, as Butterfield never tired of insisting, the social function of the historian resides in mediating between the actuality of the historical experience and contemporary perceptions of it.[33] That function acquires a particular urgency, it may be claimed, when, as in the case of Ireland, the communal memory retains a keen sense of the tragic dimension of the national history. In such circumstances the mediating function of the historian is manifestly *not* fulfilled by stoking the memory of ancient wrongs and the bitterness of bygone times. But neither is it constructive to conspire to 'remove the pain from Irish history' as a recent critic of the modern school has protested; to avert one's gaze from the sufferings of past generations or to seek to immunise against them by recourse to the distancing devices of academic discourse.[34] As sorry experience has shown, such stratagems serve only to establish a credibility gap between the professional historian's account of the past and the public perception of it: the bitter reality, recalled in song and story, continues to haunt the popular memory.[35] The historian's role of mediation must begin, therefore, by acknowledging the burden of the past. Having done so, ways may then be sought, as Butterfield suggests, to communicate an understanding of the tragic past that is both historically true and humanly responsive and that, without diminishing the tragedy, pays due regard to the propensity of the historical process for turning the least promising human situations to constructive purpose.[36] That way lies the path to liberation.

III

The second criticism of substance against the value-free approach requires lengthier consideration. The issue involved is complex and fraught with ideological implications. Moreover, it concerns an enterprise which was central to the preoccupations of the founding fathers of the school and which has

scientists to achieve 'critical distance' by Graham McCann, 'Vulnerable science and ordinary pain' in *Times Higher Education Supplement*, 13 May 1988, p. 13.
33. Butterfield, *Christianity & history*.
34. Bartlett, 'An end to moral economy'.
35. The failure of the 'demythologised' version of Irish history to make a perceptible impact at the popular level has been a source of pessimistic comment in revisionist writings. A recent instance is Foster, 'History & the Irish question', pp. 190-92.
36. Butterfield, *Christianity & history*. A similar point is made concerning the ameliorating role of the social and political scientist in McCann, 'Vulnerable science'.

come to occupy a younger generation of professional historians even more fully. This is the need to revise the version of Irish history which the triumph of nationalism in the opening decades of the twentieth century served to entrench as a form of public history.[37] The revisionist enterprise, as can now be seen, developed in two stages. A conscious reaction against the nationalist-ically-biased historical interpretation characterised the objective school from the beginning. However, the strategy in the early decades, by and large, seems to have been one of tacit demolition by means of a Rankean 'history as it actually was' style of historical narrative. The late 1960s and early 1970s saw the increasing dominance of a more overtly iconoclastic approach by a new generation, initially reflecting disillusionment with the nationalist dream in the aftermath of the celebrations of 1966, and later reacting against the contribu-tion, as they believed, of the nationalist mythology to the recrudescence of radical militant nationalism in Northern Ireland.[38] The subject of revisionism, therefore, returns the discussion to where it left off at the end of Part I.[39]

Before embarking on a critique of this revisionist enterprise, two points must be made by way of introduction. One concerns the standpoint from which the criticism is offered. In that connexion it must be emphasised that the purpose is not to question the validity of subjecting the received version of Irish history to critical scrutiny, much less to seek to rehabilitate it, myths and all. The intention is rather to question, on the basis of the historiographical evidence, the utility of the value-free principle as a means of approaching the Irish historical experience. Having noted the inherent limitations of the method earlier, what follows is intended to bring its actively destructive propensities to light. That leads to the second introductory point which concerns the hazards, discussed at the outset, in reducing the epistemological principle of value-free interpretation to practice.[40] Even at the theoretical level, the notion of a revisionist enterprise conducted in the name of 'value-freeness' suggests a contradiction in terms. And in practice in the Irish case, application of the principle in this reactive way has reduced it to a mere matter of intellectual sleight of hand The value-free interpretation turns out to be a negatively biased interpretation which, as the opposite of positive bias, lays claim to impartial-

37. The revisionist mood of the early pioneers is vividly recalled in Edwards & O'Dowd, *Sources*, pp. 201-13, esp pp. 208-9.
38. The trend was established, as can now be seen by a crudely debunking piece on the leaders of the rebellion of 1916, written by a mild-mannered Jesuit professor of Old Irish and published posthumously, Francis Shaw, 'The canon of Irish history: a challenge' in *Studies*, lxi (1972), pp. 113-52. Continuity between the modern revisionist enterprise and the 'objective' historiography of the school of the 1930s is claimed on behalf of the revisionists by Ronan Fanning in 'The meaning of revisionism' in *The Irish Review*, no. 4 (spring 1988), pp. 15-19 at pp. 18-19.
39. Above, pp. 335-6.
40. Above. pp. 337-8.

ity.[41] There lies the key to the value-free principle's destructive propensities. For it is clear that in practice, negative bias has proved no more immune than positive bias to interpretative distortion. What have changed are the forms in which distortion has manifested itself. In what follows, therefore, the cost of the revisionist enterprise is counted in terms of three forms of interpretative distortion.

One form may be described as invincible scepticism. Here the most sceptical possible reading of the evidence is preferred as the soundest canon of historical interpretation. Accordingly, a corrosive cynicism is brought to bear in order to minimise or to trivialise the significance of transcendent aspirations and dynamisms. An obvious instance of this revisionist approach is provided by their iconoclastic assault upon the so called apostolic succession of national heroes. The procedure in this instance, in effect, has been to place these figures in the dock and to conduct the case for the prosecution—in the name, of course, of professional objectivity. Invariably, they emerge discredited as the torchbearers of the national cause across the centuries, representing instead a motley collection of local warlords, defenders of narrow class-interest, or, when, at last, the play of national sentiment must be acknowledged in such people as Tone, Davis, Pearse and Connolly—as politically inept and intellectually confused ideologues.[42] Some sense of the distortion this inquisitorial approach involves may be gained by contrast in certain specific instances where such figures have been subjected to scrutiny by scholars who do not share the revisionists' predispositions. In the case of the representative sample that comes to mind—Brian Boru, Hugh O'Neill, Daniel O'Connell, Patrick Pearse—the heroes have emerged duly demythologised on the basis of a fully professional approach to the evidence while, nevertheless, retaining credibility as figures of heroic stature whose careers possess a unique significance for the course of Irish history.[43] These instances highlight the logical fallacy in applying

41. Desmond Fennell observes in 'Against revisionism', his riposte to Fanning, 'The meaning of revisionism', that revisionism is 'primarily a new moral interpretation' (*The Irish Review*, no. 4 (spring 1988), pp. 20-26 at p. 22; above, p. 185).

42. Recent examples of revisionist iconoclasm are Tom Dunne, *Theobald Wolfe Tone: colonial outsider* (Cork, 1982); idem, 'Haunted by history Irish romantic writing, 1800-50' in Roy Porter and Mikulás Teich (eds.), *Romanticism in national context* (Cambridge, 1988), pp. 68-91, at (for Davis), pp. 76-9; Ruth Dudley Edwards, *Patrick Pearse: the triumph of failure* (London, 1977). They are all the more insidious for the elegance of the treatment. The latest iconoclastic study of Connolly is Austen Morgan, *James Connolly: a political biography* (Manchester, 1989), p. pp. 196-203. A survey of recent revisionist studies of Connolly is a view article by Graham Walker, himself a revisionist, in *London Review of Books*, xi, no. 19 (12 Oct. 1989), pp. 22-3 A recent revisionist study of post-Famine revolutionary nationalism is Tom Garvin, *Nationalist revolutionaries in Ireland, 1858-1928* (Oxford, 1987).

43. On Brian Boru, see the suggestive treatment in Donnchadh Ó Corráin, *Ireland before the Normans* (Dublin, 1972), pp. 120-31. For Hugh O'Neill, I rely on Hiram Morgan's unpublished Ph.D. thesis, 'The outbreak of the Nine Years War: Ulster in Irish politics,

invincible scepticism as an antidote to the uncritical admiration of the nationalists: the effect is to invert, not to remedy, the distortion.

The second form in which revisionist distortion manifests itself also involves a process of inversion. This occurs by way of antidote to the nationalists' projection of their ideology into the past, supposing it to have provided the fundamental dynamism of Irish history down the centuries. In reaction to this misconception the revisionists have inverted the anachronism. Their response has been to seek to extrude national consciousness as a dimension of the Irish historical experience from all but the modern period. An extreme example of 'extrusion by stealth' for the medieval period is Otway-Ruthven's massive *History of medieval Ireland*. Here even the famous declaration of legislative independence in the parliament of 1460 is passed over with a dismissive footnote.[44] For the early modern period, appeals to bardic poetry as evidence of a Gaelic national consciousness have been briskly rebuffed by Bernadette Cunningham; and similarly Tom Dunne has sought to demonstrate the archaism of the Gaelic mentality in this period and, therefore, its inability to develop national consciousness.[45] For a later period still, Roy Foster has recently given us a good example of the revisionist polemic against 'the simplifying perspective of nationalist historiography'.[46] In extruding national consciousness, these revisionists echo the conventional orthodoxies of the historians and political scientists of the modern period who envisage European nationalism as the product of an historic conjuncture at the onset of modernity between the forces of Romanticism, populism and proto-industrialisation.[47]

1583-96' (University of Cambridge, 1987) On O'Connell, Oliver MacDonagh, *The hereditary bondsman: Daniel O'Connell. 1775-1829* (London, 1988), provides the first volume of a classic in the making. Pearse emerges as a credible moderniser and a practical visionary in Joseph Lee, *The modernisation of Irish society, 1848-1918* (Dublin, 1973), pp. 141-8. In the same mould is Owen Dudley Edwards's interpretative essay on de Valera, the last of the revisionists' scapegoats, *Eamon de Valera* (Cardiff, 1988).

44. A.J. Otway-Ruthven, *A history of medieval Ireland* (London, 1968), p. 387, n. 19.

45. Bernadette Cunningham, 'Native culture and political change in Ireland, 1580-1640' in Brady & Gillespie (eds.), *Natives & newcomers*, pp. 148-70; T.J. Dunne, 'The Gaelic response to conquest and colonisation: the evidence of the poetry' in *Studia Hibernica*, xx (1980), pp. 7-30. For a recent scholarly monograph along similar lines, see Joseph Th. Leerssen, *Mere Irish and fiór-Ghael: studies in the idea of Irish nationality* (Amsterdam and Philadephia, 1986). For the complementary interpretation of the colonial mentality of the Old English, see Nicholas Canny, *The formation of the Old English élite in Ireland* (Dublin, 1975), and Aidan Clarke, 'Colonial identity in early seventeenth-century Ireland' in T.W. Moody (ed.), *Nationality and the pursuit of national independence* (Historical Studies, xi, Belfast, 1978), pp. 1-35.

46. R.F. Foster, 'Introduction' in C.H.E. Philpin (ed.), *Nationalism and popular protest in Ireland* (Oxford, 1988), pp. 1-15.

47. For a representative example of studies in this vein, see Hans Kohn, *The idea of nationalism* (New York, 1945); Hugh Seton-Watson, *Nationalism old and new* (Sydney, 1965); John Plamenatz, 'Two types of nationalism' in Eugene Kamenka (ed.), *Nationalism: the nature*

On the other hand, the assumptions of the modern historian, and the *a priori* theorising of the political scientists, do not accord with the historical evidence which indicates that national consciousness recurred as a feature of European political history over a much longer period—drawing upon the rich inspirational resources of classical Roman literature and the messianic tradition of Israel.[48] Similarly, national consciousness can be discerned as a recurring cultural phenomenon in Ireland for, perhaps, a millennium before the onset of modernity. It is reflected, for instance, in the early medieval period, in the exile theme so characteristic of early Christian spirituality and in the historical outlook reflected in the recessions of the Gaelic origin-legends. Later on, it surfaces in the tropes of classical bardic poetry and in the burgeoning legend of the 'island of saints and scholars'. Finally, it surfaces in a recognisably ideological form, in the political commentary, antiquarian writing and creative literature which emerged within the two historic communities of the island in response to the cataclysm which began to engulf them from the mid-sixteenth century onwards.[49] Influenced, it seems, by the models of the political scientists, the revisionists have failed to allow such evidence any explanatory power in accounting for the course of Irish political history before the modern period. Tacitly ignoring the positive evidence they focus attention instead on the countervailing pull of dynastic particularism and on the trans-national thrust of Gaelic and Anglo-Irish cultural influences.[50] One way or another, it is clear that the revisionists have responded to the anachronistic projection of a nationalist ideology into the immemorial past by extruding the play of national

and evolution of an idea (Canberra. 1974); Ernest Gellner, *Nations and nationalism* (Oxford, 1984).

48. For an elaboration of this approach, see Johann Huizinga, 'Patriotism and nationalism in European history' in idem, *Men and ideas* (London, 1960), pp. 97-155. The evidence for a heightening of awareness of nationality in early modern Europe is overwhelming, however the phenomenon may then be interpreted. On this, see *inter alia* Orest Ranum, *National consciousness, history and political nature in early modern Europe* (Baltimore and London, 1975).

49. For support for this thesis, see Donnchadh Ó Corráin, 'Nationality and kingship in pre-Norman Ireland' in Moody (ed.), *Nationality & the pursuit of national independence*, pp. 1-36; Jarnes Lydon, *Ireland in the later middle ages* (Dublin, 1973), ch. 5; J.A. Watt, 'Gaelic polity and cultural identity in Art Cosgrove (ed.), *A new history of Ireland*, ii (Oxford, 1987), ch. 12; Brendan Bradshaw, *The Irish constitutional revolution of the sixteenth century* (Cambridge, 1979), ch. 9; idem, 'Native reaction to the westward enterprise: a case study in Gaelic ideology' in K.R. Andrews, Nicholas Canny and P.E.H. Hair (eds.), *The westward enterprise: English activities in Ireland, the Atlantic and America, 1480-1650* (Liverpool, 1978), pp. 65-80; Breandán Ó Buachalla, '*Annála ríoghachta Éireann* is *Forus Feasa ar Éirinn*: and comhthéacs comhaimseartha' in *Studia Hibernica*, xxii-xxiii (1982-3), pp. 59-105, esp. pp. 74-82; idem, 'Na Stíobhartaigh agus an t-aos léinn: Cing Seamas' in *R.I.A. Proc.*, lxxxiii (1983), sect. C, pp. 81-134, esp pp. 104-6; idem, foreword to 1987 reprint of Geoffrey Keating's, *Foras feasa ar Éirinn* (Irish Texts Society, 1988).

50. Above, p. 343 and nn 45, 46, 47.

consciousness from all but the modern period. In doing so, they have simply inverted the anachronism.

The final form of revisionist distortion subsumes the other two and constitutes the most distinctive aspect of the revisionist enterprise. This arises by way of reaction against the controlling conception of nationalist historiography, the notion of a 'national past', of Irish history as the story of an immemorial Irish nation, unfolding holistically through the centuries, from the settlement of the aboriginal Celts to the emergence of the national polity of modern times. This holistic conception the revisionists dismiss as a farrago of misconceptions, anachronisms and downright fabrications. By way of antidote, they appeal to the testimony of the documentary evidence to show the complexity, ambiguity and—above all—discontinuity that characterises the island's historical odyssey and the hybrid character of the modern national community which claims continuity with the aboriginal Celtic settlement by lineal descent.[51] Shorn of the idealisations and anachronisms of nationalist historiography, the revisionists contend, the holistic conception of Irish history stands exposed as a myth designed to validate the aspirations of modern nationalism and to provide an origin-legend for the twentieth-century nation-state. Viewed as it really was, they urge, the course of Irish history fragments into a series of more or less discrete epochs, each presenting a unique social, cultural and political configuration. Thus the island's history serves not to link the national community of modern times with the 'native race' of earlier epochs, however constituted. It serves rather to set them apart. In the words of a current historiographical catch-phrase which might well serve as the revisionists' motto, Irish history is not the past of the modern Irish nation: 'the past is a foreign country'.

For a perspective on this formidable indictment of the central motif of nationalist historiography, it is necessary to return at some length to Herbert Butterfield's *Whig interpretation*. More precisely, it is necessary to consider the caveat which he himself entered against that work in *The Englishman and his history* thirteen years later. Originally, in 1931, Butterfield inveighed against whig historians for interpreting the past in accordance with their own idealised preconceptions instead of attending to the reality in all its complexity as revealed in the documentary evidence.[52] In the later work, however, he proceeded to vindicate the whig interpretation and to warn against 'those who, perhaps, in the misguided austerity of youth wish to drive out that whig interpretation'.[53] These attitudes seem incompatible and, indeed, *The Englishman and his history* has been taken to represent a capitulation to the patriotic

51. For a recent statement of the case and a guide to the supporting literature, see Foster, 'History & the Irish question', above, pp. 122–45.
52. Butterfield, *Whig interpretation*, ch. 3.
53. Idem, *The Englishmen and his history* (Cambridge, 1944), p. 3.

mood generated by the crisis of the war period.[54] The truth is rather more subtle. Butterfield's later caveat hinges on a distinction between two forms in which, as he perceived, the whig interpretation manifested itself, a distinction which the public response to the crisis of 1939-40 served to bring to his attention. One was as a form of academic history designed, therefore, to provide a rational understanding of the past based on a scientific examination of the documentary evidence. As such, the whig interpretation fell short and it was the achievement of the young Butterfield in 1931 to diagnose and demonstrate the fatal flaw, a faulty hermeneutical procedure which allowed the interpretation of the evidence to be controlled by a set of *a priori* assumptions.[55] However, the public response to the crisis of the war years drew Butterfield's attention to the whig interpretation under quite a different aspect, as a form of public history in which the historical consciousness of the community was expressed and transmitted. Here lies the key to Butterfield's apparent *volte face*. For in that form, as he realised, the whig interpretation was not the product of a school of historiography, as such, but of the historical process itself. It had been moulded over the centuries in the public domain in consequence of the peculiarly English habit—as he believed—of appealing to the past to vindicate contemporary aspirations and values.[56] Accordingly it fell to be assessed in those terms: as the form in which the community's understanding of its past was moulded, expressed and transmitted, and, thus, as the perception of its historical experience which conditioned the community's response to current public issues. Assessed from that perspective, the whig interpretation could be seen to have exercised a beneficent influence on the public culture of England in two respects—as the response to the wartime crisis had served to highlight. One was to enshrine liberty at the forefront of the community's historical consciousness by presenting it as the central public preoccupation of the English down the centuries.[57] The other was to inculcate a stabilising sense of historical continuity by depicting English history in teleological terms as the unfolding story of 'the making of the constitution': as Butterfield pointed out, developing an insight of Macaulay, the English political system had been transformed under the guise of preserving the ancient constitution whereas in France the Revolution constituted a disturbing hiatus.[58] Contemplating this beneficent legacy, Butterfield was moved to argue in *The Englishman and his history* that the whig interpretation as a product of the historical process called rather for celebration than censure.[59]

54. On all of this, see Maurice Cowling, *Religion and public culture in England*, i (Cambridge, 1981), pp. 220-33.
55. Butterfield, *The whit interpretation*, ch. 2.
56. Idem, *The Englishmen & his history*, pp. 4-11.
57. Ibid., pp. 3-4.
58. Ibid, pp. 4-11.
59. Ibid., p. 4.

Before the insight of *The Englishman and his history* is brought to bear in the Irish context, one further aspect of the book requires a brief mention. Written to draw attention to the positive aspect of whig history—its 'wrongness' notwithstanding—it serves, by comparison, to illuminate the inadequacy of Butterfield's earlier negative approach to the subject—'in the austerity of his youth', as he implicitly admitted. In doing so, it also serves to highlight an occupational hazard to which the professional historian is peculiarly vulnerable in responding to the phenomenon of public history. The frame of mind which informs Butterfield's original study—and which provides the substance of a dire warning in the opening chapter of *The Englishman and his history*—constitutes a kind of academic puritanism. That epithet reflects the single-minded zeal for history as an academic discipline that shines through the pages of *The whig interpretation*. On the other hand, it reflects the corresponding vice, the puritan's characteristic narrow-mindedness: a narrowing of the boundaries both of the intellectual imagination and of moral tolerance that results from an élitist obsession. The unbending strictures of *The whig interpretation* against the tradition of public history in England reveal the Achilles heel of the young value-free historian and serve to exemplify the logical fallacy to which attention was drawn at the outset whereby negative bias, applied by the revisionist as an antidote to positive bias, is construed to be value-free.

In a nutshell, the issue raised by Butterfield's exposition of the positive values of English public history is whether the received version of Irish history may not, after all, constitute a beneficent legacy—its wrongness notwithstanding—which the revisionists with the zeal of academic puritans are seeking to drive out. No doubt to pose the question is to call attention to the need for a full-length study of the phenomenon of public history in Ireland in its relation to the public culture of the community—under the title, perhaps, of *The Irishman and his history*! Meanwhile, the obvious resonances of Butterfield's perceptive treatment may simply be pointed out.

A correspondence exists between the traditions of public history in the two countries and between their special characters as expressions of an historical consciousness moulded over the centuries by the invocation of history to vindicate contemporary aspirations and values.[60] When that consciousness is analysed in the light of Butterfield's appraisal, its characteristic features seem less obviously deserving of the disdainful dismissal they have received from the revisionists. If, in the first instance, as Butterfield points out, the whig interpretation has taught succeeding generations in England to sing of liberty, so, it can equally well be claimed, has the nationalist tradition of historical interpretation in Ireland. No doubt the song strikes differently on the ear,

60. Above, n. 38.

expressing, as it does, a consciousness and an aspiration moulded by the Irish historical experience. The song is, indeed, native to the place, but, for all that, no less worth the singing. To disparage it in the manner of the revisionists is to concede this central strand of the Irish political tradition, its concern with liberty, to the 'men of violence' as their peculiar heritage—which is both a betrayal of the historical truth and an abdication of social responsibility.[61]

Of, perhaps, even greater importance, if possible, the holistic interpretation of Irish history assumes a new and highly positive significance in the light of Butterfield's reappraisal of the teleological thrust of the whig interpretation. It is that interpretative perception which, as Butterfield convincingly argues, has moulded the English sense of historical continuity, 'playing providence upon the tears and rents in the fabric' so as to prevent 'the uprooting of things which have been organic to the development of the country'. The development, therefore, of a perception of Irish history as the 'nation's past' is an achievement—not least in terms of creative ingenuity—which calls for positive reappraisal in the light of Butterfield's analysis. The element of 'creative ingenuity' provides, in fact, its own special resonance, which helps to set a much derided feature of the nationalist interpretation in a new light. As Butterfield pointed out, the whig concern with history was not that of hidebound traditionalism, totally in thrall to convention and custom. It was 'present-centred', seeking 'to make capital out of the past and to put the history of earlier centuries to practical use'. 'Purposeful unhistoricity' was central to such a strategy, by which is meant the development of idealisation and anachronism in order to accommodate the past to the needs of the present.[62] And that strategy explains in turn the remarkable capacity of English public culture through the centuries to combine a deep sense of tradition with a propensity for radical innovation. Applied to Ireland, Butterfield's notion of 'purposeful unhistoricity' holds out the prospect of a more positive approach to the much maligned mythical quality of the nationalist interpretation. Hitherto the myths have been exposed with scholarly fastidiousness: their positive, dynamic thrust has remained largely ignored.[63] A case very much to

61. On the constitutional political tradition and the theme of liberty, see my 'The beginnings of modern Ireland' in Brian Farrell (ed.), *The Irish parliamentary tradition* (Dublin, 1973), pp. 68-87, and my Irish constitutional revolution, esp. pp. 21-9, 258-88.
62. For Butterfield's discussion of the 'purposeful unhistoricity' of the whig interpretation, see *The Englishman & his history*, pp. 6-8. The book is mainly devoted to demonstrating the strategy in action in the moulding of English historical consciousness.
63. No small part of the problem here is the impoverished and confused notion of myth which has been adopted. See, e.g., T.W. Moody, 'Irish history and Irish mythology' in *Hermathena*, cxxiv (1978), pp. 7-24. For a brilliant example of an analysis which explores the positive dynamic of the mythology, see Joseph Lee, *The modernisation of Irish society, 1848-1918* (Dublin, 1973), pp. 137-48. See also Gearóid Ó Tuathaigh, *Ireland before the Famine, 1798-1848* (Dublin, 1972), a work which broke new ground in its exploitation of

the point is the myth of the 'native race' which has earned the particular obloquy of the revisionists as purveying a racist and thereby an exclusivist concept of Irishness. Historically considered, in fact, its function has been precisely the opposite: by the skilful deployment of anachronism and idealisation the Gaelic origin-legend has been reworked and developed in order to graft on successive waves of new settlers to the native stock and to enable a progressively more heterogeneous national community to appropriate the rich heritage of the aboriginal Celtic civilisation. Thus, Hyde, Griffith and Pearse, in seeking to mould a notion of Irishness which would establish continuity between themselves—*arrivistes* to a man, as their names indicate—and the Gaelic past, stood in a tradition stretching back to Geoffrey Keating and, indeed, beyond him to the Gaelic recensionists of the tenth century with whom the myth originated.[64] The notorious 'backward look' of the Irish turns out on inspection, therefore, to be firmly rooted in the present.

All in all, the public history moulded within the ambience of the nationalist movement can be claimed to have played the part in Ireland which Butterfield came to claim for the whig interpretation in England, that 'of building up the centuries and creating the [Ireland] that we know'. In that light it is hardly cause for surprise—though surprise is indignantly professed—that this received version continues to exercise a tenacious hold upon the historical consciousness of the national community, despite the determined re-education campaign conducted by the revisionists.[65] Invited to adopt a perspective on Irish history which would depopulate it of heroic figures, struggling in the cause of national liberation; a perspective which would depopulate it of an immemorial native race, the cumulative record of whose achievements and sufferings constitutes such a rich treasury of culture and human experience; a perspective, indeed, from which the modern Irish community would seem as aliens in their own land—for 'the past is a foreign country':[66] in face of such an invitation the Irish have clung tenaciously to their nationalist heritage. Who could blame them?

The contention of this study is that the aspiration towards the development of a value-free history has flawed the achievement of the professional school of Irish historians since its establishment in the early 1930s. That principle has shown itself to be inappropriate as a means of approaching the Irish

literary sources in English and in Irish to illuminate the history of *mentalité*. For examples of the revisionists' puritanical response to 'purposeful unhistoricity' of this kind, see Foster, 'History & the Irish question', pp. 184-91; Fanning, 'The meaning of revisionism', pp. 16-19.

64. The studies cited above, n. 47, deal with various phases of the creation of an integral origin-legend.

65. Foster, 'History & the Irish question'.

66. A survey history which exemplifies all the virtues and all the vices of the modern professional school is R.F. Foster, *Modern Ireland, 1600-1972* (London, 1988).

historical experience in two major respects. On the one hand, the inherent limitations of the principle have been revealed in the inhibitions displayed by its practitioners in face of the catastrophic dimension of Irish history. On the other hand, its vulnerability to tacit bias has been highlighted by the negative revisionism practised in its name in exploring the Irish nationalist tradition. Perhaps the most disturbing aspect of the entire enterprise is the credibility gap which is now acknowledged by all sides to exist between the new professional history and the general public. All of these considerations lead to the conclusion which has been implicit in the discussion from the outset. The value-free principle must be abandoned as a basis on which to develop a professional historiography in Ireland. What is envisaged as an alternative, it must hastily be added, is not a capitulation to the uncritical public history moulded within the nationalist ambience. That is not the necessary alternative. In fact, the alternative lies ready to hand in the practice of a minority group within the professional school of Irish historians whose work demonstrates the feasibility of combining a fully critical methodology in the analysis of the evidence with a more sensitive response to its content.[67] The key to their interpretative procedure is summed up in two words. The first is empathy—a notion for long familiar in the social sciences to where it migrated, ironically, from the humanities.[68] The second is imagination—a quality much suspected by rational scientists of earlier generations but now generally acknowledged as equally crucial to rational investigation as to the creativity of the artist.[69] As the fruits have already shown, an imaginative and empathetic approach holds out the prospect of a professional Irish historiography which concedes nothing in the way of critical standards of scholarship, while at the same time responding sensitively to the totality of the Irish historical experience. The time has come, therefore, to resume contact with an emerging tradition of Irish historical scholarship which was thrust aside by the impatient young men of

67. To the works cited above, nn 43 and 49, might be added Ó Gráda, as above, n. 31, Bartlett, 'An end to moral economy', as above, n. 29, Ó Tuathaigh, *Ireland before the Famine*, and Lee, *Modernisation of Irish society*.
68. The notion has a long history in literature and philosophy; see Karl F. Morrison, '*I am you': the hermeneutics of empathy in western literature, theology and art* (Princeton, 1988). It has increasingly come under attention as an analytical strategy in the social sciences and in psychology over recent decades; see Robert L. Katz, *Empathy, its nature and uses* (London, 1963), and Nancy Eisenberg and Janet Strayer (eds.), *Empathy and its development* (Cambridge, 1987).
69. On imagination and historical understanding, see R.G Collingwood, 'The historical imagination' in idem, *The idea of history* (Oxford, 1946), pp. 231-49. For a more recent statement in the same tradition, see Wolfgang Van Leyden, 'Categories of historical understanding' in *History and Theory*, xxiii (1984), pp. 53-77, esp. pp. 57-61. Cf. Hugh Trevor-Roper, *History and imagination* (Oxford, 1980), passim.

the 1930s, and to recover the vision of its two great luminaries, Eoin MacNeill and Edmund Curtis.[70]

It remains to be emphasised, by way of epilogue, that the case made out here is not that historians should concern themselves with the Irish nationalist community to the exclusion of the protestant tradition of the north of Ireland. It is not a plea for green history. On the contrary, the history of the northern community seems as much in need of imaginative and empathetic elucidation as that of its southern neighbours. It too is marked by the experience of catastrophe and heroic endurance—to which the value-free school has responded with no greater comprehension than in exploring the nationalist tradition. The plea, therefore, is for an account of Irish history capable of comprehending sympathetically the historical experience of both communities, and, by comprehending them, of mediating between the island's past and its present.[71]

70. It is reassuring to find the scholarly contributions of MacNeill and Curtis linked in a handsome acknowledgement by an historian of impeccably non-nationalist 'background and training', J.A. Watt, 'Approaches to the history of fourteenth-century Ireland' in Art Cosgrove (ed.), *A new history of Ireland*, ii (1987), pp. 303-13 at pp. 303-6.
71. I wish to thank the following for their help in enabling me to develop the ideas expressed in this study: Vincent Carey, Owen Dudley Edwards, Sheridan Gilley, Willy Maley, Hiram Morgan, Jim Smyth. Needless to say, the views expressed here are entirely my own responsibility. I also wish to thank the organisers of the Conference of Irish Historians in Britain for 1988, Seán Hughes, president of the Trinity College (Cambridge) History Society for 1987-8, and John McCafferty, auditor of the History Society, University College, Dublin, for 1988-9, for the opportunity to present earlier versions of the paper. Lastly, I wish to thank Elizabeth Murray of the History Faculty, Cambridge, for her forbearance and efficiency in typing the text.

13

Revisionist Milestone[*]

KEVIN O'NEILL

Normally I avoid reading reviews of books which I have been asked to review, or which I hope to be asked to review. However presumptuous, I feel that each author 'deserves' an independent, and hopefully, original response to the fruit of his or her labours. As a result, I am often quite behind in my reading of reviews, and correspondingly slow to know how others are responding to the works which most interest me. While I have maintained my boycott of other reviews for Foster's *Modern Ireland: 1600-1792*, I have been manifestly unable to isolate myself from the warm reception which this work is receiving. 'Everyone' is talking about Foster's work and clearly Allen Lane has a smash hit on its lists. In fact, before its appearance here, it had already established itself as a major piece of historical writing. For example (even though I haven't read the review), let me quote from Owen Dudley Edward's comment in the *Irish Times* (obligingly supplied by Viking with its publications releases): 'I devoured most of it in a day, one of the happiest days of my life. . . . With this book Dr Foster becomes one of Ireland's greatest historians.' Heady stuff, and from someone who has the ability to offer such judgments.

There is no question that Foster has produced a major piece of historical writing which represents the consolidation of the current phase of revisionist historiography. He has written with clarity, precision and painstaking detail of nearly five centuries of Irish history. And although the book is a survey it provides a great deal of original insight and interpretation. Indeed, it is difficult to disagree with Edwards; this work will surely become a 'classic', and Foster must, by its merits, be considered one of the major historians of Ireland. Or to put it in more mundane terms (PhD candidates take note), all serious students of Irish history now have a 600-plus page monster to master. Fortunately, the book is so well organized, reasoned, and written that few readers will find themselves either frustrated or unchallenged. Some, however, may be disappointed.

The driving force behind Foster's work is the need to escape from the 'Anglocentric' forms of Irish historical and political debate which supposedly

[*] First published in *Irish Literary Supplement* (Fall, 1989), pp. 1, 39.

dominated the field until fairly recently. (Though given the honour roll of Irish historians from Moody and Martin through Louis Cullen, Joseph Lee and Ronan Fanning into the current generation of young historians, it is rather hard to identify any 'recent' unrevised history.) Foster makes admirable use of the avalanche of monographs produced by revisionist historians over the last 25 years, and produces a broad synthesis intended to move us away from the irredentist preoccupation with Albion's perfidy. There is no question that Foster's succeeds in providing an intelligent and coherent 'revized' synthesis of modern Irish historical experience. However, it is not nearly so clear that he has escaped from an Anglocentric mentality. He is certainly not Anglophobic; and only an Anglophobe would call him an Anglophile. Yet Anglo-Irish issues and conflicts dominate his vision to such an extent that the very purpose of the work is undermined. He has, in fact, produced an 'alternative' Anglocentric view of Irish history which is preoccupied with redefining the nature of the relationship between the two islands, and the effects which these relationships had upon the various groups into which Irish people were divided by history or historians.

The relationships he describes are more complex than simple, more assimilationist than confrontational, more symbiotic than predatory; but still these Anglo-Irish relationships dominate. And perhaps more oddly, the bulk of his discussion, especially for the critical years of the 17th century, is approached through the English perspective. (He even chooses to use the old calendar preferred by the English rather than the modern Gregorian calendar employed by the Irish.) His analysis of how the 17th-century conquerors, bureaucrats and settlers viewed the Irish is detailed and insightful, but hardly an avenue to a less Anglocentric view of Irish history. Nor does his explanation that English attitudes and actions towards Irish 'savages' were part of 'contemporary anthropological ideas of savagery' help us to penetrate the mentality of British rule in Ireland: such 'anthropological' ideas were created precisely to justify the Elizabethan élite's most savage acts against the 'savages' of the world in North America, the Caribbean, Africa, and of course Ireland. Rather than helping us to understand British action in Ireland the notion of an anthropology distinct from racism and cant obscures the pettiness of the violence which dominated 17th-century British policy in Ireland. It is such rationalization which permits Foster to characterize Mountjoy as a 'humane man' while referring to his plan to make Ireland a 'razed table'. The ability to reconcile such ideas without comment reveals more about Foster's mentality than that of Mountjoy or his compatriots.

This new synthesis is unsatisfactory for other reasons. It fails to provide an adequate sense of causality (as distinct from guilt) for the dramatic events of this era, and fails to provide a meaningful comparison with other societies which might provide the alternative perspectives that are prerequisites to a truly non-Anglocentric discussion of Irish history. Of course, it may be that, given the nature of Anglo-Irish relations since 1600, a non-Anglocentric interpretation would be a rather irrelevant historical exercise. (For an indication of where such a synthesis might lead, Raymond Crotty's *Ireland in Crisis* offers intriguing possibilities.)

This narrow British Isles focus leads to a number of lacunae. The omission most likely to disturb historians less familiar with Ireland is the nearly complete lack of interest in 'colonialism' and 'imperialism' as categories of inquiry. At several points Foster rather arrogantly dismisses attempts by others to draw Ireland into a sort of comparative colonial net as irrelevant. For example, in arguing that the intent of the Penal Laws was to restrict Catholic landowning and Catholic political power 'rather than to impose apartheid' he draws a distinction that many, including South Africans, would have some difficulty in understanding. While his insistence on Ireland's 'uniqueness' may be valid, it is hardly a unique claim, nor does it excuse him from the obligation to look beyond surface realities of parliamentary politics, and social and economic structures. Ireland, however defined, was part of the Norman feudal conquest, the Elizabethan colonial expansion, and the Victorian imperial realm. This triple jeopardy may make the Irish situation far more complex than that of most other subject nations, but it hardly removes the reality of experience for those who lived during any of these eras; nor the historian's responsibility for interpreting the complex effects of such experience on successive generations.

The clearest example of Foster's failure in this area concerns his treatment of the Irish rural economy. While he describes in great detail the imposition of British land law, he offers little analysis of the enormous significance of this process, and his subsequent discussion of Irish agriculture accepts the nature of the system itself as an inevitable phenomenon, rather than the colonial imposition it clearly was. Predicably he adopts the neo-classical economists' preoccupation with rent levels and eviction rates, and reports in considerable detail and clarity on the operations of the Irish agricultural system during the 18th and 19th centuries. Not surprisingly, he concludes that Irish landlords charged low rents and generally avoided capricious evictions. Following in his line of reasoning, a good deal of the poverty of rural Ireland was caused by the 'backwardness' of the cultivation techniques used by Irish tenants (often persisted in despite the zealous efforts of their landlords to encourage 'improved' British methods).

Unfortunately, such an analysis is ahistorical, and limits our understanding of many aspects of Irish society. Fully capitalist agricultural systems have rarely coexisted with peasant agriculture for very long without introducing the type of massive disruption and misery which Ireland experienced during the 18th and 19th centuries; and nowhere was capitalist agriculture so unrestrained in its assault upon the peasant community as in the case of the Anglo-Irish kleptocracy[1] in Ireland. Many historians of other 18th- and 19th-century peasant societies would find it difficult to understand how such a manifestly 'radical' or destructive economic system could be considered so 'normal', or how modern notions of the 'capital value' of Irish land can be used to evaluate a peasant agricultural system. Of course the Ascendancy land system was neither 'normal' nor acceptable to the majority of people who lived in it. They continued to contest its legitimacy by maintaining violent secret societies, and by other more mundane but probably more effective forms of popular action which perpetuated an alternative moral economy, which dominated peasant communities until the time of the Famine. It was the clash between this popular moral economy and the landlord/government defined legal land system which dominated the realities of rural Irish politics and society.

Foster's treatment of this popular culture is disappointing. While he does devote considerable effort to exploring this field of growing interest to Irish historians, he remains decidedly in sympathy with the perspective of elite culture. For example, when discussing the omnipresent secret societies of rural Ireland, he notes that they were committed to ' "the cause", which did not need to be defined'. Whether Foster intends to convey disapproval for slipshod peasant epistemology, or whether he recognizes that the meaning of the cause was so self-evident as to need no definition, is not clear. It is clear, however, that the author has a rather narrow sense of 'definition': the 'cause' was very clearly defined to those who believed in it; it was defined in their ritual, their use of symbol, and in the iteration of the central elements of their communal social norms. What is deficient here is the modern historian's ability to deal adequately or fairly with ideologies that do not meet our standards of erudition. This is also apparent in his treatment of Land League violence, where he sees (unmentioned) signs of 'machismo and sexual frustration'.

This difficulty in engaging with popular culture is most damaging in his treatment of sectarianism. He finds it understandable that, given the experience of violent conquest and long-term discrimination, Catholics might think and behave in a sectarian way, but he does not adequately assess either the alternatives available to the disadvantaged or the complexity of the term itself. Paradigms of political, social and economic power were determined by British and Anglo-Irish violence and authority, not peasant mentality; all of these paradigms contained the common element of sectarianism at the core of their power relationships. It is therefore not a very useful observation to note that the victims of that authority 'chose' to use parallel sectarian violence and rhetoric in their responses to authority. What is left unexplored here are the ways which Irish popular culture found of reinterpreting the meaning of élite-imposed norms and ideologies in ways which advanced their own interests

1   I am indebted to my colleague Robin Fleming for this term.

and goals. There is a wide and growing current of historical thought engaged in the hermeneutics of popular culture and discourse. Such a method moves history away from the centre of élite power preoccupations and towards the reality of human experience and understanding. It does not require the affirmation of traditional nationalist history, or 'myth' as the revisionists like to call it, but it does require an objective analysis of popular culture which goes beyond simple narrative or the frequent arrogant dismissals Foster delivers to 'archaic', 'nostalgic' or 'atavistic' popular behaviour.

There are other less significant weaknesses with Foster's synthesis. He is clearly less at home with demographic issues; his attitude towards the Irish abroad is paranoid (especially when compared to his general 'moderate' tone). He finds the 'Irish' identity of emigrant communities 'anachronistic' and 'fiercely unrealistically obsessive'. Last, the book lacks a conclusion, a real disappointment. In conclusion, let me say that I find myself in partial agreement with Professor Edwards: R.F. Foser has achieved the stature of Ireland's major historians, but it will take me much more time to fully digest this work, and I am not sure, however important it is, that I will enjoy the experience.

14

The Canon of Irish Cultural History:
Some Questions concerning Roy Foster's
*Modern Ireland**

BRIAN MURPHY

INTRODUCTION

Why, some will ask, write about Roy Foster's *Modern Ireland* at this late date?[1] His book was, after all, published in 1988 and sufficient debate took place then to last a lifetime. Many will, in fact, plead that they cannot stand any further airing of the issue of revisionism. With those sentiments I heartily concur. My concern is not with theoretical arguments about revisionism, but with particular instances of inaccuracy in the use of source material. I write because Foster's book contains serious failings relating to the treatment of original sources. He has not lived up to the dictum of Goethe that the master is known by his attention to detail. There can be no doubt that Foster has been hailed as a master: countless accolades have been showered upon him. Owen Dudley Edwards declared that 'with this book Dr Foster becomes one of Ireland's greatest historians. Not just "living" historians. Lecky may welcome him'.[2] Conor Cruise O'Brien pronounced that 'this is a magnificent book. It supersedes all other general accounts of modern Irish history'; and Kevin Kenny, writing in *The Recorder*, an American journal, stated that 'Foster has established himself as perhaps the leading Irish historian of his generation'.[3] The paeans of praise have been numerous and universal. Very few voices have been raised in criticism, and yet questions remain; and they assume a heightened gravity from the very status accorded to *Modern Ireland*. It became incumbent to write when I became aware that Foster's 'narrative with an interpretative level', as he described it in his Preface, was, quite literally, flawed at source.

---

* First published in *Studies* (Autumn, 1993), pp. 171-84.
1. R.F. Foster, *Modern Ireland 1600-1972* (London, 1988).
2. Owen Dudley Edwards, *Irish Times*, 29 October 1988, p. 9.
3. Conor Cruise O'Brien, *Sunday Times*, 30 October 1988, p. 13; Kevin Kenny, *The Recorder*, Summer 1990, pp. 97-105.

FOSTER'S REVISIONISM

Modern revisionism of the genre associated with Roy Foster first manifested itself, I believe, with the Ford lectures of Professor Lyons at Oxford University in 1978 which were subsequently published as *Culture and Anarchy in Ireland, 1890-1939* (1979). This book, which was far different in tone from Lyons's *Ireland Since the Famine* was deeply influenced by Patrick O'Farrell's *Ireland's English Question. Anglo-Irish Relations 1534-1970* (1971). The findings and sentiments expressed in O'Farrell and Lyons have been further elaborated and extended in Oliver MacDonagh's *States of Mind. A Study of Anglo-Irish Conflict 1780-1980* (1983). In these works of O'Farrell, Lyons and MacDonagh we have the inspirational voices that have, to a high degree, fashioned Foster's *Modern Ireland*.

On reading *Modern Ireland* I found that Foster's reliance on these authors was total. In the very first paragraph of his book Foster declared that he had relied on 'some masterly books that are not general histories but present general arguments'; and in his very first footnote he identified the 'masterly books' as those of O'Farrell, Lyons and MacDonagh.[4] My contention is that by accepting the findings of these authors uncritically Foster has incorporated into his work several erroneous uses of source material. His attempt, therefore, to write 'a narrative with an interpretative level' is literally impaired at source. Vagueness is a complaint that Michael Laffan has rightly levelled against much anti-revisionist literature in his excellent survey of revisionists and their critics.[5] My critique of Foster's *Modern Ireland* will attempt, therefore, to be as precise and specific as possible. While it may well be impossible to eliminate the myth that resides in the psyche, it may be possible to reduce the level of myth created by factual error.[6] Foster's treatment of the Gaelic League serves as a starting point for this exploration.

FOSTER AND THE GAELIC LEAGUE

Foster's survey of the language movement is uncompromisingly critical Writing of the Gaelic League, the Gaelic Athletic Association and other nationalist societies, he declared that 'the emotions focused by cultural revivalism around the turn of the century were fundamentally sectarian and even racialist'.[7] This startling conclusion is largely based on MacDonagh's

4. Roy Foster, op. cit., preface and p. 621. See also Roy Foster, 'Varieties of Irishness' in *Paddy and Mr Punch*, pp. 21-39 and extracts in *Irish Times*, 7 March 1989 for a more qualified acceptance of the views of Professor Lyons.

5. Michael Laffan, 'Insular Attitudes: the Revisionists and their critics', in Máirín Ní Dhonnachadha and Theo Dorgan (eds.), *Revising the Rising* (Derry, 1991), p. 119.

6. Mark Patrick Hederman, '*The Crane Bag* and Northern Ireland', *The Crane Bag* (1980) vol. 4, no.2, p. 738.

7. Roy Foster, *Modern Ireland*, op. cit., p. 453,

evidence that in 1906 Canon Hannay, a Protestant clergyman, was 'illegally excluded from participating in the organization of a League feis . . . on the ground that he was fundamentally unIrish'.[8] Indeed Foster appears to have made his own MacDonagh's generalizations that Protestants were 'alienated', 'threatened', and 'driven on to the defensive' by the early years of the present century.[9]

It is necessary to state that the Minute Book of the Gaelic League does not substantiate MacDonagh's interpretation. In January 1906 Canon Hannay delivered a lecture entitled 'Is the Gaelic League Political?' in which he declared, 'inside the ranks of the Gaelic League there is no religious strife or religious bitterness. It is an amazing thing . . . that here in Ireland there exists an organization where men and women of different creeds meet in friendliness; where a priest and parson love one another'.[10] In the same month, it became known that Canon Hannay, under the pen name of George Birmingham, had published *The Seething Pot*, a work of fiction in which a Catholic priest was ridiculed. Another novel, *Hyacinth*, seemed to cast aspersions upon the Sisters of Charity at Foxford. Despite the issues over these books Canon Hannay was elected to the Gaelic League Executive in August 1906, and it was stated that not only was the constitution of the League non-sectarian but also that anyone violating this principle was acting 'ultra vires'. It was against this background that Canon Hannay was excluded from the feis committee of Tuam in September 1906 by a Catholic priest. Despite this incident many of the League Executives stood by Hannay in November 1906 and a Catholic priest resigned because more was not done to uphold the action of the priest at Tuam.[11] Certain conclusions may be drawn from these events: the opposition to Canon Hannay was caused by the content of his books rather than by his religious affiliation—in short it was not sectarian in origin. Moreover, the Gaelic League attempted to uphold a non-sectarian policy in the most difficult of circumstances—a policy that had been warmly praised by Hannay at the start of the year. Douglas Hyde, the Protestant President of the League, who was a close friend of Hannay and who was involved in resolving the case, was able to say in 1913 that he had never known 'any member to be shaken or biased one iota

8.   Oliver MacDonagh, *States of Mind: a study of Anglo-Irish conflict 1780-1980* (London, 1983), p. 114.

9.   Ibid., p. 114 and 116.

10. J.O. Hannay, 'Is the Gaelic League Political?', Dublin: 1906, p. 8. See *Irish Times*, 24 September and 19 October 1992 for my article and reply to letters regarding Canon Hannay. Two valuable articles were mentioned during the correspondence: R.B.D. French 'J.O. Hannay and the Gaelic League', *Hermathena*, spring 1966, pp. 26-52; and Peter Murray, 'Novels, Nuns and the Revival of Irish Industries: the Rector of Westport and the Foxford Woollen Mill 1905-1907', *Cathair na Mart*, vol. 8 (1988), pp. 86-99.

11. Gaelic League Minute Book, 13 November 1906, pp. 39-41.

by sectarian considerations'.[12] That was his opinion after the Hannay incident; it is markedly different from the 'sectarian and even racialist' view of the League and the language movement that has been proposed by Foster.

Foster has also been adversely influenced by other observations made by MacDonagh in his chapter entitled 'The Politics of Gaelic'. For example MacDonagh claims that Douglas Hyde 'was reduced to a pandering type of constitutional monarch once the Gaelic League had been launched in 1893'.[13] This contention runs counter to all the evidence. The records show that Hyde, as President of the League, played a leading role in such major issues as the Mahaffy-Atkinson debate in 1899 during the Royal Commission's inquiry into Intermediate Education; the argument over the value of Irish in the Intermediate exam in 1901; and the place of 'essential Irish' for matriculation in the new National University between 1908-1910. Moreover, his presidential tour of the United States in 1905 not only enhanced the standing of himself and the League, but also brought in vital financial resources to fund the League's activities. Ernest Blythe commented on Hyde's visit to the United States that it 'added, of course, to the prestige of the President of the League'; and he concluded his thoughts on the status of Hyde in the League with the statement that 'his leadership in the fight to make Irish an essential subject in the matriculation examination of the new university raised his standing still further'.[14] This testimony of a Northern Ireland Protestant accurately reflects Hyde's position in the League. He was no mere cypher—no 'pandering type of constitutional monarch', as MacDonagh would have us believe, nor were there any Catholic designs upon his position as President. And yet this view that Catholic Gaels had suborned the position of the Protestant Hyde has gone unchallenged and has fashioned the final judgement of Foster.

In large part Foster would appear to have been influenced by equally dubious suggestions by MacDonagh about the language movement. MacDonagh claimed that the attempts of Irish Catholics to supplant the Anglo-Irish leadership of the League had been foreshadowed as early as 1876 by the election of Archbishop MacHale as Patron of the Society for the Preservation of the Irish Language (SPIL).[15] In fact the choice of MacHale as Patron, actually made in April 1877, was complemented by the appointment of Lord Francis Coyningham as President, and of Isaac Butt as one of the vice-Presidents. The selection of these two eminent Protestants along with MacHale as honorary officials reflected the true aspirations of the Society; it was a genuine attempt of Catholic and Protestant academics to develop an interest in Irish studies—

12. *Freeman's Journal*, 25 January 1913.
13. MacDonagh, *States of Mind*, pp. 113, 114.
14. Earnán de Blaghd, 'Hyde in Conflict', in Sean Ó Tuama (ed.), *The Gaelic Idea* (Cork and Dublin; 1972), p. 35.
15. MacDonagh, *States of Mind*, p. 114. See Minute Book of SPIL, 17 April 1877, for correct details.

scholarship rather than religion was the compelling interest of its members. While it is true that two Catholics, The O'Conor Don and Count Plunkett, subsequently became Presidents of the SPIL, they were also respectively President and vice-President of the Royal Irish Academy. Their roles in the Academy provide further confirmation, if any were needed, that in the field of scholarship religious differences made very little impact. The same attitude was apparent in the work of the Irish Texts Society and the School for Irish Learning. These societies and the SPIL present a very different picture from that depicted by MacDonagh: harmony rather than hostility characterized the relationship between Catholic and Protestant scholars throughout this period.

In conclusion it has to be said that Foster's view of a 'sectarian and racialist' language movement is wide of the mark. While D.P. Moran in *The Leader* was purveying anti-English and anti-Protestant sentiments, these were not adopted by the League. The positive statement of Hyde made in 1913, the character of the League as revealed in the unfolding of the Hannay incident, and the weaknesses underlying MacDonagh's depiction of the language movement all combine to confirm the non-sectarian ideals of the League. Grave doubts are cast upon Foster's contrary interpretation. The consequences for the current political debate are manifest. For underlying Foster's narrative is the implication that if the language movement was sectarian, then it was reasonable for Protestants, firstly, to distance themselves from the League and, secondly, to seek to preserve their own identity by a policy of separation. A more careful look at the historical evidence indicates such attitudes were not a reasonable response to the League's policies. While there were deep religious divisions, accentuated by the *Ne Temere* marriage decree of 1908, the Gaelic League was endeavouring, with some limited success, to bring together peoples of different religious persuasions.

FOSTER AND IRISH NATIONALISM

If Foster's attempt to depict the Gaelic League as anti-Protestant is suspect at source, so also is his attempt to place the same anti-Protestant label upon the Irish nationalist movement at large—and for the same reason. Error over source material is responsible. Foster writes that 'to a strong element within the Gaelic League, literature in English was Protestant as well as anti-national; patriotism was Gaelicist and spiritually Catholic'.[16] His words mirror those of Lyons almost exactly 'the marriage between Catholicism and Gaelicism was fatal', wrote Lyons, 'to the hopes of the Protestant Anglo-Irish protagonists of cultural fusion'; and Lyons, in turn, derived his conclusion from O'Farrell, who declared that 'the main reason why the priesthood played such an

16. Foster, *Modern Ireland*, p. 453.

important role' in the language movement was 'the conviction that British literature was spiritually destructive'.[17] One apologizes for the minutiae of this textual exegesis; but the writing of O'Farrell is a major source for the errors that have entered into the work of Lyons and, through him, Foster. Lyons was the first historian to make significant use of O'Farrell's book and acknowledged that he was 'much indebted' to him, especially for his contributions on the Gaelic League and on religious matters. It is passing strange that academic historians should have relied so unquestioningly on a book that has no footnotes conveying exact references. Of the various references to the *Catholic Bulletin* and *The Lyceum* that I could manage to identify most were either inaccurate or taken out of context.[18]

The reference that has inspired Foster's views on literature and patriotism may be taken as typical. O'Farrell used an extract from *The Lyceum* of May 1890 to make his point: 'the English literature which has come down to us is essentially Protestant', the passage reads, and goes on, 'the daily and weekly journals, the reviews, and all the lighter literature preach Protestantism with a hundred tongues'.[19] The author, however, continues, with words that are ignored by O'Farrell, to say that 'it must, however, be said that in adopting the English tongue the Irish, though losing something of their national heritage, have gained in many respects . . . with the English tongue comes too the English literature, more rich and varied than that of any modern European nation . . . (and) we gladly recognise the elevated spiritual tone, the high literary morality of such Protestants as Burke and Grattan'.[20] Far from being 'spiritually destructive', as O'Farrell would have us believe, even Protestant writers were respected for the spiritual tone that they brought to their work. By following O'Farrell uncritically, Foster, and incidentally Lyons, have distorted not only the native Irish approach to English literature, but also the character of Irish nationalism. The political effects for the present are again obvious: the anti-Protestant bias of the native Irish, as presented by Foster, would justify separation and partition; the more accurate reading of source material would indicate unity amidst diversity.

FOSTER AND 1916

Foster portrays the Rising as coloured by the 'strain of mystic Catholicism

17. Lyons, *Culture and Anarchy*, p. 82 and O'Farrell, *Ireland's English Question*, p. 228.
18. See Brian P. Murphy, 'J.J. O'Kelly, the *Catholic Bulletin* and contemporary Irish cultural historians', *Archivium Hibernicum*, 1989, pp. 71-88 for examples re the *Catholic Bulletin*. See Brian P. Murphy, 'J.J. O'Kelly and the *Catholic Bulletin*: Cultural considerations, Gaelic, Religious and National, *c.*1898-1926', unpublished PhD thesis, (1986), pp. 222-32 for examples re *The Lyceum*.
19. O'Farrell, *Ireland's English Question*, p. 228 and *The Lyceum*, May 1890, p. 215.
20. *The Lyceum*, May 1890, p. 215.

identifying the Irish soul as Catholic and Gaelic'.[21] The link with O'Farrell is evident: 'The message was loud and clear', O'Farrell wrote of 1916, 'Catholic Ireland had fought in Easter week; pious blood had been spilt for Ireland'.[22] The source for this conclusion was the *Catholic Bulletin*. After the Rising, O'Farrell contended, there took place in its pages 'a kind of canonization—in its monthly featuring brief biographies of the Irish rank and file who fell in the rebellion'. O'Farrell even gave examples such as George Geoghegan who was described as 'an earnest and almost lifelong member of the Dominick Street Sodality of the Holy Name, he received Holy Communion on Easter Sunday morning'.[23]

At first glance the text justifies O'Farrell's claim of 'canonization' and that of 'martyrolatry' made by Foster. There is, however, a simple explanation for the attitude of the *Catholic Bulletin* which not only rebuts their use of its pages, but also tells us much about their approach to history. The editor of the *Bulletin*, J.J. O'Kelly, wrote as he did because he was prevented from doing anything else by the censorship laws imposed under martial law. In the very first number after the Rising he explained that one 'has little option but to overlook the political and controversial features of the upheaval and confine comment almost entirely to the Catholic and social aspects of the lives and last moments of those who died either in action or as a result of trial by court martial'.[24] Records of the Censor's office show how O'Kelly acted with great skill and tenacity in order to present the public with any item of information at all.

He was acutely aware of the need to preserve a historic record of the men of 1916. 'To prevent the scales of history from being weighed too heavily against them', he wrote in 1917, 'the *Catholic Bulletin* has been able to put before its readers for the past twelve months the simple record of their lives. . . . When the heat and passion of today shall have subsided the records left in the back files of the *Catholic Bulletin* will be searched by students of history for material which will enable them to place in their true perspective the lives and the methods and the motives of the men of Easter week'.[25] Herein lies the real gravamen of the charge against Foster, and it must be said of many others who have simply followed O'Farrell that instead of recognizing the *Catholic Bulletin* as a valuable historical source—preserved in the most challenging of circumstances—he has misrepresented it. He has, in fact, taken

21. Foster, *Modern Ireland*, p. 479.
22. Seamus Deane, 'Wherever Green is Read', *Revising the Rising*, pp. 91-105; below, pp. 234-45; and O'Farrell, *Ireland's English Question*, p. 285.
23. Ibid., and see J.J. O'Kelly Papers, National Library of Ireland, MS 18555 for some forty letters, including one from the wife of George Geoghegan, to confirm the veracity of the accounts.
24. *Catholic Bulletin*, May/June 1916, p. 393.
25. Ibid., April 1917, p. 201.

the side of the Censor who did not wish the true history of Ireland's struggle to be recorded.

Foster delineates the events leading up to 1916 with a jaundiced eye. 'The Irish nationalism that had developed by this date' (the start of the Home Rule crisis of 1912), he writes, 'was Anglo-phobic and anti-Protestant, subscribing to a theory of "the Celtic Race" that denied the "true" Irishness of Irish Protestants and Ulster Unionists, but was prepared to incorporate them into a vision of "independent Ireland" whether they wanted it or not'.[26] The Irish nationalism is also portrayed as having an underlying revolutionary dimension. While avoiding the worst excesses of O'Farrell, Lyons and MacDonagh who branded the Gaelic League as inherently revolutionary, Foster's final verdict on Pearse is that he and MacNeill were 'cultural revolutionaries' who 'remained tactical moderates until quite late in the day'.[27]

Once again there is clear evidence linking this discernment from about 1912 of an exclusively Catholic and revolutionary nationalism with the findings of Lyons and O'Farrell; and once again it is marred at source. O'Farrell quoted Bishop O'Dwyer of Limerick to the effect that '"had the healing influence of native rule been felt for even a year" the 1913 strike would not have occurred . . . the lesson was obvious (O'Farrell adds)—the clergy should support and encourage true nationalism. This meant, not the spiritually untrustworthy Irish party, but nationalism in its Gaelic form'.[28] Serious flaws exist in this interpretation: Bishop O'Dwyer did not utter the words attributed to him; they were written by Fr Peter Dwyer, S.J.; and for him 'native rule' meant Home Rule.[29] The records that we do have of Bishop O'Dwyer show that he also was a strong supporter of Redmond and Home Rule until late 1913. Instead of supporting a revolutionary nationalism in the years before 1916 the Gaelic League and the Catholic Church were identified with the eminently constitutional policy of supporting the Irish Parliamentary Party of Redmond. This is not made clear by Foster.

The political implications for the present are again momentous. By projecting a revolutionary dimension on Irish nationalism, it becomes reasonable for Unionists to distance themselves from the nationalist movement. An argument for separation and partition is again advanced. Foster's final verdict on Irish nationalism that it was 'prepared to incorporate' Unionists into 'a vision of "independent Ireland" whether they wanted it or not', is revealed not only as partial history, but also as a highly political statement.[30] The image

26. Foster, *Modern Ireland*, p. 459.
27. Ibid. p. 461.
28. O'Farrell, *Ireland's English Question*, p. 271.
29. Fr Peter Dwyer, 'The living wage and how to get it', *Catholic Bulletin*, October 1914, p. 693. In fact, the words were taken from the joint pastoral of the Bishops of Ireland of February 1914.
30. Foster, *Modern Ireland*, p. 459.

is skilfully conveyed of a majority racial group, inspired by sectarian motives, forcing a smaller racial unit to submit to its revolutionary diktat. Many questions are begged in this analysis apart from the distorted image conveyed of religious sentiments, it should be recorded that the political wishes of Ulster had been expressed in democratic fashion to the extent that in 1916 there were 17 Home Rule MPs as opposed to 16 Unionists; and the 'independent Ireland' to which Unionists were asked to give allegiance was committed to recognize the British King as head of the state. All this Foster ignores.

By a curious coincidence, worthy of historical examination, the contemporary records defending this constitutional path of Irish nationalists, which have been ignored by Foster, were censored by the British authorities at the time. For example, the first editorial of the *Catholic Bulletin* after the Rising, having listed the revolutionary actions of the Unionists, stated that 'it is to be remembered that Mr John MacNeill and the late Mr P.H. Pearse were among the prominent speakers who, four years ago, assisted at Mr Redmond's monster Home Rule demonstration . . . we recall these circumstances to show how men of proved constitutional instincts may be driven from the constitutional path'.[31] The Censor ruled that such an interpretation of the Rising, and of the events leading up to it, was not acceptable: but the rebels had to be shown as men of violence without any redeeming features. In like manner it was not permitted to itemize the illegal activities of Carson and his followers.

FOSTER, THE 'TWO NATIONS' THEORY AND HISTORICAL PERSPECTIVE

No greater testimony to the efficacy of Foster and his mentors can be found than in the assertion of the late John Whyte, made in his *Interpreting Northern Ireland* (1990), that 'scarcely anyone. . . writing in a scholarly manner on the problem now stands over the one nation theory'.[32] Foster's own attitude to the 'two nations' theory is revealing. He observed in a detached manner that at the time of the Home Rule Crisis 'the question of whether Ireland was one nation or two hung in the air'; but he made no attempt to address the question.[33]

Alice Stopford Green, who did, is dismissed as 'a zealot', despite the recognition of her work by such varied and distinguished contemporaries as James Connolly, Eoin MacNeill and George Russell.[34] This hasty and ill tempered rejection by Foster betrays a choice of historical approach which is instructive. In the historical climate of the time Green's major book, *The*

31. *Catholic Bulletin*, May/June 1916, p. 246.
32. John Whyte, *Interpreting Northern Ireland* (Oxford, 1990), p. 141.
33. Foster, *Modern Ireland*, p. 466.
34. Ibid., p. 447.

Making of Ireland and its Undoing (1908), was seen as significant; more, it was seen as dangerous. It was banned from the library of the Royal Dublin Society. As a reviewer at the time put it, she had 'set herself the agreeable task of demolishing a political myth'.[35] That myth was the superiority of English over Irish culture and institutions. She was critical of Sir Horace Plunkett's *Ireland in the New Century* as being coloured by his 'ascendancy prejudices'; and was even more hostile to Provost Mahaffy's denial of Irish values, observing that 'in any other history than that of Ireland it would be held unfair to heap up these comprehensive accusations, taken from hostile sources'.[36]

Foster's treatment of Mahaffy is significant. Foster simply lists his scholarly publications. Having attempted to show that racial overtones inimical to Unionists were inherent in the Irish language movement, he fails to reveal that in the debate on the Irish language the most offensive remarks were made by Mahaffy. To revive the language, Mahaffy said, would be 'a retrograde step, a return to the Dark Ages to the Tower of Babel', and as for its literature it was dismissed as 'silly or indecent'.[37] Nor does Foster convey the publicly expressed view of Mahaffy that the British in Ireland 'did not destroy anything either in religion or in society which would have produced any real civilization'.[38] Most significantly of all no mention is made of Mahaffy's famous remarks made at the Irish Convention of 1917 that there are in Ireland 'two creeds, two breeds, two ways of looking at the vital interests of men'.[39] Alison Phillips cited these words with approval in his history of Ireland, and Professor Corcoran of UCD was quick to attack the assumptions upon which this idea of two nations was based. The idea, Corcoran declared 'finds constant outlet in the modern writings of Murray, Bagwell, Dunbar-Ingram, Tyrrell and their numerous disciples . . . for there can be no doubt of the mind of Trinity College as to which of the "two creeds, two breeds" . . . is the preferable choice. . . Even Sir Samuel Ferguson, as early as 1875, could see that this doctrine was really an insolent claim to racial, cultural and religious ascendancy, on the part of those who so ostentatiously proclaimed their separateness'.[40] In fairness to Mahaffy it should be recorded that, at the Convention, he advocated a very limited scheme of Home Rule on Swiss lines, because of the alternatives—'the coercion of Ulster, which is unthinkable, or the partition of Ireland, which would be disastrous'.[41] It would appear, however, that Mahaffy's underlying assumption of 'two creeds, two breeds' rather than this

35. *Times Literary Supplement*, 25 June 1908.
36. *Westminster Gazette*, 27 February 1904 and *Church of Ireland Gazette*, 3 May 1907.
37. L. Paul Dubois, *Contemporary Ireland* (Dublin, 1991), p. 414.
38. *Freeman's Journal*, 9 February 1907.
39. W.B.Stanford and R.B. McDowell, *Mahaffy: A biography of an Anglo-Irishman* (London, 1971), p. 235.
40. *Catholic Bulletin*, November 1923, p. 762.
41. Stanford and MacDowell, *Mahaffy*, p. 237.

practical proposal, may be detected in Foster's view of modern Ireland; and from this perspective it is not surprising, indeed it is eminently understandable, that the tone of his history should incline towards a 'two nations theory'.

Many commentators in the early years of the century, it should be recorded, were opposed to the theory. Alice Green, writing in 1912, agreed that two races, two religions, two factions existed in Ireland but of two nations she wrote, 'this new term seems to find favour as a convenient means of adding discredit to the notion of nationality, and thus by indirect means weakening the claim of any and every nation'. 'What', she added pertinently, 'is the name of that other nation in Ireland?'[42] John Redmond totally rejected the theory as an 'abomination and a blasphemy'.[43] George Russell (Æ), a northern Ireland Protestant, maintained that the theory was deliberately fostered by the British Government. Writing at the height of the debate on the Government of Ireland Act in 1920 he stated that 'it was not the policy of the British Government that one section of the Irish people should trust the other section; and Mr Lloyd George invented the "two nations" theory to keep Ireland divided'.[44] This suggestion has recently found some support in the findings of David Miller in his book, *Queen's Rebels*, where he makes it plain that the theory 'seems to have been introduced by British rather than Irish Unionists'; but, at the same time, he outlines the Unionist claim for special recognition as a distinct community.[45]

CONCLUSION

Judged by Foster's own criterion that he set out to write 'a narrative with an interpretative level', it may reasonably be said that the interpretations are not always sound in historical terms. Having relied uncritically on the 'masterly works' of O'Farrell, Lyons and MacDonagh, it is evident that the masters have let the master down.

The political implications of Foster's book have also been profound and require critical analysis. By branding the native Irish as racialist, revolutionaries and sectarian, Foster has made separation and partition more reasonable and respectable. He has conferred an unmerited legitimacy on the 'two nations' theory. Taken together with the writings of Garret FitzGerald and Conor Cruise O'Brien we have an historical approach that is shaping current political attitudes in a very precise manner. It creates a climate in favour of rejecting Articles 2 and 3 of the 1937 constitution; it allows the British government to

42. *Westminster Gazette*, 13 May 1912.
43. Denis Gwynn, *Life of John Redmond* (London, 1931), p. 232.
44. *Freeman's Journal*, 9 June 1920.
45. Whyte, *Interpreting Northern Ireland*, pp. 127-29 for a valuable assessment of Miller's book and others on Unionist attitudes.

say that these Articles are not helpful; and it permits Unionist politicians to attack them as acts of aggression. By focusing on internal Irish differences, and often misrepresenting the nature of these differences, Foster has (as have FitzGerald and O'Brien) failed to convey adequately the British and Unionist responsibility for the Home Rule Act of 1914 and the Government of Ireland Act of 1920. Once that historical reality is given due prominence then it becomes evident that any reconsideration of the Irish territorial claim made in Articles 2 and 3 of the 1937 constitution should only be undertaken within the framework of a similar evaluation of the British territorial claim made in section 75 of the 1920 Government of Ireland Act.

May I say, in conclusion, that in stating the case against the 'two nations' theory, one is not suggesting that Unionists be forced to submit to nationalist diktats inside a unitary state tout court, that is in its simplest form. Degrees of unity and degrees of Britishness must be examined and explored so that the two cultures, two creeds, and two traditions that inhabit the island of Ireland may live together in peace.

15

Wherever Green is Read[*]

SEAMUS DEANE

I

The Easter Rising of 1916 has been so effectively revised that its seventy-fifth anniversary is a matter of official embarrassment. Nevertheless, the revisionists are now themselves more vulnerable to revision because their pseudo-scientific orthodoxy is so obviously tailored to match the prevailing political climate—especially in relation to the Northern crisis—that its claims to 'objectivity', to being 'value-free', have been abandoned as disguises no longer needed. Conor Cruise O'Brien has declared himself to be a unionist and, in that light, his writings can be understood as a polemic in favour of that position. A less strident example, free of any such declared *parti pris*, is provided by Roy Foster in his popular *Modern Ireland 1600-1972*, in which he writes about 1916 thus:

> Any theoretical contradictions present in the 1916 rising, however, were obscured by the fact that its rhetoric was poetic. Several poets took part, and the most famous reaction to it was a poem: Yeat's 'Easter 1916', written between May and September and strategically published during the Anglo-Irish war four years later. But an intrinsic component of the insurrection (for all the pluralist window-dressing of the Proclamation issued by Pearse) was the strain of mystic Catholicism identifying the Irish soul as Catholic and Gaelic. It could be argued that this was nothing new: literary Fenianism yet again. But the message would be read more clearly than ever in an Ulster heavily committed to the war effort, for whom 1916 would be marked not by the occupation of the GPO, but the terrible carnage on the Somme. (479)

All sorts of curious assumptions and shiftings reveal themselves here. Apparently, rhetoric is a bad thing, especially when it is poetic, because it obscures 'theoretical contradictions'. (This from Yeats's biographer!) It is the kind of approach one would expect from a nineteenth-century historian (for

[*] First published in Máirín Ní Dhonnchadha and Theo Dorgan (eds.), *Revising the Rising* (Derry, 1991), pp. 91-105.

example, Lord Acton objecting to George Eliot's style on similar grounds),
but its apparent intellectual naiveté serves a useful purpose. The Rising's
'rhetoric was poetic', poets participated in it and the most famous reaction to
it was a poem by Yeats. Even if we allow that stature to Yeats's long-delayed
poem, what does it tell us about the Rising? That it was 'poetic' and *therefore*
a bad thing, an absurdity? Clearly, insurrections should avoid poets and poems
if they wish to be taken seriously. To be so taken, they should either be without
'theoretical contradictions' or, failing that, they should not obscure them.

However, poetry is not, after all, the real problem. It is 'the strain of mystic
Catholicism identifying the Irish soul as Catholic and Gaelic; that is truly
offensive. Some of the harm might be taken out of this if it is read as recycled
"literary Fenianism", and therefore "incurably verbal" ' (393). Irish revolutionaries all seem to suffer from this disease of discourse. Still, the antidote
to their implacable writerliness is provided by a section of their readership—the
Ulster unionists. Pearse's strain of mystic Catholicism 'would be read more
clearly than ever' in an Ulster undergoing the much more acceptable, if terrible,
'carnage on the Somme'. For 'the strain' has now clarified into 'the message'
that would be read in Ulster. It is surely of some importance to known *when*
this reading took place. Did 1916 have to happen before the Ulster unionists
perceived that Irish nationalists were Catholic and Gaelic? Or has Pearsean
exclusivity been borne in upon the unionists only with the passage of time?
Since it is going to be (or was) read 'more clearly than even', it is fair to assume
that it had been read before, albeit less clearly. Perhaps it is the poetic rhetoric
that previously made it obscure. The poetry of the Rising has to be separated
from its 'message'.

This is achieved by a single connective. *But* it is an 'intrinsic component'
of mystic Catholicism that would be read as the message of 1916 in Ulster
and not the 'pluralist window-dressing' of the Proclamation. It is hard to know
if that *but* is entirely meant to separate the poetry from the Catholicism or to
conjoin them, although it does seem that the poetry is not as intrinsic a
component as the Catholicism. Perhaps the real bridge word here is 'mystic',
since it links the two entities by allowing that they share the same obfuscating
and irrational function. Ulster cannot read the poetry but it can read the
Catholic strain. They may be distinct, they may be conjoined, *but* it is the
latter that counts.

The paragraph is itself an exercise in rhetoric and its central trope is that
of 'reading' clearly what has been obscured. First theory is obscured by rhetoric
(but read nonetheless); then an 'intrinsic' element, 'mystic Catholicism',
emerges as 'the message' that would be read in Ulster behind all the 'pluralist
window-dressing'. Clear reading is an Ulster prerogative and is associated with
the Somme; obscure (and, by implication, obscurantist) writing is a Southern
characteristic and is associated with the GPO. The trope is not local, of course;

it extends to the whole treatment of the 1912-16 period, in which the South consistently misreads the North (for example, the Howth gun-running as a bad reading of the Larne gun-running) while the North accurately reads the true intentions that lie behind the Gaelic-Catholic-revivalist jargon of the South. This has a very familiar ring. The perceptive Ulster readers have been displaying their interpretative skills on deceitful Southern texts up to the present day. Maybe they have classes on the hermeneutics of suspicion in Glengall Street or at the Bob Jones University. Certainly, whatever the South writes, the North will read and Ulster will be right.

That 'pluralist window-dressing' of the Proclamation, we may take it, is the residue of Connolly's contribution to the Rising. In the preceding pages, Foster wonders what persuaded Connolly to give up his 'hard-headed Marxian socialism' for the vaporous mysticism of Pearse. The relationship between a soft-focussed Irish nationalism and socialism is, in this view, necessarily contradictory and—for present purposes—Marxian socialism may be allowed to be 'hard-headed', a figurative compliment of the most strategic kind. Still, theory has taken a fair hammering. It is bedevilled by contradictions, it is obscured by rhetoric, it secretes within itself a mystic strain and yet, for all its shyness, theory can be exposed and read as a message. But it has even more blows to take. In the next paragraph it appears in another of its stereotyped adversarial roles—against practice.

'Theory apart, what about the practicalities of insurrection?' Theory always seems to be apart from, not of the Rising. The other stock opposite to theory—instinct—is also invoked. The IRB reacted to World War I in a fashion that was 'almost Pavlovian in its dogmatism' (461). I find it difficult to remember what Pavlov's experiments have to do with dogmatism, although they did indeed have a lot to do with dogs. Anyway, the verbal associationism of the sentence is almost rescued by its 'almost'.

The whole point of Foster's representation is that the Easter Rising was an exercise in irrationalism, a word entirely congruent with nationalism (of the Irish, not the British, kind) and that it was read as such in Ulster. The legacy of the Rising is the Northern crisis. The North can read the South; the South cannot read the North. Writing is the characteristic practice of the 'incurably verbal' South and it is always, explicitly or implicitly, separate from pragmatic considerations and infused with demonic, atavistic and chaotically 'spiritual' energies. Reading is what the North is good at, the extrapolation from verbiage of the real message, a capacity that is characteristically pragmatic, hard-headed, rational. Thus the North and South are constituted both as poltically and culturally distinct entities: one authorial, the other readerly; one obscure, the other clear; one poetic, the other prosaic. Foster's own writing is itself a reading, dependent on the congealed stereotype of the partitionist mentality that is subsequent to the process he effects to describe. Perhaps it is now time for the stereotype to invert, so that the South can start reading the jargon of the North's newly acquired writerly status, complete with its 'myths' of the 'Cruithin' (Ian Adamson's redaction of the Gaelic story of dispossession, much favoured by the UDA and, increasingly, by Glengall Street), its evangelical religion and, of course, its poetic rhetoric.

But, incurably verbal, 'history' legitimates its version of the present by its interpretations of the past. It has become almost a solecism to rehearse the well-known similarities between British imperial and Irish nationalist practices in the first decades of this century. Blood-sacrifice, a lot of bad and some good poetry, racist ideology, a glorification of violence, belief in the destiny of the nation, the recreation of a glorious past in fancy-dress charades (for instance, the reinvention of the British monarchy), health and strength movements (sports and body-building as a new form of morality, the Boy Scouts, predecessors of the Pearsean Fianna)—these and much else of the same kind were carefully nurtured cultural activities in Britain and in Europe between 1880 and 1914. Further, the tide of irrationalism continued to run, despite the bloodshed of 1914-18 until 1939-45.

But it would, in the current vocabulary, be 'Anglophobic' or 'atavistic' to pursue such an enquiry, especially since among its consequences might be a recognition that it was 1912, not 1916, that created the ghastly circumstances of the Northern statelet and that made religious bigotry the central organizing principle of its political life. It is, in present circumstances, an inadmissible notion. For the reaction to Easter 1916 is part of the reaction to the Provisional IRA. The lamentations about that organization's use of violence in the furtherance of political ends come most loudly from those who have a well-established notoriety for that practice themselves—the British and the unionists. They are not opposed to violence as such; they are opposed to violence directed against them. But they are perfectly happy to direct violence against their opponents and even, if need be, against one another. Yet it is the violence of Easter 1916 that is regarded as originary and therefore legitimizing.

Easter 1916 was a sorry reproduction, in its forms and its practice, of the ideology of imperialism. It was not only the immense military disadvantage that made it so. Culturally, it was armed with primitive weapons. It could not compete with the British army's regimental tradition of glorified violence; it had no evangelical fervour that could match Victorian Protestantism's euphoria, it had no war poets to compare in ferocity with Kipling or Sir Henry Newbolt; it had no theory of racial degeneration, regression and atavism to compare with those of Edwin Ray Lankester or Thomas Huxley, and those in Ireland who did promote such theories—like Standish O'Grady and Yeats—were not among the insurrection's most notable participants or supporters. At least it can be said for Easter 1916 that it tried; but as a response to its imperial mentor's example (on the Somme and elsewhere) it was a grievous failure.

Only the Ulster unionists managed to approximate the imperial example, possible because they regarded themselves (rightly) as the representatives in Ireland of the imperialist system. Their 'rebellion' in 1912 was a reminder to Westminster that any attempt to modify that status would bring the whole system into question.

Still, Irish historians and commentators are anxious to assign Easter 1916 to a curious double fate. On the one hand, it is a point of origin that should be erased as much as possible. Had it not happened, it is argued, we would be better off—without partition (possibly) and without all the bloodshed of the years 1916-22. On the other hand, it is to be remembered as a point of origin for all our ills—clientism in politics, economic illiteracy, nationalist vapourings and, above all, the Northern crisis and the IRA. Nationalism, we are told, is not compatible with democracy, nor with socialism. It is provincial and provincializing. Until 1989, it was even possible to argue that it was a nineteenth-century phenomenon, an anachronism in the modern world. Similarly, imperialism or colonialism were myths generated by nationalists, unless, that is, they are spoken of by heroic little republics struggling to free themselves from the Soviet embrace. That is reality, not myth. But British imperialism? In Ireland? Even the Workers' Party has ditched that fantasy, exchanging it for the other fantasy of the multinational system of late capitalism. The hostility to the idea that there might be a system—apart from nationalism, of course—whether it is called capitalism (a system that prides itself on not being one), imperialism or colonialism, is itself a symptom of revisionism's desire to deny the validity or the possibility of any totalizing concept, and to replace this with a series of monographic, empiricist studies that disintegrate the established history of 'Ireland' into a set of specific and discrete problems or issues that have at best only a weak continuity to link them.

II

To theorize a total system is, perhaps, a contradiction in terms, since no system that is truly total would leave any space for anyone to stand outside it and theorize it. Empiricists often manage this dilemma best by implying that if there is a system, then it can be modified, improved or altered in such-and-such a particular way so that a discernible goal or purpose can be realized. Empiricists make good liberals; that is to say, all good liberals are empiricists, but not all empiricists are good liberals. The kindest view of liberalism in present-day Ireland would credit it with the wish to improve the existing political-economic system in such a manner that people would be as economically secure and as free as possible from all the demonic influences of 'ideologies', religious and political. Its buzz word is 'pluralism'; its idea of the best of all possible worlds is based on the hope of depoliticizing the society to the point where it is essentially a consumerist organism, absorbing the whole array of goods that can be produced within the free market. No doubt there is a suspicion that the market is, in some sense of the word, a system and that consumption is allied in particular ways to production and distribution. But the emphasis is on the idea of the individual and his/her liberty within a system that is junior to the individual self. Systems change, but individuals—as an idea, not, thank heaven, as individuals—go on forever. The full realization of the individual self is regarded as an ambition that institutions exist to serve. Those that do not—religion, education, the 1937 Constitution, for example— are to be liberalized, gentrified or abolished.

Self-fulfilment is not an aim that threatens any system that produces it. Rather the reverse: it is one of the achievements of capitalism to have created it. Its ultimate political expression is pluralism, the Pearsean-Connolly 'window-dressing' in the Proclamation. Its desire is for variety and accessibility. Its pride is to be modern, its dread to be out of step with what is deemed to be modernity, or Europe—commonly assumed to be the same thing. Its general attitude to what it does not like is that it is out-of-date, out-of-place in this wonderful world of the late twentieth century. Pluralism has only one time—the present; everything else is, literally, anachronistic. It has the egregious tolerance of the indifferent to anything or anyone else who is willing to live in a hermetically sealed microclimate of individual or group privacy. Alas, it is also very expensive. The economic system must be functioning at a high level to sustain it and it can do that only in specific places at specific times. Ireland cannot afford to live in such present-ness. It must perforce live with its past. That is a matter of some resentment to this sort of liberal mind.

I do not think it is answer enough to say that, even if it could afford it, Ireland would not have pluralism. The abortion, contraception and divorce issues seem to point that way, but if Ireland could afford pluralism, it would not be for Ireland we know. What we have instead is a dilapidated version of pluralism, media-led, centred in Dublin 4, a mini-metropolis that regards the rest of Ireland as the hinterland of its benighted past. Still, in so far as it can, Ireland now treats the past as a kind of supermarket for tourists, a place well-provided with 'interpretative centres' that will allow Newgrange and Joyce, the flora and fauna of the Burren, the execution cells at Kilmainham, the Derrynaflan hoard and the Blarney stone to be viewed as the exotic debris thrown up by the convulsions of a history from which we have now escaped into a genial depthlessness. Easter 1916 or Ulster in 1912—not to mention Ulster in 1991—are altogether too present in their pastness to be commodified in this manner. It is perfectly in tune with this blandness that people in the South wonder what the killing in the North is all about. 'Why can't they live in peace together and forget the Boyne and 1916?' They are irrational creatures, those Northerners, because they are caught in the past and still have to catch up with the present. It is all the more irrational because they belong to an economic world that would allow for pluralism.

But then, on top of all that, there is the question of democracy and the need to preserve it, North and South. Any unionist will tell you now that there is no democracy left in the North. The British took it away and replaced it with a system of Orders-in-Council, issued through the Northern Ireland Office and the Secretary of State, all appointed, not elected, officials. Any nationalist or republican (or Lord Devlin) will tell you that there never was democracy in Northern Ireland, even before the proroguing of Stormont that succeeded the massacre of Bloody Sunday in 1972. (This is a well-tried tactic—a massacre of the enemies of those whom you are going to betray politically in order to make the betrayal palatable.) Still, the democracy that ain't and the democracy that never was have to be preserved from the men of violence who threaten it. That is, in case there might be doubt, not the British army or the RUC or the UDR or the UDA, but the other men of violence, the IRA. This is, in fact, a delusion. It is the Union that is to be preserved, not democracy. The mass of the Irish people did not want the Union, but they got it with the help of the corrupt Irish parliament in which those same people were regularly referred to as 'the common enemy'. The unionists of the North did not want the modifications of the Union Treaty that came in 1922, 1972 and then again in 1985, but they got them and were outraged at this treatment of the majority. But that's how democracy works in what is now a neo-colonial system. No matter how often it is abolished, the phantasm of its presence remains. If democracy is abolished legally by a parliament, then it cannot really be abolished—it is just in a state of suspended animation and will resume its life-giving contact with the people once all the objections to its suspension have been overcome.

Nevertheless, the biggest threat to democracy is that outlandishly retarded form of nationalist violence that Easter 1916 spawned and the IRA inherited. The only fully democratic system that Ireland has ever known is that developed since independence. Yet nationalism is not compatible with democracy. Maybe it could be suggested that, in colonial conditions, nationalism is often the preconditioning climate for democracy. But then, of course, colonialism probably does not exist, is merely a figment of the nationalist imagination—as phantasmal as democracy in Northern Ireland or all pluralism in the Republic. But it is precisely such 'window-dressing' that a consumerist society wants. If pluralism or democracy is too expensive to buy, then at least we can window-shop, gazing fondly at their simulacra on the TV, along with the other glamorous advertisements. In the end, it may be the 'window-dressing' that has survived best from the Proclamation. It was unreal then, we may feel, but now we have transformed it into the real unreal.

It would indeed be ironic if, in our anxiety to liberate ourselves from 1916 and its presumed legacy, we fell into such a psychosis. For one of the characteristic ways of discrediting the Rising has been to intimate that its leaders were an odd lot, psychologically unstable, given to Anglophobia and dread homoerotic tendencies. Pearse has been the favourite target of this kind of psycho-history (see Ruth Dudley Edwards, *Patrick Pearse: The Triumph of Failure*) but it is a dangerous precedent. If the same kind of attention were to be directed at, say, Carson, Asquith, Lloyd George, Churchill, who should 'scape whipping—if the phrase may be allowed in such a context. Anyway, it is just an inverse form of the 'great man' school of history, in which the agency of the individual, however disturbed (maybe because disturbed), is given priority over all the other determinant and impersonal forces of which we might otherwise believe the ostensibly free individual to be the instrument. The problem with 'forces' is that they extend over long periods of time and are readable only when they constitute patterns—or when they are constituted as patterns. Individuals whose intervention warps or alters these patterns are often seen as eccentric and freakish. But to pursue that line of polemical investigation is to go down a cul-de-sac with a mirror at the end.

So, no system, no metanarrative, just discrete issues discreetly interlinked now and then. Irish history, like any history, has to re-present the past for the present. The anxieties of the present determine what elements of the past are most in need of signification. Easter 1916 was an action predicated on a version of Irish history that has now been rewritten so that its force may be denied, particularly the force that came from the rebels' conception of themselves as the culmination of a long, single narrative that had been submerged by deceit and oppression. Revisionism attacks the notion of a single narrative and pretends to supplant it with a plurality of narratives. It downplays the oppression the Rising sought to overthrow and upgrades the oppression the Rising itself inaugurated in the name of freedom. The rewriting of modern history has, as its terminus, the Northern problem and thus explains its present intransigence by criticizing those who did not anticipate or recognize its inevitability and its depth. It is a retrospective vision—as all history must be—but its pretensions to objectivity are as much a part of its rhetoric as are the internal characteristic strategies of the discourses of its various practition-ers. Its most interesting achievement has been to place the problem of historical writing as such on the agenda. Inescapably a fiction, history, of whatever kind, owes its allegiance to fact, however selective, however organized. (This does not mean that historians do not tell lies; they do. But let us say that a writer who tells lies is not, in virtue of that, being at that moment an historian. Froude was, on that count, infrequently an historian. Sir John Temple never was.) But history is discourse; events and conditions are not. They are outside discourse, but can only be reached through it—to paraphrase Barthes. It is a slippery discipline that has the additional merit or demerit of itself being an integral part of the object it addresses. We do not know the past except through the interpretations of it. Historians do not write about the past; they create the past in writing about it. And, when they do that, they are also writing in and of and for the present. It says a good deal about historians that so many of them still believe in their capacity to be 'objective'.

III

One of the outstanding features of historical revisionism is its philosophical innocence, perhaps the basic requirement for its peculiar brand of political incrimination that pretends to be a rational form of 'detachment'. This might help to explain the paradox whereby it actually collaborates—unconsciously— with the very mentality it wishes to defeat. There is indeed a brand of Irish nationalism that is willing to deny to 'Ulster' the independent tradition that it claims for itself and to swallow it up in the fond embrace of all-Ireland nationalism proper. (This is not a brand that can, on any reading of the evidence, be legimately associated with people as diverse as Thomas Mac-Donagh, George Sigerson, Frederick Ryan, W.P. Ryan, James Connolly and many others, although they have all been huddled together under the sign of nationalist messianism.) But what the revisionists do is to deny to the 'South' the tradition that they then, perforce, accede to the 'North'. The 'two–nations' theory is an anomaly in historical revisionism, because it is conceding that idea of continuity and tradition that is the bedrock of all nationalist thinking, of whatever variety. But it is, of course a *necessary* anomaly. To legitimize partition, Northern Ireland must be allowed its separate 'identity', 'tradition', 'essence', while nationalist Ireland must have these qualities denied it. Alas, you cannot have one without the other. If Ulster is 'different', its difference can be described only in contrast with the 'sameness' of the rest of the island. Abandon the sameness and you abandon the difference. The only grounds on which partition can be legitimized are the same as those on which it can be refused. What is 'Protestant' in Christianity is defined in relation to what is 'Catholic'; both are still within the one embrace. The more one argues for two nations, the more one fuels the argument for one nation. Allow the concept of nation, nationality, tradition and all the rest of those continuities that make metanarratives possible, then the rest is history—or history of the present-day Irish kind. Revisionists are nationalists despite themselves; by refusing to be Irish nationalists, they simply become defenders of Ulster or British nationalism, thereby switching sides in the dispute while believing themselves to be switching the terms of it.

It is only the inverted nationalism of historical revisionism that makes Easter 1916 a date so central that it has to be so assiduously ignored. Roy

Foster mentioned the strategically delayed publication of Yeats' poem 'Easter 1916', perhaps to point out that it had a deeper repercussion during the War of Independence (or the 'Anglo-Irish war', as he, with comparable strategy, calls it) than it would have had earlier. But 1916 saw the equally delayed publication in New York of Joyce's *A Portrait of the Artist as a Young Man*. With the benefit of hindsight, it could be pointed out that the MacCann of *A Portrait* is modelled on Francis Sheehy-Skeffington, who was to be murdered by a British officer in 1916, and that the Davin of the same novel is a partial portrait of George Clancy, murdered in 1921 by the Black and Tans. Do these later facts add 'significance' to *A Portrait*? Perhaps it is safer and saner to say that Joyce's attack in this novel on the servility of the Irish in the face of the Roman Catholic and British imperia is of much greater historical import, although the attack is ventriloquized through Stephen Dedalus and he may not be too readily taken as a reliable narrator of Joyce's own views or of the existing state of things.

Literary discourse has its own specific problems, although they differ from those that attend historical discourse. But does retrospect not lend (dis)enchantment to the view we take either of historical or literary texts? A novel finished in 1910, but not published until 1916, a poem written in 1916 but not published until 1920, are both subject to the pressure of retrospect even before they appear in print. Even if we take their 'origin' as the moment they were completed (or begun), they produce another 'origin' at the moment they are published and yet another at the moment they are interpreted or reinterpreted according to the prevailing literary or historical paradigm inside which they are read. History would like to disembarrass itself of this 'literary' burden. Conversely, literature, in its 'humanist' mode, takes that weight gladly upon itself and dissolves the problem of time and retrospect that historians have to face, by chattering gaily about 'timeless' works of art, 'the autonomy of the artefact', and so on.

A Portrait is an artefact, the Rising is a fact. The production, transmission and consumption of a text is a process that is obviously part of its meaning, but in literary studies the endlessness of the meaning has conventionally been terminated by conferring upon the text the destiny of form. Everything else may be mobile, but form abides.

Historians would draw the bottom line elsewhere. Events took place. There is an undeniable zone that no manipulation can alter. But historical facts or events are artefacts. Once an event is characterized as 'historical', it has entered into the world of historical discourse. Even discourse itself is an event, but it is often the case—in recent historical writing in Ireland at any rate—that the written word, when treated as historical evidence, has a very peculiar relation to action, especially action of the revolutionary kind. In the Fosterian view of the 'South', there are many examples of the process by which people like the

Fenians or the Parnellites produced writing that led unwittingly to action, when 'literary rhetoric would threaten to take on a mobilizing force all its own' (428). The oddity of the phrasing does make the linkage between language and action a little obscure. Did revolutionary language produce revolution? Can that be shown by someone who is himself using language? Is 'rhetoric' the word for the kind of language that 'produces' actions of which the historian disapproves?

Similarly, it seems that actions can be tailor-made to suit a pre-existent language, as when the British foolishly commit atrocities and thereby make a 'propaganda gift' (498) to the IRA. The propaganda is, so to say, prior to the atrocities; it is a language trap into which the British stupidly fall by killing people. It is not killing people that turns the populace against the Black and Tans; it is IRA propaganda. No doubt the British progaganda machine, notoriously efficient then and since lay in wait for the IRA to kill people too. This is, perhaps, *a posteriori* 'rhetoric', where the action is inscribed beforehand and the falsity of the language is, oddly, cancelled by the performance of the kind of action imputed to be characteristic of the British. It is difficult, in such a context, to know where language begins and action ends, what is an event and what is rhetoric. The only security the reader has is that the philosopichal problems that are raised by historical writing can be ignored because the writing is so heavily coded. There is no doubt about the distribution of approval and disapproval. But such writing, while very effective, is highly polemical. Its pretence to detachment, if it has any such pretence, is part of its polemical strategy. It too is 'rhetoric'.

So, discourse validates itself in many ways. It claims either to be self-referential (literature) or to refer to facts outside itself which it neverthess includes within itself (history). This is the South and North of writing, the partitionist 'rhetoric' that confirms the partition between literature and history.

It used to be said, and is still in some quarters felt, that Irish nationalism had managed to produce a nation-state just at the moment when the 'time' for nation-states had passed. Now we are seeing the nation-state, and the theories of discourse that accompanied it, defended by those who fancy they are questioning the assumptions that underlay their formation. The sponsorship of pluralism and diversity is merely an addition to nation-state politics and the language of 'individual' discourse, not a replacement for it. Seventy-five years after the Rising, the revising of it has led to the revision of the revisionists, who, for all the pluralist window-dressing of their proclamations, are victims of a strain of mystic rhetoric of the kind that we should now read all the more clearly, precisely because of the differences between the Somme and the GPO. We do not only read and write history; history also reads and writes us, most especially when we persuade ourselves that we are escaping from its thrall into the never-never land of 'objectivity'.

SOURCES

Adamson, Ian, *Cruithin, The Ancient Kindred* (Newtownards; Nosmada Books, 1974).

Anderson, Benedict, *Imagined Communities* (London: Routledge & Kegan Paul, 1983).

Barthes, Roland, 'Le discours de l'histoire', *Poétique* (1982), 49, 13-21.

Canary, Robert H. and Henry Kozicki (ed.), *The Writing of History: Literary Form and Historical Understanding* (Madison: University of Wisconsin Press, 1978).

Edwards, Ruth Dudley, *Patrick Pearse: The Triumph of Failure* (London: Gollancz, 1977).

Foster, R.F., *Modern Ireland 1600-1972* (London: Allen Lane, The Penguin Press, 1988).

Girouard, Mark, *The Return to Camelot: Chivalry and the English Gentleman* (New Haven, Connecticut: Yale University Press, 1981).

Hutchinson, John, *The Dynamics of Cultural Nationalism: The Gaelic Revival and the Creation of the Irish National State* (London: Allen & Unwin, 1987).

Peck, Daniel, *Faces of Degeneration. A European Disorder, c.1848-c.1918* (Cambridge: Cambridge University Press, 1989).

Rigney, Ann, *The Rhetoric of Historical Representation* (Cambridge: Cambridge University Press, 1990).

White, Hayden, *Metahistory: The Historical Imagination in Nineteenth-Century Europe* (Baltimore and London: Johns Hopkins University Press, 1973).

——, *The Content of the Form: Narrative Discourse and Historical Representation* (Baltimore and London: John Hopkins University Press, 1987).

16

The Irish and Their History[*]

HUGH KEARNEY

In 1907 John Millington Synge met with bitter criticism from the Gaelic League for his alleged insults to Irish womanhood in *The Playboy of the Western World*. In 1926 Sean O'Casey ran into similar trouble in Dublin and New York for certain scenes in *The Plough and the Stars*. Both playwrights are now regarded as leading luminaries of the Irish literary renaissance. During their lifetime, however, their work seemed to touch a sensitive nerve in Irish nationalist circles, much as Caradoc Evans offended Welsh non-conformity during the same period.

Something of a similar sort seems to have occurred, though no doubt on a less elevated literary level, when historians from University College Dublin lectured in London in the late 1980s. At one sessions, on 'The Flight of the Earls', a member of the audience is said to have protested against the revisionist tone of the lecture by calling out 'For God's sake leave us our heroes'. Another speaker was denounced in *The Irish Post* as a West Briton. What the native-born scholars regarded as legitimate historical criticism seemed to London-based Irish exiles to be misleading and offensive. Within Ireland itself a clash between nationalist and revisionist interpretations of Irish history is also in full swing. Something of the same kind may also be discerned in the United States, where Kevin O'Neill recently criticized Roy Foster's study of Irish history for being Anglo-centric. It would be surprising if Irish communities in Britain remained immune from such tensions.

In recent years, revisionism, in the sense of a critical approach towards received orthodoxy, has been in the ascendant in Irish academic circles. The latest revisionist piece, Professor J.J. Lee's disenchanted look at Irish life in his successful book *Ireland 1912-1985, Politics and Society* (1989), seems to have touched a chord in the Irish public at large. As nationalist rhetoric turned sour and the early hopes of Sinn Féin failed to materialize, a certain scepticism among historians seemed appropriate. Nationalist history in the style of Mary Hayden, Dorothy McArdle and P.S. O'Hegarty no longer was acceptable.

However, there are now signs of a reaction against what was becoming

[*] First published in *History Workshop Journal* 31 (1991), pp. 149-55.

revisi   doxy. Such controversy in historiography as in other matters,
may b   a sign of health. In English history, the social interpretation
of the   volution has been subjected to severe criticism by Conrad
Russell,   Morrill and Jonathan Clark. Among Irish historians, a champion
of nationalism against revisionism has now made an appearance in the person
of Dr Brendan Bradshaw, Limerick born, but now a lecturer at the University
of Cambridge. In a recent article, 'Nationalism and historical scholarship in
modern Ireland' (*Irish Historical Studies*, November 1989), Bradshaw took to
task the revisionist school of Irish historians. He described them as having
introduced a 'corrosive cynicism' into Irish historiography. In his eyes, even
the critical methods introduced by T.W. Moody and R. Dudley Edwards in
the 1930s and hitherto much praised, served to inhibit rather than enhance
the understanding of the Irish historical experience. Bradshaw presents
especially the way in which the revisionists reject 'the controlling conception
of nationalist historiography, the notion of a "nationalist past" of Irish history
as the story of an Irish nation unfolding historically through the centuries from
the settlement of the aboriginal Celts to the emergence of the national polity
of modern times'.

Perhaps the most surprizing aspect of Bradshaw's anti-revisionist critique
is his use of Herbert Butterfield's argument that the English Whig interpretation, despite its being a historical myth, provided 'a beneficient legacy' which
enabled the English to avoid the horrors of revolutionary change on the French
model. Echoing Butterfield's phraseology, Bradshaw asks the question 'is the
received [the nationalist] version of Irish history a beneficient legacy—its
wrongness notwithstanding—which the revisionists with the zeal of academic
puritans are seeking to drive out?' His answer is in the affirmative. For
Bradshaw the function of the Irish historian is to enable 'a progressively more
heterogeneous national community to appropriate the rich heritage of the
aboriginal Celtic civilization'.

These are disturbing words coming from an academic historian and not
less so for appealing to the authority of Butterfield. The voice may be the
voice of Herbert but the hands are the hands of Machiavelli. Bradshaw in
effect is stating that the historian's duty is to propagate a myth, despite its
wrongness, for the sake of its supposedly beneficient consequences. This is
surely the role of the politician or the journalist not that of a scholar. The
problem which it raises is not of course confined to Ireland. It was discussed
in the pages of this journal (HWJ 29) by Jonathan Clark who argued that
school history was 'an initiation into a culture by the transmission of a heritage'.
For him, popular history (termed by Bradshaw 'public history') is 'a battlefield
in a battle for cultural hegemony' between left and right. History it would
appear should *either* be a story of achievement, advance and enlightenment *or*
a version emphasizing exploitation, suffering and poverty, but not both. There

is no room apparently for ambiguity. This is bowdlerized history of a paternalist kind, taking a pessimitistic view of the capacity of pupils in their early teens to deal with complexity in history, even though they might very well be dealing with some measure of complexity, at that moment, in literature. It is to study William the Conqueror at the level of Just William. The study of literature in the schools has long since abandoned the approach of Mr Bowdler. It would be sad if historians were to attempt to fill the gap with mythological history, however well-intentioned.

In reducing history to the level of myth, Bradshaw does not seem to have considered that what is sauce for the Irish goose is also sauce for the English gander. The Irish cannot complain in good faith about the persistence of long-standing myths about Irish history on one side of the Irish Sea if they are happily purveying the equivalent on the other. For Irish emigrants the beneficient legacy of such myths might be far from apparent.

Bradshaw's apparently innocent advocacy of traditional nationalism is thus open to serious criticism. It must be admitted, however, that his own hostile view of the revisionists, or some of them, is not unjustified. He is right to draw attention to the neglect of what he terms the catastrophic element in Irish history, exemplified in the long tale of massacre, conquest and colonization during the sixteenth and seventeenth centuries. Revisionists have also played down the tragic dimension of the Great Famine of 1845-1848 and the miseries of mass emigration which accompanied it. Bradshaw seems to go too far, however, in his wish to play down the role of the historian as critic. He seems to be calling for the restoration of a pantheon of Irish heroes from Brian Boru to Patrick Pearse. His reference to 'the rich heritage of the aboriginal Celtic civilization' is comparable to an English romantic's wish to return to the glories of Anglo-Saxon England.

The truth is that despite Bradshaw's criticisms, the revisionists have made a major contribution to our understanding of the Irish past. The Institute of Advanced Studies founded by Eamonn de Valera proved to be a veritable revisionist seminary, with T.F. O'Rahilly's famous (or infamous) lecture on 'The two St Patricks' as its opening salvo. Later scholars followed his lead. Donnchadh Ó Corráin showed how the myth of Brian Boru as a nationalist hero was manufactured by official historians of the O'Briens. Fr Paul Walsh in one of the early issues of *Irish Historical Studies* provided a historical criticism of a bardic life of Hugh Roe O'Donnell showing in the process how new mythologies were created in early modern Ireland. Maureen Wall, a fine Gaelic-speaking historian who died prematurely, constructed a powerful revisionist interpretation of the Penal Laws. The volume of essays on the Great Famine, edited by T.D. Williams and R.D. Edwards, for all its lack of a tragic dimension, was the first serious attempt to criticize the nationalist view, as put forward by John Mitchel, that the Famine was planned by the British

Government. Theo Hoppen, in a detailed study of Irish elections during the nineteenth century, has drawn attention to the importance of local issues in deciding the outcome of parliamentary elections. In recent years traditional views about Protestant proselytism and 'taking soup' have also come under criticism. Ruth Dudley Edwards' biography of Pearse, *The Triumph of Failure*, is criticized by Bradshaw for its revisionism. To me it seems an admirable work which treats Pearse as a human being rather than a plaster saint, and hence all the more heroic. All this work, and much else unmentioned, suggests that 'revisionism' is merely a shorthand term for modern historiography.

What the revisionists have done is remind us that history should be a matter for rational debate not a matter of dogma, whether religious or political. Bradshaw is right to draw attention to the significance of the Irish language and of the Celtic tradition. But as with all traditions there are ambiguities and contradictions. Are human sacrifice, blinding, polygamy, 'cursing' to be considered part of the 'rich heritage'? Are the marriage customs of Tory Island, as described by Robin Fox, part of this Celtic heritage? And what about 'the wake' which the Church finally succeeded in stamping out after many centuries. (To many the healing rituals of the wake must have been welcome.) It is an open question whether very much remains of the Celtic heritage today in the Irish Republic, influenced as it is by English common law, the Roman Catholic Church, the United States and the European Community.

Bradshaw seems to recognize that much of nationalist teaching about Irish history is mythical. However, he wishes to retain myth, or 'public history' as he sometimes terms it, because of its 'beneficient legacy'. One obvious problem is who decides what is beneficient. (For Jonathan Clarke this decision rests with the politicians.) For many the legacy of Irish nationalism is not as self-evidently beneficient as Bradshaw seems to believe. Yeats was not alone in thinking that the legacy of nationalism after 1922 was one of civil war and denominational narrowness, from which the Republic is only now beginning to emerge. When we look north of the Irish Border it becomes even more difficult to speak easily of the beneficient legacy of myth. Bradshaw calls for a return to the nationalist tradition of Eoin MacNeill, but MacNeill's own words on the decision to carry out a Rising in 1916 seem 'revisionist' in spirit. In February 1916 he wrote:

> We have to remember that what we call our country is not a political abstraction, as some of us, in the exercise of our highly developed capacity for figurative thought are sometimes apt to imagine—with the help of our patriotic literature. There is no such person as Caithlín Ní Uallacháin or Roisín Dubh or the Sean-Bhean Bhocht, who is calling upon us to serve her. What we call our country is the Irish nation which is a concrete and visible reality. . . . I do not know at this moment whether the time

and circumstances will yet justify revolutionary action but of this I am certain that the only basis for successful revolutionary action is deep and widespread popular discontent. We have only to look around us in the streets to realise that no such condition exists in Ireland. A few of us, a small proportion who think about the evils of English government in Ireland, are always discontented. We would be downright fools if we were to measure many others by the standard of our own thoughts.[1]

Bradshaw accuses the revisionsits of attempting 'to extrude national consciousness as a dimension of the Irish historical experience from all but the modern period'. Here he raises an issue which is fundamental for all nationalist historians, namely the question how far back in time can we trace national consciousness. As the vast historical literature concerning nationalism illustrates, we are entering an extremely problematic area. What is a nation? What is the criterion of belonging? Language? Religion? Class? Race? How many individuals can be said to be conscious of belonging to a particular nation at any one period? If ninety-nine per cent of the inhabitants of Ireland in 1014 saw themselves in terms of local feudal, tribal or social identities, does it make historical sense to speak of 'national consciousness'? Robin Dudley Edwards was fond of quoting Michael Oakeshott's dictum 'History is what the evidence obliges us to believe'. We are not obliged to believe in an extended sense of national consciousness in the age of Brian Boru.

When we come to the modern period further difficulties remain. Bradshaw speaks throughout his article of a single nationalist tradition of historical interpretation. It is clear even to an outsider that serious differences exist about the criterion of nationhood. Fr Tom Burke said in 1872:

> Take an average Irishman—I don't care where you find him—and you will find that the very first principle in his mind is 'I am not an Englishman because I am a Catholic'. Take an Irishman wherever he is found all over the earth and any casual observer will at once come to the conclusion 'Oh he is an Irishman, he is a Catholic'. The two go together.

The beneficient legacy of such a view of Irish nationality is very much open to question in the eyes of those who admire the United Irishmen and the Young Irelanders. The role of the historian is surely to stand outside all of these traditions and to attempt to view them critically but sympathetically, to rescue them, in Edward Thompson's words, from the enormous conde-scension of posterity'.

1. F.X. Martin, 'Select Documents: Eoin MacNeill on the 1916 Rising', *I.H.S.* xii (1960-61), pp. 239-40.

It may be that some historians in an excess of zeal have erred more on the side of criticism than sympathy. However, to dismiss as Bradshaw does the modern critical tradition of Irish historical scholarship from 1938 onwards, the date of the founding of *Irish Historical Studies*, seems to be extraordinarily idiosyncratic. It involves ignoring, for example, the distinctive revisionist tradition in early Irish history, unrelated to *Irish Historical Studies*. Binchy (1900–89), whom many would regard as the Irish Maitland, was an arch revisionist in this field. He was well aware that his critical articles would have little effect upon widely held myths about the 'instant Christianization' of Ireland and he commented ruefully upon the way in which high Irish ecclesiastics provided a diet of myth rather than history during the papal visit. Patrician studies are surely one of the areas in which the revisionists made a definite contribution.

All this may seem remote to the readers of *History Workshop Journal*. What is at stake, however, is the status of history as a detached scholarly activity. Brendan Bradshaw following in the wake of the late Herbert Butterfield, claims a privileged position for a particular interpretation of Irish history. He advocates a return to the nationalist tradition of Eoin MacNeill and Edmund Curtis, and a rejection of what he terms the revisionist 'value-free' interpretation of modern Irish historiography. Not all revisionism is rejected. Bradshaw attempts to have it both ways in this regard by approving a short list of those historians who have shown the appropriate qualities of empathy and imagination. But suppose, as seems to be the case with Professor Lee, they are orthodox in one book and revisionist in another?

The truth is that Bradshaw's attempt to turn the clock back to the 'golden oldies' like MacNeill and Curtis is seriously misleading. For they in terms of their own time were also revisionist. We should discard the concept of revisionism itself and return to the notion of historical scholarship as an endless debate, in which it is possible to discuss people and movements in a spirit of relative detachment. Two examples of such history come to mind. My friend and colleague Robin Dudley Edwards used to recommend J.F. Kenney's introduction to *The Sources for the Early History of Ireland: Ecclesiastical* to all newcomers to Irish history. It is still excellent advice. I would also add the various essays by Daniel Binchy in *Studia Hibernica*. Kenney and Binchy seem to me to be examples of historians who transcend the categories of 'nationalist' and 'revisionist'.

We are still left with the problem with which we began, namely how to reconcile the critical comments of Irish-born historians with the sensitivities of the emigrant Irish in Britain, the United States and elsewhere. The answer to this is surely not to return to the violent prejudices of 'the day of the rabblement'. The Irish and their friends must learn to see Irish history in a multi-dimensional context rather than as partisan simplicities (as must of course the English).

It is also worth pointing out in conclusion that Bradshaw has raised an issue which though relevant to Kilburn in 1991 is as old as the Renaissance and Reformation, namely the moral role of history. Hugh Trevor-Roper in his Neale lecture on William Camden, 'Queen Elizabeth's first historian', showed how Camden was pressed by the Puritans to depict Mary Queen of Scots as an example of moral depravity rather than as a human being caught up in a tangled web of events. It was the Puritans who saw history in clear cut terms of black and white with Foxe's Book of Martyrs as their favourite text. By this criterion, Bradshaw is laying himself open to the very charge of puritanism which he levels at others. History makes strange bedfellows.

17

Unionist History*

ALVIN JACKSON

I

The Irish, north and south, are as bound by their history as they are divided by it. Their abuse of the past has for long been shared. Their historical inheritance, though different in content, shares the same form: Derry besieged or Limerick besieged, 1641 or Drogheda, 1916 on the banks of the Liffey or on the banks of the Somme. History for all the Irish is a mantra of sacred dates, an invocation of secular saints: though the enshrouding flags differ, the martyr's coffin is a shared icon. Ethnicity for both sides is a cocktail distilled by external assault and internal confidence. Most nations, colonial or indigenous, have produced clearly defined notions of their community's strengths and weaknesses, of the experiences of injustice and the superior qualities which permit survival or triumph: the 'varieties of Irishness' are not exceptional in this respect.

The Protestant sense of history in Northern Ireland is as fragmentary and limited as more popular historical awareness, but this is not to suggest that the demands of political unity have wholly spirited away those aspects of a complex inheritance which do not suit contemporary exigency. The Protestant past is an uncomfortable and ugly garment, and a gaudy Orange sash never fully conceals the stains of denominational tension, or the patches of class division. Rural Protestant communities in eastern Ulster retain tortured memories of 1798, of the struggle for tenant right, and of the sectarian rivalries between Presbyterian and Episcopalian. As Terence Brown has argued, Protestant history *is* more complex than contemporary rhetoric would suggest. But, then, a fundamental aspect of the Irish tragedy is that the past is continually and ritually sacrificed to a caricature of the present. Threads are plucked from both past and present, and woven into a smothering ideological blanket of a uniform green, or orange, or red, white and blue. A monochrome history deceives only a minority, but it is the few, purblind zealots who have sculpted so much of our environment.

Unionism does not demand a complex vision of its own past. This is very

* First published in *The Irish Review* (Autumn 1989), pp. 58-65 and (Spring 1990), pp. 62-9.

far from saying that the Unionist historiographical tradition is as sporadic and mono-dimensionsal as the needs and perceptions of its beneficiaries would appear to imply. On the contrary, early Unionist visions of the past were as varied and shifting as the demands of political debate. The fissiparous nature of Irish Unionism, no less than that of Nationalism, meant that there was always a tendency towards producing a simplified historical creed for the consumption of the pious. But the emphases of this creed certainly changed according to political necessity, and a more complex historiographical dogma has always been available to a material and intellectual elite.

Unionism remains fissiparous, and retains a need for its catechisms of historical faith. The broadening of political debate since 1972 has made ideological and strategic demands for which the Unionist movement, schooled disastrously at Stormont, has had no response. As the demands of Anglo-Irish politics have become more intricate, so the political and historical perceptions of Unionism have become simplified. The historical and historiographical legacy is rich and complex, but the legatees squander their inheritance by their very frugality.

II

The definition of Unionist history is as intangible as the definition of Unionism itself, but in the interests of clarity the arguments here are structured around two alternative propositions. Unionist history may be at once a matter of Unionists engaged in the writing of history and, at the same time, the study of the Unionist tradition in Ireland by those not necessarily politically committed in one direction or another: the distinction between 'Unionist historian' and 'historian of Unionism'. Defining the definition—defining the 'Unionist historian'—is by no means easy, partly because of the diversity of Unionist political commitment, and partly because it is self-evidently unreasonable to ascribe political sentiments to those contemporary historians (like J.C. Beckctt) who have not made some unambiguous expression of political faith. No, the intention here is not to speculate about personal conviction from uncertain evidence, or to offer a definition of Unionism so flaccid as to be meaningless, but rather to identify a type of historian who has either been politically active in the interests of Unionism, or who (like A.T.Q. Stewart) has unequivocally publicized his or her political sentiments. Against this grouping I want to juxtapose a tradition of scholarship concerned with the evolution of Unionist politics and society in Ireland. Clearly the two categories—'Unionist historian' and 'historian of Unionism' are not mutually exclusive, as the mention of Stewart suggests—but the overlap is, in practice, much slighter than one might expect. And it will become clear that the categories are also discrete, judged within the context of the historical profession's evolution in Ireland.

The period between the emergence of Home Rule within the mainstream of Irish politics and the emergence of two states in Ireland saw a dramatic upsurge both in political pamphleteering and in the manipulation of history, or exploitation of historical evidence, for partisan intent. The historical profession, defined as those pursuing the discipline of history within a university environment, emerged in Ireland at the same time as the national revival, and it should come as no disappointment (especially given continental precedents) that the two events should be so intricately interwoven. The dialogue between the Irish cultural revival and political nationalism is an obvious historical phenomenon, as are the political commitments of historians like Eoin MacNeill and Alice Stopford Green—R.B. McDowell's 'passionate historian'. Of course parliamentary Nationalists like T.M. Healy were no less eager to seek legitimization through the writing of history, whether in works like *The Great Fraud of Ulster* (a title which signals that this is no work of mealy-mouthed moderation), or through tendentious autobiographical reminiscence. But the phenomenon of the scholar-politician was as much a Unionist as a Nationalist creation, and the frequently historical nature of the Home Rule debate ensured that the writing of history had a central role in the political priorities of the Unionist intelligentsia. If, as Lloyd George and other British pragmatists so often complained, Irish politics were a matter of perceived historical grievance, then the all-too-familiar centuries of 'English occupation' were as actively scrutinized by Unionists as by Nationalists.

Unionist historical scholarship had several institutional focuses in Ireland, but chief amongst these was Trinity College Dublin. Trinity College was landowning and Anglican, and (as its parliamentary representation repeatedly indicated) predominantly Unionist. Its law school supplied technically adroit advocates to the Irish Unionist leadership, and its lawyers and historians supplied Unionism with ideological substance, and with a shifting vision of the Irish past. Among the Protestant intellectual elite of Victorian Dublin a recognizable cultural Irishness and constitutional anti-separatism were for long compatible, married within the Royal Irish Academy, among the pages of the *Dublin University Magazine*, or the writings of a Samuel Ferguson. Of course mainstream politics in the Ireland beyond College Green were pressing towards a more ambitious nationalism and a more rigorously exclusivist definition of Irishness (whether judged in terms of religion, perceptions of ethnicity, or anti-Englishness). The radicalization of Irish politics after the 1870s outstripped the expectations and desires of most Trinity intellectuals, however liberal or Irish in terms of self-perception. Certainly an historian like Lecky, as Donal McCartney has demonstrated, was being shunted from an early and generous liberalism in the 1860s towards an increasingly circumspect conservatism by the 1890s, an evolution to be traced in the successive revisions to his *Leaders of Public Opinion in Ireland*. In his preface to the edition of *Leaders* which appeared in 1903 Lecky repudiated 'the worst specimens of the boyish rhetoric' evident when the volume first appeared in 1861, as well as the contemporary political analysis which prefaced the version of 1871. And Lecky was only the most prominent of a group of Trinity and other scholars who, by the end of the nineteenth century, had emerged as active proponents of Unionism, and active investigators of the origins of the Unionist tradition in Ireland.

Unionist historiography was therefore, as with its Nationalist counterpart, essentially a response to the prevailing political climate in Ireland. C.L. Falkiner, an important yet neglected Unionist historian, admitted candidly in the preface to his *Studies in Irish History and Biography* (1902) that it was impossible to approach his subject with 'absolute colourlessness'; and he found himself in agreement with Lord Rosebery's dictum that 'the Irish question has never passed into history because it has never passed out of politics'. Predictably, given this interrelationship of history and politics, scholars like Falkiner were active in defiance of the Unionist interest. Falkiner and his contemporary F.E. Ball, the historian of County Dublin and of the Irish judiciary, fought comfortable crusades for the Union in the suburbs of south Dublin at the turn of the century: Ball in fact stood in south County Dublin as a rogue Unionist candidate at the election of 1900. Lecky, their mentor, sat as parliamentary representative for Trinity College between 1895 and 1903, having migrated from Liberalism (indeed from a limited form of nationalist sympathy) to Liberal Unionism in 1886. Other scholars were associated with these Trinity historians: Richard Bagwell from Clonmel, active as a Liberal Unionist, S.H. Butcher, the classics scholar and Kerry man, and Edward Dowden, dismissed by Yeats as the archetypal Victorian drudge, but rated rather more highly within the hierarchy of the Irish Unionist Alliance.

But conspicuous though scholar-politicians like Butcher and Dowden were, it was the historians who were of the greater ideological importance to the development of Unionism. Falkiner, Ball and Lecky supplied Irish Protestants with histories of the Anglo-Irish political tradition, and with celebrations of its values and achievements. Lecky offered an account of the Ascendancy in the eighteenth century in the form of a five volume *History of Ireland*—one of the first and most obviously Anglo-centric general histories of Ireland, if only because it was directly a by-product of a survey of English history. Falkiner sketched sympathetic portraits of Castlereagh and John Fitzgibbon, Earl of Clare, the architects of Union between Britain and Ireland.

The strength of the bond between Unionist politics and Unionist historical scholarship is indicated both by the political concerns of the historians themselves, but also by the evolving form of their scholarly interests. The historical nature of Gladstone's promotion of Home Rule and the encouragement which he gave to others similarly disposed to argue from historical principles (like the Parnellite J.G. Swift MacNeill) created a need for an Irish Unionist response. Thomas Dunbar Ingram, a Belfast born lawyer and historian rose to the occasion, composing *The Passing of the Act of Union* (1887) to demonstrate the strength of contemporary support for the Union and the purity of the circumstances surrounding its passage. Successive Unionist historians and writers returned to consider and to vindicate the measure— Falkiner through his biographical essays, Lord Ashbourne, the Unionist Lord Chancellor of Ireland, through his biography of Pitt, and J.R Fisher through his *The End of the Irish Parliament*, published—significantly—in 1911, on the eve of the crisis arising from the third Home Rule Bill.

More widely ranging Nationalist indictments of British rule in Ireland, which proliferated in 1886 and after, were countered by Unionist historical propaganda, scouring the centuries for a sharper illumination of the present. Lord Midleton's *Ireland: Dupe or Heroine* (1932), hailed by the *Evening Standard* as 'this authentic record by the greatest living authority on Ireland' was merely a late addition to a peculiar form of Irish historical apologetic, which sought to annex the lessons of history in the service of present political need. The point of Midleton's polemic was a defence of W.T. Cosgrave and has Cumann na nGaedheal administration (his last chapter, entitled 'St Patrick or De Valera', came down decisively on the side of St Patrick); but earlier Unionist historians and controversialists (A.W. Samuels, Peter Kerr-Smiley) had shaped their narratives along similar lines in order to impugn a Parnell or Redmond.

The responses of Irish historians and historical polemicists were not exclusively tied to either Home Rulers or to the Home Rule debate. Celebrating the loyalist tradition in Ireland also, inevitably, meant celebrating the contribution of Irish soldiers to the British war effort in the years 1914-1918. War simultaneously united and divided the Irish people; 1916 came to represent a different sort of 'magic number' to different types of Irishman, even if Protestants and Catholics were fighting and dying together on the Western Front. The War, the Somme in particular, dominated Unionist history-writing in the 1920s, when the Irish Free State was being supplied with a revolutionary mythology and hagiography by its scholarly and polemical defenders. Celebratory accounts of the struggle against the British and of its protagonists were paralleled within Unionist historiography by celebratory accounts of the Irish struggle against Kaiser Wilhelm. Piaras Béaslaí's portrayal of Michael Collins (1926) appeared only months before the commemoration of another Irish commander assassinated in 1922—Field Marshal Sir Henry Wilson, whose *Life and Letters* were devoutly compiled by a fellow Irish Unionist and war veteran, General Charles Callwell. Other Irish Unionist writers supplied regimental and divisional histories: Bryan Cooper, Unionist MP for South Dublin in 1910, and subsequently a convert to Cumann na nGaedheal, commemorated the Irish dead of Gallipoli through his account of the action of the *Tenth (Irish) Division*. Cyril Falls, son of a prominent Fermanagh Unionist, began a distinguished scholarly career with the publication of his *History of the 36th (Ulster) Division* (1922), and his *History of the Royal Irish Rifles* (1925). Lord Ernest Hamilton a rather less skilled but no less committed historian, paid his homage to the war dead through *The First Seven Divisions* (1916). In the midst of these war requiems only W.A. Phillips, holder—significantly—of the Lecky chair of Modern History at Trinity, offered—a substantial, near-contemporary and Unionist analysis of the Anglo-Irish struggle.

The blood sacrifice called for by Pearse had been offered, but by different loyalties and on different altars. War had fully exposed the tensions within Irish politics, and historians, divided both politically and now by their choice of subject matter, compounded these tensions. Commemorating their respective dead, historians supplied two distinctive devotional literatures to the two Irish states, and helped to fashion two distinctive iconographical traditions.

III

Although commentators as diverse as Peter Gibbon and Tom Paulin have recognized the partitionist sympathies of individual Irish historians, the extent and importance of the work celebrating 'Ulster' and the origins of Northern Ireland have too rarely been grasped. In aggregate, northern historians and historical writers, working from the end of the first World War through to the 1940s, supplied a comprehensive legitimizing and apologist literature. War histories were only one, indirect contribution to the historical vindication of loyalism and of the Unionist state: indeed historians themselves only offered one form of contribution to a more complex literature which had for its subject matter the Ulster Protestant condition. Popular Unionist historians like Ernest Hamilton followed in the path of the Victorian Orange novelist and politician, William Johnston, in celebrating the planter tradition, delineating its qualities and publicizing its tribulations. The onslaught of 1641 was a recurrent theme, taken up by Johnston in his novel *Under Which King?*—a strangely lachrymose document from an Orange commander—and expounded in detail by Hamilton in his *The Irish Rebellion* (1920). Hamilton himself offered semi-fictional accounts of 1641 in his *Tales of the Troubles* (1925). Both Hamilton in *Elizabethan Ulster* and Cyril Falls in his *The Birth of Ulster* explored the development of the Ulster plantations, Falls referring to his own planter origins and to his admiration for that tradition.

The period of the foundation of Northern Ireland was characterized by a literature, equally partitionist in implication, which commemorated specifically the Ulster Unionist achievement and celebrated 'the Ulsterman'. The ubiquitous Ernest Hamilton—provided a schematic and selective history of his native province in *The Soul of Ulster* (1917), pointed towards a condemnation of Sinn Féin. Ramsay Colles supplied a marginally less tendentious and certainly more comprehensive *History of Ulster* in 1919—an enterprise justified by 'the Province's magnificent record, and the greatness of her achievements in so many spheres of activity'. The inevitability of partition was further adduced through the work of contemporary historians and political commentators in the 1920s such as H.D. Morrison and J.W. Logan. And the events leading to the foundation of Northern Ireland were interpreted with a piety worthy of a P.S. O'Hegarty or a Béaslaí by the Ulster Unionist MP Ronald McNeill in his influential *Ulster's Stand for Union* (1922).

All these works, whatever their scholarly merits or demerits, were essentially period pieces, because consciously or unconsciously, they represented an Ulster Unionist response to the partition question. The writers were often politically active, and where, like Cyril Falls, they were professional scholars, they expressed their particular communal loyalty. This was Unionist history, not necessarily because it was uniformly and absolutely committed, but because it was written by Unionists on historical themes of particular relevance to the Unionist community, and occasionally with a contemporary political purpose. James Craig's Northern Ireland had therefore a more formidable literary vindication than is frequently assumed. If Northern Ireland was an instant and arbitrary political formulation, then Unionist writers saw, with Whiggish confidence, only a more ancient pedigree and an inevitable constitutional denouement.

Ronald McNeill's work was important, and not simply because he was the most able exponent of Unionist historiography in the 1920s. His *Ulster's Stand for Union* represented a key historiographical transition as the first substantial, documented and public account of organized Unionism. McNeill looked forward to the evolution of scholarly interest in the structures of the Unionist movement, and his narrative, important as much for its personal insights as for its political balance, is still required reading. A Unionist historian of organized Unionism, McNeill pioneered a shift away from other forms of partitionist historiography, and was the precursor of an historiographical tradition which is sustained through the work of scholars like A.T.Q. Stewart.

McNeill was, therefore, the father to the literature which celebrated the Unionist founders of Northern Ireland, and the events surrounding its foundation. In the 1930s and after, celebratory biographies of Carson and Craig appeared, written by historians and propagandists, like McNeill, from within the Unionist tradition, and frequently drawing upon McNeill's own narrative. Edward Marjoribanks and Ian Colvin wrote the first major assessment of Carson, published in three volumes between 1932 and 1936: this was followed in 1953 by Montgomery Hyde's *Carson*, and in 1981 by a brilliant synthesis of these pioneering works written by A.T.Q. Stewart. The early assessments were essentially positive, as indeed the nature of their authorship might have suggested: Colvin was leader-writer on the ultra-Tory *Morning Post* and Hyde was a Unionist MP at Westminster in the 1950s. James Craig was nearly as fortunate in his biographers, Hugh Shearman writing sympathetically though professedly from a non-partisan standpoint (*Not an Inch*, 1942), while St John Ervine's massive, semi-official biography (1949) was composed partly 'to expound and interpret . . . the beliefs and political faith of Ulster Unionists' of whom he declared himself to be one. Through works such as these the cult of Unionist commanders like Carson, so vital a political phenomenon in their own lifetime, was sustained after death. Celebratory biographies helped to reaffirm the integrity of the state's purpose and leadership in Northern Ireland no less than popular portrayals of Collins in the Irish Free State. These were the lives of the Founding Fathers, and as such they fulfilled an essential ideological function for successive Stormont governments. One need not look any further than the career of Ian Paisley to observe the influence and burden of Carson's mystique; and panegyrical biographies were crucial in the bequest of such political reputations and mythologies.

Celebrating the origins and founders of Northern Ireland also occasionally involved a reconsideration of some of the more dramatic and controversial aspects of Ulster Unionist politics. The gun-running of 1914 was of crucial political and psychological significance, bringing credibility to Unionist threats, and representing a successful defiance by an embattled and minority community of an unsympathetic government: as such it was a focal point for Ulster Unionist self-congratulation and pride. A leading gun-runner, like F.H. Crawford, though an idiosyncratic, even apocalyptic figure, enjoyed patronage from the Northern Ireland government; indeed leaders of that government (Craig for example) had themselves been indirectly involved with Crawford's activities. Ronald McNeill celebrated the gun-running in his *Ulster's Stand for Union*. Crawford offered his own, often inaccurate memories of the episode in *Guns for Ulster* (1947); and more minor figures like R.J. Adgey were equally anxious to recall their participation in the events of April 1914. A.T.Q. Stewart provided a vivid and intricately researched portrayal of the gun-running through his *The Ulster Crisis of 1967*. The date of publication is significant. Stewart's was a highly acclaimed work of professional scholarship, and therefore to be distinguished from earlier accounts; but it was written by a friendly observer in the context of a still stable Stormont administration. *The Ulster Crisis* was among the last works of Unionist Whiggery, works which cast the founders of Northern Ireland and their actions in an heroic mould. In this sense the Stewart of 1967 stood as virtually the last representative of an historiographical tradition which had its roots in the origins of Northern Ireland itself.

IV

Since 1969 the historical analogy which has dominated the minds of the Unionist leadership has been that supplied by the events of 1912–1914. Previous generations of loyalist validated their actions by evoking comparison with 1641 or with 1690; but, while the Boyne is never far from the historical consciousness of the Unionist movement, the precedents suggested by loyalist activity in 1912 have lately exercised a more thorough fascination and restraint. This may be partly related to divisions within Unionism, and to the search by the Democratic Unionist Party for domination of the Unionist past, no less than of the Unionist present. Ian Paisley has repeatedly identified himself as the successor to Edward Carson—from his association with Carson's son in 1966 through to the Carson Trail campaign tour of 1981. In doing so, he has implicitly challenged the validity of rival claimants, as Terence O'Neill and his successors within mainstream Unionism have speedily recognized. But both Democratic and Official Unionists have agreed in seeing their resistance to the Anglo-Irish Agreement as a reconstruction of their forefathers' opposition to the third Home Rule Bill—even if they differ over the inheritance of individual roles. The immutability of their dilemma has impressed all types of Unionist. As with Frank McGuinness's Kenneth Pyper, ancestral hands exercise a guidance and constraint from beyond the grave. A particular sense of history and a particular cast of mind permit the present to be fulfilled by the events of a long-dead struggle.

If Unionist commentators, from Dr Paisley to the newly-formed Ulster Society, have been engaged by the events of 1912–1914, then recent scholarship has opened up broader perspectives on the historical development of the Unionist movement. The resurgence of violence in Northern Ireland after 1969 has radically altered the character of the study of Unionism. Broader interest in the politics of the North has promoted a more comprehensive and politically complex examination of Unionist history, even if—as I shall argue—there remain striking imbalances within this literature.

Setting aside ephemeral anti-partitionist polemic (such as James Winder Good's *Irish Unionism* 1920), those writing on Unionism before 1969 tended themselves to be Unionist: indeed, as has been indicated, some of the most important commentators were active in contemporary Unionist politics (Ernest Hamilton, Ronald McNeill). Well-publicized violence since 1969 has attracted a more diverse range of analysis, for—as John Whyte has pointed out—'Northern Ireland is a small stage on which great issues can with relative ease be tested'. External comment, combined with the exponential growth of historical research in Ireland, has created new historiographical traditions within the study of Unionism, as well as a more weighty literature. 'Unionist history' is no longer the preserve of Unionist principle; indeed, as has been noted,

Unionist commentators are now effectively confined by the consideration of Carson's achievement.

V

Much has been written about the nature of contemporary Protestant politics, but this lies largely beyond the parameters of the present essay. The concerns here are with the historical development of organized Unionism and not with any broader treatment of Irish Protestant politics. It may be briefly observed, however, that there *is* a bias within much of the most recent literature towards the consideration of radical loyalism. In part this reflects a general weighting within Irish and British historiography, which, as Brian Harrison has argued, tend to neglect centrist themes, and to favour the radical periphery of politics. So Ian Paisley and his movement have been anatomized in three important works (Moloney and Pollak's *Paisley* (1986), Clifford Smyth's *Paisley: Voice of Protestant Ulster* (1987), Steve Bruce, *God Save Ulster!* (1980)), whereas James Molyneaux has been almost thoroughly neglected: there is one conversational essay in biography, and no extended analysis of his leadership. Equally, since 1972 there have been at least three substantial examinations of loyalist paramilitary politics—David Boulton's *The UVF* (1973), Sarah Nelson's *Ulster's Uncertain Defenders* (1984), Martin Dillon's *The Shankill Butchers* (1989) but no published study of Official Unionism—since its evolution in 1973-4 the single largest Unionist party, and indeed, to purloin W.D. Flackes's label, 'the largest political entity in the province'. There have been no detailed assessments of Molyneaux's predecessors, Harry West, Brian Faulkner, and James Chichester-Clark; Terence O'Neill's epochal rule has, setting aside the general histories, been examined only once—in David Gordon's stimulating and polemical *The O'Neill's Years* (1989). After twenty years of violence the plain of Unionism, suburban and constitutional, remains apparently more inaccessible than the ganglands stalked by Lennie Murphy.

The historical development of organized Unionism has stimulated even less scholarly enthusiasm, yet it is probably true that more has been written on this theme in the twenty years since 1969 than in the fifty years preceding the re-emergence of widespread violence. The intellectual origins and implications of this work are exceedingly diverse, but a starting point may be made with the broad organizational dichotomy employed by Whyte in his reviews of the literature on Northern Ireland: that separating Marxist and non-Marxist commentator.

Of course the divisions within the Marxist literature are as striking as the differences between Marxist and non-Marxist works. Divisions over the national question and partition have coloured Irish socialism from the Edwardian disputes between William Walker and James Connolly: such divisions were bequeathed to the Labour Party in Northern Ireland, and are reflected in Marxist and socialist analysis of Ulster Unionism. The now disbanded British and Irish Communist Organization produced an important and partitionist analysis, *The Birth of Unionism*, which links that movement to the uneven development of Irish capitalism, and to the existence of two nations, a British and an Irish, on the island. Anti-partitionist Marxists such as Desmond Greaves and Michael Farrell have had a more traditional conception of a single Irish nation, with the island of Ireland as its natural territory: partition, for Greaves, was a cynical British imposition favouring an economically privileged and dissident minority of the Irish people. Farrell's conception of Ulster Unionist nationality is more ambiguous, for while he accepts that Protestants may perceive themselves as part of a British nation, he has also inherited Connolly's bemused impatience with the Unionism of the Protestant working classes: populist Unionism, rather than being a corollary of Britishness, is instead an unhealthy admixture of bigotry and bourgeois manipulation.

Starting from intellectual premises so opposed, the analysis of Unionism proffered by BICO and by Greaves and Farrell embodies very different emphases: indeed Parnell and BICO have come into direct polemical confrontation, the BICO pamphlet *The Two Irish Nations* being cast, in its edition of 1975, as a rejoinder and rebuke to Farrell. Farrell, particularly in his *Northern Ireland: The Orange State* (1976), dwells on the injustices experienced by the northern minority at the hands of Unionist government. Unionism, as embodied in its governmental structures, reflects superannuated economic relationships, and inevitably—though ineffectually—tends towards repression. For BICO commentators it is Unionism, rather than its Nationalist critics, which reflects the historically more advanced economic conditions; and it is Nationalism, through its relationship with Catholicism, which is socially and politically regressive and oppressive. BICO commentators frequently stress the radical political and social potential of Ulster Protestantism, expressed whether in the United Irishmen, or in farmer agitation, or in the populist opposition to Belfast Toryism. The BICO analysts and Farrell have had at least this in common—that they have approached Unionist historiography from the perceptive of contemporary commitments, Farrell representing his *Orange State* as being a partisan work designed as a call to political action. BICO activists were, by definition, political crusaders first and historians second, working from a comprehensive critique of contemporary politics supplied by commentators such as Brendan Clifford and Peter Brooke.

Paul Bew, Peter Gibbon, and Henry Patterson constitute a third school of Marxist comment on Irish Unionism: in John Whyte's terms they represent the apex of the Marxist dialectic on Northern Ireland—the 'synthesis' to Farrell's 'thesis' and the BICO 'antithesis'. Influenced by the work of Louis Althusser, Bew, Gibbon and Patterson have sought to break away from the more banal aspects of the partition controversy, and have concentrated on examining the internal dynamics of Unionism. As with BICO and Farrell, Bew and Patterson are each anxious to offer a political critique of British government in Northern Ireland: they share with BICO an emphasis on the uneven development of Irish capitalism. But their contemporary and historical analyses are more sharply distinguished than those of BICO and Farrell, and their writing is more subtle and expansive in terms of ideology, methodologically more innovative, and more generous in its sympathies. Their fundamental achievement has been to probe the depth of economic and political tension within, particularly, urban Unionism, whether at the level of the Stormont cabinet (*The State in Northern Ireland* (1978)), or among the Protestant working classes of Belfast (Patterson's excellent *Class Conflict and Sectarianism* (1980)). Peter Gibbon has explored the interrelationship of urban and rural Unionism, and the political supersession of landlordism by a dynamic, export-oriented Unionist manufacturing and mercantile elite (*The Origins of Ulster Unionism* (1975)). Through these works Bew, Gibbon and Patterson have shifted from re-mapping the interface between Unionism and Nationalism towards a new dimension in the analysis of Unionist development. The nature of the partition question is much less important than the nature of the partitionists themselves; qualitative distinctions between Unionism and Nationalism are much less important than qualitative distinctions *within* Unionism.

Recent non-Marxist historiography represents rather less of a break with earlier analyses of Unionism than the work of Bew, Gibbon and Patterson. Works such as John Biggs Davison's and George Chowdharay-Best's *The Cross of St Patrick* (1984) certainly share similarities with an older, laudatory historiography both in terms of the political sympathies of their authors, and in terms of source material. More recent celebrations by Unionist politicians and writers living in Ireland tend to appear rather lightweight when judged in comparison with their late Victorian precursors—yet they also stand as clearly within a tradition of loyalist self-assessment as *The Cross of St Patrick*. The fiftieth anniversary of Carson's death stimulated James Allister, a democratic Unionist Assemblyman, and Peter Robinson, Democratic Unionist MP for East Belfast, to compose a reverential essay on their perceived political forebear. This, and a number of works on the 1912-14 period produced by the Ulster Society, a body created in 1985 'to promote an awareness and appreciation of our distinctive Ulster-British culture', recall in both their tone and purpose the historical reflections of Victorian Unionist activists. Neatly packaged, well-illustrated, and cheaply priced, these recent publications are evidently designed for a mass market—designed to promote a more active consideration of the loyalist tradition. Standing within a Unionist historiographical lineage, it is ironic that the evangelical tone of these works should recall the zeal of Gaelic revivalist literature no less than the apologetic of Victorian loyalism.

But the work of the majority of non-Marxist commentators is less overtly politically committed, and therefore less uniformly centred on Ulster Unionism, than either loyalist or Marxist reflection. Southern Unionism was virtually rediscovered by Patrick Buckland after a political and scholarly neglect of almost fifty years. His seminal articles and monograph (*Irish Unionism I: The Anglo-Irish and the New Ireland* (1972)) opened the way in the 1970s to a succession of studies of southern loyalism or ex-loyalism (those of Ian d'Alton, Jack White, Kurt Bowen). Indeed, although Professor Buckland wrote two studies of pre-partition Unionism, one on the south and one on the north, the former is physically a more substantial volume than the latter. And the doyen of the Irish historical profession, Professor J.C. Beckett, has contributed to this debate and to the emphasis on southern Unionism through his *The Anglo-Irish Tradition* (1976). Professor Beckett concludes with, and endorses the call of William Drennan—words which echo through Stewart Parker's 'Pentecost' and other northern literature, and which have flavoured, ironically, Unionist rhetoric: that 'the Catholics may save themselves, but it is the Protestants must save the nation'. 'The words are as true today as when they were written', comments Beckett drily, 'and as little likely to be heeded'.

D.C. Savage and F.S.L. Lyons have provided studies of Ulster Unionism during two key phases of its evolution, in 1885-6 and in 1904-5; John Harbinson has written a pioneering general account of organized Ulster Unionism from its foundation through to 1973. David Miller, through his *Queen's Rebels* (1978), and Andrew Gailey, in *Ireland and the Death of Kindness* (1987), have explored aspects of the Ulster loyalist's relationship with British government. But, even allowing for these works, it is arguably the case that as much is known about the institutional evolution of southern Unionism as of northern Unionism for the period before 1933—a curious imbalance given the numerical weakness and ultimate demise of the southern movement. And, although the literature on Unionism in Northern Ireland is relatively large, little has been written on many aspects of Protestant and Unionist society, or of the Unionist Party itself. Only in 1987 was the first dissection of Nationalist attitudes towards Ulster Unionism offered (Clare O'Halloran's *Partition and the Limits of Nationalism*); only in 1988 were the first studies of the Unionist press and of Viscount Brookeborough offered by, respectively, Dennis Kennedy and Brian Barton.

The impact of contemporary political debate on these non-Marxist scholars is certainly subtle, yet it is as profound as for the more deterministic. To some extent political controversy has dictated both the subject matter and evidence of those scholars researching Unionism. Just as the struggle surrounding the first Home Rule bill had an historical dimension, so critics of partition have looked to the historical record of Unionism in order to substantiate their allegations. The Government of Ireland Act plays much the same role in late twentieth century polemic as the Act of Union in the Home Rule controversies of the late nineteenth century; the record of successive British Chief Secretaries for Ireland was analysed minutely in 1880 and 1893 in much the same way as the record of Stormont ministers has been tested in work published since the late 1960s. The issues of polemical concern have become the issues attracting scholarly research; polemical literature has become the substance of historical research. To a limited extent the polemicists have *become* the scholarly researchers, just as historiographical and party political activities were not deemed to be incompatible in the nineteenth century (before the popularization of a 'scientific' methodology).

The critics of Unionist government have indirectly encouraged greater consideration of the subject. Michael Farrell has, through *Northern Ireland: The Orange State* and *Arming the Protestants* (1983), provided more thoroughly researched versions of his own work as an ideologue and leader within People's Democracy. Volumes such as these both reflect an increasing research interest in Stormont, itself the offspring of polemical discussion, and in turn excite further scholarly rejoinder. John Whyte, for example, has subjected a central feature of the critique of the Unionist record—the allegation of sustained discrimination—to a comprehensive analysis, weighing the available historical evidence against verdicts of commentators such as Farrell and the Unionist A.J. Walmsley. Tom Wilson, a distinguished economist and adviser to Terence O'Neill, has taken up this theme, and other aspects of the debate over Stormont government, in a measured defence of the Unionist record (*Ulster: Conflict and Conciliation* (1989)).

More generally, there has been a proliferation of commentary on the politics and history of Northern Ireland, as scholars respond to the demands of heightened public awareness, and of political discussion. Works such as Patrick Buckland's intricately researched *Factory of Grievances* (1979) or his valuable *History of Northern Ireland* (1981) offer considered assessments of the Unionist record, and help to satisfy the popular appetite for reliable historical comment on Northern Ireland: David Harkness's excellent *Northern Ireland since 1920* (1983) fulfils a similarly useful function. Naturally these works address issues of contemporary political concern, and from the historical perspective—whether economic performance, employment practice, or security policy.

Contemporary debate also, inevitably, intrudes into the historian's sources. There is both an institutional and personal dimension to this intrusion. Governments and civil service in London, Dublin and Belfast have proved to be extremely cautious over the release of material bearing on Unionist government. The restrictions governing such material tend to be much more oppressive than for other, less controversial, areas of administration; and the processes of selection are performed with apparently much greater vigour. To some extent all historians working in official archives are informally bound to an agenda devized by government—but this is more obviously the case with the records of the Stormont ministries. Nor is there much consolation to be gained elsewhere. Leading Unionist politicians have been—understandably— reluctant to place their archives on public access, and their descendants, often fearful of the consequences of publicity, are generally no less coy. Autobiographical reminiscence (Terence O'Neill's *Autobiography* (1972), Brian Faulkner's posthumously-published *Memoirs of a Statesman* (1978)) is, almost by definition, less concerned with factual reconstruction than with the protection of political reputations. The opponents of Unionism are generally as unforthcoming as the targets of their invective. Violence in Northern Ireland, allied to the peculiarly acrimonious nature of political exchange, means that the penalties of unconsidered frankness, of sweeping disclosure, are very considerable. Given these constraints of evidence, even the most disinterested historian is as bound to the sectarian arena as the most vitriolic polemicist.

VI

A more diverse and vibrant historiography has therefore emerged since 1969—but an historiography characterized by both old and new varieties of emphasis and imbalance. The historiography of Unionism remains an historiography of crisis, detailed examinations of politics in 1885-6 or in 1912-14 proliferating at the expense of the investigation of either institutional evolution or Unionist society. Southern Unionism before 1922 has evoked a comparatively great scholarly regard, while many features of the early development of popular Unionism in the North remain obscure. Perhaps scholars have found Belfast, MacNeice's 'country of cowled and haunted faces', a less congenial territory than the 'islands' of Anglo-Irish civilization inhabited by Somerville and Ross, or by Elizabeth Bowen. Or perhaps the general predominance of elite history within European political historiography has an Irish reflection in a literature which says more about Ascendancy landowners than about Orange labourers.

Unionist historiography retains an inevitable connection with contemporary political perspectives, but this connection has been both tempered by the development of professional scholarship and mitigated by new varieties of interpretation. Moreover, the evolution of Unionist historiography has reflected the evolution of Unionism itself, from early political triumphs and an uncertain command of parliamentary power at Stormont through to division and defeat. The confident tones of Trinity Unionists, defending the constitutional *status quo* of the 1890s, or of the Unionist polemicists of the 1920s, hailing their particular Brave New—northern—World, have scarcely survived 1969 and 1972: the evangelical tone of recent popular historiography seems more firmly rooted in despair than in hope. A schismatic and fissile Unionism is reflected in a scholarship which, itself divided by political and methodological sympathy, focuses on analyses of Unionist division. In this sense, therefore, the political revolution in Northern Ireland has evoked a revolution among its chroniclers.

WORKS CITED (OTHER THAN THOSE GIVEN IN THE TEXT)

Frank McGuinness, *Observe the Sons of Ulster Marching Towards the Somme*, London, 1986.
John Whyte, 'Interpretations of the Northern Ireland Problem: An Appraisal' in *Economic and Social Review*, ix, 4 (1978), pp. 257-82.
John Whyte, *Is Research on the Northern Ireland Problem Worthwhile?* (Belfast, 1983).
John Whyte, 'Interpretations of the Northern Ireland Problem' in Charles Townshend (ed.), *Consensus in Ireland* (Oxford, 1988).
Brian Harrison, 'The Centrist Theme in British Politics' in *Peaceable Kingdom: Stability and Change in Modern Britain* (Oxford, 1982).
Anne Purdy, *Molyneaux: The Long View* (Antrim, 1989).
Peter Robinson & James Allister, *Edward Carson: Man of Action* (Belfast, 1985).
David Hume, *'For Ulster & Her Freedom': the Story of the April 1914 Gunrunning* (Lurgan, 1989).
Gordon Lucy (ed.), *The Ulster Covenant: a Pictorial History of the 1912 Home Rule Crisis* (Lurgan, 1989).
Ian d'Alton, 'Southern Irish Unionism: a Study of Cork Unionists 1884-1914', in *Transactions of the Royal Historical Society*, xxiii, 3 (1973), pp. 71-88.
Ian d'Alton, 'Cork Unionism: its Role in Parliamentary and Local Elections, 1885-1914' in *Studia Hibernica*, xv (1975), pp. 143-61.
Ian d'Alton, *Protestant Society and Politics in County Cork, 1812-1844* (Cork, 1980).
Jack White, *Minority Report: the Anatomy of the Southern Irish Protestant* (Dublin, 1975).
Kurt Bowen, *Protestants in a Catholic State: Ireland's Privileged Minority* (Dublin, 1983).
D.C. Savage, 'The Origins of the Ulster Unionist Party, 1885-6' in *Irish Historical Studies*, xii (1960-61), pp. 185-208.
F.S.L. Lyons, 'The Irish Unionist Party and the Devolution Crisis 1904-5' in *Irish Historical Studies*, vi (1948-9), pp. 1-21.
John Harbinson, *The Ulster Unionist Party, 1882-1973* (Belfast, 1973).
Dennis Kennedy, *The Widening Gulf: Northern Attitudes towards Partition* (Belfast, 1988).
Brian Barton, *Brookeborough: the Making of a Prime Minister* (Belfast, 1988).
Louis MacNeice, 'Belfast' in *Poems* (London, 1935).

18

Making History in Ireland in the 1940s and 1950s: The Saga of *The Great Famine**

CORMAC Ó GRÁDA

Foillsítear gach ní le haimsir[1]

Shortly before presenting their typescript to the publisher, one of the editors of *The Great Famine: Studies in Irish History*[2] mused that explaining its long gestation 'in even one paragraph [would] not be easy'.[3] The brief preface to the book gives little hint of the delay. The story is worth disentangling and retelling for the light it sheds on Irish history-writing in the 1940s and 1950s. In the preface, the editors thanked J.H. Delargy (Seamus Ó Duillearga), Director of the Irish Folklore Commission, for first suggesting the proposal of a history of the Great Famine. What they failed to mention is that the idea for such a history had stemmed from a conversation between the Taoiseach, Eamon de Valera, and Delargy in late 1943 or early 1944. The ensuing contacts between civil servants and historians are chronicled in a recently released official file. The file suggests that de Valera kept up an interest in the idea, and indeed after publication, one of the editors remembered that 'it was the Taoiseach, he thought, who first proposed a book on the great famine'. De Valera wanted a study to mark the centenary of the famine 'for publication, if possible, in 1945'.[4] The director of the National Library of Ireland, Dr Richard Hayes, was consulted in the quest for 'a trained historian whose name is already favourably known, and who would be a specialist in the period. Hayes brought the proposal to the notice of the recently-constituted Irish

* Reprinted from *The Irish Review*, 1992, pp. 87-107.
1. I am very grateful to Kevin B. Nowlan, Thomas P. O'Neill, Ruth Dudley Edwards, Joyce Padbury, and Patrick Lynch, for sharing their reminiscences and for correcting me on several points. Austin Bourke, Louis Cullen, David Dickson, Ronan Fanning, Tom Garvin, Michael Laffan, Moore McDowell, James McGuire, Peter Neary and Kevin Whelan provided useful comments. The standard disclaimer applies with greater force than usual.
2. Ed. R. Dudley Edwards and T. Desmond Williams, Dublin: Browne & Nolan.
3. R. Dudley Edwards' academic diary, December 1954. I am very grateful to Ruth Dudley Edwards for allowing me to consult and quote from her father's diary. Subsequent references to the diary are given as 'RDE'.
4. National Archives, D/T S. 13626.

Committee of Historical Sciences. The ICHS at first hoped to subsume the project under a broader scheme of monographs in Irish history to be published by Faber & Faber, but that plan was rejected by the government. An author's fee plus a subsidy towards publication by Irish publishers was thought to constitute the best arrangement.

However, another aspect of the ICHS's proposal—history-writing by committee—survived. The ICHS proposed a volume based largely on essays by graduate students, who would be supervised by members of the ICHS. These essays would comprise the results of new masters' dissertations on various aspects of the Famine, and part of the government grant would be passed on to the students involved. According to Hayes, Professor Theodore W. Moody (Trinity College, Dublin), Professor Robert Dudley Edwards (University College, Dublin) and Dr. David B. Quinn (Queen's University, Belfast), who would act as joint editors, believed the work would take three to four years. Nothing seems to have happened for six months, when Muiris Ó Muimhneacháin (Maurice Moynihan), secretary of de Valera's department, issued the first of many reminders and queries to the historians. Edwards (who happened to be a close friend and neighbour of Moynihan) replied by phone, saying that 'the arrangements he would propose for the production of the book formed part . . . of a general scheme for the production of historical works'. Moynihan's request for an outline in writing produced the following letter from Dudley Edwards, acting in his capacity as secretary of the ICHS:

'The great famine, 1845-52.'

It is proposed to issue a book of approximately 1000 pages under this title to be edited by T.W. Moody and R. Dudley Edwards. (Dr. Quinn whom it had been intended to include is leaving Belfast for Swansea.) The work will include separate contributions dealing with the events, medical history, relief (including poor law amendment), emigration, population, agriculture, the people, political implications, the place of the famine in Irish history. A few of the contributors will be paid some fee and the total under this head should not exceed £250. Cost of printing 1000 pages should not exceed £1250. It is proposed to ask the government of Eire for a grant of £1500 the expenditure to be supervized by this committee. Contributors are already at work. The book should be in print in 1946.

R. Dudley Edwards.
9.ix.1944

In 1944 none of the three intended editors could have claimed an expertize

in the Famine or even in the nineteenth century, though Moody was beginning
to concentrate his researches on that century. Edwards thus based his list of
topics on the suggestions of Thomas P. O'Neill, then a graduate student in
history at U.C.D. The proposed publication date would have been appropriate,
since 1846 marked the true beginning of the Great Famine. In February 1945
Maurice Moynihan passed the project on to the Department of Education,
who already had some experience in dealing with the ICHS and with
publishing. A few weeks later Proinsias Ó Dubhthaigh of Education sought
approval from the Department of Finance for a grant to the ICHS, adding
that the money would be refunded to the government if sales of the book
warranted it. The figure envizaged was the £1,500 mentioned in Edwards'
letter, a considerable sum in those days. The plan was announced in the *Irish
Press* on 28 April 1945. Five of the authors eventually included in the published
volume were recruited around this time. In addition to O'Neill, they were
Oliver MacDonagh (a graduate history student at U.C.D.), Roger McHugh
(a lecturer in English at U.C.D.), Rodney Green (then completing his study
of the industrial revolution in the Lagan Valley at Trinity College Dublin),
R.B. McDowell (about to return to Trinity as a member of the Department
of Modern History), and the noted medical historian Sir William MacArthur.
Green and McDowell, besides being competent scholars, were Belfastmen and
gave the project the ecumenical, all-Ireland character sought by the ICHS.[5]
The original choice for the medical chapter, Sean Moloney, was replaced by
Belfast-born MacArthur (1884-1964), a noted medical historian, after a visit
by the latter to Dublin to address the Irish Historical Society.[6] Folklore was
not included in the original list of topics: McHugh, a friend of Dudley Edwards
and author of a series of articles in *Studies* on pre-famine Irish authors,[7] was
the radical of the group. The seventh contributor, Kevin B. Nowlan, was
recruited somewhat later.

5.   On Oliver MacDonagh's academic career, see Tom Dunne's tribute in F.B. Smith (ed.),
     Ireland, England and Australia: Essays in Honour of Oliver MacDonagh (Cork and Canberra,
     1991), pp. 1-13. On Kevin Nowlan, *Report of the President University College Dublin 1985-6*,
     pp. 159-60; on Roger McHugh, *Report of the President University College Dublin 1977-8*,
     pp. 125-6; on Rodney Green, the memoir by R.D.C. Black in *Irish Economic and Social
     History* 8 (1981), pp. 5-7. Moody had invited Michael Yeats, then a student in TCD, to
     participate, but Yeats opted for a legal career instead.
6.   The original choice had been Sean Moloney. Moloney had completed his M.A. in history
     before embarking on medical studies. MacArthur's lecture to the Irish Historical Society
     on 'The Identification of Some Pestilences Recorded in the Irish Annals' (subsequently
     published in *I.H.S.* vi (1948-9), pp. 169-188) was not quite germane to the Great Famine,
     but he had recently published 'Famines in Britain and Ireland', *Journal of the British
     Archaeological Association* 3rd ser. 9 (1944), pp. 66-71.
7.   William Carleton: A Portrait of the Artist as Propagandist', *Studies* xxvii (1938), 47-62;
     'Maria Edgeworth's Irish Novels', *Studies* xxvii (1938), pp. 556-70; 'Charles Lever', *Studies*
     xxvii (1938), pp. 247-60.

The Irish Folklore Commission through Delargy also made a considerable contribution at this stage to what was described in its minutes as 'an scéim a bhí bunaithe ag an Rialtas chun staidéar mór údarasach a chur ar fáil don phobal ar an mór-imtheacht san (the government scheme to provide the public with a large authoritative study on that important event). The Commission first submitted its standard questionnaire to most of its correspondents and this produced 908 pages of reports. A larger questionnaire (devised by T.P. O'Neill) followed, accompanied by special notebooks, and these were sent to collectors and to other potential contributors. This produced almost four thousand pages of accounts, which were lent to the ICHS.[8] The accounts inevitably are very uneven in quality, yet non-historian Roger McHugh's chapter on this material—again largely completed in 1945-6—turned out to be the most evocative contribution in the book.

The next item in the Department of an Taoiseach's file is a request from the ICHS, through a letter from Moody in August 1946, that the agreed money be paid over. This prompted Proinsias Ó Dubhthaigh to seek information on the project's progress. In reply Edwards claimed that substantial portions of this work have already been submitted to the editors, and that Messrs Cahill & Co., Dublin, have agreed to print and publish it in 1947'.[9] Edwards added that the ICHS had agreed to pay the publishers £600 towards the cost of printing, give £600 to contributors, and 'the remaining £300, it is hoped, will cover typing, secretarial and supplementary expenses'.

Edwards' reply caused some consternation in the Department of Education. Indeed an official had noted on the margin of his original letter, 'What about receipts from sales?', and Ó Dubhthaigh wondered why 'it [was] not proposed to adhere closely to the arrangements already made'. Further equivocation from Edwards (29 September 1946) led to a sterner response from the Department of Education. Had the Committee sought estimates from other publishers? Was there a contract? If so, what were the details? The Department was justifiably concerned about complaints from rival publishers. The big increase in payments to contributors elicited a request for details about their distribution. Finally, had contributors not sent in their material ready for the printers? If so, why the provision for typing costs? While such questions were aimed at eliciting a less cavalier attitude about public moneys from the historians, at the same time the Department of Education tried to rectify matters with the Department of Finance.

8. Comhairle le Béaloideas Éireann, Annual Report 1945-6, p. 4; minutes of meetings, 22 June 1945 and 1 February 1946. The replies are to be found in Irish Folklore Commission Mss. 1068-1075 and 1136. I am grateful to Séamus Ó Catháin for showing me the relevant C.B.E. files.

9. James Carty, a member of ICHS, probably provided the link with Cahills. His brother Francis, later editor of the Sunday Press and the Irish Press, worked for the firm at the time.

After a promising start, the sources suggest that the project was put into cold storage for three years or so. However, on 10 May 1950, the Secretary at the Taoiseach's Department asked for an update. The reply from Tarlach Ó Raifeartaigh (or Terry Rafferty), Deputy Secretary of the Department of Education, a historian himself, friend and neighbour of Dudley Edwards, and also a friend of Sir William MacArthur and later president of the Irish Historical Society), provided chapter outlines. The ICHS promised nine chapters, plus an epilogue:[10]

Section (1)	Ireland in 1845—R.B. McDowell	(Complete in first draft)
Section (2)	Course of the Famine—Kevin B. Nowlan	"
Section (3)	Relief—T.P. O'Neill	"
Section (4)	Emigration—Oliver MacDonagh	"
Section (5)	Economics—J.F. Meenan	"
Section (6)	Agriculture—E.R.R. Green	(In 2nd draft)
Section (7)	Medical Aspects—Sir William MacArthur	"
Section (8)	English Public Opinion—Brian Osborne	(Complete in first draft)
Section (9)	Folklore—R.J. McHugh	(In 2nd draft)
Section (10)	Epilogue—the Famine in history.	(Must await revision of Sections 1 to 9 inclusive).

Moody had resigned from the project in 1946. In January 1947 his place was taken by John Francis O'Doherty, until recently professor of ecclesiastical history at St Patrick's College, Maynooth. The choice of O'Doherty (a medieval specialist and an active member of the Irish Historical Society), who had resigned from Maynooth in rather difficult circumstances to become a curate in Omagh, was a curious one. He was charged 'with full responsibility for the final revision of the work'. In an era long before xeroxes and faxes, O'Doherty's location in Tyrone would have made progress difficult, but other distractions ensured that the project would mark time in 1946-8. They included the Foyle Fishery court case, which involved several historians as expert witnesses, and academic intrigues in connection with the plan to create a School of Irish Historical Research within the Dublin Institute of Advanced Studies. The last-mentioned was the brainchild of Moody and Edwards, and its collapse in 1948 was a crushing blow for Dudley Edwards in particular.[11] O'Doherty was replaced by Desmond Williams in 1949, after the latter's return to University College, Dublin, as professor of modern history.[12]

10. D/T S. 13626, T. Ó Raifeartaigh to An Runaí, Roinn an Taoisigh, 17 August 1950.
11. On the proposed school of historical research see Edward MacLysaght, *Changing Times* (Gerrards Cross, Bucks., 1978), pp. 167-70.
12. Tenth Annual Report of the ICHS', *I.H.S.*, vi (1948-9), p. 67. O'Doherty, a friend of Dudley Edwards and editor of the ICHS Bulletin, was clever and by all accounts a kind

When work on the book resumed in 1950, efforts at enticing Moody back as a third editor failed, and R.B. McDowell also refused to join the editorial team, which Williams put down to the influence of Moody who 'wished to be out of this long-delayed project'.[13] Edwards and Williams also briefly hoped that Kenneth Connell (whose classic *Population of Ireland* had recently been published) would join them on the editorial team, and later that he would contribute 'a statistical section' to the volume. Such hopes were not to be realized, but Connell did comment astutely on several chapters for the editors. Connell's suggestions had little impact on the final product, however. He had considered Green's work 'very slipshod, possibly as he was not interested', but there is no evidence that the editors forced Green to make any substantial amendments.[14]

The ICHS hoped—rashly, as events proved—to have revised versions of Sections 1 to 9 completed by the end of 1950, 'when they will be in a position to arrange for the preparation of the final Section'. The Committee had received the grant in three instalments of £500, in 1946/7, 1947/8, and 1948/9. But little had been achieved in that period, and the Committee now anticipated that it might require another grant.

Only seven of the nine 'sections' [sections (1), (3), (4), (6), (7), and (9) above] ever saw the light of day, though Kevin Nowlan was to contribute an excellent chapter on the high politics of the period. Osborne, whose contribution was soon excluded on Moody's 'implied condemnation', was a Peterhouse connection of T. Desmond Williams. The decision to axe his chapter was later regretted by Edwards.[15] The promised epilogue never appeared.

Dudley Edwards' academic diary, full of astute comments and asides and disappointments, captures the fitful progress of the project after 1951. Late in 1951 the editors promised the Department of Education the finished product before the end of the financial year. Edwards deemed the chapters by McDowell, MacArthur, McHugh and Green 'virtually finished', but 'Nowlan,

man; he died in Strabane in May 1954. On Williams see James McGuire's obituary in *I.H.S.* xxvi (1988–9), pp. 3–7; on Dudley Edwards, Aidan Clarke's in *I.H.S.* xxvi (1988–9), pp. 121–7.

13. RDE, 22 December 1951.
14. RDE, 29 October 1952. Green's footnotes suggest that he consulted no manuscript sources. Edwards also noted (15 December 1953):

> Reading Rodney Green's section on Agriculture one can now see precisely how much better it could have been if he had attempted to reconstruct the sources. It is clear enough in talking to him that he realizes this and as he says no one has yet attempted a systematic study of an Irish estate so that the work suffers from being a study surveyed before the real groundwork has been surveyed.

T P. O'Neill recalls being asked to rephrase a few sentences in response to Connell's comments.

15. RDE, 23 December 1954.

MacDonagh, and O'Neill will have to revise within 20,000 words or their sections will not go in'. The original plan of a thousand-page book would have encompassed the masters' theses of the last-mentioned three without much pruning, but the scaled-down work now contemplated required considerable re-writing. For O'Neill, this entailed omitting a great deal of useful material on privately-funded relief.[16] Edwards still hoped for an epilogue, though he added—presumably with Desmond Williams in mind that 'future collaborative work must only be undertaken in circumstances in which every associate's control of his own time can be assured'. Later Edwards was to complain about 'TDW pursuing his own Cambridge, London and Berlin interests while assuring me that he had drafted his Famine contribution'.[17] There were to be several other setbacks. Economist James Meenan, whom Edwards had known since their days together at the Catholic University School, had been recruited at the outset of the project, and attended some meetings in connection with it, but 'flopped' on his promised contribution.[18] Edwards and Williams hoped for a time that Kenneth Connell (then external examiner to the National University of Ireland) would fill in for Meenan, and also hoped for a co-authored chapter from graduate student Joseph Maher and Dr R.C. Geary of the Central Statistical Office on the land question on the eve of the Famine. Other names mentioned around this time included George Duncan of Trinity College and R.D.C. Black of Queen's University.[19] The annual reports of the ICHS, published in *Irish Historical Studies*, reflect the painfully slow progress of the project. They also capture the editors' diminishing expectations as regards the scope of the final product. At the outset the book was referred to as 'The History of the Great Famine', but from the 14th report onward (that for 1951-2) there was an ominous shift to 'Studies in the History of the Irish Famine'.[20]

Edwards' diary in 1951-3 reflects a recurring concern with bringing the project to a conclusion. Another look at MacArthur's medical chapter in February 1952 proved reassuring, and a query from Kenneth Connell about the book's progress in June was optimistically interpreted as a willingness to

16. Much of it was published elsewhere, e.g.: 'The Society of Friends and the Great Famine', *Studies*, xxxix (1950), pp. 203-13; 'Sidelights on Proselytism', *Irish Ecclesiastical Record* (1951).
17. RDE, 23 October 1951; 21 July 1955.
18. R.B. McDowell remembers a genial meeting with James Meenan in a Dublin club to discuss the allocation of subject-matter. Meenan mirthfully conceded all requests from McDowell for topics that the latter wanted included in his own chapter.
19. RDE, 17 November 1351, 22 December 1951. Moody had suggested Duncan and Black ('now lecturing in economics in Queen's and a TCD prodigy ten years ago') to Dudley Edwards. Edwards (23 October 1951) had also considered including a brief section on education from W.J. Williams, recently-retired professor of education in U.C.D., and father of Desmond Williams.
20. *I.H.S.* viii (1952-3), p. 162.

cooperate. Maurice Moynihan (presumably egged on by de Valera) kept up the pressure from Merrion Street, with repeated inquiries about the project's progress. In October 1953 Ó Raifeartaigh, very much the historians' advocate throughout, relayed word that the publishing company of Browne & Nolan Ltd. had agreed to produce the book on condition that they kept all the proceeds from sales. Michael Tierney, president of University College, Dublin, was a director of Browne & Nolan, and provided the link between the company and the ICHS. Browne & Nolan had a very cosy relationship with University College, Dublin, and held the contract for the U.C.D. Calendar.[21] Ó Raifeartaigh added (on behalf of the historians) that the State should keep its distance from publishing 'ós rud fíorachrannach cursaí staire (as history is a complicated business)', and that his own reading of the proposed book revealed that 'cé go bhfuil a leagan amach féin ag gach údar [nach] bhfuil éinní ann go bhfeadfaí claon-stair a thabhairt air ná go bhfeadfaí ceann a thógáil de ó thaobh polaitíochta ná eile (though each author had his own approach, there was nothing which could be termed biased history or which might cause political controversy)'. The Taoiseach's Department's reaction was that other Irish publishers should be given a chance to bid before Browne & Nolan were handed the contract. This put Edwards and Williams, anxious not to appear ungrateful to Tierney, in somewhat of a dilemma. A further communication elicited a reply from Tarlach Ó Raifeartaigh, who enclosed the following letter from Desmond Willlams to Ó Raifeartaigh dated 30 March 1954:

> Dear Mr. Ó Raifeartaigh,
> In reference to my letter of 28 July, 1953 concerning the 'Studies in the history of the famine', and in reply to your letters of August 10 and October 24, I have been directed by the Irish Committee of Historical Sciences and by the editorial sub-committee, to express our view that we are satisfied that no other Irish publisher would be prepared to publish suitably, as an academic production, 2,000 copies of the proposed work on the conditions which you mention in your letter of October 24.
> It is true that publishers could be found to produce some copies of the work, under some of the conditions you mention, but Dr Edwards and I, as editors, are entirely satisfied with the proposal put forward by Messrs. Browne and Nolan Ltd.
> In these circumstances we would point out that a rejection of our views on this matter would be considered by us as representing a lack of confidence in the performance of our duties, and that we would have to take the logical steps arising out of such a decision.

21. Browne & Nolan also published the *Irish Ecclesiastical Record*. Was it for fear of giving offence in clerical quarters that the publishers, through the editors, forced one author (T.P. O'Neill) to excise a reference to a mother suckling her hungry ten-year-old son?

Furthermore, we would stress the desirability for the publishers, for the public interested in the history of the famine, as well as for ourselves as University people with other duties to attend to, of a decision being taken as soon as possible in this matter. We would also point out that our services in connection with the production of the work have taken a considerable amount of time, and that (a fact that perhaps does not need to be stressed) they have been entirely of an honorary nature.

Yours sincerely,
(Sgd.) T. Desmond Williams

Other public servants might have been upset by the tone of Williams's letter, but Ó Raifeartaigh (who may well have seen a draft of the letter before receiving it in the Department of Education) merely passed on a copy in a reply to Merrion Street, where Williams's request for a quick decision elicited an irate marginal note from Nioclas Ó Nunáin (Nicholas Noonan): 'After taking over 5 months to reply to Mr. Ó Raifeartaigh's letter!' The departmental file reveals that de Valera was not 'ró-shásta' ('too pleased') either with Williams's reply. Nevertheless, the plan was agreed.

In the end the publication of the book was largely due to the commitment of Dr Kevin Nowlan, Joyce Padbury, and the late Maureen Wall (*née* Maureen McGeehin).[22] It was Kevin Nowlan, quite late in the day, who 'ghosted' the introduction at the request of Desmond Williams. Edwards and Williams appended their initials to Nowlan's essay without changing a word; only the crisp writing style (reminiscent of Nowlan's earlier contributions to *The Leader*) and the references to 'the Baltic lands' and 'Lettish peasants' (hints of Nowlan's year-long stay at Marburg in 1953-4) provided clues to the *cognoscenti*.[23] It was left to Joyce Padbury to prepare the index: that it contained only references to names and places was the editors' decision, not hers. Padbury, Nowlan, and Wall helped with tidying the material that had lain for several years in U.C.D.'s history department, and organizing the more recent contributions. The end-product contained not a single word from the pen of Desmond Williams; Dudley Edwards was responsible for the brief acknowledgements section. The illustrations, with one exception, were suggested by T.P. O'Neill. Browne & Nolan were probably responsible for the only unattributed illustration, that facing the title page: though purporting to show paupers outside a Dutch-gabled workhouse in New Ross in 1846, it seems to have been first published

---

22. See the memoir of Maureen McGeehin by Tom Dunne in Gerard O'Brien (ed.), *Catholic Ireland in the Eighteenth Century: The Collected Essays of Maureen Wall* (Dublin, 1989).
23. J.J. Lee, *Ireland 1912-1985* (Cambridge, 1990), p. 590, incorrectly attributes the 'short, brilliant introduction' to Williams and Edwards.

in 1887 in an illustrated golden jubilee biography of Queen Victoria.[24]

The typescript of the book was finally deposited with Browne & Nolan on 29 December 1954, with some misgivings. Edwards hoped that 'the individual impression of the contributors [would] emerge without any formalizing in the name of academic sameness'.[25] The book appeared just too late for the Christmas market in 1956, well over twelve years after the idea had first been mooted. On receiving advance copies, Dudley Edwards expressed satisfaction in his diary, but with the following sobering caveat:

> The overall impression is that the team can stand up to it. But would they do so in a Butterfield sense? Hardly. If it is studies in the history of the Famine, it is because they are not sure all questions are answered. There are still the fundamental matters whether its occurrence was not due to the failure of the sophisticated to be alert.

The end-product, though a substantial volume, contained slightly over one-half the thousand pages promised earlier by the ICHS in 1944. For all its good points, the book showed several signs of lackadaisical editing. First and foremost, lacking a narrative structure or even an overall narrative chapter, *The Great Famine* was far from being the comprehensive history of the Famine commissioned in 1944. Rather, it reads more like an *administrative* history of the period, with the core chapters (those by Nowlan, O'Neill, MacDonagh, and Mac Arthur) dwelling on the tragedy mainly from the standpoint of the politician, the poor law administrator, those who controlled passenger movements, and the medical practitioner. But there were less serious shortcomings too. While there is little overlap between the individual contributions, there is little sense either of this being a collaborative venture, and cross-references from chapter to chapter are lacking. On the crucial matter of excess mortality, the lack of coordination produces a ludicrous outcome. In its foreword the book eschewed discussion of the tragedy's demographic toll—'what is certain is that many, many died'—but this did not deter several contributors from producing their own 'conflicting' guesses.[26] None of the surviving contributors remembers a single joint meeting of the entire group.

24. I owe this information to T.P O'Neill.
25. RDE, 22 December 1954.
26. Edwards and Williams, pp. vii, 126, 255, 312. This is noted by Joel Mokyr, *Why Ireland Starved: A Quantitative and Analytical History of the Irish Economy 1800-1850* (London, 1983), p. 263. The issue of excess mortality has been addressed several times since; see Joel Mokyr, 'The Deadly Fungus: An Econometric Investigation into the Short-term Demographic Impact of the Irish Famine, 1846-51', *Research in Population Economics* 2 (1980), pp. 237-77; Phelim P. Boyle and C. Ó Grada, 'Fertility trends, excess mortality, and the Great Irish Famine', *Demography* 23 (1986), pp. 542-62. Roy Foster (*Modern Ireland*

Few of the contributors relied on the wealth of manuscript sources available even then on the famine years. Moreover, while paying lip-service to the need for context, the book lacked any proper analysis of economic conditions during the famine period. Sir William MacArthur's frequently-cited chapter on the medical history of the famine appeared virtually without references, because one of the editors (Desmond Williams) had mislaid the author's notes, allegedly in a London taxi-cab; the editor attempted to placate the aggrieved MacArthur by noting that the text of a historian of his reputation stood on its own ground—which turned out to be true![27] For all this the blame ultimately rested with the editors, who were not properly geared to the task. Dudley Edwards had a fine intuition and an astute mind, but found great difficulty in expressing himself on paper.[28] He was a great originator of ideas and schemes; the Irish Historical Society, the Irish Catholic Historical Committee, the Intervarsity History Students Congress, the Irish Society for Archives, and the Archives Department of University College, Dublin, all owe their beginning in large part to Dudley Edwards. But Edwards was no great organizer. Neither was Desmond Williams, who in any case was preoccupied with other things (notably with editing *The Leader* and with academic politics in Dublin and Cambridge) in the period discussed here. It was rather late in the day in January 1955 for Dudley Edwards' self-criticism that 'the Famine book could be more justifiable if the editors had first cast down and assessed O'Rourke and O'Brien and on that basis planned the whole'.[29] And yet, despite all this, *The Great Famine* contained some excellent material that is of enduring value.

Dudley Edwards and his colleagues in University College, Dublin were reasonably happy in the end, and duly celebrated the book's completion. The book was widely, and favourably, reviewed.[30] The publishers, too, had every

1600-1972, p. 324) on a single page both cast doubts on Joel Mokyr's aggregate figures, and invokes his estimates of excess mortality by county!

27. Several accounts of how the footnotes went 'missing' survive, but I am assured by Paddy Lynch that this is the correct one! Margaret Crawford tells me that MacArthur derived much of his information from articles by William Wilde in the *Dublin Quarterly Journal of Medical Science* (vols. VII (1849), pp. 64-126, 340-404; VIII (1849), pp. 1-86, 270-339), and Wilde's better-known contributions to the 1851 population census Crawford's own 'Epidemic Diseases in the Great Famine of Ireland 1845-50' (presented at the Famine and Disease Conference, Christ's College, Cambridge, July 1991) builds on and in part supersedes MacArthur's chapter.

   MacArthur was accorded every facility while working on his chapter in Dublin. Two cartons of the Chief Secretary's papers were temporarily transferred from the State Papers Office to National Library for his use, but he hardly used them in the end.

28. It is clear from his diary that Dudley Edwards in these years worried a good deal about writer's block. James McGuire tells me that Edwards later on would recommend a work diary as a cure for this problem.

29. John O'Rourke, *The History of the Great Irish Famine of 1847*, 3rd ed. (Dublin, 1902); W.P. O'Brien, *The Great Famine in Ireland* (London, 1896).

30. E.g. in the *Irish Times*, 11 January 1957 by F.S.L. Lyons, in *Irish Historical Studies*, xi

reason to be satisfied. The volume sold well, and in late 1958 only one hundred copies of the print run of two thousand remained, and another fifteen hundred unbound copies had been sold to an American co-publisher, New York University Press. These excellent sales, one of the contributors opined, had been achieved 'despite mismanagement in regard to the publicity'.[31] However, one publicity ruse on Browne & Nolan's part produced some hard feelings. On the eve of publication excerpts from the book had appeared in the *Sunday Independent* without the permission or prior knowledge of contributors. With some reluctance, Browne & Nolan eventually made ex gratia payments to the long-suffering contributors. The book was reprinted in 1962, and an American firm specializing in reproducing classic works produced a new printing in 1976. Second-hand copies of *The Great Famine* have grown quite scarce, and this justified an Irish publisher's decision to produce a new paperback version in 1991.

The editors sent de Valera (then in opposition) a complimentary copy of their book. He thanked them graciously enough, though he also felt it necessary to remind them in his reply of the conditions endured by 'ordinary people' in Bruree (the Limerick village where he had spent his childhood) during the Famine. Later he expressed unhappiness with the book, presumably because it seemed to downplay those aspects of the tragedy that had been etched in his own memory.[32] That he much preferred Cecil Woodham-Smith's *The Great Hunger* tells its own story. *The Great Hunger* was published in 1962, and immediately became a runaway success.[33] Late in 1963, when Woodham-Smith gave a public lecture in Trinity College about her experiences in writing the book, de Valera paid her the honour of attending,[34] and when some months later, the National University of Ireland awarded her an honorary doctorate, de Valera, as Chancellor of N.U.I , may well have been responsible. On that occasion he organized a lunch in her honour at Aras an Uachtaráin, to which he also invited his old-time comrades Jim Ryan, Frank Aiken, Sean T. O'Kelly, and their wives. T.P. O'Neill—then at work on de Valera's biography—was also present, the only link with the Edwards-Williams volume. Curiously, the

(1958-9), pp. 60-4 by Nicholas Mansergh; in *History* vol. 42 (1957), pp. 155-6 by Norman Gash; in the *American Historical Review*, vol. 63 (1957-8) by Helen Mulvey; in the *English Historical Review*, vol. 73 (1958), pp. 316-8 by W.L. Burn.

31. D/T S.13605.
32. I am grateful to T.P. O'Neill for this information.
33. By 1987 hardback sales in Britain had reached 45,225, book club sales 5,634, and export sales 4,304 (letter from Hamish-Hamilton to author, 16 March 1987). In the United States, Woodham-Smith topped *Time Magazine's* best-seller list for several weeks. Penguin issued a new reprint in 1991.
34. The lecture was organized by Muintir Mhuigheo in aid of the Irish Freedom from Hunger Campaign (*Irish Times*, 9 November 1963). The Woodham-Smiths had been frequent visitors to Mayo since the 1940s. For de Valera's views on Woodham-Smith I am grateful to T.P. O'Neill and Mairtín Ó Flatharta (de Valera's private secretary for several years).

introductory address by the Vice-Chancellor of N.U.I. (and President of U.C.D.), Michael Tierney, at the conferring ceremony struck a note that anticipates some later criticisms of Irish famine historiography:

> The lady whom I have the honour to introduce today has proved that while remaining a science, [history] can be a great deal more; and what in her case above all has contributed to this enlargement is not merely her mastery of a vivid, subtle and delicate style. It is above all the quality of sympathy with her subject, a sympathy that shines so brightly from every page she has written . . . *The Great Hunger*, which by reason of the thorough research on which it is based, the vividness of its style and the sympathy with which the terrible subject is treated, has received the praise of the world. By this book . . . Mrs. Woodham-Smith has shown herself not only a great historian and a great writer, but also a great benefactor to Ireland.

The immense popular success of *The Great Hunger* was a measure of the opportunity lost by Edwards and Williams. Woodham-Smith's work has rarely been out of print since publication, and probably still ranks as the all-time best-seller among Irish history-books.[35]

Yet Dudley Edwards never treated Woodham-Smith as a rival. He had befriended her when she first broached the topic of her planned book with him in January 1954, and that friendship endured. She publicly acknowledged his help and that of T.P. O'Neill and R.B. McDowell in due course. Years later she was to travel to Dublin at Dudley Edwards's request to attend the inauguration of the Irish Archives Council.[36] For his own part, Edwards was alive from the outset to one of the real weaknesses in Woodham-Smith's approach to the subject:[37]

How will Cecil Woodham-Smith tackle the Famine? It seems a safe bet

---

35. Ireland had featured largely in *The Reason Why: A Behind-the-Scenes Account of the Charge of the Light Brigade* (London, 1953), and indeed Woodham-Smith's interest in the Famine was prompted by her study of the papers of Lord Lucan of Crimean War fame. Michael Egan, custodian of the Lucan papers in Castlebar, also introduced Woodham-Smith to some Mayo workhouse material. The over-simplified model of the pre-famine economy presented in *The Reason Why* reappears in *The Great Hunger*. Though not an academic historian, Woodham-Smith was a formidable researcher. Much of her work is based on previously unused archival material.

36. It was therefore rather churlish of Leland Lyons to take Woodham-Smith to task for singling out Dudley Edwards in her acknowledgements, and ignoring Williams. Edwards was an old friend by 1962, while Williams could hardly claim to be an authority on the Famine. See F.S.L. Lyons, review of *The Great Hunger*, *I.H.S.* xiv (1964-5), p. 76.

37. RDE, 31 October 1955; also 3 January 1954.

that she will tie it to a few personalities—administrators, landlords, gombeenmen. There will also be a chance to enliven the generalisation that Ireland has in consequence bedevilled the good relations of Britain and America.

In the last resort this is in danger of not being history. The pouncing upon the conspicuous personality and the vivisecting of him may create a charicature (sic) and impose upon him a type which is only partly illustrative (could one get 2 or 3 of each type in each of say three areas). There is also the danger of accepting some contemporary thesis such as that of the *Economist* that the landlords were to blame.

This showed great prescience, because several critics were to fault Woodham-Smith for organizing her narrative around 'key' personalities, and the demonization of Prime Minister Lord John Russell and Treasury under-secretary Charles Trevelyan. While Woodham-Smith's was a highly effective rhetorical device, it over-emphasized the importance of those individuals in the tragedy. Moreover, Edwards correctly noted Woodham-Smith's propensity to oversimplify issues such as culpability and international relations.[38]

The Great Hunger had many other flaws. Still, it is my belief that most Irish historians have been less than fair to Woodham-Smith. Roy Foster's memorable but cutting depiction of her as a 'zealous convert' captures the condescending professional consensus. But since I have made the point before,[39] let me add just one further, comparative illustration here. It concerns F.S.L. Lyons, whose remarkably indulgent review of Edwards and Williams bears comparison with his delayed, rather snide reaction to Woodham-Smith. Lyons' only criticism of Edwards and Williams concerned the limitations of the index. His belated review of *The Great Hunger* in *Irish Historical Studies* made several valid points, but there was also a great deal of nit-picking, and in one important respect at least, Lyons stands accused of double standards. Thus in 1957 he wrote of the Edwards and Williams volume: 'We can see now that the Great Famine was a logical consequence of a vicious system of land-holding, a pitifully backward agriculture, and a social structure which invited disaster'. Historians today might question Lyons' undue emphasis on land tenure and the underlying determinism, but as an argument against facile populist notions, this was fair enough. Yet when Woodham-Smith reasoned that 'all this wretchedness and misery could, without exception, be traced to a single source'—the land system—Lyons pounced: 'that phrase "a single

---

38. Woodham-Smith stuck to her guns: 'the Famine left hatred behind. Between Ireland and England the memory of what was done and endured has lain like a sword' (*The Great Hunger*, p. 412).

39. Roy Foster, 'We Are All Revisionists Now', *The Irish Review* 1 (1986), p. 3; C. Ó Gráda, *The Great Irish Famine* (London, 1989), p. 10-11.

source" betrays an attitude of mind which is not, in the deepest sense, historical'!⁴⁰ Woodham-Smith's book has many weaknesses but, to its lasting credit, it laid bare anew the horrors of the tragedy glossed over in *The Great Famine*. That Irish historians in the 1950s should have sought to rid Irish history of its undue emphasis on the tragic is understandable; but the appalling catastrophe of the 1840s was an unhappy choice for that campaign. There was thus undoubtedly an element of sour grapes in the Irish historians' reaction to Woodham-Smith. After all, had the ICHS performed its task properly and on schedule, Woodham-Smith might never have embarked on her own book in the mid-1950s.

In defence of those involved in *The Great Famine*, the raw state of Irish historiography in the 1940s must be not be forgotten. In May 1943 Moody had addressed fellow-members of the Irish Historical Society on things to be done in [nineteenth-century] Irish history'. The lecture survives only in summary form, but reading that summary nearly half a century later, it is striking how little scholarly dispassionate research had been produced in the field by that date. Moody noted the lack of even a satisfactory general historical outline, and referred those interested to the *Oxford History of England*! For a general bibliography, he recommended appendices to the *Cambridge Modern History*. The few specialist works on Irish history that Moody considered worth mentioning—George O'Brien's *Economic History of Ireland from the Union to the Famine* (1921), John O'Donovan's *Economic History of Live Stock in Ireland* (1940), Nicholas Mansergh's *Ireland in the Age of Reform and Revolution* (1940), and the works on land tenure by Elizabeth Hooker (1938) and N.D. Palmer (1940) would be considered dated or unimpressive today.⁴¹

Individual contributors to *The Great Famine* faced other obstacles easily forgotten today. In the 1940s the National Library of Ireland's collection of catalogued manuscripts barely exceeded a thousand, compared to well over twenty thousand now; while the authors were doing their research, thousands of potentially useful documents lay in large wooden boxes with their lids

---

40. F.S.L. Lyons, reviews of Edwards and Williams, *The Great Famine*, in *Irish Times*, 21 January 1957, and of Cecil Woodham-Smith, *The Great Hunger*, in *I.H.S.* xiv (1964-5), 76-78. Woodham-Smith is not cited at all in Lyons' *Ireland Since the Famine* (London, 1971).

   The Great Hunger, a 'trade' book, was less widely reviewed in the professional journals than *The Great Famine*. See, however, the reviews by Kevin Nowlan, *Studia Hibernica* 3 (1963), pp. 210-11; Francis Finnegan, *Studies* 52 (1963), pp. 329-31; E.A.J. Johnson, *Journal of Economic History* 24 (1954), pp. 120-1.

41. T.W. Moody, 'Things to be Done in Irish History, VI: Nineteenth Century', *Bulletin of the Irish Committee of Historlcal Sciences*, No. 28 (December 1943), pp. 1-2. The list omitted William Forbes Adams' brilliant *Ireland and Irish Emigration to the New World* (New Haven, 1938). To be fair to the late George O'Brien, he was the first to admit that his works in economic history were written as a passport to a position in UCD (Patrick Lynch to author, 16 June 1991).

screwed on. The Library had yet to appoint a permanent keeper of manuscripts. No list of land estate materials had been compiled, and Irish parish registers had not been microfilmed.[42] The records of Workhouse Boards of Guardians lay scattered around hospitals and county council offices, and no location list of them existed.[43] In the mid-1940s, the hundred year rule still applied to famine-related material in the State Papers Office.[44]

In such circumstances, that *The Great Famine* might 'not claim to be a definitive history of the Great Famine but rather a contribution towards such a history'[45] is more understandable. Yet if the cream of Irish historians could not organize such a history in twelve years, then who could? Almost three decades later, that 'definitive history' remains to be written, though a great deal of work has been done in the interim. In the end, the ICHS failed to provide de Valera with what he had sought—and offered good money for—in 1944, a comprehensive account of the Great Famine. I suspect that the kind of collective history-writing instituted in 1944 could not have provided that. Overall, the episode does not reflect well on the professionalism of the Irish historical establishment of the 1940s and the 1950s. At a more parochial level, while 'history in U.C.D. [may have] had a special air of excitement and innovation'[46] about it during the period discussed here, its strengths lay in teaching and post-graduate research. Publishing was another matter, and the delays and the nature of the final product points to serious organizational shortcomings too.

That Eamon de Valera, nurtured on stories of perceived wrongs from his grandmother in a cottage in Bruree, should have sought a book on the Great Famine is almost predictable; that the Irish historical establishment should have denied him the kind of reassurance that he sought is almost equally predictable. Yet, ironically, Dudley Edwards clearly anticipated the kind of criticism that would be made of Irish famine historiography later, though he could not bring himself to do anything about it. Reading E.C. Large's brilliant

---

42. The usefulness of parish registers as a source for historians had recently been brought home by Domhnall Mac Carthaigh, 'Marriage and Birth Rates for Knockainy Parish, 1882-1941', *Cork Historical and Archaeological Society Journal* xlvii (1942).

43. Compare J.A. Robins, 'Charter School and Poor Law Records', *Irish Archives Bulletin* 3(1) (1976), pp. 2-6.

44. As T.P. O'Neill recounted to the author 'To get access to any official papers was an achievement and one was hemmed in by regulations. All my notes had to be left behind to be 'vetted' by the Keeper of State Papers before I could take them out of the building. What I was allowed to take was censored. This happened in regard to information regarding a landlord who refused to subscribe to a local relief committee—he was Lord Conyngham who held vast estates in Donegal and Clare as far as I recollect' (T P. O'Neill to author, 6 June 1991).

45. Edwards and Williams, p. xv.

46. Tom Dunne, 'Oliver MacDonagh', pp. 2-3.

Advance of the Fungi early in 1952 turned his mind 'rather uneasily' to the Famine work. With some foreboding, he noted:[47]

> I begin to feel that there is real danger that the sections of the specialists will fail to convey the unity of what was clearly a cataclysm in the Butterfield sense. The modern Irish of the countryside are largely predestinarian. Was the famine inevitable? and was the belief in its inevitability a factor which has tended to strengthen a tendency which one can well believe was always an Irish belief? I doubt if I can answer either but the need to ensure that at least in the final result the Famine book will contain some attempt to see the explosion as a whole, mark its beginnings and indicate its short and long term limits. Neither politics, relief, agriculture, emigration (not to say history or folklore) can bring this out. It requires a careful assessment of the cumulative factors and a demarcation of how they became explosive. This will also answer the question of responsibility, so unhesitatingly laid at England's door by John Mitchel.

Such thoughts lay behind Edwards' plan, alas never acted upon, to produce a volume of documents to accompany the book. This would not only allow people 'to see the truth of what is written down, [but] enable the historians [to] control interpretation, and see how one another behave in their work of reconstruction'.[48] Edwards returned to the alleged shortcomings of the contributions again on 9 September 1952:

> I feel a little depressed at the dulling effects of academic discipline. . . In our anxiety to bring out this book we must not be satisfied with pretty academic studies which fall dead from the press. Carleton and Liam O'Flaherty have at least an equal right to be taken for history as such. McHale and Mitchel are the prophets and must be treated as such. The logic of all this—and TDW agrees—is that the historiography of the famine (and a brief introduction) will have to state the real (as opposed to the administrative) position.[49]

There Edwards put his finger on a real weakness of the contributions to

---

47. E.C. Large, *Advance of the Fungi* (London, 1940); RDE, 20 January 1952. The reference to 'Butterfield' was to Herbert Butterfield of Peterhouse, Cambridge.
48. RDE, 27 July 1952.
49. The references are to William Carleton, *The Black Prophet* (Dublin, 1847) and Liam O'Flaherty, *Famine* (London, 1937).

the project, taken together. That was their largely administrative focus. Further doubts were recorded a few days later:[50]

> *The Famine: danger of dehydrated history.* [emphasis in the original].
>
> The more one thinks of the Famine the more the approach of contributors makes it necessary to take effective action. An integration could be attempted in the introduction and the stage set with some vivid contemporary extracts such as the Catholic hierarchy's address to the LL of 21 October 1847. The historiography is crucial when one recollects how the Mitchel-McHale story is as effective on the next generation as the depositions story on the post-1641 world. It had probably more effect on the writing of Irish history than the Young Ireland nationalism which really acted as a medium for translating Irish ideas (often wrongly) for foreigners.

The preoccupation persisted:[51]

> The essential weakness of the Famine studies came to me very clearly after reading Dr. T. O'Herlihy's booklet published seven years ago with its obvious analogies to Mrs. Woodham-Smith's ability to be on fire. 'The circumlocution office' was not exactly the same as Dublin Castle, but the fact remains that we have failed to include anything on the Castle and KBN [i.e. Kevin Nowlan] admits they were a sorry lot. In the light of what we see today of a Kenya such a factor should get some proper treatment.

Again, re-reading Roger McHugh's chapter on the famine in folk memory convinced Edwards that something was lacking in the other chapters: 'Mitchel's popularity is explainable not because he was merely defiant. It was because he correctly interpreted the feeling of the people. The attitude to relief, to the soup kitchen comes well out of McHugh.'[52] Edwards should not be seen here as claiming that the resentment of the starving provides a full or coherent explanation of the Famine, merely that Mitchel was articulating widely-held views. My own belief is that a thorough analysis of the contents of the replies to the questionnaire would return a more equivocal verdict on popular feeling (or folk memory), and indeed McHugh's contribution let slip the opportunity to weigh folklore and literary evidence against other sources. Still, Edwards' comment about folklore and Mitchel captures something that is lacking in the

---

50. RDE, 11 September 1952.
51. RDE, 5 March 1954. The reference is to T. O'Herlihy C.M., *The Famine 1845-1847: Ravages and Causes* (Drogheda, 1947).
52. RDE, 28 December 1954.

book, read whole. It also begs the question why Irish historians since—with a few exceptions such as Kenneth Connell—have been so reluctant to invoke or confront folklore evidence.[53] Roger McHugh's essay is so much out of tune with the other contributions that one may well wonder whether the chapter on folklore 'was a sop to Seamus Ó Duilearga because of his involvement in the early idea of the book'.[54]

A final comment on Dudley Edwards' reservations about the project and famine historiography. The relevant passages in his diary—and his remarks on Woodham-Smith—suggest a healthy scepticism towards nationalist 'genocide' interpretations of the Great Famine. Yet Edwards worried that in their eagerness to produce an antidote to the 'ochón, ochón' emphasis of Irish nationalist historiography and what the introduction deemed its undue reliance on 'the political commentator, the ballad singer and the unknown maker of folk-tales', some of the contributors might come across as too unfeeling about what was, after all, an immense human tragedy. To this extent, *The Great Famine* might be seen as contributing to 'a version of Irish history . . . which downplayed the tragic dimension of Ireland's historical experience'.[55] Edwards anticipated such a reaction, and indeed sympathized with it.

Completion of *The Great Famine* provided a morale boost to historians in Earlsfort Terrace and led to a resolution to beef up nineteenth-century studies there. But in nearby Merrion Street, the departmental file on *The Great Famine* closed on a further request for funds from the ICHS, this time for a subvention towards a book on the Fenian era. The government denied that request. Once bitten, twice shy?

53. A recent case in point: Oliver MacDonagh's much-lauded biography of Daniel O'Connell chose to ignore Rionach Uí Ogáin's *An Rí Gan Choróin* (Dublin, 1987), the most comprehensive study to date of 'the Great Dan' in folklore. Moreover, reviewers on McDonagh failed to note the omission.
54. T.P. O'Neill to author, 6 June 1991.
55. Edwards and Williams, p. viii; Brendan Bradshaw, 'The Emperor's New Clothes', *Fortnight* (Supplement on 'Free Thought in Ireland'), No. 297 (1991), p. 18.

19

Ireland's Marxist Historians

ANTHONY COUGHLAN

'There is no stronger political force than a people's desire for independence.'

Charles de Gaulle

The controversy on historical 'revisionism' is relevant to assessments of Ireland's Marxist and neo-Marxist historians as well as those writing mainstream academic history. Both Marxist and non-Marxist writers have faced the same intellectual issues in recent decades: the revaluation of Nationalism and Unionism and how England's historical involvement in Ireland influences present-day Anglo-Irish relations. Since the 1960s, in parallel with non-Marxist revisionist criticism of traditional Irish nationalist history, a younger school of Marxist or neo-Marxist writers, among them Austen Morgan, Helga Woggon, Paul Bew and Henry Patterson, have criticised the conclusions of historians of the older Marxist tradition who have been sympathetic to nationalist interpretations, principally James Connolly, Erich Strauss, Thomas Alfred Jackson and C. Desmond Greaves. The central tenet of classical Marxism in contention is the view held by Marx and Engels themselves that it is English intervention in Ireland rather than internal Irish conditions that historically has been the prime political cause of the country's problems.

A SOCIOLOGY OF HISTORY

The Marxist historical tradition aspires to be a sociology of history as well as to give a scientific account of the past. It holds that to understand history one must understand its historians, and how politics and economics condition their values and the circumstances in which they write and publish. By corollary, historians need to be aware of themselves as part of the phenomena they study, especially when they are writing on what has formed their own lives and times. They should be conscious of how their values and social interests influence their selection of what they regard as significant facts about the past and their judgements of them. The truth is the whole, as Hegel once said, so that all accounts are necessarily partial and one-sided. One can no more avoid bias in history than one can in food.[1] In this perspective value-free history is inherently impossible. To claim to write it is to show philosophical bad faith and to assert a spurious universality for one's personal value position. The good historian knows that he is a moral and political being involved in an enterprise that is also moral and political. He will follow the scientific method in weighing facts and evidence, while being conscious of, and desirably declaring, his own values. He strives for objectivity while being simultaneously 'engaged'. As a political being the historian will be concerned with how knowledge of the past enables us to understand where we have got to in history and how such knowledge may help us tackle the problems that confront us. Most of the older generation of Ireland's Marxist historians not only regarded history-writing as a political act, but were themselves actively engaged in contemporary affairs, principally in democratic and working-class politics. Such involvement is rare among 'revisionist' Marxists, whose preferred ambience is the academy rather than the polis.

While traditional Marxist historiography on Ireland was sympathetic to Irish Nationalism, it regarded the simplifications of much nationalist history, with its story of a centuries-old heroic and 'pure' national struggle against alien oppression, culminating in the establishment of an independent Irish State, to be part of the myth of origin of that State's bourgeoisie. Following the 'disestablishment' of the Irish Republic proclaimed in 1919, the acceptance of Partition under the Treaty and the subsequent Civil War, the business and political elites that constituted the Southern Irish bourgeoisie found themselves in charge of a State that was significantly different, both as regards its territorial boundaries and its development possibilities, from that historically aspired to by Irish nationalists. Despite this they understandably sought to emphasise their State-building achievements in face of potentially threatening hard-line Republicanism to their Left. To the various myths of origin of the Irish bourgeois Establishment, writers like Strauss, Jackson and Greaves counter-posed a typical Marxist concern with the role of classes and class interest as the prime motive force of history and as explaining the origin and contemporary character of the Irish State. Nonetheless, the generality of Irish historians, non-Marxist and Marxist, were at one in stressing the value of such political independence as had been achieved, despite its limitations, and hence of the movements in Irish history that could be interpreted as pointing towards that independence. This was the case so long as the Irish bourgeoisie retained

---

1. An aphorism of the late C.D. Greaves. It seems to the present writer that such of the insights of modern 'deconstructionism' as have validity—for example, the interconnections between viewpoint and viewer, the social relativity and ideological character of both text and interpretation—are implicit if not explicit in the Marxist tradition. (Cf. Marx's definition of the human being as 'the ensemble of social relations'.)

enough self-confidence to aspire to playing an independent role in the world, which was broadly the period from the 1920s to the 1950s.

Then the intellectual climate receptive to nationalist history, whether academically orthodox or Marxist, changed. The mass unemployment and high emigration of the 1950s led the Republic's business and political elites to abandon the attempt to construct an independent national capitalism. Irish Governments turned away from Eamon de Valera's policy of economic self-sufficiency and adopted instead a policy of industrialization through attracting foreign capital investment. Henceforth economic independence was to be dismissed as a pipedream. If the rationale of the Sinn Féin ideal had been that social salvation came from within, economic salvation was now seen as coming from without. The period from the 1960s to the 1980s saw the culmination of a long-growing disillusionment with the achievement of independence among the Irish intelligentsia.[2]

The policy of economic integration with Britain under the Anglo-Irish Free Trade Agreement of 1965 and Irish membership of the European Economic Community from 1973, encouraged further reassessment of the value and potential of independent statehood and the nationalist assumptions traditionally underpinning that. The climate became favourable for the popularization of the work of the first generation of 'revisionist' historians, that of Professors Moody, Edwards and Lyons. Fr Francis Shaw's article, 'The Canon of Irish History—A Challenge', which had been turned down as too shocking by the editor of *Studies* in 1966, the year of the 50th anniversary of the Rising, appeared in the more intellectually congenial climate of 1972, the year the Irish Government signed the Treaty of Rome.[3] The recrudescence of IRA violence in the North after 1970 alienated further Southern liberal and media opinion. Increasingly the dominant Irish intellectual consensus tended to conflate nationalism with support for physical force. The violence led to a more sympathetic attitude to British Government policy and to Ulster Unionism, the strength of whose objections to Irish independence and unity Irish nationalists, it was held, had traditionally underestimated. With the zeal of converts to a new religion the country's young liberal intelligentsia threw off the values of their fathers. 'Revisionism' in history and cultural commentary became fashionable with publishers and the media. In a further development the Irish Government's commitment to political integration with the European Community and the possible development of a quasi-federal European Union under the Maastricht Treaty, seemed to put a question-mark over the very

2. Declan Kiberd and Seamus Deane discuss this disillusionment in their contributions to M. Ní Dhonnchadha and T. Dorgan (eds.), *Revising the Rising* (Field Day, Derry, 1991). Kiberd refers to examples of similar disillusion among middle-class intellectuals in other post-colonial societies.
3. Fr Francis Shaw, 'The Canon of Irish History: A Challenge', *Studies*, 61, 1972.

future of the sovereign Nation State itself, that key parameter of political history in modern Western Europe. Courses in 'European studies' proliferated in the universities and colleges. Events posed the question, and not only in Ireland: did national political history need to be reinterpreted henceforth as a mere stage in the evolution of a 'European' rather than a national political formation?[4] These trends form the background to the revisionist controversy.

MARX AND ENGELS ON IRELAND

It is surprising how few references historians of nineteenth-century Ireland make to the work of Marx and Engels, in view of the fact that they were among the few non-Irish writers on Irish affairs at the time who were sympathetic to nationalist aspirations, about which they wrote extensively and interestingly. The volume of their collected writings on Ireland amounts to some five hundred pages, of which eighty consist of notes by Marx on the course of Irish history from the American Revolution to the Union with Britain in 1801 and over a hundred are preparatory materials by Engels for a History of Ireland which he embarked on but did not complete.[5] The rest are mostly articles, letters, excerpts from speeches and reports, but with numerous remarks on Irish history overall, that together constitute a commentary on the successive phases of Irish national struggle up to their time. They are testimony to the importance of Ireland in the eyes of the founding fathers of Marxism, who pioneered the systematic analysis of the country's social class relations.

Engels described Ireland as England's first colony and he and his colleague traced the process of its subjugation from the 12th century. They analysed the landlord system as a foreign implant, upheld by the English Government or its surrogate in Dublin, that led to an intertwining of the popular struggle against landlordism with the national struggle for democracy and independence. Marx's analysis in Volume I of *Capital*[6] of the 19th century land clearances as a special case of capital formation, in which the replacement of tenantry by cattle entailed the expropriation of the necessary means of subsistence of the former, and not just the surplus they produced, is a valuable insight into the land question of the time.

Marx and Engels used Irish data in developing their theory of rent[7] and it was primarily in relation to Ireland that they evolved their theory of

---

4.   In the present writer's opinion, the attempt at West European political and economic integration, far from making nationalism out of date, is likely to make the national question, the assertion of national independence and democracy against the forces that seek to diminish these, the main issue of West European politics over the coming decades.
5.   K. Marx and F. Engels, *Ireland and the Irish Question* (Progress Publishers, Moscow, 1978).
6.   Ibid., pp. 109-126.
7.   Ibid., pp. 69-75, p. 127, p. 469. See also *Capital*, 3, ch. 37.

imperialism. Colonial conquest, as well as distorting the social development of the conquered nation, held back progressive development in the conqueror. They judged that by confiscating Irish land Cromwell strengthened aristocracy, ditched his more radical supporters and paved the way for the Stuart Restoration. 'By engaging in the conquest of Ireland Cromwell threw the English Republic out the window', Marx commented on the 17th-century English revolution.[8]

In Marx's view the Act of Union turned Ireland into an agricultural district of England, supplying that country with corn, wool, cattle and industrial and military recruits. It at once made the Irish question a major issue in English politics and brought an accretion of Irish immigrants to the British working class. It strengthened aristocratic power in England as well as Ireland, so delaying reform in both countries and justifying the maintenance of a larger standing army. He wrote in 1870:

> Every industrial and commercial centre in England now possesses a working class divided into two hostile camps, English proletarians and Irish proletarians. The ordinary English worker hates the Irish worker as a competitor who lowers his standard of life. In relation to the Irish worker he feels himself a member of the ruling nation and so turns himself into a tool of the aristocracy and capitalists of his country against Ireland, thus strengthening their domination over himself. This antagonism is the secret of the impotence of the English working class, despite its organisation. It is the secret by which the capitalist class retains its power.[9]

Consequently, he advocated that for English workers 'the national emancipation of Ireland is no question of abstract justice or humanitarian sentiment, but the first condition of their own social emancipation'.[10] It was in relation to Ireland that Marx coined his famous aphorism: 'Any nation that oppresses another forges its own chains.'[11]

In 1867 Marx wrote to Engels: 'What the Irish need is: (1) self-government and independence from England; (2) an agrarian revolution. . . ; (3) protective tariffs against England. . . . Once the Irish are independent, necessity will turn them into protectionists, as it did Canada, Australia etc.'[12] In the 1840s and 1850s Marx had held that Ireland would gain her national freedom through working class ascendancy in England. But in 1869 he wrote: 'Deeper study

8.   Ibid., p. 138.
9.   Ibid., pp. 407-8.
10. Ibid., p. 408.
11. Ibid., p. 255.
12. Ibid., p. 158.

has now convinced me of the opposite. The English working class will never accomplish anything before it has got rid of Ireland. The lever must be applied in Ireland.'[13]

Partly history, partly political prescription, the founding fathers of Marxism shift continually between 'Is' and 'Ought'. The alliance they adumbrated between Irish nationalism and English democracy has more often been a potential than a reality, but its possibilities are likely to remain as long as the Irish question remains an issue in English politics.

Sympathetic though they were to the Irish national movement, Marx and Engels were well aware of its heterogeneous character. In a letter to Bernstein in 1882 Engels outlined the two trends within it. The first was the agrarian, rooted in peasant secret societies, democratic and radical in character. The second was the 'liberal-national opposition of the urban bourgeoisie which, as in every peasant country with dwindling townlets . . . finds its natural leaders in lawyers'.[14] The bourgeoisie needed the social muscle of the peasantry to lend weight to their own demands, but they sought to confine agitation within bounds that would not disturb their class privileges or rouse social forces they could not control. O'Connell's relations with the peasantry and Parnell's with the Fenians illustrated the pattern. Marx and Engels make few references to the Irish working class. In their day this was modest in size outside the Belfast area and did not as yet play a politically significant independent role. They do not discuss Ulster Unionist opposition to the 1886 Home Rule Bill, apart from referring to 'the Protestant braggarts of Ulster, who threaten to rebel', and noting as instructive the defence by Conservatives like Randolph Churchill and others of Ulster's right to resist Home Rule by force 'as a part of constitutional theory—though only so long as they form the opposition . . .'[15]

Their strongly positive attitude to Irish nationalism may be summed up in a comment of Engels in 1882: 'I hold the view that *two* nations in Europe have not only the right but even the duty to be nationalistic before they become internationalistic: the Irish and the Poles. They are most internationalistic when they are genuinely nationalistic.'[16]

IRISH MARXIST HISTORY-WRITING

James Connolly's stature as a socialist theoretician of the national question is likely to receive new recognition in the light of developments in Eastern Europe and elsewhere in recent years. The birth of a couple of dozen new Nation States, as forgotten national communities of those parts establish political units

13. Ibid., p. 398.
14. Ibid., p. 451.
15. Ibid., p. 466.
16. Ibid., p. 449.

to represent them internationally, shows that the historical momentum of the French Revolution, with its proclamation of the democratic principle of the right of nations to self-determination, is far from being exhausted and may still in fact be nearer its commencement than its close. The likely advent of dozens, possibly hundreds, of new Nation States to the international community over the coming century as peoples in Africa, Asia and the Middle East pass beyond kinship-based and tribal society, develop a national and linguistic identity and consciousness and find themselves restricted by the boundaries of the multinational States established by colonialism, is surely now inevitable. As the Labour movements of these countries aspire to some form of 'socialism'—entailing the imposition of social controls on private capital in the collective interest—they will find themselves facing the problem Connolly wrestled with in the days of the Second International: how to define the relation between national independence and socialism, between democratic struggle embracing all the people and working class struggle for the special interests of a particular class. In seeking to deal with it they might do well to emulate Connolly's counsel when he wrote that 'the Irish socialist was in reality the best patriot, but in order to convince the Irish people of that fact he must first learn to look inward upon Ireland for his justification, rest his arguments upon the facts of Irish history, and be a champion against the subjection of Ireland and all that it implies.'[17] Connolly's intellectual originality was to link the working-class ideal of socialism with the categories of the citizen and the native, with the republicanism of the former and the nationalism of the latter.

His book *Labour in Irish History*, published in 1910, was the first attempt by an Irish writer to analyse the country's history in terms of the Marxist class categories. It inaugurated Irish labour history and is still indispensable reading for students for its insights and force of style. It is a remarkable achievement for a self-educated working-man. Connolly disclaimed any intention of writing an academic history of labour in Ireland. 'It is rather a chronicle of labour in Irish History,' he said.[18] The chapters on the Jacobites, the 18th-century peasant movements, Grattan's Parliament, the United Irishmen, the Emmet conspiracy and Daniel O'Connell illustrate his thesis that 'the Irish question is a social question. The whole age-long fight of the Irish people against their oppressors resolves itself in the last analysis into a fight for the mastery of the means of life, the source of production, in Ireland.'[19] His judgements on the relations between the main social classes at the climactic moments of Irish history have stood the test of time. Subsequent criticism has been mainly about details. They parallel the treatment of the same topics by Marx and Engels,

17. Quoted in C.D. Greaves, *The Life and Times of James Connolly*, p. 60.
18. *Labour in Irish History* (New Books Publications, Dublin, 1967), p. 128.
19. Ibid., p. 139.

the full extent of whose writings on Ireland Connolly was not aware of, as many were not published until after his death.

As Dr Priscilla Metscher remarks in her study of republican and socialist ideology in 19th- and early 20th-century Ireland,[20] Connolly's book presents us with a radically different picture of Irish history to the conventional view. For him British imperialism is not merely armed occupation but an expression of a highly developed form of capitalism that was supported by a large section of the Irish capitalist class. Connolly regarded historical materialism as the key to the understanding of the Irish question, for 'without this key to the meaning of events, this clue to unravel the actions of "great men", Irish history is but a welter of unrelated facts, a hopeless chaos of sporadic outbreaks, treacheries, intrigues, massacres, murders and purposeless warfare.'[21]

Connolly has been criticised for over-simplified views and an over-mechanistic attempt to apply the materialist theory of history by too rigidly seeking to separate political and economic causes.[22] His very negative assessments of Grattan and O'Connell are partly an attempt to counter the hagiography of the romantic nationalist history of his day. In 1910 he was still under the influence of syndicalist conceptions. Thus he wrote, 'The Irish toilers from henceforward will base their fight for freedom not upon winning or losing the right to talk in an Irish Parliament, but upon their progress to the mastery of those factories, workshops and farms upon which a people's bread and liberties depend.'[23] Connolly's attitude at this stage was that only the Irish working class could be relied on in the struggle for national independence. He had not yet reached the position of seeing the importance of an alliance with the more progressive forces of bourgeois nationalism, which he developed after the outbreak of World War I.

This alliance is still at the heart of historical controversy over Connolly. It is an issue vitally relevant to contemporary considerations of what should be the attitude of the Labour movement and socialists to national independence struggles, whether in Ireland or other countries. In his biography C. Desmond Greaves summarised the evolution of Connolly's views on the subject as follows:

> Connolly held that the national revolution was a prerequisite of the socialist revolution. But he did not arrive easily at a clear conception of their mutual relationship. At first he was inclined to *identify* them. Later

20. P. Metscher, *Republicanism and Socialism in Ireland* (Verlag Peter Lang, Frankfurt am Main, 1986), p. 365.
21. *Labour in Irish History*, p. 139.
22. Cf. J. Hoffman, 'James Connolly and the Theory of Historical Materialism' in *Saothar*, 2, pp. 53-61, 1976.
23. *Labour in Irish History*, p. 139.

he distinguished them as the political and economic *aspects* of one process. Finally he reached the conclusion that they were two stages of one democratic reorganisation of society, each involving economic changes which it was the function of political change to promote. This is the significance of his phrase 'the first stage of freedom'.[24]

Connolly's participation in the Easter Rising was in line with the resolutions and slogans of the parties of the Second International to 'turn the imperialist war into a civil war.' The aspirations of the 1916 men accorded with Marx's view that what Ireland most needed was political independence to enable it deal with its own problems itself. The rebel cause was championed by Lenin, though condemned by Trotsky. Subsequent controversies have echoed their assessments. The logic of Connolly's writing and actions in the period leading up to 1916 was that of socialist republicanism: that socialists should participate in, and indeed seek to lead, national independence and other democratic movements. The alternative view was that by taking up nationalism Connolly had abandoned socialism. As C.D. Greaves points out, there were two variants of this. One, typical of Belfast, was for socialists to capitulate to sectarian pressure, ignore the national question, concentrate on work in the trade union movement and reform within the UK, professing a kind of Unionism of the Left. The other, typical of Dublin, was to admit that national independence was important, but to see it as separate from Labour struggle and the aspiration to socialism. This was effectively to hand over leadership of the national struggle to the bourgeoisie, represented by Fianna Fáil, or the small bourgeoisie, represented by the post-1920s IRA and Sinn Féin. Thus 'non-republican socialism, of the right, or the ultra-left, is inspired from one common ideological source—British imperialism.'[25]

The historical works of Strauss, Jackson and Greaves, though differing in detail, subscribe to the classical Marxist view that English involvement in Ireland is the political root of the country's problems. At the time they were writing this involvement principally took the form of Partition. Erich Strauss's study, *Irish Nationalism and British Democracy*[26] is the first Marxist work to analyse thoroughly the class basis of the Unionist-Nationalist split in the Irish bourgeoisie. This lay in the export-orientation of Ulster's shipping, engineering and textile trades, which made the Northerners feel threatened by the protective tariff policy aimed at developing the domestic market that Southern

24. C.D. Greaves, *The Life and Times of James Connolly*, p. 342. The phrase referred to, which was accidentally mistranscribed by Greaves and should read "the first *days* of freedom", occurs in an article in the *Workers' Republic*, 15 January 1916.
25. Ibid., p. 343.
26. E. Strauss, *Irish Nationalism and British Democracy* (Methuen, London, 1951; reprinted by Greenwood Press, Connecticut 1975.

nationalists advocated for a Home Rule Ireland. This aligned Ulster Unionism with the Empire-free-trading interest in Britain which swung increasingly behind the Tory Party after the 1886 Home Rule crisis. Ulster business also felt threatened by the prospect of facing higher taxes to finance land purchase and industrialisation under Home Rule. The popular basis of urban Unionism lay in the Protestant aristocracy of Labour in the North-East, where Protestants predominated in the skilled trades and Catholics in the unskilled. The failure of the Larkin and Connolly movement to establish political solidarity on class lines between Catholic and Protestant workers in the first decade of the century meant that the Protestants lined up behind their employers in Carson's Ulster Volunteer Force in 1912, in what might perhaps be regarded as the first proto-fascist movement of modern times.

Strauss's brilliant book surveys the relation of Ireland and Britain from the 17th century to the 1940s, and in particular what he terms 'the time-honoured English policy of disciplining the Irish people by detaching the middle class from the masses'.[27] He sees Britain's interest in Ireland as both economic and strategic and Ireland's influence on Great Britain as 'the most powerful influence ever exerted by a colony on an imperial power since the cultural penetration of the Roman Empire by Greece'—though Ireland's influence was of course political rather than cultural.[28]

Ireland Her Own, by the English working-class intellectual T.A. Jackson,[29] was written in response to a suggestion by Connolly's lieutenant Con O'Lyhane that he write the first comprehensive history of Ireland from a Marxist standpoint. 'I write frankly as a partisan,' says Jackson, 'I have done my best to be candid, but impartiality is beyond my scope. My concern is to help forward the cause I uphold.'[30] Such candour has laid him open to criticism. Wartime paper shortages led his publishers to cut the final text of this fine stylist by over half its original length, but the resultant rather bare treatment of events, especially in the early period, has not detracted from its popularity, for the book has remained continually in print, with an epilogue by C.D. Greaves that brings the story to 1970. Jackson argued for a shift in the balance of political forces in Britain towards anti-Unionism as being essential for undoing Partition: 'Partition was imposed from England. In England the work of undoing Partition must be, and will be, begun.'[31]

27. Ibid., p. 163.
28. Ibid., p. 70.
29. T.A. Jackson, *Ireland Her Own, An Outline History of the Irish Struggle* (Cobbett Press, London, 1947; 5th impression Lawrence and Wishart, London, 1990). There is a lengthy biographical entry on Jackson in J. Bellamy and J. Saville, *Dictionary of Labour Biography*, Vol. 4 (Macmillan, London, 1977)
30. Ibid., p. 20.
31. Ibid., p. 432.

C. Desmond Greaves's books on Tone, Connolly, Mellows and O'Casey, as well as his history of the Irish Transport and General Workers Union, are widely recognized as major contributions to Irish labour history and Marxist scholarship.[32] His study of Wolfe Tone aims to give what he terms 'a bird's-eye view of Irish history' that traces the development of Irish kinship society under the impact of English conquest and feudalism and seeks to show that a movement for national political independence could only come about when the political allegiances of clan society had been uprooted. This happened with the United Irishmen of the late-18th century. The 1800 Act of Union, Greaves contends, following Marx, was aimed not only against Irish nationalism but against British democracy. The accretion of landlord strength that it brought to Westminster possibly delayed parliamentary reform in Britain for a generation, while the Union broke the alliance of Catholics and Dissenters, who did not attain complete emancipation until 1829, causing the latter to look not to the Irish Catholics but to their co-religionists in Britain for support.[33]

In writing the *Life and Times of James Connolly* in the 1950s Greaves had the advantage of being able to meet many of those who knew and worked with Connolly personally. This enabled him establish several hitherto unknown facts about Connolly's career, for example his Scottish birth and youthful service in the British Army. Greaves's own estimate of his second biography, *Liam Mellows and the Irish Revolution*, as being his most important historical work, will surely stand the test of time.[34] Greaves regarded the whole period 1913-1922 as encompassing what he termed 'the Irish Revolution'—the struggle to establish an independent Irish State—in which the 1913 lockout, the Ulster crisis, the Easter Rising, the War of Independence and the Civil War were episodes. So defined, that Revolution is still unfinished and will remain so until Northern Ireland becomes part of an independent Irish State.

In this book a study of the complex social dynamics and class relations of the revolutionary period 1916-23 is woven round the biography of the Left-Republican leader Liam Mellows, who was executed by the Provisional Government in 1922. It shows how the destruction of Redmond's Home Rule Party in the two years after the 1916 Rising left the southern Irish bourgeoisie without a party. For a time the small bourgeoisie, then numerically the country's largest social class, filled the gap through Sinn Féin, Labour having

---

32. C.D. Greaves, *Theobald Wolfe Tone and the Irish Nation* (Fulcrum Press, Dublin, 1991); *The Life and Times of James Connolly* (Lawrence and Wishart, London, 1961); *Liam Mellows and the Irish Revolution* (Lawrence and Wishart, London, 1971); *Seán O'Casey, Politics and Art* (Lawrence and Wishart, London, 1979); *The Irish Transport and General Workers Union: The Formative Years, 1909-1923* (Gill and Macmillan, Dublin, 1982).

33. Op. cit., p. 106.

34. See the account of Greaves's life and work in A. Coughlan, *C. Desmond Greaves, 1913-1988, An Obituary Essay* (Irish Labour History Society, Dublin, 1991).

opted to remain uninvolved organizationally so as to preserve the unity of the trade union movement.[35] This fatal renegation, in the crucial period of formation of an Irish State, left the radical small bourgeoisie without allies when Sinn Féin split on the Treaty and the forces of large property and conservatism rallied to the Free State. Political Labour sidelined itself thereby and the leadership of the national movement passed thereafter to the national bourgeois Fianna Fáil and the small bourgeois militant Republicans.

For much of his life Greaves was politically active in Britain in opposing the Stormont Unionist regime. There is a case for regarding him as the originator of the *idea* of a civil rights campaign as the way to shatter Unionist political domination in the North of Ireland, which was taken up by the late 1960s Civil Rights movement. His book *The Irish Crisis*[36] is the first study of the history and politics of Northern Ireland from a Marxist standpoint. While being well aware of the internal factors making for Northern Ireland's political and sectarian divisions, he regarded British Government policy in upholding Unionism as the fundamental cause of the continuance of Partition. This book was written as an expansion of an earlier reply to Barritt and Carter's *The Northern Ireland Problem: A Study in Group Relations*,[37] which was the progenitor of numerous subsequent 'internal conflict' analyses of the problem. The common feature of these studies, which have been reviewed by the late Dr John Whyte,[38] is the relegation of British Government policy to, at most, a secondary role in the historical causation and contemporary continuance of the Northern crisis.

Greaves opposed the abolition of Stormont in 1972 as likely to strengthen the Union rather than weaken it, much as the abolition of the corrupt College Green Parliament in 1800 had strengthened Ireland's links with Britain then. He advocated instead the conception of a Bill of Rights imposed by Westminster as a legislative straitjacket on the subordinate Stormont assembly. This would at once outlaw discriminatory practices, so satisfying the civil

35. 'So losing the whole of Ireland for the sake of Belfast', as the late Peadar O'Donnell once put it to this writer.
36. C.D. Greaves, *The Irish Crisis* (Lawrence and Wishart, London, 1972 and Seven Seas Books, Berlin, 1974). Editions of this book were also published in Italian, Russian and Hungarian. It was based on an earlier work, *The Irish Question and the British People: A Plea for a New Approach* (Connolly Publications, London, 1963), that had been written as a reply to the book by Barritt and Carter published the year before.
37. D. Barritt and C. Carter, *The Northern Ireland Problem: A Study in Group Relations* (Oxford University Press, 1962).
38. J. Whyte, *Interpreting Northern Ireland* (Oxford University Press, 1990). Whyte discusses Marxist as well as 'internal-conflict' interpretations in this survey of the literature on the Northern Ireland problem. He mentions *The Irish Crisis* only in passing, preferring, as he put it (p. 179), to consider the 'more substantial Marxist works' that were soon to follow, and so avoids having to deal with Greaves's argument. He does however discuss Barritt and Carter's book sympathetically and at some length (v. the index references).

rights aspirations of the Northern nationalist population, while at the same time permitting, and preferably encouraging, a devolved administration in the North to develop closer relations with the South.

This was a policy issue that separated Greaves from the Marxist-oriented leaders of the student-based People's Democracy of the time, who welcomed the abolition of Stormont and the imposition of 'direct rule' from London. A number of these—Michael Farrell, Eamon McCann, Geoffrey Bell, John Gray and Paul Arthur—have subsequently written books on Northern politics.[39] Farrell's works in particular—*The Orange State* and *Arming the Protestants*— have been major contributions to the history of Northern Ireland from a Marxist standpoint. Another issue distinguishing Greaves from these others was his more positive attitude to the Irish State, while they tended to emphasize its conservative and denominational features. But all of these writers share a common subscription to the classical nationalist view of the Northern problem as being primarily due to Britain's insistence on maintaining sovereignty and politically underwriting Ulster Unionism. This is what principally differentiates them from revisionist Marxist or neo–Marxist historians.

REVISIONIST MARXIST HISTORY

Revisionist Marxist history-writing, like other intellectual trends, can be assumed to have social roots. In the 19th and early 20th centuries Marxism was a theory used by working-class political activists to guide them in their political work and help solve practical problems. Then in the mid-20th century Marxism became the creed of millions, the official ideology of several States and a dangerous ideological challenge to the West. Perhaps what could no longer be intellectually ignored or suppressed might be sapped of its subversive potential through a strategy of cooption? One may speculate that from the 1960s onwards one of the responses of political Establishments in various countries to this ideological challenge was to encourage the development of a form of 'katheder Marxismus', or scholastic Marxism, mainly sited in university politics and sociology departments, where the theory purveyed was far from being Frederick Engels' 'guide to action'. Much of the academic neo-Marxism produced there, which has filled whole libraries with exegesis and polemic, is an eclectic ideology, a kind of Establishment socialism, Marxism

---

39. M. Farrell, *Northern Ireland, The Orange State* (Pluto, London, 1980), *Arming the Protestants* (Pluto, London, 1983); E. McCann, *War and an Irish Town* (Penguin 1974 and Pluto, London, 1980); G. Bell, *The Protestants of Ulster* (Pluto, London, 1976), *Troublesome Business, The Labour Party and the Irish Question* (Pluto, London, 1982), *The British in Ireland, A Suitable Case for Withdrawal* (Pluto, London, 1984); J. Gray, *City in Revolt: James Larkin and the Belfast Dock Strike of 1907* (Blackstaff, Belfast, 1985); P. Arthur, *The People's Democracy 1968-1973* (Blackstaff, Belfast, 1974).

without commitment, though often extremely dogmatic in form, that revises key concepts of the classical tradition, in the process frequently using left-wing terminology to produce an apologia for contemporary conservative practice. Far from using the insights of Marxism to help solve practical political problems, these Establishment or academic Marxists, radical-sounding dominies, tend to be compilers of bibliographies, dissectors of texts—some of which have been written solely for journalistic purposes—and above all inventors of jargon. As regards Ireland the political thrust of this neo-Marxist school has, broadly speaking, been to produce an apologia for British involvement in Irish affairs, and for Ulster Unionism, that parallels the work of non-Marxist revisionist historians. Some examples will illustrate the genre.

Dr Austen Morgan's book *James Connolly, A Political Biography*[40] is a self-proclaimed polemical work that seeks, as its blurb succinctly explains, to pose the 'unanswered question. . . why a man who lived as a socialist died an Irish nationalist'. The question remains unanswered, one may say, because its premise is a nonsense. Connolly died, as he lived, a socialist internationalist. What is presented for explanation did not happen. Morgan's thesis is essentially that of the 1919 Seán O'Casey: that when at the outbreak of the 1914-18 war Connolly contemplated an Irish national revolution, 'Labour lost a leader'. Left-wing terminology is used to represent Irish nationalism, the ideology of the movement for an independent Irish State, as reactionary.

The early chapters of Morgan's biography concentrate on Connolly's socialism, playing down his consistent stand for Irish independence. His later chapters describe Connolly's 'nationalism' during the last twenty months of his life. The author seems unaware of the principle that the emancipation of a small nation is an act of internationalism, as it enables that nation to take its place in the world and relate to other nations in the international community. Connolly, like other leaders of the Second International, hoped for a revolution that would lead to the 'dethronement of the vulture classes that rule and rob the world.' When it was clear in 1914 that this was not going to happen and that workers required the experience of war to develop a revolutionary consciousness, Connolly was left with the need for fresh tactics.

A 'one-stage' revolution that would bring about socialism simultaneously with national independence, was not in sight. All Dr Morgan's talk about 'stages theory' is therefore redundant. There is no absolute rule. Under the conditions of the time Connolly outlined 'two stages of Irish freedom', which Dr Morgan refers to only to dismiss. As with many academic Marxist works, Morgan's book gives one the impression of being written by someone with

---

40. A. Morgan, *James Connolly: A Political Biography* (Manchester University Press, 1988). The same writer repeats his criticisms of Connolly in the context of a general apologia for Ulster Unionism and an attack on Irish Nationalism in his book *Labour and Partition: The Belfast Working Class 1905-23* (Pluto, London, 1991).

little practical experience of political activity who inhabits a world of abstractions where there is no such thing as adapting a consistent principle to transformed circumstances.

Dr Helga Woggon, in the most voluminous study of Connolly so far produced and the first biography of him in the German language,[41] also manipulates '-isms' as she sends Connolly's 'nationalism', in classic philosophically idealist fashion,[42] into battle with his 'socialism'. Despite her scholarship she seems to forget that the matter is one of real things rather than their theoretical reflections: of how national independence, as embodied in the establishment of a democratic State, may relate to socialism, a mode of organizing that State's economy and institutions. Dr Woggon begins with a model of what she calls 'integrative socialism', that is, a special form of socialist politics that consists of socialist concepts developed in a situation of national and colonial dependence. These, she says, are derived from national tradition and are 'integrated' into it. The political challenge is then stated to be how to turn the national revolution into a socialist one. By this standard she judges Connolly not to come up to the mark. Instead of transforming the national revolution, his socialism became swallowed up by nationalism. She subscribes to Eric Hobsbawn's thesis that Connolly's 'national Marxist' politics failed because alliances by socialists with national movements tend to weaken socialism, as it is identified thereby with anti-socialist traditions without being able to transform them.[43]

41. H. Woggon, *Integrativer Sozialismus und nationale Befreiung: Politik und Wirkungsgeschichte James Connollys in Irland* (Vandenhoeck and Ruprecht, Gottingen, 1990).
42. Philosophical idealism—treating ideologies and interpretations as primary rather than the social movements and objective reality that produce them—seems to be particularly common among historians and sociologists of the national question. Thus far more attention is typically given to 'nationalisms' and the political ideas of national movements than to the genesis and evolution of nationality and national communities themselves. The notion of the nation as an imagined rather than a real community is a typically idealist one (cf. Benedict Anderson, *Imagined Communities*, Verso, London, 1983). An egregious local instance of this tendency is the opening sentence of Tom Dunne's essay 'New Histories: Beyond "Revisionism"' (*Irish Review*, No. 12, Institute of Irish Studies, Belfast 1992), which reads: 'The interpretation of Ireland's traumatic history has long been at the root of its political and ideological divisions. . .' Here the country's divisions are seen as caused by its historians rather than the historians seen as explaining the divisions. More academic modesty is surely called for!
43. E. Hobsbawm, 'Some Reflections on "The Break-Up of Britain"', *New Left Review*, 105, 1977. Hobsbawm's views on the national question are criticised and, in the present writer's opinion, comprehensively refuted by J.M. Blaut in *The National Question: Decolonising the Theory of Nationalism* (Zed Books, London, 1987). A non-idealist approach to the development of national and ethnic communities in ancient and moder times is exemplified in the works of A.D. Smith, Professor of Sociology at the London School of Economics: *National Identity* (Penguin Books, London, 1991), *The Ethnic Origin of Nations* (Blackwell,

Dr Woggon maintains that Connolly worked with the concepts of 'true' and 'false' nationalism. 'False' was bourgeois nationalism, 'true' was nationalism from below and reflected Connolly's alleged belief that 'every nationalist worker because of his class identification and nationalism was predestined to be a socialist revolutionary, regardless of his political opinions'.[44] Throughout her book she treats republicanism and nationalism as interchangeable. In fact Connolly differentiates much more than she gives him credit for. After all Pearse, not Griffith, was his alliance partner in 1916. He was well aware of the political and class differences between those who shared his own socialist republicanism and the non-socialist republicans of Pearse and the IRB, the monarchical nationalists of Griffith's Sinn Féin and the constitutionalists of John Redmond's Home Rule Party. Like other left-wing revisionist historians Dr Woggon interprets modern Irish labour history since Connolly in terms of the subordination of 'socialism' to 'nationalism', for which the dead Connolly is allegedly responsible.

Bew, Gibbon and Patterson's *The State in Northern Ireland 1921-1972, Political Forces and Social Classes* claims to be a Marxist history of Northern Ireland.[45] Its value is to tell the story of Unionism during the days of Stormont and to give details, based on newly available archival material, of the differences between various Unionist factions over how best to maintain Protestant working-class support for Unionism. At the same time the authors hold that national independence and reunification of the national territory have no relevance to the future of Ireland. This of course is no novel thesis. It is the view of Unionists, of the Orange Order, of transnational capital and of Her Majesty's Government of the moment. The originality of the authors and of their several imitators is that no one previously had thought of presenting it as Marxism.

One of the central conceptions of classical Marxism is that in the era of capitalist imperialism the national and colonial struggles for independence, formerly part of the bourgeois-democratic revolution, have become part of the socialist revolution, the attempt to subordinate capital to the interests of the working-class. China, Vietnam and Cuba would be examples. The three authors deny that this principle applies to Ireland and spend thirty pages attacking the position of those Irish Marxists who assert it. Once more the only novelty is that the writers consider they are Marxists themselves.

They speak throughout of Northern Ireland as a 'State' rather than as part

Oxford, 1986), *Theories of Nationalism* (Duckworth, London, 1983) and *The Ethnic Revival* (Cambridge University Press, 1981).

44. Op. cit., p. 187.
45. P. Bew, P. Gibbon and H. Patterson, *The State in Northern Ireland, Political Forces and Social Classes* (Manchester University Press, 1979). In discussing this work the present writer has drawn extensively on a review of it by C.D. Greaves, 'Irish Marxism', *Irish Democrat*, London (July 1980).

of the British State and fail to address the question why Britain should seek
to maintain sovereignty there. Part of their case is that Marx, Engels, Connolly
and Lenin failed to see what might be called 'Ulster exceptionalism', based on
the uneven development of capitalism in Ireland. But they had before them
the extremely uneven development of English capitalism, which did not create
demands for exclusion. The authors excuse Marx because he 'died in 1883,
before Protestant opposition to any form of united Ireland had become
completely clear'.[46] Marx is rightly excused but the authors have grasped the
wrong issue. For thirty years after Marx died Ulster Protestants continued to
live in a united Ireland and were perfectly content to do so. The objection
raised by Carson and his friends was to separation from England. Even today
one could not guarantee Protestant objection to a united Ireland if they were
sure England would rule the whole of it. Reunification is spurned because she
cannot rule the whole.

In their final paragraph Messrs Bew, Gibbon and Patterson call for 'a
decisive break with Irish Marxism's subordination to bourgeois ideology', that
is to say, to Republican objectives.[47] What the authors substitute is an ideology
of Unionism expressed in Leftist vocabulary. It is an old pattern—the
ultra-Left using radical-sounding language to adopt or advance the political
positions of the Right. It illustrates the political tendency of Ireland's
neo-Marxist revisionist historians, which aligns them intellectually with their
non-Marxist counterparts. Their history is neo-unionist in its values and,
whether intentionally or no, is akin to conventional revisionism in providing
an apologia for British Government policy in Ireland.

In his survey of the voluminous literature on the Northern problem,
Interpreting Northern Ireland,[48] Dr John Whyte discusses John Martin's
contention in the journal *Capital and Class*[49] that the weakness of traditionalist
Irish Marxist historians is that they have underestimated the autonomy of the
Protestant working class, but that this is outweighed by the greater failure of
the revisionists in accepting the progressive nature of the British State and
ignoring its reactionary role in Northern Ireland. Clearly the issues remain in
contention. Only the evolution of history itself will decide whether Northern
Ireland's existence as part of the British State is going to be temporary or
permanent, or indeed whether Britain itself will continue in being as a State
into the coming century. On these outcomes will depend the retrospective
validity or otherwise of the interpretations of Irish 'revisionists' and 'anti-
revisionists', whether non-Marxist or Marxist, in so far as their work seeks to

46. Ibid., p. 3.
47. Ibid., p. 221.
48. Op. cit., p. 189.
49. J. Martin, 'The Conflict in Northern Ireland: Marxist Interpretations', *Capital and Class*,
    18, 1982.

point to the future. Marxists in particular should have no difficulty in accepting that historical practice is the ultimate test of the validity of their social science.

Surprisingly, Dr Whyte seems to align himself with what is probably the most extreme form of Irish historical revisionism—the idea that there are two national communities in Ireland—when he writes archly, though surely with exaggeration, that 'virtually no one who has put themselves to the discipline of researching on Northern Ireland still defends the one-nation theory'.[50] Yet who are these two nations that supposedly inhabit the area? Protestant and Catholic? These are religions, not nations. British and Irish? Britain is the name of a multinational State, inhabited by English, Scots and Welsh, not a nation. Northern Ireland Protestants do not claim rights to national self-determination. What they assert is a supposed unilateral right to union with Britain, a State whose own future looks problematic in the light of Scottish aspirations to independent statehood, when there surely can only be rights of separation.

The least that those who contend that there are two nations in Ireland should be able to tell us is the names of the supposed nations. Yet this they fail to do. 'Two-nationism' has a long lineage in Unionist apologetics.[51] That a scholar of Dr Whyte's standing should seem to give it his intellectual blessing demonstrates that when it comes to contemporary issues there are no neutral men among historians, that the concerns of academic history and social science are intimately intertwined with the cut-and-thrust of politics and partisanship, and that the beginning of wisdom in historical scholarship is honestly and openly to acknowledge that fact.

50. Op. cit., p. 191.
51. James Anderson has shown that the idea of an 'Ulster Protestant nation' was first floated by the Liberal Joseph Chamberlain and the Conservative leader Lord Salisbury in 1886 during the crisis over the first Home Rule Bill, though to a marked lack of response from within Ireland (v. 'Ireland's First Home Rule Crisis', in C.H. Williams and E. Kofman (eds.), *Community Conflict: Partition and Nationalism*, Routledge, London, 1989). His examination of ideological reactions in Ulster at the time, based on a study of contemporary local newspapers, leads him to repudiate the contention of such writers as Heslinga and Gibbon that what might validly be designated a distinctive Ulster nationalism was evident either then or later (cf. M. Heslinga, *The Irish Border as a Cultural Divide*, Van Borcum, Assen, 1962; and P. Gibbon, *The Origins of Ulster Unionism*, Manchester University Press, 1975). The 'two-nations' view was also advanced during the third Home Rule crisis, in particular by the English journalist W.F. Moneypenny in *The Two Irish Nations* (John Murray, London, 1913).

20

Irish Historical 'Revisionism': State of the Art or Ideological Project?*

M.A.G. Ó TUATHAIGH

During the course of 1991 there was considerable controversy in the Republic of Ireland concerning the appropriate manner in which the seventy-fifth anniversary of the Easter Rising of 1916 ought to be celebrated, by the Irish people and by the Irish national state. The controversy arose principally because of the implications which any form of commemoration might have for the continuing violent conflict and communal division in Northern Ireland. Indeed, the invocation of 'history' by various parties to that conflict had already become so problematic, on moral and political grounds, that many academic historians had become circumspect about the audiences they would address and the auspices under which they would lecture in public.[1] But, in seeking a wider context for the controversy, one would have to acknowledge a more general uncertainty among sections of the Irish intelligensia regarding the achievement and the achievements of an Irish national state and the historical forces which had made the project of an Irish national state their political objective down through the centuries: were their assumptions valid, were their objectives realistic, were their methods acceptable, was their legacy a benign one or not, particularly in the light of the continuing conflict and loss of life in Northern Ireland? In the wider context, Ireland's membership of the European Community, with the diminishing significance, as it seemed, of national sovereignty (economic and cultural, no less than political), seemed to portend the increasing obsolescence of a large part of the rhetoric of Irish nationalism, over the past two centuries at least. The basis of the nationalist case for an Irish national state was under serious scrutiny, not least because

---

*   An earlier version of this paper was presented at the ACIS Conference in the University of Wisconsin-Madison in April 1991. I am grateful to those who commented on it, formally and informally, on that occasion: Tom Bartlett, Nicholas Canny, David Dickson, Mary O'Dowd, Kevin Whelan.
1.   See, for example, the controversy which followed the decision in early 1986 of a number of Irish historians to decline an invitation to participate in a lecture series in London in memory of Terence MacSwiney: *Irish Post*, 25 January 1986; *The Terence MacSwiney Memorial Lectures* (London G.L.C. published 1986).

of a growing body of scholarly writing severely critical of independent Ireland's 'performance' since 1922 (principally, but by no means exclusively, in terms of its economic 'performance').[2]

While it is imperative that this wider context be kept in view, the particular controversy surrounding the seventy-fifth anniversary of the 1916 Rising prompted, among other things, a renewal of public interest in a matter which had been crackling on the margins of political debate in Ireland since the early 1970s, that is, the 'rights' and 'wrongs' of so-called revisionist historical writing on Irish history. This renewed public interest in what, in essence, is a rather complex and arcane debate among academics, commanded a position of unusual prominence in the popular media of newspapers, radio and television in Ireland throughout 1991.[3] This may not be altogether surprising. After all, for more than two decades the public discussion of 'historical revisionism' had been conducted principally in overtly political and moral terms, and its protagonists had included many notable intellectuals and publicists, among whom Conor Cruise O'Brien and Desmond Fennell were especially prominent.[4] The most recent phase of the debate has, however, acquired a more strictly academic focus, while in no way ceasing to be an issue of acute public controversy. In particular, Dr Brendan Bradshaw's intervention, together with the controversy which has attended it, has focused on a number of key aspects of the writing

2. On 'assessments', see in particular: Kieran Kennedy, T. Giblin and D. McHugh, *The Economic Development of Ireland in the Twentieth Century* (London, 1988); Eoin O'Malley, *Industry and Economic Development: the challenge for the latecomer* (Dublin, 1989); J.J. Lee, *Ireland 1912-1985: Politics and Society* (Cambridge, 1989); Raymond Crotty, *Ireland in Crisis: a study in capitalist colonial undevelopment* (Dingle, 1986); P. Bew, E. Hazelhorn and H. Patterson, *The Dynamics of Irish Politics* (London, 1989); Brian Girvin, *Between Two Worlds* (Dublin, 1989). For a sample of the general examination of conscience on national sovereignty, a useful starting point would be the journal of ideas, *The Crane Bag* (1977-85); the pamphlet publications of the cultural group, *Field Day*; the occasional publications of the *Irish Sovereignty Movement*; and, Desmond Fennell, *The State of the Nation* (Dublin, 1983), and *Beyond Nationalism* (1985).

3. Among many programmes, a special current affairs television programme centred on a lengthy and at times technical panel discussion of Revisionism. See transcript of *Today Tonight Special*, 31 March 1991. The controversy was rehearsed at several well-publicized summer schools in 1991, including the Merriman Summer School and the Desmond Greaves Summer School.

4. See, for example, Fennell, op. cit. n. 2 above, and Conor Cruise O'Brien, 'The Embers of Easter 1916-66', in Owen Dudley Edwards & Fergus Pyle (eds.), *1916:The Easter Rising* (London, 1968), pp. 223-40, and *States of Ireland* (London, 1972). Early indications of the academic ramifications of the debate can be found in publications relating to the 1916 Rising: F.X. Martin, '1916—Myth, Fact and Mystery', *Studia Hibernica*, no. 7 (1967), pp. 7-126, and 'The 1916 Rising: a Coup d'Etat or a Bloody Protest?', *Studia Hibernica*, no. 8 (1968), pp.106-37; Francis Shaw, 'The Canon of Irish History: a challenge', in *Studies*, lxi (1972), pp. 113-52; Pádraig Ó Snodaigh, *Comhghuallaithe na Réabhlóide 1913-1916* (Baile Átha Cliath 1966), and for a digest of the early battles Pádraig Ó Snodaigh, *Two Godfathers of Revisionism* (Dublin, 1991).

of Irish history, the systematic examination of which is both desirable and overdue.[5] While Bradshaw's intervention was, in the first instance, a response to the provocatively original contribution of Dr Steven Ellis regarding the appropriate or most fruitful 'settings' or 'contexts of explanation' for the consideration of the Irish historical experience in the late medieval and early modern period, the actual grounds of Dr Bradshaw's indictment of the revisionist agenda went well beyond the areas of his disagreement with Dr Ellis.[6] The revisionist writing on the modern period, its historiographical roots, and, most problematically, its ideological and social function, were all matters upon which Bradshaw threw down the gauntlet. In addition to Dr Bradshaw (and to such veteran critics of the revisionist enterprise as Dr Desmond Fennell, Pádraig Ó Snódaigh and Anthony Coughlan), the main corpus of revisionist writing on the modern period has also been strongly criticized by Dr Kevin Whelan. For Whelan the charge against the 'revisionist' writing is that it is too present-centred, too Anglocentric, too narrowly political in its focus, historiographically naive, methodologically stale and unexciting.[7] It is also worth noting, perhaps, that, more obliquely, two highly-regarded economic historians have expressed some reservations on certain key works generally considered part of the revisionist canon.[8] It is to be expected that

5. In point of time, the opening of the latest phase of the debate may be traced to R.F.Foster, 'History and the Irish Question', above, pp. 122-45. The main contributions, several of which are collected above, include: Steven G. Ellis, 'Nationalist historiography and the English and Gaelic worlds in the late middle ages', above, pp. 161-80; Brendan Bradshaw, 'Nationalism and historical scholarship in Modern Ireland', above, pp. 191-216; Ronan Fanning, "The great enchantment": uses and abuses of modern Irish history', above, pp. 146-60); Ronan Fanning, 'The meaning of Revisionism', *The Irish Review*, no. 4 (Spring 1988); and Desmond Fennell, 'Against Revisionism', above, pp. 183-90; Roy Foster, 'We Are All Revisionists Now', in *The Irish Review*, no. 1 (1986); *Modern Ireland 1600-1972* (London 1988); Editor, *The Oxford Illustrated History of Ireland* (Oxford 1989); 'Varieties of Irishness', in Maurna Crozier (ed.), *Cultural Traditions in Northern Ireland* (Belfast 1989); K. Theodore Hoppen, *Ireland since 1800: Conflict and Conformity* (London 1989), and his review of Foster's *Modern Ireland* in *I.H.S.*, xxvi, no. 103 (May 1989), pp. 304-6; Hugh Kearney, 'The Irish and their History', above, pp. 246-52.

6. See Ellis, art. cit. n.5 above; and also, Ellis, S.G. 'Historiographical debate-representations of the past in Ireland: whose past and whose present?', in *I.H.S.* xxvii, no. 108 (November 1991), pp. 289-308; and Art Cosgrove, 'The writing of Irish medieval history', in *I.H.S.*, xxvii, no. 106 (1990-1), pp. 97-111.

7. Kevin Whelan, 'Clio agus Caitlín Ní Uallacháin', in Seosamh Ó Murchú *et al.* (eag.), *Oghma 2* (Baile Átha Cliath, 1990), lgh 9-19 is his most incisive intervention.

8. See, for example, Cormac Ó Gráda's review of Mary Daly's *The Famine in Ireland* (1986) in *I.H.S.*, xxv, no. 99 (1987); 'For Irishmen to Forget?; recent research on the great Irish famine' (University College Dublin: Centre for Economic Research Working Papers 88/3); *The Great Irish Famine* (London, 1989); and ' "Making History" in Ireland in the 1940s and 1950s: the saga of *The Great Famine*' below, pp. 269-87; See, also, Kevin O'Neill's review of Foster's *Modern Ireland* (above, pp. 217-21).

the number of contributors to the debate will grow, and, as it does, that the central issues will emerge with greater clarity. What follows here is a modest 'commentary' on some of the key issues that have emerged to date, and which, I would argue, require further debate and refinement. The perspective is that of academic history, and the concerns of the commentary relate mainly to the implications of the revisionist debate for the writing of Irish history by professional historians.

Firstly, it is worth noting that while the revisionist controversy raises fundamental questions for historians, the actual grounds of the controversy are, in some respects, relatively narrow. Thus, for example, none of the parties involved is against 'revising' historical accounts in the light of new evidence or the application of new techniques (e.g. quantification) to known data. Furthermore, no moral or ideological indignation seems to have been aroused by what, at a casual evaluation, might seem to have been highly sensitive areas of 'settled' history which have been energetically 'revised' over the past thirty years: for example, the particular revision of 'traditional' Irish Catholicism launched by Emmet Larkin, and the more general wave of revisionist writing on many aspects of Irish economic and social history (demography, land ownership and use, emigration, migration, urban and labour studies) which has flowered on both sides of the Atlantic in the past twenty years.[9] Likewise, the radical revisions in recent decades of many aspects of early Irish history (e.g. regnal succession, the laws, social and family structure), while they have provoked lively debate and disagreement among professionals in the field, have had nothing like the same seismic impact within the profession as the controversy surrounding the modern period. Indeed, apart from the significant and understandably urgent demand of feminist historians for the 'reclamation' of the place and perspective of women in Irish history, the very substantial body of revisionist writings on Irish economic and social history has not, in the main, led to any public or academic indignation or renunciation. In fact, the real heat has centred on a relatively limited corpus of historical writing—but writing which has become influential both within the profession and, for a variety of reasons, among the wider public.[10]

9. The extraordinary growth in the volume and range of publications in economic and social history (partly a function of the increasing number of specialist historians of Ireland in North America as well as on this side of the Atlantic and in Australia and New Zealand) is reflected in several contributions to J.J. Lee (ed.), *Irish historiography 1970-79* (Cork, 1981), but especially in the editor's own chapter. The annual bibliographical listings published in the journals, *Irish Economic and Social History* and *Saothar: Journal of the Irish Labour History Society*, are further evidence of this growth.

10. Both Foster's *Modern Ireland* and Lee's *Ireland 1912-85* were awarded prestigious literary prizes and received very considerable attention in the popular media; senior historians such as John A. Murphy and Ronan Fanning regularly reach a wide public through their

It may be useful and sensible, therefore, to look closely at this corpus of 'contested' writing, and to begin with some statements from those who are generally considered 'revisionist' historians, and who, themselves, seem to be quite comfortable with the appellation. It will be clear that for the several writers described or describing themselves as in favour of a revsionist approach, definitions and perspectives are quite distinctive and variable. Professor Ronan Fanning has stated that 'a striking characteristic of modern Irish historiography [is] a continuous compulsion to confront myth and mythology'.[11] For reasons that pertained to the belated and partial opening of official Irish archives, and also to the relatively late growth of interest (and output) in economic and social (as distinct from political) history, the encounter between the professional historians and the settled myths of Irish nationalism and Ulster unionism coincided with, but was not caused by, the eruption of violence in Northern Ireland after 1969. Certainly, that encounter was given a particular urgency and was made more contentious by the northern convulsion, in which 'old mythologies were revived and new mythologies created', often with lethal consequences. The conflict in Northern Ireland rendered even more difficult and controversial what, in any case, would have been a bruising task, namely, the task of applying historical scholarship to the simplistic accounts of the revolutionary period (1912-23) which had become the ideologically licensed 'official history' of the Irish national state. In this 'official' version, the Rising of 1916 was seen as the climax and culmination of the Irish nationalist historical project, as the Proclamation itself had claimed. Because, as Fanning argues: 'Nowhere else in the European, North American or antipodean democracies does the writing of twentieth century history demand so constant a confrontation with mythologies designed to legitimize violence as a political weapon in a bid to overthrow the state'. This, then, for Fanning, is the essence of the revisionist enterprise: the actual writing of the political history of twentieth century Ireland, and of the revolutionary era in particular, in accordance with the rules and rubrics of academic history, constantly alert to the pull of deeply-entrenched myths, and operating at all times with a scrupulous regard for the available historical evidence. However, Fanning recognizes that the term 'revisionist' in the popular controversy has other connotations, that it is often a term of 'abuse for defenders of the republican ideological commitment to use about those nationalists *who seek to undermine that tradition*' (my italics). This may indeed be the case, as a matter of fact. But it must not be inferred (nor does Fanning suggest) that the writing of scholarly or academic history should be taken as synonymous with seeking to undermine the tradition of

journalistic writings; and Irish historians and political scientists are invited to comment as a matter of course on issues in current affairs and historical debate on radio and television.
11. Fanning, 'The great enchantment', p. 142, above, p. 156.

physical force nationalism; the different meanings and usages of 'revisionist' must be recognized.

In a separate contribution to the revisionist debate Fanning provides a further elaboration of his views, in terms such as the following:[12] 'In its simplest sense, it [revisionism] merely means re-ordering or revising our knowledge of the past in accordance with such new evidence as we may unearth'. Or, 'What historians are revising is not history but myth and legend'. Or, again, 'The truth is that writing history involves repudiating myths and legends. And, of course, the myths and legends of any community are not the preserve of its historians, but of all its people'. It does not surprise Professor Fanning, therefore, that 'because it falls to historians to overthrow popular legends, they incur popular obloquy'. This overturning of popular legend in Ireland has resulted in 'a national loss of innocence', and this loss is widely resented. But Fanning is in no doubt that this loss of innocence was inevitable following the outbreak of violence in Northern Ireland after 1969; inevitable and, it seems reasonable to infer, salutary, in the long term.

Roy Foster's defence of revisionism is, in certain respects, more indiscreet and revealing.[13] Professor Foster sees revisionism's virtues as an 'ability to appreciate half-tones, to be sceptical about imputing praise or blame, to separate contemporary intentions from historical effects. By exploring nineteenth and twentieth century Irish politics in all their density, sophistication and ramifications, scholars . . . have made it impossible to interpret Irish history in the rousing terms of P.S. O'Hegarty (as) "the story of a people coming out of captivity"; it signals an end once and for all to 'the compelling Manichean logic of the old "Story of Ireland", with a beginning, a middle and what appeared (up to about 1968) to be a triumphant end'. This unsettling/subversion of the old nationalist story has been achieved by exercising 'the most robust scepticism about the pieties of Irish nationalism'. According to Foster, revisionism is not, as its critics frequently assert, a school of history 'hostile to Irish nationalism', but, rather, something along the following lines: 'To the scholars it is quite simply a desire to eliminate as much as possible of the retrospectively "Whig" view of history, which sees every event and process in the light of what followed rather than what went before; the effort to get behind hindsight. Along the way, many simple assumptions need to be questioned'. More than that, Foster especially approves of 'the slightly blasé and sceptical way in which many Irish people view the institutionalized pieties of Irish history'. It is not surprising, therefore, that Foster reserves some of his sharpest barbs for the 'pieties' written by such a 'zealous convert' as Cecil Woodham Smith, or the 'innocent and sometimes naively hilarious works of

---

12. Fanning, 'The Meaning of Revisionism', pp. 15-16.
13. Foster, 'We Are All Revisionists Now', pp. 1-5.

piety about the Fenians or Young Irelanders, written by amateur historians of the British left'.[14] In a television interview during the public controversy in 1991, Foster spoke of the impact of revisionism as being, in effect, subversive of the uncritical certainties of determinist nationalist history, and, most interestingly, of involving a necessary iconoclasm and a significant dimension of counterfactual argumentation.[15]

What is clear, therefore, is that the particular task which the advocates of the 'revisionist enterprise' see as desirable and necessary in respect of the political history of modern Ireland is that of confronting the myths and legends which constituted an obsessively determinist nationalist historiography; an historiography which, endorsing or ratifying the claims of the 1916 Proclamation, saw the underlying logic of Irish political history as the urge towards an independent Irish state, and which rested on the assumption that this urge towards national sovereignty ('freedom') was itself predicated on an enduring and ineradicable 'Irish national consciousness' which, though drawing on different or constantly shifting elements of cultural particularity down through the centuries, retained for all that a core of 'national identity' sufficiently strong to sustain the urge to 'nationhood'. An additional, but secondary, feature of the traditional 'story of Ireland' under revisionist scrutiny was the valorization of those who, through the centuries, could be presented as having been most committed, or most uncompromisingly committed, to achieving this freedom, this Irish national sovereignty. This so-called determinist nationalist historiography (in truth, a relatively easy target in terms of its scholarly credentials up to the 1940s) has, accordingly, been subjected by the revisionists to interrogation in a spirit of 'robust scepticism', in significant areas of the political history of modern Ireland. It is the outcome of this interrogation—the fruits of the confrontation of nationalist myth by academic history—that is the matter of contention between the revisionists and their critics.[16]

14. Ibid., p. 3.
15. Transcript of special *Wednesday Report* programme, RTE, 27 March, 1991. For discussion of the historian and the counter-factual see David Lewis, *Counterfactuals* (1973), Jon Elser, *Logic and Society* (1978), and Geoffrey Hawthorn, *Plausible Worlds: Possibility and Understanding in History and the Social Sciences* (1991).
16. This relates to the modern period. See, T.W. Moody (ed.), *Irish historiography 1936-70* (Dublin 1971); J.J. Lee, 'Some aspects of modern Irish historiography', in Ernst Schülin (ed.), *Gedenkschrift Martin Göhring: studien zur Europäischen geschichte* (Wiesbaden, 1968), pp. 431-43; also, *Ireland 1912-85: Politics and Society*, pp. 587-97; R.W. Dudley Edwards and Mary O'Dowd, *Sources for early modern Irish history 1534-1641* (Cambridge, 1985), especially pp. 201-14; R.B. McDowell, *Alice Stopford Green a passionate historian* (Dublin, 1969); Aidan Clarke, 'Robert Dudley Edwards (1909-88), in *I.H.S.* xxvi, no. 102 (November 1988), pp. 121-27; Helen Mulvey, 'Theodore William Moody (1907-1981): an appreciation', in *I.H.S.*, xxiv, no. 94 (1985); R. Dudley Edwards, 'T.W. Moody and the origins of *Irish Historical Studies*, in *I.H.S.*, xxvi, no. 101 (May 1988). For achievements in the early period,

It is not the intention to spend time here on the tangled, but immensely important, terms of the controversy regarding 'revisionism' as a factor in shaping public debate and public policy in respect of Anglo-Irish relations, and specifically on Northern Ireland, during the past two decades. This would require an evaluation of the influence of revisionist writings—mediated through conferences, lectures and contacts—on the thinking and policies of various political actors, influential journalists, commentators and administrators, in the vital arteries of public opinion and in the specific context of policy-making. But, in passing, it is interesting to quote Ronan Fanning (citing Bernard Lewis) to the effect that: 'those who are in power control to a very large extent the presentation of the past and seek to make sure that it is presented in such a way as to buttress and legitimize their own authority, and to affirm the rights and merits of the group which they lead'. To which Fanning adds: 'One could scarcely find a more succinct statement of what motivated the Irish political establishment after 1969 to adopt that interpretation of modern Irish history commonly described as "revisionist"'.[17] It is precisely this ideological aspect that is of prime concern to such critics of revisionism as Desmond Fennell. For Fennell, 'Revisionism, both in its ultimate thrust, and as a matter of objective fact, is the historiography of the counter-revolution. . . . Primarily, it is a new moral interpretation of the known major facts'. Fennell rejects 'the pretension of revisionist history to be a value for the nation', on the grounds that: 'First . . . its moral interpretation is not correct; second, because such history does not serve the well-being of the nation'.[18] These are serious charges, and Fennell is not alone in making them. But neither of the charges is, in essence, a matter of historical scholarship, and, accordingly, they will not be examined in detail here.

What must be examined thoroughly, however, is Brendan Bradshaw's charge-sheet against the revisionists—a charge sheet heavy with indictments and containing very few mere misdemeanours.[19] First, let us consider the issue of whether the revisionist writings—in their interpretative approach (the hermeneutic aspect) or in their style of exposition—are unable to handle the Irish historical experience on the grounds that the revisionist approach cannot and does not come to terms with the 'catastrophic' dimension of a history like Ireland's, that it filters out the trauma and the pain of Irish history. There is, here, a profound and extremely difficult issue in historical writing raised by Bradshaw. According to Bradshaw the value-free approach of the revisionists (inherited from Edwards and Moody and the foundation principles of *Irish*

see Michael Tierney, *Eoin Mac Neill: Scholar and Man of Action 1867-1945* (edited F.X. Martin, Oxford, 1930).

17. Fanning, 'The great enchantment', pp. 142-3, above, pp. 156-7.
18. Fennell, 'Against Revisionism', above, pp. 187.
19. Bradshaw, art. cit. n. 5 above; unless otherwise stated quotations in the text attributed to Bradshaw are from this article.

Historical Studies in the thirties), filters out the trauma of Irish history through strategies of tacit evasion (sometimes actually ignoring the evidence); of normalization (playing down the exceptional or abnormal character of violence and colonization in early modern Ireland); and, as in the case of certain studies of the Great Famine, by achieving distance (emotional and moral) 'through assuming an austerely clinical tone', and through 'resorting to sociological euphemism and diometric excursi, thus cerebralizing and, thereby, desensitizing the trauma'. All of these failings, in Bradshaw's view, arise from a fatally-flawed adherence to the precepts of (bogus) value-free history-writing, which 'denies the historian recourse to value judgements and, therefore, access to the kind of moral and emotional register necessary to respond to human tragedy'.

It seems to me that there are a number of separate issues here that need to be addressed. The basic concept of a 'catastrophic dimension' in the historical experience of certain peoples or nations is, at several levels, a challenging concept. But the issue may, on the one hand, be primarily one of sources or evidence; the charge being that the historians have given insufficient attention to 'history from below', that they have not registered clearly, or have chosen to ignore, the voices and the experience of those who have suffered the trauma of Irish history. It is worth noting that this particular concern with the variety, the provenance and the potential of different kinds of source-material for Irish history has emerged in some recent contributions of Cormac Ó Gráda to the debate on Irish historiography and revisionism.[20] There is, however, a very different issue raised by Bradshaw's charge against the value-free approach. This is the problematic issue of the voice of the historian being insufficiently resonant with moral indignation, or, alternatively, the historian's vocabulary failing to find the descriptive power appropriate to describing great pain and suffering. (In T.S. Eliot terms, a case of the historian's language being inadequate to the 'objective correlative' of trauma, pain and suffering, at an individual and at an aggregate level.) On this latter point, which arises in the context of holocaust studies or writings on the slave trade, there is, one has to say, no easy answer. But it is hard to see that the problem is basically the fatal consequence of trying (with a great deal of self-deception) to write value-free history. Seeking a critical distance from the historical events under review, through the adoption of a dispassionate tone (more concerned to explain than to evoke the historical events/processes being discussed) has become the dominant contemporary mode of professional, academic history-writing in the western democracies. Of course, it begs many important questions. But it is not incompatible with an acute sense of, and a

20. Cormac Ó Gráda, 'Literary Sources and Irish Economic history', in *Studies*, vol. 80, no. 319 (Autumn 1991), pp. 290-99; and also the same author's ' "Making History" in Ireland', pp. 269-87 above.

sympathetic imaginative engagement with, the pain and trauma of human tragedy. (The individual reader's response to various kinds of history-writing is itself a complex matter; this is an aspect 'reception-theory' with which literary critics in particular have been grappling for some time.)[21]

For my own part, I can only state that accounts (for example, in the early modern period) which seek to provide a comparative framework for Irish colonization and conquest, or which attempt to contextualize more precisely the shaping of colonial policy, or the changing norms of warfare, seem entirely praiseworthy, in so far as they enlarge our 'contexts of explanation' for certain critical events and processes in Irish history. This is not in any way to advocate 'normalization' or the 'tacit evasion' of the historical reality of pain and trauma involved in dispossession or subjugation: any serious attempt at providing a 'rounded' study of colonization in early modern Ireland will, of course, have to come to terms with the voices and the testimony of the defeated and the dispossessed as well as with the colonists and the governing elites. But, surely, there must be room for different perspectives, different concerns, different emphases, in the discussion and analysis of historical events, however much these events/processes may have been marked by human trauma and pain? Likewise, in the more modern period, accounts of the Great Famine which employ the most up-to-date statistical techniques and an expository style heavily influenced by highly-quantified economic history seem to me to add an important dimension to our understanding of that great human tragedy (even if the language of cliometics grates from time to time!). What one may find 'cold and clinical' as an expository style should not preclude acknowledgement of new insights achieved through the application of new techniques and concepts to the available evidence.[22] Differences of emphasis, perspective and, indeed, temperament, must be accommodated in the interests of that debate on evidence and explanation which sustains the practice of historical scholarship as an academic discipline.

When we turn to the matter of the direct and deliberate assault by the revisionists on the 'nationalist historiography', we are close to the heart of Bradshaw's unease. Bradshaw sees the reaction against nationalistically-biased history as having proceeded in two phases: the first, the pioneers of the 1930s school, who sought a tacit demolition of the nationalistic 'story' through a neo-Rankean style of historical narrative, overwhelmingly document-centred and document-led.[23] The second phase of revisionism Bradshaw describes in

---

21. A difficult but absorbing treatment is Wolfgang Iser, *The Implied Reader: patterns of communication in prose fiction from Bunyan to Beckett* (Baltimore, 1974).

22. See, for exarnple, Joel Mokyr, *Why Ireland Starved: A Quantitative and Analytical History of the Irish Economy 1800-1850* (London, 1983). See,also, Margaret Crawford (ed.), *Famine; The Irish Experience 900-1900* (Edinburgh, 1989).

23. See Edwards and O'Dowd, *Sources,* n. 16 above. Butterfield's connection with Ireland and

the following terms: 'The late 1960s and early 1970s saw the increasing dominance of a more overtly iconoclastic approach by a new generation', which, in place of a positive bias towards the nationalist view in earlier accounts, simply substituted a negative bias as its value-base. The three main forms of 'interpretative distortion' which, according to Bradshaw, characterize this recent revisionist wave are: i. Invincible scepticism—opting for the most sceptical possible reading of the evidence, resulting in 'a corrosive cynicism [that] is brought to bear in order to minimalise or to trivialise the significance of transcendant aspirations and dynamisms'. A significant feature of this is the iconoclastic assault on the so-called nationalist apostolic succession of heroes.[24] ii. Inverted anachronism: where nationalist 'myth' projected national consciousness' (and the political instinct for freedom) back through the centuries, in order 'to provide the fundamental dynamism of Irish history down through the centuries', the revisionist bias (inverted anachronism) attempted 'to extrude national consciousness as a dimension of the Irish historical experience from all but the modern period'. iii. The rejection of 'the controlling conception of nationalist historiography, the notion of a 'national past', of Irish history as the story of an immemorial Irish nation, unfolding holistically through the centuries, from the settlement of the original Celts to the emergence of the national policy of modern times. This holistic conception the revisionists dismiss as a farrago of misconceptions, anachronisms and downright fabrications'. . . In its place they emphasize 'the complexity, ambiguity and above all the discontinuity that characterise the island's historical odyssey; . . . viewed as it really was, they urge, the course of Irish history fragments into a series of more or less discrete epochs, each presenting a unique social, cultural and political configuration'. In short, they urge that 'Irish history is not the past of the modern Irish nation: "the past is a foreign country".'

Making generous allowance for the normal caveats regarding emphasis, selectivity and exaggeration, I think it can be conceded that certain salient features of some of the more influential texts of recent revisionist political history can be recognized in Bradshaw's presentation (and indictment) of the

his role in shaping Irish historiography will be discussed in the forthcoming Butterfield biography by Patrick Higgins of New Hall, Cambridge.

24. Studies which are frequently cited as examples of the revisionist iconoclasm are Ruth Dudley Edwards, *Patrick Pearse: The Triumph of Failure* (London 1977); Tom Dunne, *Theobald Wolfe Tone: colonial outsider* (Cork, 1982); Marianne Elliott, *Wolfe Tone: Prophet of Irish Independence* (New Haven, 1989). For Tone, see Preface by Anthony Coughlan to C. Desmond Greaves, *Theobald Wolfe Tone and the Irish Nation* (Dublin, 1991), pp.1-7. For Connolly, see Austen Morgen, 'Connolly and Connollyism: the making of a myth', *Irish Review*, no. 5, (Autumn 1988), pp 44-55. In this context of iconoclasm E.R. Norman, *A history of modern Ireland* (London 1971) is *sui generis*. It is worth noting, however, that 'iconoclasm' didn't begin even with Fr. Shaw: Hedley McCay's biography of Pearse (Cork, 1966) and Frank McDermot's of Tone (1939), were both, to say the least, critical of their subjects.

genre. The burden of his criticism relates to matters of style and of substance (though in the work of some of the most prominent revisionists the two are especially intimately related). On the matter of historical consciousness of nationhood/nationality—its antiquity and its manifestation—it is clear that this is primarily a question of evidence rather than belief, and as such is susceptible of historical investigation and 'proof'. It is an historical problem that requires more thorough investigation than it has been given to date, and it requires subtlety and linguistic mastery of some problematic sources. To speak plainly, it is difficult to see how a discussions of cultural or 'national' consciousness in Ireland in the early modern period can be conducted very sensibly by those who cannot handle confidently source material in Gaelic. Some useful work has been done in recent years on this vexed question of 'national consciousness', but a great deal more is required; to calibrate more closely, for example, the changing (or unchanging) nature of the Gaelic mentalité over time (from, say, the sixteenth to the nineteenth century), and to determine to what extent it may have been mediated by such factors as region/locality, or, over time, social class.[25] Indeed, it is worth noting in passing that, in this matter of mentalité of colonizer and colonized, it is not only source material in Gaelic which is proving problematic.[26] What we need to remember in all of this debate is that national or communal historical consciousness is itself an historical construct; the transmission of foundation or other 'bonding' communal myths is a deliberate exercise in both primitive and technologically advanced societies. In the case of the debate on the antiquity and endurance of the consciousness of 'a distinct sense of peoplehood' among the Irish, it may well be that the concept of 'ethnicity', as employed in the discourse of the social sciences and notably by Barth, may prove to be the most useful conceptual tool for discussing the 'constructions' of Irishness which have been attempted down through the centuries.[27] Certainly, the relative weight of

25. See, most recently, Michelle O'Riordan, *The Gaelic Mind and the Collapse of the Gaelic World* (Cork, 1990), the bibliography of which lists the relevant work by, among others, Brendan Bradshaw, Nicholas Canny, Breandán Ó Buachalla, Bernadette Cunningham, Tom Dunne. See also, Joseph Th. Leerssen, *Mere Irish and fíor-Ghael: studies in the idea of Irish nationality* (Amsterdam & Philadelphia, 1986), and Brian Ó Cuív's survey of Gaelic sources in T.W. Moody, F.X. Martin and F.J. Byrne (eds.), *A New History of Ireland*, vol. 3, *Early Modern Ireland 1534-1691* (Oxford, 1978).

26. See, for example, Ciaran Brady, 'Spenser's Irish Crisis: Humanism and Experience in the 1590s', *Past and Present*, no. 111 (May 1986), pp. 17-49; and exchange between Ciaran Brady and Nicholas Canny on this matter in *Past and Present*, no. 120 (August 1988), pp. 201-15.

27. F. Barth, *Ethnic Groups and Boundaries* (London 1969). See, further, John Hutchinson, *The Dynamics of Cultural Nationalism* (London, 1987), and Damian Hannan, Hilary Tovey and Hal Abramson, *Why Irish?* (Dublin, 1989). For a critical note see Tom Garvin, 'The Return of History: Collective Myths and Modern Nationalisms', *Irish Review*, no. 9 (Autumn 1990), pp. 16-30.

religion and language in constructions (and the articulation) of Irish ethnicity is an issue requiring more careful attention than it has received to date from historians of Irish mentalités.

As to the iconoclastic zeal and the 'corrosive cynicism' which Bradshaw deplores in the revisionist writings, it seems to me that he has here a point worth some attention, though he may be mistaken in his identification of the historiographical tradition to which this particular aspect of revisionist 'style' or 'tone' belongs. Of course, in matters of this kind one must be especially circumspect, and eschew dogmatism; the issue is one of style, of emphasis and nuance, of tone and texture, in short, of the 'literariness' of the historical text; where one scholar's 'corrosive cynicism' may be another's 'critical distance' or 'robust scepticism' (and likewise, indeed, for different readers). Moreover, so personal and individual is the work of any important historian that identifying key historiographical influences in his/her work is always a very difficult undertaking, even in cases where intellectual debts are explicitly acknowledged. Yet, for all that, I do believe that the zeal for debunking myths of traditional nationalist determinism (the teleological version of the story of Ireland as a project whose 'appropriate' end was an independent Irish state for the immemorial Irish nation) has indeed produced what we may describe as the predictable excesses of an avowedly—indeed evangelically—corrective mission. Thus, for example, while Theo Hoppen's masterly study of Irish elections in the nineteenth century very properly stresses (and massively documents) the importance of local factors in Irish political life in the last century, yet his 'scepticism' with regard to the traditional nationalist belief in 'national consciousness' as the over-riding condition of Irish political sentiment in recent centuries, does, at times, tempt him into a style which moves from jaunty irreverence to more caustic dismissal when some of the rhetoric of nationalist (and, indeed, unionist) ideologues are being discussed.[28] Or, again, the frequency with which the adjectives 'curious' and 'bizarre' occur in sections of Roy Foster's narrative on Irish political rhetoric (again Orange as well as Green) is interesting, and has been remarked upon. Now, it is important not to exaggerate the importance of these tropes; it would be absurd to become overheated and indignant about them. Were sections of the writings of any productive historian to be subjected to this kind of 'content and style' analysis, the outcome would, most likely, turn up literary devices and habits that might prove more disconcerting to the author than they had ever been to his readers. Nevertheless, in respect of this particular criticism of the 'temper' of some

28. His latest work, *Ireland since 1800: Conflict and Conformity* (London, 1989) provides a number of examples. For the major statement of the primacy of 'localism' see K. Theodore Hoppen, *Elections, Politics and Society in Ireland 1832-1885* (Oxford, 1984). It is only proper to add that this is only one aspect of style; the works of Hoppen and of Foster are generally characterized by an enviable lucidity and elegance.

revisionist writing, there seems to this reader, at least, a case for arguing that the cumulative effect of this astringent—and at times heavily-ironic—critique of the nationalist myth (simplistic as it may have been) is to create a sense of pervasive idiosyncracy about Irish nationalist (and to a considerable degree, also, unionist) political rhetoric and ideas. I am not here concerned with whether or not this mode of exposition does or doesn't 'do justice' to the inherent worth, or coherence or interest of the ideas themselves (though I happen to think that in some instances it does not). What I am saying, however, is that it does constitute a particular and recognizable expository style, a particular way of countering a referentially deterministic commentary on Irish nationalism with a narrative that is resolutely anti-determinist, emphasizing paradox and irony, accident and inadvertence, inconsistency and contradiction, disjunction and discontinuity. It regularly deploys the ludic as an antidote to the pietistic.[29]

It would, however, be a mistake to see this particular aspect of the revisionist 'style' as being animated by anti-Irish, or indeed anti-nationalist, bias.[30] Nor, *pace* Bradshaw, does it seem entirely convincing to see the writings of Foster or Hoppen or Fitzpatrick, or others described as revisionists, as the latest crop from the seed of the Edwards-Moody logical-positivist Rankean history of the 1930s vintage (cradled in the Institute of Historical Research), nor, save at a considerable remove, composed under the shadow of the young, anti-Whig Herbert Butterfield. What may be suggested—tentatively and with due regard for the range and variety of intellectual sources which have shaped this company of highly individual historians—is that these revisionist writings, at least in respect of a common astringency of tone and hard-nosed scepticism in dealing with public political rhetoric, are related to a more recent historiographical current or vogue. This is the 'high politics' school of history-writing, associated with, and heavily influenced by Maurice Cowling at Cambridge since the mid-1960s. The historians who, for all their intellectual and stylistic individualism, exhibit, to a greater or lesser extent, certain common features of philosophical temper, certain common notions about the writing of political history, and certain common features of expository style, are, in addition to Cowling himself, Andrew Jones, John Vincent, Alistair Cooke and Michael Bentley.[31] Significantly, one of Roy Foster's most

29. An exaggerated example is Norman, op. cit. n. 24 above; but see also David Fitzpatrick's essay, 'Ireland since 1870' (including captions for illustrations) in R.F. Foster (ed.), *The Oxford Illustrated History of Ireland* (Oxford, 1989), pp. 213-74. For the theme of discontinuity and disjunction, see the Editor's Introduction to R.F. Foster (ed.), *Oxford Illustrated History*, pp. v-vii; and also R.F. Foster, Introduction in C.H.E. Philpin (ed.), *Nationalism and Popular Protest in Ireland* (Cambridge, 1987), pp. 1-5.

30. Both Hoppen and Foster, as indicated, are equally sceptical and astringent in discussing Orange/unionist rhetoric.

31. Key texts include, Maurice Cowling, *1867: Gladstone, Disraeli and Revolution* (Cambridge,

impressive books—his perceptive study of Randolph Churchill—belongs firmly in the 'high politics' genre.[32] This is not the occasion for even a brief enquiry into the rich and complex origins of the high politics school of history-writing (though any such enquiry would undoubtedly encounter the presence of Michael Oakshott and, indeed, Herbert Butterfield, at an early stage). But, for present purposes it must suffice to note that among the important features of the practitioners of 'high politics' history (apart from a commendable rigour in the matter of sources) have been a 'robust scepticism' towards public political rhetoric (as a language of real intention or belief), and a severe antipathy to all varieties of schematic Marxian determinism.[33] In applying this general intellectual disposition to Ireland, it is not surprising that Marxist writings (with imperialism and colonialism as key analytical concepts in their interpretations of Irish history and of Anglo-Irish relations) would come under particular critical review. But for certain British historians of Ireland, 'robust scepticism' was also generously applied in reassessing what was perceived as a soft-centred, guilt-ridden, sentimental, and insufficiently critical English liberal interpretation of Anglo-Irish relations, and, in particular, the neo-Gladstonian acceptance of the Irish nationalist critique of British control in Ireland as having been oppressive and mistaken.[34]

I am, I must confess, acutely aware of the difficulties and pitfalls inherent in offering any kind of generalization on this particular area of intellectual history. Matters of style and tone and philosophical temper are ineluctably personal to each individual historian. I would not wish to be misunderstood. I am not suggesting that the particular revisionist Irish historians whom I have mentioned are part of a coherent 'school', still less that they share a 'programme', as it were, of historical tasks requiring completion. For example, Michael Bentley, in his review of Roy Foster's *Modern Ireland*, seems to detect (approvingly, as I think) echoes of Edward Norman; yet Foster explicitly distances himself from Norman's treatment of Irish history.[35] Again, Joseph Lee (in virtually all of his writings on Ireland, but notably in his *tour de force*

1967); *The Impact of Labour 1920-1924* (Cambridge, 1971); A.B. Cooke and John Vincent, *The Governing Passion* (Brighton, 1974); Andrew Jones, *The Politics of Reform 1884* (Cambridge, 1972); Michael Bentley, *The Liberal Mind 1914-1929* (Cambridge, 1977). For necessary distinctions, see Michael Bentley, 'Party, Doctrine and Thought', in M. Bentley and John Stevenson (eds.), *High and Low Politics in Modern Britain* (Oxford, 1983), pp. 123-153.

32. R.F.Foster, *Lord Randolph Churchill: A Political Life* (Oxford, 1981).

33. A context for the general intellectual disposition is provided in Maurice Cowling, *Religion and Public Doctrine in Modern England*, vol. 1 (Cambridge, 1980), vol. 2 (Cambridge, 1985).

34. See, for example on Gladstone, John Vincent, *Gladstone and Ireland* (Raleigh Lecture of the British Academy 1977), *Proceedings of the British Academy*, vol. LXIII (1977), pp. 193-238, and, for an alternative reading, H.C.G. Matthew, *Gladstone 1801-1874* (Oxford, 1986), and Introduction to *The Gladstone Diaries*, vol. x (Oxford, 1990), pp. xxvii-cxcii.

35. Michael Bentley, 'A Sense of Style', in *The Irish Review*, no. 6 (Spring 1989), p. 98; but

on twentieth century Ireland), is not particularly inhibited in his use of irony, paradox and wickedly extended metaphors in his critical commentary on the 'failings' and poor 'performance' of Ireland, north and south, in this century. Yet, despite the fact that, technically, he is relentlessly revisionist in his assessments of a broad range of issues and themes in the history of modern Ireland, he is not considered a 'revisionist' by the main critics of revisionism.[36] Clearly, there are revisionists and 'revisionists'; and there is need for more careful examination of the criteria of differentiation. But, in the meantime, it may be suggested that, for all the differences which undoubtedly mark the varied writings of a clutch of distinguished historians, the writings of some of the revisionists and of some of the high politics group have enough in common to warrant closer examination, as an 'historiographical curiosity', so to speak.

Turning from the specifically academic aspects of the debate on revisionism, let us consider briefly the gap—the unhealthy gap in his view—which, Bradshaw claims, has opened up between the revisionist version of recent Irish history and 'the modern Irish community'. This gap doesn't altogether surprise Brendan Bradshaw: 'Invited to adopt a perspective on Irish history which would depopulate it of heroic figures, struggling in the cause of national liberation; a perspective which would depopulate it of an immemorial native race, the cumulative record of whose achievements and sufferings constitutes such a rich treasury of culture and human experience; a perspective, indeed, from which the modern Irish community would seem as aliens in their own land: in the face of such an invitation the Irish have clung tenaciously to their nationalist heritage. Who could blame them?'[37] What, then, is to be said on this contentious issue—the social role and responsibility of the historian in contemporary Ireland? That (s)he has a significant role is accepted by the main disputants in the revisionist controversy. Thus, for example, Ronan Fanning urges: 'We must take new bearings, not least because of the enormous public appetite for information about our most recent political past. That appetite is most marked in the young, both in and out of the universities, and we will fail to satisfy it at our peril'.[38] Or, 'Historians cannot escape the duty of treating as history what is so widely perceived as history, no matter how difficult or distasteful that duty might be to discharge . . . to shirk that task would materially contribute to conditions fertile for the creation of new mytholo-

see Foster, 'History and the Irish Questions', *Transactions of the Royal Historical Society*, 5th series, xxxiii (1983), p. 179.

36. Thus, for Bradshaw, Lee's *The Modernisation of Irish Society 1848-1918* (1973) provides 'a brilliant example of an analysis which explores the positive dynamic of the mythology' (p. 349; above, p. 214); while the same Lee's *Ireland 1912-1985: Politics and Society* is, for Hugh Kearney, 'The latest revisionist piece . . . [a] disenchanted look at Irish life' (Kearney, p. 149; above, p. 246). He is recognizably the same Lee in both works.

37. Bradshaw, art. cit., p. 214.

38. Fanning, 'The great enchantment', p. 144; above, p. 158.

gies'.[39] Or, again: '[History is] much, much too important to be abandoned to those who would prostitute it for political purposes. The corrollary is that Ireland's historians must, and I believe do, accept that in their quest for objective historical truth they may be maligned as anti-national'.[40] Roy Foster, likewise, has concerns that 'the judicious reassessments' which the new historical revisionism has produced may not be reaching the popular audience. The findings of the new social and economic history may be getting through, but, 'as regards political history, the old pieties have it their own way and historians tread carefully for fear of the "anti-nationalist" smear. . . . Need "nationalism", defined as a commitment to Irishness, presuppose obsessive Anglophobia and a dedication to the mentality of the conspiracy theory? A historical habit of mind has been the mark of the Irish since such things began to be noticed; this establishes a ready-made audience for Irish historians, but at the same time ensures that the audience will be "parti pris". . . . In a country that has come of age, history need no longer be a matter of guarding sacred mysteries'.[41] These words, it is worth noting, were written in 1986; the enormous popular success of Foster's *Modern Ireland* would seem, at least on face value, to signify a sizeable Irish audience prepared to 'entertain' the new history. In fact, it is hard to know on what evidence Bradshaw (with relief) and Foster (with resignation or regret) conclude that among the plain people of Ireland 'the old pieties have it their own way' or that the temptation to taste the treacherous apple of revisionism is proudly scorned!

On the general question of the role of the professional historian in providing 'public history'—his role as social utility, as it were—I have to confess to a deep sense of unease at Bradshaw's invitation to Irish historians to countenance a certain degree of 'purposeful unhistoricity', i.e. 'the development of idealization and anachronism in order to accommodate the past to the needs of the present'. This invites historians to embark on an undertaking in which they should connive in the interests of a socially beneficient public history, for the construction and propagation, as public history, of an historical narrative in which the Ireland of to-day is the outcome of 'the building up of the centuries', a narrative which sees the story of Ireland (from a present-centred perspective) as the holistic unfolding of a people's odyssey through to its present position and predicament. While acknowledging that, in introducing the concept of 'purposeful unhistoricity' into the current debate, Bradshaw (following Butterfield) is attempting to grapple with the thorny distinctions between public history and 'professional' history (conducted between consenting academics, as it were), nevertheless, it is not clear to me that this conniving at 'purposeful unhistoricity' is something in which the professional historian

39. Ibid., p. 145; above, p. 159.
40. Fanning, 'The meaning of Revisionism', p. 19.
41. Foster, 'We Are All Revisionists Now', p. 5.

can easily participate, if indeed (s)he can participate at all. It would, of course, be tidy to say that the politicians and the ideologues and the propagandists will be more than willing to provide this particular kind of comforting 'popular history' (of ratification or legitimation), and that the role of the historian ought surely to be very different—to interrogate, to subject unhistorical notions, purposeful or not, to rigorous examination and, as appropriate, refutation. To say this is, in a sense, easy and inexpensively virtuous for an academic historian. But it is not sufficient as a reply. Historians do not live only in the ivory tower. It is incontestable that some wider social role is performed by the historian: as textbook-writer for schools, as advisors to government and educational bodies, to publishers and the providers of historical resources for learning, as contributors to popular newspapers, to radio and television programmes; and the thorny question of the role of 'school history' (described by Jonathan Clark as 'an initiation into a culture by the transmission of a heritage') is not an issue which the academic historian can honestly ignore.[42] And, yet, even if one concedes a significant role for school history in propagating a version of 'public history' (and the effectiveness of school history in doing this is open to question, to say nothing of the propriety of using school history for this purpose), it still remains the case that 'the past' is, to coin a phrase, 'user-friendly'. We need to remind ourselves that the historian shares the past with many other 'users', trained and untrained, using it purposefully and unconsciously—as memory, as sanction, as excuse, as emotional resource. It is vital also that the historian be constantly aware of the complex process through which 'historical consciosness' is formed (mediated, for example, through 'street' history, the 'felt experience' of authority and power, of oppression and poverty, class, gender, race). But whatever role historians may play in the shaping of public history and the formation of popular historical consciousness for their own or a later generation, I am not persuaded that this role requires, or can best be discharged by the production of 'purposeful unhistoricity', however beneficial may be its anticipated or intended social consequences.

In concluding this brief commentary on some key aspects of the current state of the revisionist debate, it is only fair, perhaps, to ask the question, 'where do we go from here'? It seems to me that what Irish history-writing does not need at the present time is a protracted and, inevitably, recriminatory exercise in the categorization of Irish historians into rival camps of nationalist and anti-nationalist; helpful to national well-being (writing affirmative public history) on the one side, and on the other side, debilitating to historically-rooted national pride and self-esteem (compulsive iconoclasm); revisionists versus anti-revisionists; imaginative empathizers versus corrosive cynics. This, it

42. Clark cited in Kearney, p. 150; above, p. 247.

seems to me, would not be calculated to advance the cause of historical scholarship (or, unless I am greatly mistaken, any other cause either). It would inevitably, especially as it attracted a motley cast of opportunist pundits to the game, be shot through with a kind of double-edged McCarthyism which would serve nobody. What the debate may prompt, however, if we respond honestly and responsibly, is a re-examination (and, in some instances, a first examination) of some significant questions which the controversy has brought into sharper focus. I would instance the following, as issues worthy of historical enquiry in the light of the revisionist debate:[43] Firstly, we need to apply ourselves more systematically to the study of popular historical consciousness in Ireland over the *longue durée*, with a view to establishing what constituted this 'consciousness' at different times; what factors shaped it, how did it manifest itself at different times, in different forms, to different purposes down through the centuries; what the evidence is for continuities and discontinuities, and what implications will follow from this enquiry for our assessment of the dynamics of popular politics in Ireland in the modern period. This work—an investigation of mentalité as an historical construct (i.e. as a time-bound and context-bound historical phenomenon)—will require careful attention to a wide range of sources and texts of a kind that many Irish historians are not accustomed to handling. A start has been made in this task, but no more than a start. It is only fair to point out, in passing, that this agenda formed part of the plea made by Kevin Whelan for our 'moving on' from the narrow political terms in which the revisionist debate, as he read it, had become enmeshed.[44] Secondly, Irish historians clearly need to give their attention to a more systematic, and a more subtle, examination of the various historiographical currents which have marked the writing of Irish history, particularly in the academy, for more than a century. By raising these historiographical issues, the disputants in the revisionist debate have placed all practitioners of Irish history in their debt.[45] Thirdly, in the light of the discussion of purpose, tone and style in these contested writings, it would be most desirable if Irish historians were to pay some attention to the issues in critical theory which have been addressed in recent years in the field of historical narratives or historical representation. If historians in recent decades have shown a healthy willingness to familiarize themselves with (and, where appropriate, make use of) concepts and techniques from other disciplines in the social sciences (notably, economics, anthropology and sociology, political science, applied

43. These, it must be stressed, are only some issues arising directly from the debate to date. The 'revisionism' of unionist (and especially Ulster unionist) myth requires an exegesis of its own.
44. Whelan, art. cit. n. 7 above, pp. 14-16.
45. The intellectual and cultural background to the flowering of professional history-writing on Ireland in North America and, to a degree, in Australia and New Zealand is a subject worthy of detailed examination.

statistics), they have, on the whole, been less courageous—or at least less enterprising—in looking to critical theory for insights into how the activity of historical writing/representation is conducted. One is reminded here of Hayden White's unexceptional observations on the composition of historical texts: '. . . historians gain part of their explanatory effect by their success in making stories out of mere chronicles; and stories in turn are made out of chronicles by an operation . . . called . . . "emplotment". . . . No given set of casually recorded historical events in themselves constitute a story; the most that they offer to the historian are story elements. The events are made into a story by the suppression or subordination of certain of them and the highlighting of others, by characterization, motific representation, variation of tone and point of view, alternative descriptive strategies, and the like—in short, all the techniques that we would normally expect to find in the emplotment of a novel or a play. . . . This suggests that what the historian brings to his consideration of the historical record is a notion of the types of configuration of events that can be recognized as stories by the audience for which he is writing'.[46] This, of course, is not to ignore the special way in which the 'truth claims' of historical writings rest primarily on evidence rather than imagination. Nevertheless, it is disappointing how few practising historians seem prepared to contemplate or, more accurately, to address the implications for their work of the writings of White and other critical theorists.[47] It is especially sad when a most distinguished practitioner of academic history feels impelled to warn young historians against exposure to the language of critical theory, in terms such as the following: '. . . we are fighting for the lives of innocent young people beset by devilish tempters who claim to offer higher forms of thought and deeper truths and insights—the intellectual equivalent of crack, in fact. Any acceptance of those theories—even the most gentle or modest bow in their direction—can prove fatal'.[48] In the context of the debate on Irish history, one can only say that when notions of 'robust scepticism', 'de-mythologizing', 'imagination' and 'empathy' become part of the currency of an historiographical

46. Hayden White, 'The Historical Text as Literary Artifact', in Robert H. Canary and Henry Kozicki (eds.), *The Writing of History: Literary Form and Historical Understanding* (Milwaukee, 1978), pp. 46-7. White's major contributions in this field include *Metahistory: The Historical Imagination in Nineteenth Century Europe* (Baltimore, 1973) and *The Content of the Form: Narrative Discourse and Historical Representation* (Baltimore, 1987). A perceptive recent study is Ann Rigney, *The Rhetoric of Historical Representation* (Cambridge, 1990).

47. For experimentation by a professional historian, see Simon Schama, *Dead Certainties (unwarranted speculations)* (London, 1991). For recent developments see Peter Burke (ed.), *New Perspectives on Historical Writings* (London, 1991). Encouraging signs on dialogue in Ireland include W.J. McCormack, *Ascendancy and Tradition in Anglo-Irish literary history from 1789-1939* (Oxford, 1985); Tom Dunne (ed.), *The Writer as Witness* (Belfast, 1987); and the recently published ambitious Seamus Deane (ed.), *The Field Day Anthology* (1991).

48. G.R. Elton, *Return to Essentials* (Cambridge, 1991), p. 41.

debate, there is probably a case for looking to the insights and propositions of literary theory with a more open mind.

In any case, the activities of historians in these three areas of enquiry that I have listed—as well as in other areas—will, I hope be conducted not in any intemperate spirit of contest on the grounds of the ideologically orthodox or 'politically correct' approach; but with historians alert to their own pre-conceptions, observing due scholarly scruple for the evidence as it presents itself, and taking some care to try to suit their expository style to their narrative intentions. Whether the outcome of these investigations will be socially or politically re-assuring or unsettling in Ireland, is a matter which can not be predicted, and which must not be predetermined.

Select Bibiography

This list includes the most important works cited as well as some additional titles which bear directly on the central issues raised during the course of the debates. The items reprinted in this anthology are not listed.

Adams, Michael, *Censorship: the Irish experience* (Dublin, 1968).

Adams, William Forbes, *Ireland and Irish emigration to the new world* (New Haven, 1938).

Adamson, Ian, *Cruithin: the ancient kindred* (Newtownards, 1974).

'Agenda for Irish history', *Irish Historical Studies*, vol. 4 (1946-7), pp. 254-69.

Anderson, Benedict, *Imagined communities* (London, 1983).

Arthur, Paul, *The people's democracy 1968* (Belfast, 1974).

Attridge, Derek (et al. eds.), *Post-structuralism and the question of history* (Cambridge, 1987).

Bann, Stephen, *The clothing of Clio: a study of the representation of history in nineteenth-century Britain and France* (Cambridge, 1984).

—— *The invention of history: essays on the representation of the past* (Manchester, 1990).

Barrit, D., and C. Carter, *The Northern Ireland problem: a study in group relations* (London, 1962).

Barthes, Roland, 'Le discours de l'histoire', *Poétique*, 49 (1982) pp. 13-21.

Bartlett, Thomas, 'An end to moral economy: the Irish militia disturbances of 1793', *Past and Present*, 99 (1983) pp. 41-63.

Beckett, J.C., *The Anglo-Irish tradition* (London, 1976).

—— *Confrontations: studies in Irish history* (London, 1972).

—— *The making of modern Ireland, 1603-1923* (London, 1966).

—— *A short history of Ireland* (London, 1958).

Bew, Paul, *Land and the national question in Ireland 1858-1882* (Dublin, 1978).

—— P. Gibbon and H. Patterson, *The state in Northern Ireland, political forces and social classes* (Manchester, 1979).

—— F. Hazelhorn and H. Patterson, *The dynamics of Irish politics* (London, 1989).

Binchy, D.A., *The origins of the so-called high kingship* (Dublin, 1959).

Booth, Wayne C., *A rhetoric of irony* (Chicago, 1974).

Bourdé, Guy, et Henri Martin, *Les écoles historiques* (Paris, 1983).

Bowen, Kurt, *Protestants in a Catholic state: Ireland's privileged minority* (Dublin, 1983).

Boyce, D. George, *Nationalism in Ireland* (2nd ed., London, 1991).

Bradshaw, Brendan, *The dissolution of the religious orders in Ireland* (Cambridge, 1974).

—— *The Irish constitutional revolution of the sixteenth century* (Cambridge, 1979).

—— 'The Opposition to the ecclesiastical legislation in the Irish reformation parliament', *Irish Historical Studies*, 16 (1969-70), pp. 285-303.

Brady, Ciaran (ed.), *Ideology and the historians: Historical Studies XVII* (Dublin, 1991).

Brown, Terence, *Ireland: a social and cultural history, 1922-85* (2nd ed., London, 1985).

Buckley, M., 'John Mitchel, Ulster and Irish nationality 1841-1848', *Studies*, 65 (1976), pp. 30-44.

Burke, Peter (ed.), *New Perspectives on historical writing* (Cambridge, 1992).

Butterfield, Herbert, *Christianity and history* (London, 1949).

—— *The Englishman and his history* (Cambridge, 1944).

—— 'Tendencies in historical study in England', *Irish Historical Studies*, 4 (1944-5), pp. 209-23.

—— *The Whig interpretation of history* (London, 1931).

—— *see* McIntire, C.T.

Canary, R.H. and Henry Kozicki (eds.), *The writing of history: literary form and historical understanding* (Madison, Wisconsin, 1978).

Carrard, Philippe, *Poetics of the new history; French historical discourse from Braudel to Chartier* (Baltimore, 1992).

Carroll, Bereneice A. (ed.), *Liberating women's history* (Urbana, Ill., 1976).

Carty, James, *A junior history of Ireland* (Dublin, 1932).

Clarke, Aidan, 'Robert Dudley Edwards (1909-1988)', *Irish Historical Studies*, 26 (1988-9), pp. 121-7.

Collingwood, R.G., *The idea of history* (Oxford, 1943).

Comerford, R.V., 'Patriotism as pastime: the appeal of Fenianism in the mid-1860s', *Irish Historical Studies*, 21 (1981), pp. 239-50.

Connolly, James, *Labour in Irish history* (Dublin, 1967).

Cook, Albert, *History/writing* (Cambridge, 1988).

Cosgrove, Art, 'The writing of Irish medieval history', *Irish Historical Studies* (1990-1), pp. 97-111.

—— and Donal McCartney (eds.), *Studies in history presented to R.D. Edwards* (Dublin, 1979).

Coughlan, Anthony, C., *Desmond Greaves 1913-1988: an obituary essay* (Dublin, 1991).

Cowling, Maurice, *Religion and public doctrine in England*, vol. i (Cambridge, 1980).

Cronin, Sean, *Irish nationalism: a history of its roots and ideology* (Dublin, 1980).

Croce, Benedetto, *My philosophy*, trans. E.F. Carritt (London, 1949).

Crotty, R.D., *Ireland in crisis: a study in capitalist undevelopment* (Dingle, 1986).

—— *Irish agricultural production: its volume and structure* (Cork, 1966).

Curtis, Edmund, 'Irish history and its popular versions', *Irish Rosary*, 39 (1925), pp. 321-9.

D'Alton, Ian, *Protestant society and politics in county Cork, 1812-1844* (Cork, 1980).

Daly, Mary, *The famine in Ireland* (Dundalk, 1986).

de Paor, Liam, *Divided Ulster* (Harmondsworth, 1969).

Deane, Seamue (gen. ed.), *The Field Day anthology of Irish writing*, 3 vols (Derry, 1991).

Dewar, M.W. (et al.), *Orangeism: a new historical appreciation* (Belfast, 1967).

Dilthey, Wilhelm, *Pattern and meaning in history*, trans. H.P. Rickman (New York, 1972).

Donnelly, James S., *The land and the people of nineteenth-century Cork* (London, 1974).

Dowling, P.J., *The hedge schools of Ireland* (Dublin, 1935).

Dunne, Tom, 'New histories: beyond revisionism', *The Irish Review*, 12 (1992), pp. 1-12.

—— *Theobold Wolfe Tone: colonial outsider* (Cork, 1982).

—— (ed.), *The writer as witness: literature as historical evidence, Historical Studies XVI* (Cork, 1987).

Eagleton, Terry, 'A postmodern Punch', *Irish Studies*, 6 (Spring, 1994), pp. 2-3.

Edwards, Owen D., *Eamon de Valera* (Cardiff, 1988).

Edwards, Owen D., and Fergus Pyle (eds.), *1916: The Easter Rising* (London, 1968).

Edwards, R.D., 'Agenda for Irish history, 1978-2018, *Irish Historical Studies*, 21 (1978-9), pp. 3-19.

—— *Church and state in Tudor Ireland* (Dublin, 1935).

—— 'Things to be done in Irish history', *Bulletin of the Irish Committee of Historical Sciences* nos. 2, 12, 21, 28 (1938-44).

—— 'T.W. Moody and the origins of *Irish Historical Studies*', *Irish Historical Studies*, 26 (1988-9), pp. 1-2.

—— and Mary O'Dowd, *Sources for early modern Irish history, 1534-1641* (Cambridge, 1985).

—— and T.D. Williams, *The great famine* (Dublin, 1956).

Edwards, Ruth D., *Patrick Pearse: the triumph of failure* (London, 1977).

Eisenberg, Nancy and Janet Strayer (eds.), *Empathy and its development* (Cambridge, 1987).

Ellis, Steven, 'Historiographical debate: representations of the past in Ireland: whose past and whose present;, *Irish Historical Studies*, 27 (1990-1), pp. 289-308.

—— *Tudor Ireland: Crown, community and the conflict of cultures, 1470-1603* (London, 1985).

Elser, Jon, *Logic and society* (Chichester, 1978).

Evans, E. Estyn, *The personality of Ireland: habitat, heritage and history* (rev. ed., Belfast, 1981: Dublin, 1992).

Fanning, Ronan, *Independent Ireland* (Dublin, 1983).

—— 'The meaning of revisionism', *The Irish Review*, 4 (1988), pp. 15-19.

Farrell, Brian (ed.), *The Irish parliamentary tradition* (Dublin, 1973).

Farrell, Michael, *Arming the Protestants* (London, 1983).

—— *Northern Ireland, the Orange state* (London, 1980).

Farrell, Desmond, *Beyond nationalism* (Dublin, 1985).

—— *Heresy* (Belfast, 1993).

—— *The revision of Irish nationalism* (Dublin, 1989).

Fitzpatrick, David, *Politics and Irish life 1913-1921: provincial experience of war and revolution* (London, 1977).

Foster, R.P., *Charles Stewart Parnell: the man and his family* (Brighton, 1976).

—— *Modern Ireland 1600-1972* (London, 1988).

—— *Paddy and Mr Punch: connections in Irish and English history* (London, 1993).

—— 'We are all revisionists now', *The Irish Review*, 1 (1986), pp. 1-5.

Foucault, Michel, *The Foucault reader*, ed. Paul Rabinow (Harmondsworth, 1986).

—— *Language, counter-memory, practice* (Ithaca, 1977).

—— *The order of things, an archaeology of the human sciences* (London, 1970).

Frame, Robin, 'Power and society in the lordship of Ireland', *Past and Present*, 76 (1977), pp. 3-33.

—— *The English lordship in Ireland 1318-1361* (Oxford, 1983).

Gardiner, Patrick (ed.), *The philosophy of history* (London, 1974).

Garvin, Tom, *The evolution of Irish nationalist politics* (Dublin, 1981).

—— *Nationalist revolutionaries in Ireland, 1858-1928* (Oxford, 1987).

—— 'The returns of history: collective myths and modern nationalisms', *The Irish Review*, 9 (1990), pp. 16-30.

Gellner, Ernest, *Nations and nationalism* (Oxford, 1984).

Girvin, Brian, *Between two worlds* (Dublin, 1989).

Glassie, Henry, *Passing the time: folklore and history of an Ulster community* (Dublin, 1982).

Goldstrom, J.M. and Clarkson, I.A. (eds.), *Irish population, economy and society: essays in honour of the late K.H. Connell* (Oxford, 1982).

Gorman, J.L., *The expression of historical knowledge* (Edinburgh, 1982).

Gossman, Lionel, *Between history and literature* (Cambridge, Mass., 1990).

Grannell, F., 'Early Irish historical studies' in Michael Hurley (ed.), *Irish Anglicanism 1869-1969* (Dublin, 1970).

Gray, John, *City in revolt: James Larkin and the Belfast dock strike of 1907* (Belfast, 1985).

Greaves, C.D., *The Life and times of James Connolly* (London, 1961).

Hall, A. Rupert, 'On Whiggism', *Journal of the History of Science*, 21 (1983), pp. 45-59.

Hampson, Norman, *The life and opinions of Maximilien Robespierre* (London, 1974).

Harbison, John, *The Ulster Unionist Party, 1882-1973* (Belfast, 1973).

Hardwerk, Gary J., *Irony and ethics in narrative: from Schlegel to Lacan* (New Haven, 1985).

Harmon, Maurice, *Sean O'Faolain, a biography* (London, 1994).

Hawthorn, Geoffrey, *Plausible worlds: possibility and understanding in history and the social sciences* (Cambridge, 1991).

Hayden, Mary and G.A. Moonan, *A short history of the Irish people from the earliest times to 1920* (Dublin, 1921).

Heslinga, M.W., *The Irish border as a cultural divide* (Assen, 1962).

Hexter, J.H., *Reappraisals in history: new views on history and society in early modern Europe* (2nd ed., Chicago, 1979).

—— *Doing history* (Bloomington, 1971).

Hofstadter, Richard, *The progressive historians: Turner, Parrington and Beard* (New York, 1968).

Hoppen, K.T., *Ireland since 1800: conflict and conformity* (London, 1989).

Huizinga, J.H., *Men and ideas* (London, 1960).

Hutchinson, John, *The dynamics of cultural nationalism: the Gaelic revival and the creation of the Irish national state* (London, 1987).

Hyde, H. Montgomery (ed.), *A Victorian historian: private letters of W.E.H. Lecky*

1859-1878 (London, 1947).

Iser, Wolfgand, *The Implied reader: patters of communications in prose fiction from Bunyan to Beckett* (Baltimore, 1974).

Jackson, T.A., *Ireland her own: an outline history of the Irish struggle* (London, 1947).

Jameson, Fredric, *The ideologies of theory: essays 1971-86*, 2 vols (London, 1988).

Kamenka, Eugene (ed.), *Nationalism: the nature and evolution of an idea* (Canberra, 1974).

Katz, R.L., *Empathy, its nature and uses* (London, 1963).

Kearney, Hugh, *The British Isles* (Cambridge, 1989).

Kearney, Richard, *The wake of imagination: ideas of creativity in western culture* (London, 1988).

Kelleher, J.V., 'Early Irish history and pseudo-history', *Studia Hibernica*, 3 (1963), pp. 113-27.

—— 'Matthew Arnold and the Celtic revival' in Harry Levin (ed.), *Perspectives of Criticism* (Cambridge, Mass., 1950), pp. 197-221.

Kennedy, Dennis, *The widening gulf: northern attitudes towards partition* (Belfast, 1988).

Kennedy, Kieran, T. Giblin and D. McHugh, *The economic development of Ireland in the twentieth century* (London, 1988).

Kiberd, Declan, *Men and feminism in modern literature* (London, 1985).

Kohn, Hans, *The idea of nationalism* (New York, 1945).

Krieger, Leonard, *Time's reasons: philosophies of history, old and new* (Chicago, 1989).

Lebow, N., 'British historians and Irish history', *Éire/Ireland*, 8, no. 4 (1973), pp. 3-38.

Lecky, W.E.H., *A history of Ireland in the eighteenth century*, ed. and abridged by L.P. Curtis (Chicago, 1972).

Lee, J.J., *Ireland 1912-1985, politics and society* (Cambridge, 1989).

—— *Irish historiography 1970-79* (Cork, 1981).

Lévi-Strauss, *Anthropolgy and myth* (Oxford, 1987).

—— *Structural anthropology* (London, 1969).

—— *Myth and meaning* (London, 1978).

Lewis, Bernard, *History—remembered, recovered, invented* (Princeton, 1975).

Lewis, David, *Counterfactuals* (Oxford, 1973).

Lyons, F.S.L., *Charles Stewart Parnell* (London, 1977).

—— *Culture and anarchy in Ireland 1890-1939* (Oxford, 1979).

—— 'The dilemma of the Irish contemporary historian', *Hermathena*, 115 (1973), pp. 45-56.

—— *Ireland since the famine* (London, 1971).

—— 'The shadow of the past', *Irish Times*, 11 September 1972.

—— and R.A.J. Hawkins (eds.), *Ireland under the union: varieties of tension* (Oxford, 1980).

McCartney, Donal, 'James Anthony Froude and Ireland: an historiographical controversy' in T.D. Williams (ed.), *Historical Studies VIII* (Dublin, 1971), pp. 171-90.

—— 'The political use of history in the work of Arthur Griffith', *Journal of Contemporary History*, 8 (January, 1973), pp. 3-19.

—— 'The writing of Irish history 1800-1830', *Irish Historical Studies*, 10 (1956-7), pp. 347-63.

—— *W.E.H. Lecky, historian and politician, 1838-1903* (Dublin, 1994).

Mc Cormack, W.J., *Ascendancy and tradition in Anglo-Irish literary history from 1789 to 1939* (Oxford, 1985).

—— *The battle of the books: two decades of Irish cultural debate* (Mullingar, 1986).

—— *The Dublin paper war of 1786-1788: a bibliographical and critical inquiry* (Dublin, 1993).

—— *From Burke to Beckett: ascendancy, tradition and betrayal in Anglo-Irish literary history* (Cork, 1994).

—— *Sheridan Le Fanu and Victorian Ireland* (2nd ed., Dublin, 1991).

MacCurtain, Margaret, Mary O'Dowd and Maria Luddy, 'An agenda for women's history in Ireland, 1500-1900', *Irish Historical Studies*, 28 (1992-3), pp. 1-37.

MacDonagh, Oliver, *States of mind: a study of Anglo-Irish conflict, 1780-1980* (London, 1983).

—— 'Time's revenges and revenge's time: a view of Anglo-Irish relations', *Anglo-Irish Studies: an interdisciplinary Journal*, 4 (1979), pp. 2-14.

McDowell, R.B., *Alice Stopford Green: a passionate historian* (Dublin, 1969).

—— *Irish public opinion, 1750-1800* (London, 1944).

McGuire, James, 'T. Desmond Williams', *Irish Historical Studies*, 26 (1988-9), pp. 3-7.

Maier, Charles, *The unmasterable past: history, the holocaust, and German national identity* (Cambridge, Mass., 1988).

Mannheim, Karl, *Ideology and Utopia* (London, 1954).

Martin, F.X., '1916—myth, fact and mystery', *Studia Hibernica*, 7 (1967), pp. 1-126.

—— 'The 1916 Rising: a coup d-état or a bloody protest?', *Studia Hibernica*, 8 (1968), pp. 106-37.

—— 'Select documents: Eoin MacNeill on the 1916 Rising', *Irish Historical Studies*, 12 (1960-1), pp. 239-40.

—— 'The Thomas Davis lectures, 1953-1967', *Irish Historical Studies*, 15 (1966-7), pp. 276-302.

Martin, John, 'The conflict in Northern Ireland: Marxist interpretations', *Capital and Class*, 18 (1982).

McIntire, C.T. (ed.), *Herbert Butterfield: writings on Christianity and history* (Oxford, 1979).

Marx, Karl and Engels, F., *Ireland and the Irish question* (Moscow, 1978).

Metscher, Priscilla, *Republicanism and socialism in Ireland* (Frankfurt, 1986).

Miller, David, *Church, state and nation 1898-1921* (Dublin, 1973).

Mitzman, Arthur, *The iron cage: an historical interpretation of Max Weber* (New York, 1970).

Mokyr, Joel, *Why Ireland starved: a quantitative and analytical history of the Irish economy 1800-1850* (London, 1983).

Moody, T.W., *The Londonderry plantation 1609-41* (London, 1939).

—— 'Twenty years after', *Irish Historical Studies*, 11 (1958-9), pp. 1-4.

—— *The Ulster question, 1603-1973* (Cork, 1974).

____ (ed.), *Irish historiography 1936-1970* (Dublin, 1971).

____ (ed.), *Nationality and the pursuit of national independence, Historical Studies XI* (Belfast, 1978).

—— and F.X. Martin (eds.), *The course of Irish history* (rev. ed. Cork, 1984).

____ (et al. eds.), *A new history of Ireland: vol. 3: Early Modern Ireland 1534-1691* (Oxford, 1976).

Morgan, Austen, 'Connolly and Connollyism: the making of a myth', *The Irish Review*, 5 (1988), pp. 44-55.

—— *Labour and partition: the Belfast working class 1905-23* (London, 1991).

Morgan, Hiram, 'Making history: a criticism and a manifesto', *Text and context*, 4 (1990), pp. 61-5.

—— 'Writing up early modern Ireland', *Historical Journal*, 36 (1993), pp. 701-11.

Morrison, K.F., *I am you: the hermeneutics of empathy in Western liberature, theology and art* (Princeton, 1988).

Mulvey, Helen F., 'Theodore William Moody (1907-1984): an appreciation', *Irish Historical Studies* 24 (1984), pp. 121-30.

Murphy, John A., 'Nationalism revisited', *The Crane Bag*, 2 (1979), pp. 304-11.

Murray, Alice, *Commercial and financial relations between England and Ireland from the period of the restoration* (London, 1903).

Ní Dhonnchadha, Máirín and Theo Dorgan (eds.), *Revising the Rising* (Derry, 1991).

Norman, E.R., *A history of modern Ireland* (London, 1971).

Novick, Peter, *That noble dream: the objectivity question and the American historical profession* (Cambridge, 1988).

Oakeshott, Michael, 'The activity of being an historian' in T.D. Williams (ed.), *Historical Studies I* (London, 1958), pp. 1-11.

—— *Experience and its modes* (Cambridge, 1933).

—— *On history* (Oxford, 1983).

O'Brien, Conor Cruise, *The great melody: a thematic biography and commented anthology of Edmund Burke* (London, 1992).

—— *Parnell and his party, 1880-90* (Oxford, 1957).

—— *Passion and cunning and other essays* (London, 1988).

—— *States of Ireland* (London, 1972).

____ (ed.), *The shaping of modern Ireland* (London, 1960).

O'Brien, Gerard (ed.), *Catholic Ireland in the eighteenth century: the collected essays of Maureen Wall* (Dublin, 1989).

Ó Broin, Leon, *Dublin Castle and 1916* (Dublin, 1966).

O'Callaghan, Margaret, 'Language and religion: the question for identity in the Irish Free State' (National Univ. of Ireland MA thesis, 1981).

O'Faolain, Sean, *De Valera* (Harmondsworth, 1939).

—— *The great O'Neill* (London, 1942).

—— *The king of the beggars* (Dublin, 1938).

—— 'Standards and tastes', *The Bell* (June, 1941), pp. 2-5.

—— 'This is your magazine', *The Bell* (December, 1940), p. 1.

O'Farrell, Patrick, *Ireland's English question: Anglo-Irish relations 1534-1970* (Dublin, 1971).

—— and Peter Murray, 'The canon of Irish cultural history: a reply to Brian Murphy', *Studies,* 82 (1993), pp. 481-98.

Offen, Karen (et al., eds.), *Writing women's history: international perspectives* (London, 1991).

Ó Gráda, Cormac, *For Irishmen to forget? Recent research on the great Irish famine* (Dublin, 1988).

—— *Ireland before and after the famine* (Manchester, 1988).

—— 'Literary sources and Irish economic history', *Studies,* 80 (1991), pp. 290-9.

O'Halloran, Clare, 'Irish re-creations of the Gaelic past: the challenge of Macpherson's Ossian', *Past and Present,* 124 (1989), pp. 69-95.

Ó Snodaigh, Padraig, *Comhghuallaithe na Réamblóide 1913-1916* (Baile Átha Cliath, 1966).

—— *Two godfathers of revisionism: 1916 in the revisionist canon* (Dublin, 1991).

Ó Tuama, Sean (ed.), *The Gaelic Idea* (Cork, Dublin, 1972).

Pollard, A.F., 'An apology for historical research', *History,* 7 (1992), pp. 161-77.

—— 'Historical criticism', *History,* 5 (1920), pp. 21-29.

—— 'History and science', *History,* 1 (1916), pp. 25-39.

Philpin, C.H.E. (ed.), *Nationalism and popular protest in Ireland* (Oxford, 1988).

Popper, Karl, *The open society and its enemies* (London, 1945).

—— *The poverty of historicism* (London, 1957).

Ranum, Orest (ed.), *National consciousness and political culture in early modern Europe* (Baltimore, 1975).

Rickert, Heinrich, *Kulurwissenschaft und Naturwissenshaft* (Tubingen, 1921).

Richter, Michael, 'The interpretation of medieval Irish history', *Irish Historical Studies,* 24 (1984-5), pp. 289-98.

Rigney, Ann, *The rhetoric of historical representation: three narrative histories of the French revolution* (Cambridge, 1990).

Rousso, Henri, *Le syndrome de Vichy, 1944-* (Paris, 1987).

Rumpf, Erhard, *Nationalism and socialism in twentieth-century Ireland* (Liverpool, 1977).

Said, Edward W., *Orientalism* (London, 1978).

Savage, D.C., 'The origins of the Ulster Unionist Party, 1885-6', *Irish Historical Studies,* 12 (1960-1), pp. 185-208.

Schama, Simon, *Dead Certainties (unwarranted speculations)* (London, 1991).

Schulin, Ernst (ed.), *Gedenkschrift Martin Gohring: Studien zue europaischen Geschichte* (Wiesbaden, 1968).

Seton-Watson, Hugh, *Nationalism, old and new* (Sydney, 1965).

Shaw, Francis, 'The canon of Irish history: a challenge', *Studies,* 61 (1972), pp. 11-157.

Sheehy, Jeanne, *The rediscovery of Ireland's past: the Celtic revival 1830-1930* (London, 1980).

Smith, F.B. (ed.), *Ireland, England and Australia: essays in honour of Oliver MacDonagh* (Cork, Canberra, 1991).

Smyth, Jim, ' "An entirely exceptional case" Ireland and the British problem', *Historical*

Journal, 34 (1991), pp. 99-107.

Solow, Barbra, *The land question and the Irish economy 1870-1903* (Cambridge Mass., 1971).

Stern, Fritz (ed.), *Varieties of history: from Voltaire to the present* (London, 1970).

Stout, Cushing, *The pragmatic revolt in Irish history* (New Haven, 1958).

Strauss, E., *Irish nationalism and British democracy* (London, 1951).

Streuner, Nancy, 'The study of language and the study of history', *Journal of Interdisciplinary History,* 4 (1974), pp. 401-15.

'The teaching of history in Irish schools', *Administration* (1967), pp. 268-85.

Terrill, Ross, *R.H. Tawney and his times* (London, 1973).

'Thirty years' work in Irish history', *Irish Historical Studies,* 15 (1966-7), pp. 359-90; 16 (1968-9), pp. 1-32; 17 (1970-1), pp. 1-31, 151-87.

Tierney, Michael, *Eoin MacNeill: Scholar and man of action 1867-1945* (Oxford, 1981).

—— 'Eugene O'Curry and the Irish tradition', *Studies,* 15 (1962), pp. 449-62.

Tosh, John, *The pursuit of history* (London, 1984).

Vance, Norman, 'Celts, Carthaginians and constitutions: Anglo-Irish literary relations 1780-1820, *Irish Historical Studies,* 22 (1980-1), pp. 216-38.

Ban Leyden, Wolfgang, 'Categories of historical understanding', *History and Theory,* 23 (1984), pp. 53-77.

Vincent, J.R., 'Gladstone and Ireland', *Proceedings of the British Academy,* 63 (1977), pp. 193-238.

Wall, Maureen, *see* O'Brien, Gerard (ed.).

Whelan, Kevin, 'Clio agus Caithlín Ní Uallacháin' i Seosamh Ó Murchú (et al., eag.), *Oghma* 2 (1990), lgh 9-19.

—— The recent writing of Irish history', *UCD History Review* (1991), pp. 27-35.

White, Hayden, *The content of the form* (Baltimore, 1988).

—— *Metahistory: the historical imagination in the nineteenth century* (Baltimore, 1973),

—— *Topics of discourse* (Baltimore, 1978).

White, Jack, *Minority report: the anatomy of the southern Irish protestant* (Dublin, 1975).

Whyte, John, *Church and State in modern Ireland* (2nd ed., Dublin, 1980).

—— *Interpreting Northern Ireland* (Oxford, 1990).

Williams, C.H. and Kofman, E. (eds.), *Community conflict: partition and nationalism* (London, 1989).

Wilson, Adrian and Ashplant, T.G., 'Whig history and present centred history', *Historical Journal,* 21 (1988), pp. 1-16.

Woggon, Helga, *Integraviter Sozialismus und nationale Befreiung: Politik und Wirkungs-geschichte James Connollys in Ireland* (Gottingen, 1990).

Woodham-Smith, Cecil, *The great hunger* (London, 1962).

Wyatt, Anne, 'Froude, Lecky and "the humblest Irishman"', *Irish Historical Studies,* 19 (1974-5), pp. 261-85.

Zeldin, Theodore, *Happiness* (London, 1974).

Index I

Principally of twentieth-century historians and other writers etc. featuring in the historiographical debates documents above.

Index II

Selected Historical Terms and Themes.